LBJ'S AMERICA

In innumerable ways, we still live in LBJ's America. More than half a century after his death, Lyndon Baines Johnson continues to exert profound influence on American life. This collection deftly explores his seminal accomplishments – protecting civil rights, fighting poverty, expanding access to medical care, lowering barriers to immigration – as well as his struggles in Vietnam and his difficulty responding to other challenges in an era of declining US influence on the global stage. Sweeping and deeply researched *LBJ's America* probes the ways in which the accomplishments, setbacks, controversies and crises of 1963 to 1969 laid the foundations of contemporary America and set the stage for our own era of policy debates, political contention, distrust of government, and hyper-partisanship.

Mark Atwood Lawrence is an award-winning historian who has taught for two decades at the University of Texas at Austin. His books include, most recently, *The End of Ambition: The United States and the Third World in the Vietnam Era.* He has been director of the LBJ Presidential Library since 2020.

Mark K. Updegrove is a presidential historian for ABC News and author of five books on the presidency, including, most recently, *Incomparable Grace: JFK in the Presidency.* He is a former director of the LBJ Presidential Library and now serves as President and CEO of the LBJ Foundation.

LBJ'S AMERICA

The Life and Legacies of Lyndon Baines Johnson

Edited by

Mark Atwood Lawrence

Mark K. Updegrove

November 2023

For Pam —

With thanks for all you do for the LBJ Library,

[signature]

[signature]

CAMBRIDGE
UNIVERSITY PRESS

Shaftesbury Road, Cambridge CB2 8EA, United Kingdom

One Liberty Plaza, 20th Floor, New York, NY 10006, USA

477 Williamstown Road, Port Melbourne, VIC 3207, Australia

314–321, 3rd Floor, Plot 3, Splendor Forum, Jasola District Centre,
New Delhi – 110025, India

103 Penang Road, #05–06/07, Visioncrest Commercial, Singapore 238467

Cambridge University Press is part of Cambridge University Press & Assessment,
a department of the University of Cambridge.

We share the University's mission to contribute to society through the pursuit of
education, learning and research at the highest international levels of excellence.

www.cambridge.org
Information on this title: www.cambridge.org/9781009172530

DOI: 10.1017/9781009172547

First published 2024

Printed in the United States of America by Sheridan Books, Inc.

A catalogue record for this publication is available from the British Library.

A Cataloging-in-Publication data record for this book is available from the Library of Congress

ISBN 978-1-009-17253-0 Hardback

Contents

Illustrations

Contributors

Melody C. Barnes is executive director of the University of Virginia's Karsh Institute of Democracy and the W. L. Lyons Brown Family Director for Policy and Public Engagement for the Democracy Initiative in the College and Graduate School of Arts & Sciences. She is the J. Wilson Newman Professor of Governance at the Miller Center and an affiliated faculty member at the School of Law, where she is also a senior fellow at the Karsh Center for Law & Democracy. She was Assistant to the President and director of the White House Domestic Policy Council during the administration of President Barack Obama and chief counsel to the late Senator Edward M. Kennedy on the Senate Judiciary Committee. She is narrator and host of the podcast "LBJ and the Great Society" and co-editor of *Community Wealth Building & the Reconstruction of American Democracy* (Edward Elgar Publishing, 2020).

Geraldo Cadava is Professor of History at Northwestern University, where his courses focus on Latino, borderlands, and immigration history. He is writing an overview of Latino history over the past 500 years, to be published by Crown in 2026. He is the author of two books – *Standing on Common Ground: The Making of a Sunbelt Borderland* (Harvard University Press, 2013) and *The Hispanic Republican: The Shaping of an American Political Identity from Nixon to Trump* (Ecco, 2020). His essays have appeared in the *New Yorker*, the *New York Times*, and *The Atlantic*.

Francis J. Gavin is the Giovanni Agnelli Distinguished Professor and the inaugural director of the Henry A. Kissinger Center for Global Affairs at Johns Hopkins SAIS. Previously, he was the first Frank Stanton Chair in Nuclear Security Policy Studies at MIT and the Tom Slick Professor of International Affairs and the director of the Robert S. Strauss Center for International Security and Law at the University of Texas at Austin. Gavin's writings include *Gold, Dollars, and Power: The Politics of International Monetary Relations, 1958–1971* (University of North Carolina Press, 2004); *Nuclear Statecraft: History and Strategy in America's Atomic Age* (Cornell University Press, 2012); and *Nuclear Weapons and American Grand Strategy* (Brookings Institution Press, 2020), which was named a 2020 *Choice* Outstanding Academic Title.

Nicole Hemmer is Associate Professor of History and director of the Carolyn T. and Robert M. Rogers Center for the American Presidency at Vanderbilt University. She is the author of *Messengers of the Right: Conservative Media and the Transformation of American Politics* (University of Pennsylvania Press, 2016) and *Partisans: The Conservative Revolutionaries Who Remade American Politics in the 1990s* (Basic Books, 2022). She is co-founder of the American Political History Conference and "Made by History," the historical analysis section of the *Washington Post*, and hosts the podcasts "Past Present," "This Day in Esoteric Political History," and "A12: The Story of Charlottesville."

Madeline Y. Hsu is Professor of History and Asian American Studies at the University of Maryland, College Park. Her books include *Dreaming of Gold, Dreaming of Home: Transnationalism and Migration between the United States and South China, 1882–1943* (Stanford University Press, 2000); *The Good Immigrants: How the Yellow Peril Became the Model Minority* (Princeton University Press, 2015); and *Asian American History: A Very Short Introduction* (Oxford University Press, 2016). With Maddalena Marinari and Maria Cristina Garcia, she co-edited *A Nation of Immigrants Reconsidered: U.S. Society in an Age of Restriction, 1924–1965* (University of Illinois Press, 2019). She is one of five co-editors for the two-volume *Cambridge History of Global Migrations* (2023).

Sheyda Jahanbani is Associate Professor at the University of Kansas focusing on the history of the United States and the world in the twentieth century. An expert on US relations with the "Third World," the history of development, and the emergence of distinctly global social problems in the post–World War II period, Jahanbani is author of *"The Poverty of the World": Discovering the Poor at Home and Abroad, 1940–1970,* forthcoming in September 2023 from Oxford University Press, and is working on a book tracing the history of "global citizenship" during the Cold War.

Peniel E. Joseph is the Barbara Jordan Chair in Ethics and Political Values; founding director of the Center for the Study of Race and Democracy; Associate Dean for Justice, Equity, Diversity, and Inclusion at the LBJ School of Public Affairs; Professor of History; and Distinguished Service Professor at the University of Texas at Austin. He is the author or editor of seven books, most recently *The Third Reconstruction: America's Struggle for Racial Justice in the Twenty-First Century* (Basic Books, 2022). Professor Joseph is a fellow of the Society of American Historians, a contributor to CNN.com, and a frequent national commentator on issues of civil rights, race, and democracy.

Laura Kalman is Distinguished Research Professor at the University of California, Santa Barbara. She is the author of *Legal Realism at Yale, 1927–1960* (Lawbook Exchange, 1986); *Abe Fortas: A Biography* (1990); *The Strange Career of Legal Liberalism* (1996); *Yale Law School and the Sixties: Revolt and Reverberations* (University of North Carolina Press, 2005); *Right Star Rising: A New Politics, 1974–1980* (Norton, 2010); *The Long Reach of the Sixties: LBJ, Nixon, and the Making of the Contemporary Supreme Court* (Oxford University Press, 2017); and *FDR's Gambit: The Court-Packing Fight and the Rise of Legal Liberalism* (Oxford University Press, 2022). Professor Kalman received her BA from Pomona College, JD from UCLA, and PhD from Yale. She is a member of the California Bar Association and is a past president of the American Society for Legal History.

Mark Atwood Lawrence is Professor of History at the University of Texas at Austin. He is author of *Assuming the Burden: Europe and the American Commitment to War in Vietnam* (University of California Press, 2005); *The Vietnam War: A Concise International History* (Oxford University Press, 2008); and *The End of Ambition: The United States and the Third World in* *the Vietnam Era* (Princeton University Press, 2021), which won the Robert H. Ferrell Prize from the Society for Historians of American Foreign Relations, in addition to numerous articles, essays, and reviews. He has also edited or co-edited several books on aspects of US foreign policy. He has served as director of the LBJ Presidential Library and Museum since 2020.

Fredrik Logevall is the Laurence D. Belfer Professor of International Affairs and Professor of History at Harvard University. He is the author or editor of eleven books, including most recently *JFK: Coming of Age in the American Century, 1917–1956* (Random House, 2020), which won the Elizabeth Longford Prize and was a *New York Times* Notable Book of the Year. His book *Embers of War: The Fall of an Empire and the Making of America's Vietnam* (Random House, 2012) won the Pulitzer Prize and the Parkman Prize, among other awards.

Marc J. Selverstone is Associate Professor in Presidential Studies and chair of the Presidential Recordings Program at the University of Virginia's Miller Center of Public Affairs. He is the author of *Constructing the Monolith: The United States, Great Britain, and International Communism, 1945–1950* (Harvard University Press, 2009), which won the Stuart L. Bernath Book Prize from the Society for Historians of American Foreign Relations, and *The Kennedy Withdrawal: Camelot and the American Commitment to Vietnam* (Harvard University Press, 2022). He is also the editor of *A Companion to John F. Kennedy* (Wiley-Blackwell, 2014) and general editor of *The Presidential Recordings Digital Edition* (University of Virginia Press, 2014–).

Mark K. Updegrove is a presidential historian and the author of five books on the presidency, including *Indomitable Will: LBJ in the Presidency* (Skyhorse, 2014); *The Last Republicans: Inside the Extraordinary Relationship between George H. W. Bush and George W. Bush* (Harper, 2017); and, most recently, *Incomparable Grace: JFK in the Presidency* (Dutton, 2022). He is the president and CEO of the LBJ Foundation. Earlier in his career, he was the director of the LBJ Presidential Library and publisher of *Newsweek*.

Joshua Zeitz is a contributing editor at *Politico Magazine* and author of *Building the Great Society: Inside Lyndon Johnson's White House* (Viking, 2018). He earned his BA at Swarthmore College and his PhD in American History from Brown University and has held faculty positions at Harvard University and Cambridge University.

Julian E. Zelizer is the Malcolm Stevenson Forbes, Class of 1941 Professor of History and Public Affairs at Princeton University, as well as a CNN Political Analyst and a regular guest on NPR's "Here and Now." He is the author, co-author, or editor of twenty-five books, including *The Fierce Urgency of Now: Lyndon Johnson, Congress, and the Battle for the Great Society* (Penguin, 2015), which won the D. B. Hardeman Prize for the Best Book on Congress; *Fault Lines: A History of the United States since 1974* (Norton, 2019); *Abraham Joshua Heschel: A Life of Radical Amazement* (Yale University Press, 2021); and *Burning down the House: Newt Gingrich, the Fall of a Speaker, and the Rise of the New Republican Party* (Penguin Press, 2020). He is co-editor of *Myth America: Historians Take on the Biggest Legends and Lies about Our Past* (Basic Books, 2023). Zelizer has published more than 1,200 op-eds and has received fellowships from the Brookings Institution, the Guggenheim Foundation, the Russell Sage Foundation, the New York Historical Society, and New America.

Introduction

Mark Atwood Lawrence

WE LIVE IN LBJ'S AMERICA. MORE THAN ANY OTHER INDI-
vidual, Lyndon Baines Johnson shaped the era of American
history that has played out since the 1960s and established the political
and social milieu within which we live. Above all, his legislative accomplishments represent a breathtaking leap forward that profoundly
reshaped the nation. LBJ championed transformative bills that extended
civil rights to African Americans, Latinos, and other historically marginalized groups, definitively ending the Jim Crow era and opening the way
to a more just America true to its founding principles. More broadly,
under the banner of the Great Society, he extended the social safety net
by creating economic opportunity for impoverished citizens left behind
even as the nation experienced a level of prosperity never before seen in
human history.

Bills signed by LBJ touched a myriad arenas of national life. The
Immigration Act of 1965 transformed America's demographic makeup
by opening the nation's doors to vastly expanded flows from non-white
parts of the world. LBJ signed similarly important new laws aimed at
protecting the environment, channeling federal dollars into education,
assuring health care for vulnerable and elderly Americans, protecting
consumers, and promoting the arts and humanities. Whenever
Americans use their Medicare benefits, obtain a Pell grant for college,
cast a vote free of racial barriers, send their kids to a Head Start program,
buckle a seat belt, or flip on "Sesame Street," they are, often unknowingly, harkening back to the Johnson years. In so many respects, America
saw advances during the Johnson administration that fulfilled its most
basic and often elusive promises of opportunity.

On a more fundamental level, Lyndon Johnson led the way in establishing a new social contract at the core of American life by assigning the federal government a central role in assuring economic uplift, expanding rights, and even promoting more aesthetically and fulfilling lives for its citizens. Unquestionably, the United States had passed through periods of ambitious reform before, most notably during Reconstruction, the Progressive era, and the New Deal. But LBJ, ranging far beyond the ideas he had promoted as a young New Dealer in the 1930s, gave liberalism a new, modern form by promoting governmental activism not just to overcome political or economic crisis but to spread the benefits of the nation's spectacular post-1945 economic boom more widely and fairly. In an increasingly complex society, LBJ believed, Americans could not protect their interests and prosper simply by exercising individual freedom. Rather, full citizenship could be exercised only when government played an active role in removing structural barriers to individual success and leveling the playing fields on which Americans vied for opportunity. The purpose of government, as LBJ put it on one occasion in 1965, was to "do for others what they are unable to do for themselves" – a conception that remains persuasive to many Americans in the twenty-first century.[1]

Yet LBJ's accomplishments also hang heavy more than half a century later because of the reaction they inspired among many other Americans hostile to his expansive vision of government-driven reform. Hindsight enables us to see Johnson's presidency not only as a time of remarkable social advances but also as a period of acceleration for the conservative politics that gained further steam across the 1970s and became dominant in the 1980s. The modern conservative movement has taken different forms at different moments, but one theme has stayed constant: suspicion of a large and ostensibly invasive federal government. Expanded bureaucracy, contend conservatives from William F. Buckley in the 1950s to Donald Trump in the 2010s, empowered an unrepresentative technocratic elite while feeding on the earnings of hard-working Americans and stifling the genius of the free-enterprise system. In this view, LBJ-era projects to protect voting rights, assure medical care, and protect consumers, to name just a few, smacked of government overreach into areas best left to the states, if not to individuals. "Government is not the solution to the problem; government *is* the problem," Ronald Reagan famously asserted in his 1981 inaugural address, rejecting the liberal creed that Johnson had espoused so energetically just a decade and a half earlier.[2] Reagan, another contender for the most influential American of recent decades, gained traction as a kind of anti-LBJ by blending traditional social mores with neoliberal economic principles. First as governor of California and then as president, Reagan persistently attacked the Great Society as wasteful, antithetical to core American principles, and conducive to social licentiousness by privileging the opinions of remote elites over the desires of ordinary citizens.

These reasons for antipathy to government dovetailed with another trend that surged as a consequence of LBJ's decisions: a widening sense that government could not be trusted. Opinion data show that faith in governmental institutions, including the federal government, increased steadily in the years leading up to about 1965. From that point onward, however, the trend turned strikingly in the opposite direction. True, confidence in government increased in the mid 1980s and again following the September 11 attacks, but it never came close to the levels (more than 75 percent expressing overall trust) reached in the early 1960s and sank to new lows (less than 20 percent expressing trust) in the 2010s.[3] This decline, a central feature of American life in the first quarter of the twenty-first century, flows, of course, from numerous causes, including the litany of scandals dating back to Watergate and the rise of antagonistic and increasingly fractured media eager to highlight government malfeasance. The turn toward distrust in the mid 1960s suggests, however, that the "credibility gap" flowing from LBJ's management of the Vietnam War played an outsize role in establishing a trend that would persist long after the last shots were fired in Southeast Asia. Again and again, LBJ declared either that the United States would not send combat forces to fight in Vietnam or, after that promise was broken, that US forces were accomplishing their objectives. Mounting evidence to the contrary called LBJ's competence and honesty into doubt. Consequently, trust in government sank from a high of 77 percent in 1964 to 62 percent just before LBJ left office. Later access to the administration's secret decision-making record affirmed that LBJ, like John F. Kennedy before him and Richard Nixon afterward, had consistently failed to level with the American public. Trust in government generally – and in the presidency in particular – has never recovered.[4]

In the arena of international affairs, too, we live in LBJ's America. True, the first years of Johnson's presidency feel far removed from the global environment confronting the United States in the early twenty-first century. In 1964 and 1965, the United States arguably sat at the very zenith of its postwar power, wielding economic, military, political, and cultural influence on a monumental scale. The Soviet Union, meanwhile, struggled to exert power beyond its borders. The following years, however, confronted Washington with the question that has bedeviled American leaders ever since: how to shore up US power in the face of economic and strategic overreach and relative decline. During the 1990s and again for a moment following the September 11 attacks, US policymakers seemed to have mastered the problem; new eras of American dominance and purpose seemed to be at hand. For the most part, though, presidents since the mid 1960s have faced the questions of how to balance international commitments against the demands of domestic renewal, and how to exert US leadership in a world less eager for American solutions than it had once been. LBJ compounded his own difficulties by choosing to Americanize the war in Vietnam, but he also confronted problems that would have existed even without the chaos in Indochina: a weakening American position in the global economy, declining prestige in the developing world, and rising challenges from superpower rivals whose material capabilities increasingly matched their pretensions to global authority. LBJ also faced – and, to a largely unrecognized degree, creatively engaged – emerging global problems all too familiar in the twenty-first century: disease, environmental degradation, resource depletion, food scarcity, and family planning.[5] Viewed with a sufficiently wide lens, Lyndon Johnson was the first president of the era in which we still live.

Rooted in a conviction of LBJ's profound importance to American life, this volume brings together some of the most accomplished scholars of American history in the 1960s and offers a fresh look at Lyndon Baines Johnson. The chapters delve into different dimensions of LBJ's life and presidency, drawing on deep research to offer new insights about his approach to politics and policymaking while providing a fresh gloss on the vast existing scholarship on the Johnson presidency.[6] Chapters examine the administration's momentous decisions in both the domestic and international realms while setting them within the context of the 1960s. In this way, the book explores "LBJ's America" in a literal sense; it examines the country whose main stage he bestrode from 1963 to 1969. But the chapters also explore the ways in which LBJ's legacies lived on after his departure from the White House and, in fact, long after his death in January 1973, almost exactly half a century before the publication of this collection. Taken together, the essays highlight the transformative quality of the Johnson presidency and the profound ways it, for good or ill, created a nation that might reasonably be called "LBJ's America."

In some respects, admittedly, Lyndon Johnson hardly seems to merit this sort of stature in contemporary American history. Born into poverty in 1908, LBJ led an early life that harkened back to the nineteenth century far more than it heralded the twenty-first. The Texas Hill Country of his youth, an outwardly verdant but fundamentally fragile ecosystem, was a land of rare booms and inescapable busts for families like the Johnsons. To be sure, the young LBJ enjoyed certain unusual advantages that gave him a broader perspective than most of his peers. His father, Sam, who served five terms in the Texas legislature, exposed Lyndon to the comparatively cosmopolitan world of Austin and encouraged his son's interest in politics. His college-educated mother, Rebekah, encouraged her son to get an education and to think broadly. From his earliest days, Rebekah would later boast, Lyndon "possessed a highly inquisitive mind."[7] Still, the basic realities of his early life were poverty, physical hardship, and limited horizons that hardly bespoke a career of accomplishment at the highest echelons of national, much less global, power.

Of course, Lyndon Johnson, driven by relentless ambition as well as a sense of humiliation about his humble origins, managed to overcome those circumstances and forge a remarkable career in national politics spanning three decades. Hindsight enables us to see, though, that his rise through the House and Senate to the vice presidency and presidency owed as much to his mastery of the mid twentieth-century idiom of American politics as any feel for the future. He won a House seat in

1935 by hitching himself to Franklin Delano Roosevelt and casting himself as a loyal foot soldier of the New Deal. During the next two decades in Congress, Johnson rose to prominence not by crafting forward-looking legislation but through his command of relatively mundane political arts: skillfully distributing funds from wealthy Texas donors, channeling federal largesse back to his patrons and constituents, cultivating the party bosses who controlled Mexican American votes, and exploiting the potential of minor leadership positions that no one else wanted.[8] When it came to substantive policy issues, LBJ was, in the words of historian Kent Germany, "a cliché of postmodernism" who repeatedly shifted shape "to fit whatever the moment demanded."[9] Only in the late 1950s did LBJ start to identify closely with the strongly liberal agenda he would pursue as president. But even in those years LBJ's most conspicuous assets as a leader – his pragmatism, willingness to work across party lines, and aversion to both ideological extremes – seem remote from the partisan and ideologically charged political world of the twenty-first century.

Surely the most important reason for LBJ's low profile in the long flow of American history is the wariness among later liberals to spotlight his accomplishments. For many political leaders and intellectuals broadly supportive of Johnson's Great Society agenda it was John F. Kennedy – or perhaps the Kennedy family more generally – who gets the lion's share of credit for bold leadership during the 1960s. Pervasive anti-Southern biases in elite American society, fascination with JFK's youthful charisma and enduring image, and broad sympathy for a heroic figure cut down in his prime made it almost impossible for LBJ to reap the accolades he deserved, precisely as the Texan feared during his vice presidency and presidency. Still more damaging to Johnson's historical profile was his pivotal role in the escalation of the Vietnam War, a catastrophe that led to more than 58,000 American deaths, deep divisions among the American public, and profound damage to the very liberal agenda that LBJ championed. For many Americans across the political spectrum, the stench of Vietnam clung so heavily around LBJ as to obscure almost everything else that he achieved across his long career. A public opinion poll conducted in 2009 showed just how dimly Americans regarded Johnson. Of nine presidents who held office from 1953 to 1993, Johnson ranked seventh, beating out only the one-term Jimmy Carter and the scandal-ridden Richard Nixon. (Kennedy finished first, significantly ahead of Ronald Reagan and Dwight Eisenhower in second and third places, respectively.)[10] Unsurprisingly, liberals running for office, including Democratic candidates for president, proudly connected themselves to FDR and JFK while mostly avoiding any mention of LBJ; there was nothing to be gained from associating with so unpopular a figure.

Much has changed in recent years, however, enabling us to understand Lyndon Johnson in fresh ways. For at least three reasons, LBJ's crucial roles in shaping contemporary America, especially his positive achievements, are now easier to see than ever before. First is the simple availability of abundant new evidence about LBJ's life and times. Ongoing declassification of national security records and continued processing of other textual materials have provided historians and biographers with an ever-larger trove of documents to comb through at the National Archives, the LBJ Presidential Library, and other repositories. But the biggest development came with the public release of audio recordings LBJ had secretly made during his presidency, an astonishing resource capturing some 632 hours of the president's telephone conversations with aides, members of Congress, family, world leaders, and other interlocutors. Through periodic releases of this material, the last of which occurred in 2008, it became possible to appreciate Johnson with unprecedented nuance and complexity. A man well known for his larger-than-life persona became even more intriguing when it became possible to hear him, in real time, agonize about Vietnam, strategize about the legislation he supported, joke with his associates, order new trousers, and wield the famous "Johnson Treatment" – the blend of persuasion and coercion with which he bent other people to his will. Such rich material, combined with the breathtaking paradoxes of the man in question, help account for the fact that LBJ remains a popular subject of new research a half-century after his death.[11]

A second reason for LBJ's new stature in American life is the dulling of passions stirred by the Vietnam War, easily the darkest mark on Johnson's legacy and the principal barrier to viewing him in richer hues. Changed perceptions do not, it is important to note, flow from any fundamental reappraisal of LBJ's role in the decisions that led to the debacle in Southeast Asia. Many historians agree that newly available evidence casts an unfavorable light on Johnson by demonstrating his failure to heed innumerable warning signs that escalation would lead to disaster.[12] Rather, perceptions of LBJ have shifted as Vietnam lost some of its radioactivity in American political culture over the decades since the end of the Cold War. The decline of Vietnam as a theme in American politics played out to some extent during the 1990s but has been particularly striking since 2008, when the American electorate rejected Republican presidential contender John McCain, a military hero of the Vietnam era, in favor of Democratic candidate Barack Obama, who had little to say about the war and embodied a new, post-Vietnam generation gradually assuming its place in US leadership circles. Deepening frustrations in Iraq and Afghanistan may also have blunted controversies connected to Vietnam by showing that the latter was hardly a unique fiasco in American history.

Whatever the cause, dwindling preoccupation with Vietnam created space for thinking anew about the Johnson presidency. The fiftieth anniversaries of LBJ's biggest legislative achievements in 1964 and 1965 provided abundant opportunities for fresh looks at his presidency in 2014 and 2015. In May 2014, the *Washington Post* ran a four-part series highlighting the breadth and ambition of the Great Society.[13] Around the same time, the LBJ Presidential Library hosted a three-day event branded the "Civil Rights Summit" to mark the half-century of the Civil Rights Act of 1964, an event that drew heavy media attention. A bipartisan trio of former presidents – Jimmy Carter, Bill Clinton, and George W. Bush – along with the incumbent, President Obama, attended the event, each paying tribute to LBJ's political courage in pursuing the cause of civil rights and social justice. "Because of the Civil Rights Movement, because of the laws Lyndon Johnson signed, new doors of opportunity swung open," Obama asserted in his celebratory keynote address. "They swung open for you, they swung open for me. ... That's why I'm standing here today, because of that effort, because of that legacy."[14] Taking stock of the event, the *New York Times* noted LBJ's "evolving" legacy. A president long lambasted by critics for Vietnam and defended by staunch loyalists increasingly appeared in a more complicated light that allowed attention to his remarkable accomplishments in the domestic arena.[15]

Media and popular culture also took another look at Johnson as the domains where he scored his biggest legislative triumphs – race relations, voting rights, poverty, immigration, and the environment – gained new urgency in American life. Polls of presidential historians conducted by C-SPAN in 2017 and 2021 ranked Johnson in the top quarter of American presidents (tenth in 2017 and eleventh in 2021), not quite in the pantheon reserved for Washington, Lincoln, and FDR but in a "near-great" category with JFK, Reagan, and Harry Truman.[16] Meanwhile, playwright Robert Schenkkan presented LBJ in a mostly sympathetic light in his Emmy Award–winning Broadway play *All the Way*, starring Bryan Cranston, which debuted in 2014 and was later adapted as an HBO movie.[17] Johnson's accomplishments in the field of civil rights also took center stage in *LBJ*, a Hollywood film directed by Rob Reiner and starring Woody Harrelson in the title role.[18] Although LBJ received less favorable treatment in HBO's *The Path to War* (2002), Ava DuVernay's 2014 film *Selma*, and the third season of Netflix's *The Crown* (2019), the flurry of attention still helped elevate Johnson as a major historical figure who played key roles in some of the most important decisions of his era.[19]

If the declining salience of the Vietnam War encouraged new efforts to see LBJ in all his complexity, another major trend of the early twenty-first century – the rise of ideologically driven hyper-partisanship – provides a third reason for resurgent interest in the Johnson presidency. In sharp contrast to national leaders who could barely tolerate being in the same room together, Johnson stood out as the epitome of level-headed moderation and skill in the arts of persuasion and coalition-building. Many pundits saw his commitment to rational problem-solving and his ability to work across the aisle as qualities sorely lacking – and desperately needed – in a later era. A leader sometimes mocked as the archetype of the flesh-pressing, arm-twisting, deal-making political animal could, it turned out, be a model to be emulated in the right circumstances. LBJ's non-doctrinaire brand of politics drew particular attention in 2020, when former Vice President Joe Biden emerged as the Democratic Party's nominee for president and then won the White House in November. Numerous commentators highlighted remarkable similarities between the two men. Both came from humble backgrounds, made names for themselves during long years in the Senate, and rose to the vice presidency as understudies to younger, more charismatic leaders. More to the point, pundits enthused about the commitment to political pragmatism and bipartisanship that the two leaders seemed to share.

Most of all, LBJ's Great Society seemed relevant as a model for what might be accomplished by a leader who combined such skills with a commitment to transformational change. In a roundabout way, Donald Trump helped highlight Johnson's accomplishments by targeting signature Great Society achievements like voting rights, Medicare, and early-childhood education.[20] But it was Biden's sweeping early initiatives to rebuild the nation's infrastructure, fight climate change, expand childcare, revise the federal tax code, and much else that shined a bright spotlight on LBJ's legislative victories during the 1960s. Along with Franklin Roosevelt's New Deal, Johnson's Great Society suddenly became a reference point for understanding the breadth and scale of change that Biden had in mind. The *New Yorker* asked in the spring of 2021 if Biden might be the "second coming" of LBJ or FDR, while National Public Radio inquired whether the new chief executive might ultimately join the "Democratic Party's Pantheon" headed by the same two forebears.[21] Never before had a sitting president been compared so extensively – and positively – to Lyndon Johnson.

Biden's legacy will no doubt be a matter of impassioned debate for many years, but LBJ's new stature in American life seemed likely to last. For some Americans, he appeared sure to endure as the embodiment of liberal ambition targeted at expanded rights and opportunities for the most vulnerable Americans. The salience of race, immigration, structural inequality, environmental degradation, and educational inadequacies in the twenty-first century made LBJ, rather than FDR (much less any Democrat since the 1960s), the obvious model of a president determined to mobilize the federal government to tackle urgent domestic woes. The Supreme Court's 2020 ruling that Title VII of the 1964 Civil Rights Act protected gay and transgender Americans – categories that LBJ and his colleagues scarcely considered – from employment discrimination showed just how important the Johnson presidency might be to progressive ambitions more than half a century later.[22]

On the other side of the spectrum, conservative critics of government overreach have numerous targets to choose among, including Ted

Kennedy, Obama, Biden, and others who have made their marks in relatively recent times. But, shorn of at least some of his Vietnam baggage, Johnson might come into sharper focus, at least for historically minded commentators, as the president who ushered in the massive backlash against the expanded rights and federal activism that he espoused. In the words of columnist Matt Lewis, LBJ set "inordinately high expectations domestically that he just couldn't meet," precisely the same phenomenon that conservatives saw playing out among liberal champions of costly new social programs in the twenty-first century.[23] For evidence of the fundamental failures of Johnson's Great Society vision, critics often point to statistics showing the long-term failure of anti-poverty programs to cut into the nation's poverty rate. To be sure, the complexity of the data makes it possible to defend almost any position about the overall impact of Johnson's programs, but the critics will continue to find plenty of ammunition in the trends that have played out since 1969.[24] No matter where one comes down on the impact of LBJ's programs, there can be little doubt of his importance in answering a fundamental question that confronts the United States as urgently in the third decade of the twenty-first century as it did in the 1960s: How does American society best produce the opportunity and social uplift so central to the nation's identity?

***

LBJ's America has four parts. The first section positions Lyndon Johnson within the broad contours of his era. Marc Selverstone's chapter examines LBJ's persona, delving into the ways in which his character and early experiences informed his transformative presidency. Selverstone also complements this introduction by exploring Johnson's shifting place in popular culture and political memory. In Chapter 2, Julian Zelizer examines LBJ's place in the long history of American liberalism stretching back to the early twentieth century. Zelizer teases out a major paradox surrounding Johnson, who was both a product of that liberal tradition and the president who held office as it rapidly disintegrated in the late 1960s. Nicole Hemmer explores LBJ's place in the rise of the modern conservative, which was fueled by broad societal backlash against the ambitious liberalism of the early 1960s.

The book's second section dives into LBJ's domestic policies. First, Peniel Joseph looks at perhaps the best known of Johnson's accomplishments: the spectacular advances during his administration in the arena of civil rights. But Joseph's story is not only one of triumph. Examining the ups and downs of LBJ's relationship with Rev. Martin Luther King Jr., he reveals the limits of collaboration between white liberals and Black activists during the 1960s and teases out the implications for later eras. In the next chapter, Geraldo Cadava takes a similarly balanced approach in exploring Johnson's attitude toward Latinos. Cadava shows that LBJ, from a young age, sincerely sympathized with Mexican Americans and helped bring major civil rights advances for Latino citizens. But the essay also reveals the strong political and demographic pressures that drove LBJ's policy preferences and notes that many Latino activists grew to distrust LBJ as the limits of the Great Society became clear toward the end of his presidency.

Joshua Zeitz takes on LBJ's War on Poverty, examining the origins and content of the administration's wide-ranging efforts to target parts of the American population left out of the era's prosperity. But Zeitz focuses too on the long-term impacts of Johnson-era programs, arguing that retrospective evaluation of their effectiveness depends on understanding what Johnson and his allies intended – and did not intend – to accomplish. In the next chapter, Laura Kalman delves into an underappreciated aspect of the Johnson presidency: the controversies that erupted around LBJ's Supreme Court appointments. Kalman argues that fierce contention about the composition of the court – a major focus of political controversy in the twenty-first century – has distinct roots in the Johnson presidency. Madeline Hsu's ensuing chapter on immigration policy, another underappreciated but highly consequential part of Lyndon Johnson's legacy, highlights the progressive motives that underlay efforts to overturn overtly racist quotas dating from the 1920s. But, like other authors in this volume, she also highlights limitations that created problems in later decades.

The book's third section turns to foreign affairs, the arena in which Lyndon Johnson scored some little-recognized successes but undeniably suffered his gravest setbacks. First, Fredrik Logevall explores Johnson's motives for escalating the war in Vietnam by sending US combat troops in

1965. Logevall notes the array of influential individuals who counseled against that step and explores the mix of reasons why Johnson ignored their advice, embracing instead a hawkish policy that would destroy his presidency, shroud his legacy, and sow social distrust that lingered for decades thereafter. But, as Francis J. Gavin observes in the next chapter, there is more to LBJ's record as a foreign policy leader than the Vietnam War. To an extent that has often gone unappreciated, the Johnson administration confronted pressing problems far from Southeast Asia, such as nuclear proliferation, growing strains within the NATO alliances, and the accelerating drain of America's gold reserves. The Johnson administration's management of these problems set patterns for the decades to come and deserves to be part of LBJ's legacy, Gavin argues. Finally, Sheyda Jahanbani shifts the focus from superpower and transatlantic relations to the Third World, where dozens of new countries gained their independence just before or during the LBJ presidency. The resulting transformation of the global order confronted Washington with profound questions about how to respond to the needs of impoverished, politically unstable nations that appeared vulnerable to communist influence, if not takeover. Jahanbani highlights LBJ's desire to bolster economic development and democratization but also his ultimate failure to realize those goals in a world that increasingly defied American leadership.

In the fourth part, the collection concludes with reflections by Melody C. Barnes, the only contributor to this collection who is not a historian with long experience writing about the LBJ period. Rather, Barnes brings the expertise of a policymaker and public intellectual who has witnessed the legacies of Lyndon Johnson in the halls of power in Washington, DC. An attorney by training, she served as chief counsel to Senator Edward M. Kennedy on the Senate Judiciary Committee before joining the Obama administration as assistant to the president and director of the White House Domestic Policy Council. These positions, combined with her more recent academic appointments at the University of Virginia and involvement in an award-winning podcast about the Great Society, enable Barnes to view LBJ's America through a unique lens and make her an ideal author to draw out the broad implications of Lyndon Johnson's presidency in contemporary America.

This collection, then, covers an exceedingly broad range of topics that generated intense concern during Lyndon Johnson's presidency and did much to shape the nation and the world in the decades that followed. To be sure, some worthy topics are omitted. The collection contains no chapter focused on education, medical care, the environment, the arts, or law and order, all of which were central to the Great Society. Nor does the book directly address the administration's approach to the condition of women, American Indians, LGBTQ communities, or other categories of Americans who demanded expanded rights during the 1960s. In connection with foreign affairs, US policymaking toward the Soviet Union, China, Cuba, Brazil, Indonesia, and many other nations central to global affairs receives attention only in the course of chapters devoted to broader themes. All of these subjects deserve fresh research to appreciate both LBJ-era decisions and the importance of those decisions to everything that followed. Still, *LBJ's America* covers far more than enough ground to highlight broad continuities and overarching questions to help guide and provoke historians drawn to other aspects of the Johnson era. Renewed attention to race, voting, immigration, a chaotic international order resistant to American control, and so many other issues reminiscent of the 1960s makes one thing certain in the third decade of the twenty-first century: LBJ and his legacies will continue to draw deep interest and debate for a long time to come.

Lyndon Johnson's words in 1968 echo across the decades. Three months before leaving the White House, LBJ sat in the Oval Office behind the desk he had brought from his old Senate office, looked into a television camera, and spoke not just to fellow Americans of his time but to history. "Most people come into this office with great dreams and leave it with many satisfactions and some disappointments," he mused, "and always, some of their dreams have not come true. I am no exception. But I am so grateful and so proud that I have had my chance, and as to how successful we've been in doing the greatest good for the greatest number, the people themselves and their posterity must ultimately decide."[25] It is a debate that continues to play out passionately over a half a century after Johnson's passing, as the following chapters show. But there is little doubt that in the five years and two months in which he held the presidency, Lyndon Johnson shaped America in more ways than even he may have imagined.

CHAPTER 1

Power and Purpose: LBJ in the Presidency

Marc J. Selverstone

HE COULD BE AS RUTHLESS AS HE WAS COMPASSIONATE, AS volcanic as he was composed, as callous as he was considerate, and as confident as he was insecure. He was, as presidential assistant Bill D. Moyers recalled, "thirteen of the most interesting and difficult men I ever met."[1] Lyndon Baines Johnson – a man with outsized appetites and boundless ambition, and almost equally bottomless doubts – is a figure so compelling that he has inspired Hollywood movies, a Broadway play, and multi-volume biographies. Indeed, the force of his personality and the magnitude of his impact make him a character of operatic proportions. From his foundational achievements on civil rights, health care, education, and the environment, to his role in expanding a disastrous war in Southeast Asia, to his imprint on the role of government in American life, Johnson occupies a central place in the modern history of the United States.

We have come to know LBJ most intimately through numerous studies of his life and times.[2] Upwards of twenty major books have chronicled the former president, depicting him as a "flawed giant," the "master of the Senate," an "architect of American ambition," and as "Big Daddy from the Pedernales."[3] These assessments have evolved as several archives, especially the LBJ Presidential Library, have released their records on the man and his administration. Initially, these titles painted Johnson with a broad brush but have since rendered him in greater detail; they have also come to treat him as a more complicated figure. Early accounts found him to be a benevolent populist or a power-hungry politico, but recent works are more nuanced, acknowledging his flaws and his strengths, as well as his achievements and failures. The writing has also advanced from presenting LBJ as focused largely on domestic affairs – mostly approvingly – toward highlighting his broader engagement with foreign policy, oftentimes for ill. This trend toward presenting a more multifaceted Johnson has become standard fare in studies of his full career. Johnson's manifold flaws, inconsistencies, and paradoxes, and their impact on his policymaking, now enliven a broader literature that incorporates the increasing complexity of the America he sought to govern and the world he tried to understand.

LBJ's approach to those challenges provides a window into his persona and its impact on his presidency. His strengths and weaknesses are evident in several dimensions of his management style, including his use of people, his workday habits, his pursuit of information, and his decision-making process. Each of them shaped his triumphs as well as his failures and persisted throughout his life and career, as would the principles he gleaned at an early age – both the idealistic as well as the less ennobling. Collectively, these aspects of LBJ reveal much about the man and his presidency and provide a backdrop for deeper exploration of his legacy and significance.

RISE TO POWER

Biographers have often described LBJ's identity as rooted in the twinned dynamics of family and geography. Johnson grew up in the hardscrabble Texas Hill Country, west of the state capital in Austin. The product of a mother who was alternately distant and attentive, and a father who was harsh and often absent, Johnson, the eldest of five children, grew up as "an emotional orphan," in the words of historian Robert Dallek. Yet it was from his parents, according to another biographer, Randall Woods, that Johnson acquired his commitment to social justice, an ethic he absorbed while accompanying his father – a member of the Texas state legislature – on campaign stops, eventually traveling to Austin to witness the hurly-burly of state house politics.[4] Lessons about compassion and privation also came from family circumstances, as faulty land speculation left his parents' finances in shambles; the attendant humiliations would haunt Johnson thereafter. Ever in need of attention, young Lyndon acted out, his restless energy and keen intellect contributing to bratty, oppositional, and unruly behavior. Ultimately channeling those impulses, Johnson succeeded in school, excelling in debate and graduating as president of a miniscule senior class (see Figure 1.1). He then made his way to Southwest Texas State Teachers College. Short of money to finish his studies, Johnson briefly left San Marcos to teach a group of largely impoverished Mexican American children in Cotulla. The experience made a deep impression on him, sparking a desire to help the disadvantaged and to engender within them a sense of dignity and possibility.

After graduating from college, Johnson took a teaching position in Houston before heading to Washington in 1931 to work for Rep. Richard Kleberg (D–Texas), who hailed from a sprawling cattle and oil district. Johnson worked tirelessly for Kleberg – much harder than the congressman, actually – and ingratiated himself with coworkers,

1.1. Debate coach Lyndon Johnson poses with his championship team on the steps of Sam Houston High School in Houston, Texas.
Credit: LBJ Presidential Library photo, photographer unknown

constituents, and other congressional staffers, amassing a knowledge of rules and procedures and the power that flowed from them. It was during this period that Johnson met and married – within the span of three months – Claudia Alta "Lady Bird" Taylor, who would remain central to Johnson's life and career, providing sage advice, keen insight, and extraordinary industry.

By 1935, Johnson had left Kleberg to become state director of the National Youth Administration, one of the projects President Franklin D. Roosevelt created under the banner of the New Deal. Johnson's frenetic pace and constant networking stood him in good stead two years later when he pursued and won a congressional seat representing his own Hill Country district. Thereafter, he supported Roosevelt to the hilt, earning the president's appreciation during his "court-packing" and executive reorganization controversies, as well as during the economic recession of 1937–38. Roosevelt, in turn, became a model for the congressman's own career. Johnson even adopted the moniker "LBJ" out of admiration for FDR and sought to emulate, and ultimately surpass, his hero as both a politician and a president.

For Johnson, though, the road to the White House ran through the Senate. After a failed bid in 1941, he emerged victorious in 1948, but only after prevailing in the Democratic primary by a mere eighty-seven votes – a contest replete with charges of malfeasance that earned him the sardonic nickname "Landslide Lyndon." (See Figure 1.2.) His political talents on full display thereafter, Johnson became Democratic whip and, in 1953, Minority Leader; after reelection the following year in a cycle that produced a Democratic majority, LBJ became Senate Majority Leader. For the next six years, he proved himself that body's master, forging party unity between Southern conservatives and Northern liberals and passing the first civil rights bill since Reconstruction. He also positioned himself for national office, distancing himself from Southern senators on voting rights, on the Senate's cloture rules requiring supermajorities to end debates, and on school integration. Johnson declined to sign the Southern Manifesto opposing the Supreme Court's 1955 Brown decision mandating school desegregation. Though the compromises he struck limited the impact of several legislative measures, they served his personal and policy needs, preserving

1.2. Among Lyndon Johnson's innovations during his run for Senate in 1948 was his use of a helicopter to travel around Texas. Here, he uses a microphone hung around his neck to address a crowd in Caldwell on June 26.
Credit: LBJ Presidential Library photo by Harry H. Bowers

his stature as a party leader while seeding the ground for more substantive advances toward racial justice. But aware of his waning power in an expanding liberal caucus – the 1958 election altered the composition of the Democratic bloc in the upper chamber – Johnson recognized the difficulties ahead in balancing his colleagues' interests and ideologies. Increasingly, he eyed a run at the White House.

THE VICE PRESIDENCY

Johnson had long thought about the presidency and actively considered mounting a bid in 1956. But he failed to declare his candidacy publicly – not the last time he exhibited ambivalence at a pivotal moment in his career. He also turned down a proposal from Joseph P. Kennedy, the former ambassador to the United Kingdom and father of Massachusetts Senator John F. Kennedy, to bankroll a Democratic ticket with Johnson in the top spot and JFK as his running mate; his snub contributed to lasting enmity between Johnson and Robert F. Kennedy, if not between LBJ and JFK. Although Jack fell short in a spirited race for the vice-presidential slot, he emerged from the 1956 convention a rising star, gaining national exposure in the process. But even as Johnson acknowledged Kennedy's strong showing and his stirring oratory, he failed to grasp the import of the Kennedy phenomenon, seriously underestimating the power of Jack's ambitions and resources. By the time Kennedy announced his presidential candidacy in January 1960, he had assembled a powerful machine and collected pledged delegates across the country. With a sizable war chest and field-tested experience, Kennedy scored primary wins in Wisconsin and West Virginia, and cruised to the convention in Los Angeles with considerable momentum. Johnson, late once more to the presidential field, tried to slow the rush, playing up Jack's medical issues and Joe's appeasement of Hitler, but to no avail. Kennedy won the nomination on the first ballot.

Still, Kennedy's background posed problems for the general election. As a young, Catholic, and comparatively inexperienced senator from the Northeast, JFK needed to balance the ticket with a seasoned politician who could offset his perceived liabilities. Lyndon Johnson – Senate Majority Leader, Protestant, and Southwesterner – fit the bill. Despite the now heightened rancor between the Kennedy and Johnson organizations, the wisdom of choosing LBJ for the second slot was undeniable. Johnson, anticipating his diminished role in the Senate and his presumed culpability for a Kennedy loss should he stay off the ticket, accepted Kennedy's invitation. He also saw the vice presidency as a backdoor to the presidency. "I'm a betting man," Johnson remarked, knowing that one out of four American presidents had died in office, "and this is the only chance I got."[5] But confusion and consternation reigned in Los Angeles after Bobby sought to talk Lyndon out of running, thereby deepening the acrimony between the two men and the two camps. Johnson proved his worth nonetheless as Kennedy won Texas and several Southern states that November, despite JFK's progressive signaling on civil rights.

The bitterness remained, however, and marked the thousand days of Johnson's vice presidency. Widely regarded as the low point in his life and career, the period was littered with indignities and humiliations. Kennedy rebuffed LBJ's bid for a more robust portfolio, and Senate Democrats resisted his effort to lead their caucus. He then became the butt of jokes among the Kennedy crowd. Aides addressed him by his first name instead of by his honorific and lampooned him as "Uncle Cornpone" at social gatherings. Kennedy looked to stroke Johnson's ego and include him on major decisions, but staffers tried to freeze him out. The president got on well enough with Johnson – he was partly amused by him, partly cautious of him – but their time together in the Senate likely left a residual wariness that never fully subsided.[6]

Still, Johnson played his part in the administration, combining the substantive with the ceremonial. He chaired the President's Committee on Equal Employment Opportunity (PCEEO), headed the Space Council, and represented the country abroad. But even those duties occasioned nasty rebukes. Criticizing Johnson's leadership of the PCEEO, Attorney General Robert Kennedy and others – including the president – complained about Johnson's performance and sullen demeanor at White House meetings. Johnson thought he should make his views known to JFK only in private and thus largely refrained from speaking at cabinet or National Security Council (NSC) discussions. But his silence continued to alienate him from colleagues who failed to consult him proactively on policy or even on legislative strategy, underscoring his lack of power and further undermining his sense of self.[7]

Compounding his troubles, the rumor mill was rife with speculation that Kennedy might drop LBJ from the 1964 presidential ticket. Johnson suspected that Robert Kennedy was behind the effort and saw Justice Department inquiries into the disgraced Bobby Baker, Johnson's protégé during his Senate days, as part of a plan to undermine LBJ's standing. Johnson may not have wanted the nomination anyway, telling aides of his interest in returning to Texas and running a newspaper or becoming president of his alma mater. According to aide Horace Busby, Johnson allegedly looked to inform Kennedy of those plans on the evening of Friday, November 22, 1963, when he and Lady Bird were to host the president and Jacqueline Kennedy at the LBJ Ranch as part of a pre-campaign swing through Texas.[8]

TRANSITION

Developments that afternoon changed his calculations, along with those of everyone else. The traumas of the day and the decisions that followed have long been retold from several angles. For Johnson, they included the protocols for leaving Dallas, assuming the presidency, investigating Kennedy's murder, and mourning JFK. Johnson's every move conditioned appraisals of his leadership, his previous irrelevance now vanishing in an instant. Landing in Washington early that Friday evening, the new president caucused for roughly three hours in his suite at the Executive Office Building, just west of the White House. Congressmen, staffers, secretaries, personal aides, the Secret Service – a raft of people came in and out while LBJ worked the phones. He then returned to his residence in northwest Washington, accompanied by Cliff Carter, Bill Moyers, and Jack Valenti – aides and associates who also hailed from Texas – strategizing until 3 o'clock in the morning. Indicative of his ability to focus and project calm in moments of crisis, Johnson coolly and competently mapped out an agenda for the road ahead.[9]

His plans included an address to Congress following Kennedy's burial to convey a sense of stability and continuity. Of signal importance, Johnson pledged to ratify Kennedy's foreign aid, tax cut, and civil rights bills, making their passage tributes to a martyr's cause. But he also sought to expand upon the Kennedy program. Pronouncing JFK "a little too conservative for my tastes," Johnson intended to provide broader access to health care, more educational opportunities, and a better standard of living – in effect, to build a more compassionate and equitable society. His commitment to those goals, and particularly to civil rights, revealed more than just political good sense; when asked about the wisdom of moving forward with civil rights legislation, Johnson, replied, "Well, what the hell's the presidency for?" It was an early sign of his fealty not only to Kennedy's full agenda, which he would now expand, but to the moral force behind it.

Aside from sketching out his legislative goals, Johnson's first order of business was to prevent a mass resignation of Kennedy aides. He did so by telling cabinet and White House officials that he needed them more than

JFK ever did. Johnson succeeded, and his ability to win over those who had showed him little but contempt revealed a political genius that had remained largely dormant since 1961. Speechwriters Ted Sorensen and Dick Goodwin agreed to stay on, as did Appointments Secretary Kenny O'Donnell, legislative liaison Larry O'Brien, and presidential assistant Arthur Schlesinger. The most senior officials, serving in White House and cabinet positions, continued to serve as well, including, for a time, Attorney General Robert Kennedy. For Johnson, the political optics of their retention were at least as important as the substantive advice they provided. Were they to leave en masse or even in dribs and drabs, the loss of confidence would be devastating for LBJ's immediate priorities, as well as for his electoral prospects that November.[10]

To help him personally navigate the turbulence of those difficult weeks and months, Johnson turned to more familiar faces. Most of them hailed from Texas and had been with him for years. Moyers had been a Senate staffer, a liaison between the Johnson and Kennedy camps, and then deputy director of the Peace Corps; Jack Valenti had run an advertising firm before managing the 1960 Kennedy–Johnson campaign in Texas; Cliff Carter had helped Johnson contest a House seat in 1937; Horace Busby was a liberal journalist who worked for Johnson's Senate campaign in 1948 and remained connected to him thereafter; and George Reedy, the only non-Texan in the group, had been writing speeches for Johnson since 1951. But first among equals was Walter Jenkins, who had been with Johnson since 1939 and was the most loyal of aides, the one who often smoothed the waters that Johnson left in his wake. Collectively, they had accustomed themselves to Johnson's operating style and were best positioned to help him succeed.

Yet his most important adviser, arguably, was Lady Bird. She had seen him climb every rung of the political ladder, counseled him through doubt and depression, managed his office during his absences, and nursed him back to health after his many maladies; through the generosity of her father, she had even bankrolled his early political rise. According to historian Julia Sweig, Lady Bird was nothing short of central to LBJ's entire political career, furnishing tactical advice and strategic counsel. Her critique of a 1964 LBJ press conference, captured on a White House recording system that taped many of the president's phone calls, is a masterclass in unvarnished critique. The First Lady assessed not only the substance of LBJ's answers but also his delivery, his appearance, and his cadence; ultimately, Mrs. Johnson gave her husband's performance a "good B-plus."[11] She also played the key role in steeling him for the 1964 presidential campaign, a contest Johnson repeatedly thought of abandoning. Lady Bird outlined LBJ's options that spring, a time when he felt "trapped" in the presidency, and later in August, when he considered declining the Democratic nomination. She did likewise in 1967 and 1968 when LBJ was considering his political future.[12] She was, quite simply, indispensable.

Johnson relied on Lady Bird and his other advisers not only to realize Kennedy's agenda but also to continue the work of Democratic presidents dating back to Franklin Roosevelt. In fact, he aimed to surpass FDR's achievements and secure what Roosevelt had termed "freedom from want." By the first week of January 1964, Johnson had declared a "War on Poverty," to be waged with all the energy he and his administration could muster. He regarded it as a moral duty, inspired not only by his own experiences of privation but also by his religiosity and its call for social justice. Beyond his commitment to enhancing the social and economic safety nets, Johnson sought to enable his fellow citizens to develop their own gifts and thereby contribute to a more productive and inclusive country. Through a range of measures related to the arts, the land, and the environment, as well as through foundational advances in civil rights, immigration, education, health care, transportation, and housing, Johnson's "Great Society" sought to protect Americans from the ravages of economic inequality and racial prejudice and to help the least fortunate, as well as the more privileged, lead lives of greater meaning and dignity. In short, he aimed to transform the qualitative experience of what it meant to be an American.

JOHNSON IN ACTION

He would do so by outworking, outthinking, and outhustling those around him, habits he had long ago adopted and brought with him into the White House. Aides describe his schedule as "unending," with LBJ using "every waking minute of the day."[13] Even his exercise regimen, which involved brisk walks around the White House or swims in its pool, were occasions for chatting up journalists and strategizing with advisers. His days began early, with Johnson usually waking between 6 and 7 a.m., and aides flowing into his second-floor bedroom shortly thereafter (see Figure 1.3); these included Moyers and Valenti during the transition period, Valenti, Jake Jacobsen, and Marvin Watson after LBJ's election in 1964, and Larry Temple and Jim Jones in the final years of his presidency. Remaining in bed, Johnson reviewed memos from the previous

1.3. During his presidency, as throughout his career, Lyndon Johnson rarely stopped working. Aides often briefed him in the early morning before he changed out of his pajamas, as in this photo taken on April 27, 1966.
Credit: LBJ Presidential Library photo by Yoichi Okamoto

night's reading, a stack of documents that would often number 100 pages or more. He frequently passed them to Lady Bird if she was awake; if asleep, she would cover her head with the bedding. Upon starting her own day, she would excuse herself to an adjoining bedroom in the presidential suite while LBJ continued his briefing.

Breakfast and the morning newspapers would arrive – tea and toast for the president, along with the *Washington Post*, the *New York Times*, the *Baltimore Sun*, and the *Wall Street Journal* – plus the overnight cables and the previous day's *Congressional Record*. Johnson digested them all, with one eye on a specially constructed television console that allowed him to watch all three networks at once. Thereafter, he reviewed the day's schedule with aides, amending it based on his reading and placing phone calls from bed. He would continue his morning run-down while showering, shaving, and attending to all manner of hygiene in full view of his assistants before heading downstairs to the West Wing.

Johnson usually arrived in the Oval Office by 10 a.m. to continue what had begun hours earlier. He worked the phones – a vital facet of his management style – and met with White House staffers, legislators, cabinet officials, visiting dignitaries, and influential private individuals; guests might include journalists, lawyers, labor leaders, civil rights activists, and business executives. Meetings stretched into the afternoon, with Johnson eating lunch in the mansion between 1 and 4 p.m., either before or after a midday nap; he had begun the practice of afternoon napping following a heart attack in 1955. Changing into pajamas and climbing into bed, he sometimes succeeded in falling asleep, though he frequently worked straight through the next couple of hours, surrounded by aides and, at times, by Lady Bird. After another shower and change of clothes, Johnson reemerged in the Oval Office ready to start his "second day," which often extended well into the evening, sometimes past midnight. Those hours included state functions as well as private dinners, with the meals themselves beginning as late as 8:30 or 9 p.m. Johnson frequently received a massage before bedtime, and on those occasions when Lady Bird was out of town, he made sure he had company until the moment he fell asleep. As he told Califano, "I don't like to sleep alone ever since my heart attack," a scare he suffered in July 1955.[14] He then turned to his reading, marking up memos with actions to pursue the following day.

Operationally, Johnson preserved and augmented Kennedy's use of task forces to address a range of policy matters. He used them frequently in the formation of domestic policy, assembling teams of academics, government officials, and business and labor leaders to study and then make proposals on a host of subjects. Much of his Great Society emerged out of this process, with Moyers coordinating the workings of fifteen such bodies during 1964, and Califano developing and coordinating a more integrated interagency process beginning in 1965. By the end of the administration, Johnson had relied on the insights and recommendations of over 100 task forces.[15]

Johnson used this ad hoc approach less frequently in managing foreign policy, but he was no less partial to the improvisation it offered. In fact, he came to prefer the less structured approach of smaller, makeshift gatherings to formal meetings of the NSC, which, by statute necessitated the presence of officials Johnson sometimes sought to exclude. As a result, Johnson relied on frequent but episodic "Tuesday Lunches" to consider the thorniest of issues with his most senior aides. Those sessions not only allowed for more candid discussions but also reduced the risk of leaks. Assessments of their value varied; attendees generally appreciated the ability to speak frankly, while the uninvited abhorred the lack of rigor and structure. Although they were hardly the primary vehicles for exploring pressing policy matters, the lunches did serve as a means for addressing the most critical issues confronting the administration. But they also derailed the more robust give-and-take that would have benefited LBJ's decision-making, particularly on Vietnam.[16]

As for his approach to legislating, Johnson understood the dynamics of moving bills through Congress as well as any lawmaker in American history. Central to his talents was his ability to align the interests of disparate groups around a common proposal by making sure that each could enjoy sufficient benefits to garner their support. His knowledge of the Senate – both its power centers and its rules – was particularly important in advancing Kennedy's program and then his own. Prying the tax cut out of the Senate Finance Committee, for instance, involved Johnson grasping that its chair, Senator Harry

F. Byrd (D-Virginia), wanted the federal budget for fiscal year 1965 to come in under $100 billion. Likewise, his maneuvering to force the 1964 civil rights bill out of the House Rules Committee and onto the House floor, or his courting of Senate Minority Leader Everett Dirksen (R-Illinois) to help break a Southern filibuster on civil rights, testified to his political savvy.

Aside from marshaling that vast institutional knowledge, Johnson made great use of his formidable persuasive skills. Honed during a lifelong pursuit of power in its many forms, they served as the bedrock of Johnson's political climb and success. Collectively, they came to be known as "the treatment," a full-body assault that often overwhelmed those on the receiving end. According to columnist Mary McGrory, it involved "an incredible, potent mixture of persuasion, badgering, flattery, threats, reminders of past favors and future advantages."[17] It often came with a dose of physicality, as the *Washington Post*'s Ben Bradlee noted, leaving its recipients feeling as though "a St. Bernard had licked your face for an hour" and "pawed you all over."[18] The treatment could take many forms. Examples from Johnson's White House tapes are legion, including the president's strongarming of Senator Richard B. Russell (D-Georgia) onto the Warren Commission, his badgering of Rep. Charles A. Halleck into granting a rule on civil rights legislation, and his bullying of Sargent Shriver into running the War on Poverty.[19] Califano also recalls a novel instance in which Johnson peppered him on urban renewal, transportation, and fair housing during a swim at the LBJ Ranch, all while the president maneuvered him into the deep end of the pool; only later did Califano realize that he was treading water while LBJ was standing on the pool floor.[20] Photographs of Johnson leaning over hapless figures – friends and foes alike – offer visual confirmation of the treatment's more physical dimensions. The president plied his talents on whole groups as well. Historian Randall Woods recounts LBJ's deft absorption of complaints about Medicare from the American Medical Association, in turns flattering and appealing to its delegates' better instincts during a July 1965 meeting at the White House. Not only did Johnson gain their support, but he convinced several to volunteer for medical service in Vietnam.[21]

Johnson's ability to prevail in these encounters often flowed from his unwillingness to take no for an answer. Again, the examples are voluminous. One involves the president convincing Governor Carl Sanders (D-Georgia) to visit the LBJ Ranch after the 1964 election, a politically delicate trip, since Johnson had lost Georgia and Sanders was its only senior official to have supported Johnson in the contest. Not only did Johnson wear down Sanders in a series of phone calls, but he also apologized for putting him in such an uncomfortable position, something Johnson rarely did in a meaningful way. He was simply relentless, a trait he exhibited in politics as well as in his personal life, including in sexual relationships. As he framed it – graphically – for labor leader Walter Reuther, "You don't ever get something unless you ask for it."[22]

But Johnson also succeeded because he was simply an effective communicator, at least in private, informal settings. He would charm and cajole, tailoring his language to whomever he was addressing. Conversations with Southern politicos, for instance, often featured more syrupy cadences than those with Northern figures, with LBJ calibrating his identity, according to historian Kent Germany, to great effect.[23] He was also funny, as his White House tapes reveal again and again; the finding aids for those recordings at the Johnson Library even include a subject section for "humor and mimicry," an apt category given the frequency with which he entertained those on the other end of the line. The humor was frequently ribald and very much of an era that presupposed traditional gender norms. But it also transcended them. Lecturing his speechwriters about their need for brevity, Johnson asked whether they could count to "four." It was "like making love to a woman," Johnson explained. "If you don't get your idea across in the first four minutes, you won't do it. Four sentences to a paragraph. Four letters to a word. The most important words in the English language all have four letters. Home. Love. Food. Land. Peace. I know, 'peace' has five letters, but any damn fool knows it should have four."[24]

LBJ's use of people was as comprehensive as his efforts to lobby them. As Califano recalled, Johnson "felt entitled to every available lever, to help from every person, every branch of government, every business and labor leader. . . . He wanted to control everything." So complete was his desire for command that LBJ chafed at aides being beyond his reach and even complained when cabinet officials were away from Washington.[25] He often compensated by providing them with additional phone lines for their bathrooms or cars – wherever they might be when he needed their counsel. And that input often included topics outside their areas of expertise; Johnson frequently asked his most senior aides, including cabinet officials, to chime in on administrative matters, political considerations, and personnel. This was especially true as Johnson closed out his caretaker administration and looked toward a full-term presidency. For instance, after acknowledging that National Security Adviser McGeorge Bundy was "carrying more work" than he should, Johnson nevertheless asked Bundy to extend his "influence" over a range of additional matters. "I'm going to tell them all, all the staff, that you're number one here at the White House, and I want all of them to carry out any suggestions you make. And if you see something you don't like, why, say so."[26]

Johnson wanted all his assistants to be similarly flexible. As he told Marvin Watson, a Texas friend who became his de facto chief of staff in 1965, White House aides were to be generalists, "can-do" people who were "willing and able to undertake any task" the president asked them to perform; there was to be "no order or rank" among them, as all reported directly to the president.[27] His was a "hub and spoke" approach to management, as Moyers describes it, with Johnson's staff reflecting "the personal needs of the President" rather than some formalized structural design. As much as that model provided Johnson with the hands-on contact he desired, his impulse to control White House and administration operations, especially its messaging, had its downsides. As political scientist Larry Berman observes, that centralization often resulted in the White House, rather than the executive branch departments, taking flack on a host of issues, a dynamic that generated conflict within the administration and often friction between Johnson and the press.[28]

Johnson's management style also featured his frequent use of contacts outside of Washington. These figures included elected officials – usually but not exclusively Democrats – as well as businessmen, lawyers, labor leaders, and financiers. He was particularly fond of speaking with current or former governors and big city mayors who could provide him with political insight, especially on dynamics in their locales. His conversation with newspaper magnate John S. Knight, whom Johnson wanted to deputize as a font of information, is indicative of these exchanges: "Pick up that phone and call me and tell me your ideas on things," Johnson said, "particularly when they differ from mine." Knight had numerous "sources of information" that Johnson lacked, and the president needed to "hear the other side." Indeed, Johnson wanted "to get it with the bark off."[29] It was a posture as vital to his own purposes as it would be for scholars researching them later on, as Johnson would note upon dedicating his presidential library in 1971.[30]

More sensitive conversations took place with figures LBJ had known for years, dating either to his time in the House or his run for the Senate. Political insiders James Rowe and Tom Corcoran, along with lawyer Eddie Weisl Sr., were valuable sounding boards as Johnson considered legislative, personnel, and administrative matters. His most trusted consiglieres were Abe Fortas and Clark Clifford; his association with Fortas dated to the late 1930s and with Clifford to the 1948 election, and both provided counsel on the most delicate of matters. They also functioned as head-hunters, tapping their networks for various administration positions. As two of the country's top lawyers, they provided legal as well as political strategy, with Fortas often backing the president's gambits and Clifford providing a more objective voice.[31]

As suggested by the variety and frequency of those many contacts, Johnson's desire for information was insatiable. In addition to his almost inhuman work habits, much of Johnson's success resulted from his absorption and mastery of detail about legislation, polling figures, and district concerns, as well as of lawmakers and their needs (and weaknesses); so consuming was his desire for knowledge about matters affecting him that he even prodded the staff at his Texas ranch for regular updates on crops, cattle, and the weather. His memory was extraordinary, and he used it to great effect. But he availed himself of every source of information at his disposal. Aside from his morning consumption of national and regional newspapers, Johnson remained current on late-breaking developments, hovering over the AP and UPI tickers in the Oval Office and barking out their contents to all within earshot. He was as least as consumed by the television news, which he watched on a three-set console in his office, just as he did in his bedroom and at the ranch. He even installed one of those units in his room at the Bethesda Naval Hospital while recuperating from gall bladder surgery in October 1965.[32]

He was frequently dismayed, however, by what he heard on those broadcasts and read in the press. Reports of reckless driving (and drinking) at the ranch or boorish behavior with aides and guests infuriated Johnson, who complained that the media routinely depicted him in the least favorable of lights. Its shabby treatment of him during the vice presidency now became darker, offering a more caricatured version of the man and his antics. Johnson, in turn, fed the beast. According to Woods, LBJ's response "to being portrayed as a coarse, crude cowboy was to act the coarsest, crudest cowboy he could imagine."[33] It did him no favors. Even when the opportunity arose to present himself more sympathetically, he was unable to do so. Insecure and resentful of the media's east coast bias – reinforced by LBJ succeeding the camera- and print-friendly JFK – Johnson overcompensated by trying to look "presidential." In so doing, he tightened up, coming across as stiff and calculating, devoid of the magic that worked so well in more personal and free-wheeling encounters.[34]

Johnson sought to improve that image by shuffling his staff and surrounding himself with more responsive aides. In fact, the turnover of personnel had been ongoing since 1964, when several Kennedy holdovers left due to their affection for JFK, their contempt for LBJ, or their absorption with Robert Kennedy's political fortunes. Others who stayed into 1965 and 1966, including Bundy and O'Brien, did so largely out of duty to the office or the country, or both. But the demands of working for Johnson – his incessant hectoring and obscenely long hours, which compounded the normal pressures of the White House – led some of his longest serving aides to leave as well. Two of Johnson's most thoughtful assistants, speechwriter Horace Busby and Press Secretary George Reedy, resigned in late 1965, having grown frustrated with and alienated from LBJ.

Of greater consequence was the loss of Walter Jenkins. Arrested on a "morals charge" in October 1964 related to a sexual encounter with another man at a local YMCA – gay sex was illegal at the time and associated with security risks and psychological instability – Jenkins left his position after Johnson learned of the incident. Although Jenkins had been with Johnson since 1939 and was serving as de facto chief of staff, LBJ's demand that he resign was swift and without much remorse. Johnson was concerned primarily with his electoral prospects, fearing Republicans would link the incident to corruption allegations surrounding Johnson aide Bobby Baker and rumblings about a scandal-plagued White House. But LBJ also feared its harm to the presidency and sought to shield the office – and his stewardship of it – from charges of lax security and a slow response.[35]

Arguably, though, Johnson's actions damaged his presidency more than the episode itself. He eventually replaced Jenkins, his most trusted and coolheaded aide, with Marvin Watson, a fellow Texan whose obsession with leaks and conspiracies mirrored the president's own, reinforcing his fears and destructive tendencies. More changes were to come. Moyers stepped in to fill Reedy's role, but he, too, fell short in Johnson's eyes, leaving at the end of 1966; thereafter, George Christian, another Texan but with no longstanding ties to Johnson, served out the remainder of the administration.[36] In the interim, Johnson hired former network executive Robert Kintner to help improve his standing. But Kintner's advice, including his recommendation that LBJ hold more press conferences, failed to turn the tide. Johnson continued to rail about his coverage, as well as about the ubiquity and perceived damage of press leaks.[37]

By then, the tenor of his presidency had shifted. Growing unrest about the pace and direction of societal change became manifest in Johnson's approval ratings, which tumbled from a high of 79 percent in February 1964 to the low 40s in 1966 and 1967 before bottoming out at 35 percent in August 1968; they would average 50 percent or less for most of his full term in office.[38] Those numbers tracked alongside an increasingly volatile electorate. Republican gains in the 1966 midterm elections – in Congress, state houses, and governors' mansions – rankled LBJ in the wake of his groundbreaking achievements, especially in the field of civil rights. But civil disorders and resistance to the spending and sweep of the Great Society – both of which contributed to GOP victories – heightened his frustrations. So did his running feud with Senator Robert Kennedy (D-New York), who, for Johnson, had become not just a nettlesome but also a dangerous figure. Bobby's challenge threatened Johnson's control of the Democratic Party and command of the policy narrative, and his critique of the administration positioned him for a possible presidential run. Collectively, these developments vexed and angered LBJ, an increasingly agitated and beleaguered figure seemingly trapped inside his own White House.

Most disturbing were developments in South Vietnam, an ally convulsed by civil strife, Cold War conflict, and the repeated collapse of its ruling regimes. Johnson had worried about escalating the war, a conflict he inherited from Kennedy with over 16,000 US military advisers already in country. But fearing the slide of Saigon's fortunes and Republican charges of weakness, LBJ initially increased America's troop strength by roughly 7,000 and authorized bombing attacks against North Vietnam. Those strikes, reprisals for the August 1964 incidents involving American ships in the Tonkin Gulf, effectively neutralized Vietnam as an issue in the 1964 election. But questions about those episodes reverberated throughout Washington, leaving Johnson unable to shake the skepticism surrounding his statements about them, as well as about other US actions abroad. His inflated description of hostilities in the Dominican Republic the following April and the alleged dangers they posed to Americans living there raised further questions about Johnson's truthfulness. The resulting "credibility gap" between presidential rhetoric and objective reality would last through the end of his term. Along with growing opposition to his handling of the Vietnam War, which Johnson continued to Americanize via the deployment of more than 500,000 troops, those doubts eroded the support he earned through his triumphs at home.[39]

In search of solace, Johnson frequently repaired to his ranch, located outside of Stonewall in the Texas Hill Country, roughly 70 miles west of Austin. Aside from his faith – Johnson was a member of the Disciples of Christ, though he was ecumenical in his church attendance – the ranch had become his spiritual center. It was "our heart's home," as Lady Bird put it, where LBJ took comfort in the land and its people and re-energized himself for his battles ahead. Acquired in 1950 from a relative's estate, the expansive homestead comprised approximately 400 acres, with the living quarters standing less than a mile from the spartan house of Johnson's birth. Its procurement ushered LBJ, as historian Hal Rothman notes, into the club of national leaders who laid claim to landed estates, conferring upon him a sense of arrival within the corridors of power.[40]

For LBJ, though, the ranch was more than just a symbol of his new-found status. It served as a refuge, allowing Johnson to move among people he understood and who, in turn, understood him. His trips to Stonewall invariably included visits with locals, including relatives who still lived in the area; they provided the sustenance largely missing from Washington. Indeed, the more grounded existence the ranch repre-sented stood in contrast to the transience of DC, with its volatility and political posturing. Of course, the local land and weather were always fickle – no one was more aware of that than Johnson, given their impact on his youth – but his control over the Texas White House exceeded his command over the one up north. His exercise of that authority and the security it gave him brought increasing comfort to LBJ. So did the joys of managing its operations, which included a thriving cattle business and related water and crop concerns. The ranch was so vital to Johnson's well-being that he spent approximately 500 days there during his presidency, roughly a quarter of his time in office, as the challenges of Vietnam, civil unrest, and his own declining popularity became more evident and intractable.[41]

Indeed, Vietnam increasingly roiled the ranks of the White House itself. The war was a significant factor in the departures of Goodwin and Moyers, as well as Bundy, who was replaced by ardent hawk Walt Rostow, a figure who enabled Johnson's rigidity on the war. Secretary of Defense Robert McNamara was yet another casualty, his exit the result of accumu-lated doubts and internal demons. In fact, of the ten cabinet officials LBJ inherited, only four of them – Dean Rusk at State, Stewart Udall at Interior, Willard Wirtz at Labor, and Orville Freeman at Agriculture – remained to the end, while those Johnson elevated were largely known to him previously. Most significantly, longtime confidante Clark Clifford, who became secretary of defense in March 1968, played a major role in moving Johnson toward a negotiated settlement in Vietnam, a position LBJ adopted late that month. Baffled by the Tet Offensive, stung by a challenge for the Democratic presidential nomination, fearful of troub-ling economic indicators, and faced with the skepticism of the business and diplomatic elites, Johnson trimmed his sails. Not only did he scale back the bombing of North Vietnam and move toward peace talks, but he also withdrew himself as a candidate for president.

Although Johnson had long debated whether to run again, by 1968 he saw himself as a spent force. Speaking with Treasury Secretary Henry Fowler, he bemoaned his inability to win over legislators as frequently or as convincingly as he had during the glory years of 1965 and 1966. Rejecting Fowler's description of him as "master of the Senate," Johnson shot back, "I'm not master of a damn thing." He could not "make this Congress do one damn thing that I know of, or the last one, either."[42] While Johnson exaggerated his difficulties with the legislature, his power and standing were clearly cratering. Conversations about the 1968 presidential race with aides and associates, and particularly with Lady Bird, reveal a man racked by frustration and doubt. Health concerns, declining popularity, challenges to his leadership, the endless war in Vietnam – these were among the factors that led Johnson to forgo another term as president.

There were more shocks to come. The murder of Robert Kennedy, the odds-on favorite to win the Democratic nomination, made Vice President Hubert Humphrey the party's de facto standard bearer, a development that left many Democrats uneasy. Among them was the president himself. The Johnson–Humphrey relationship was never close, and LBJ was particularly scornful of Humphrey's talkative nature with the press.[43] Further, Humphrey's February 1965 memo to LBJ, in which he counseled the president to reject escalation in Vietnam, prompted a bitter response and his banishment from the highest counsels of power. Nor was Johnson much more inclined to solicit Humphrey's input on domestic affairs, telling Califano that he was "never" to let Humphrey attend any planning meeting on Great Society legislation.[44] That his vice president was now the Democrats' likely nominee inspired Johnson's less than full-throated support.[45] So conflicted was Johnson about the presidential contest that he briefly considered grabbing the nomination himself. But Lady Bird again provided sage advice at a critical moment, convincing her husband to let the thought pass.

The die cast, LBJ counseled Humphrey on his selection of a running mate. It was yet another chance for Johnson to talk about personnel – a favorite topic – and to wax about the personal attribute he valued most: loyalty. Certainly, Johnson looked to hire uber-competent people with good judgment. But time and again, the president made clear that it was loyalty he prized above all. In conversation with Humphrey, he reflected on what might have been. "If I had one thing back," he said, "I'd appoint everybody like I appointed you vice president. If I had done that – started over new, why, I'd do it. Now … So that's what I want you to be careful about. And this thing loyalty, Hubert, there's not many of them that got it." It was, Johnson maintained, "the number-one quality."[46]

Humphrey would not get to test the proposition, as he lost that November to the Republican candidate, Richard Nixon. The popular vote was exceedingly close and might well have been affected by some dirty pool. Just days before voters went to the polls, the Nixon team injected itself into delicate diplomacy surrounding Vietnam, secretly and cynically discouraging Saigon from participating meaningfully in talks to end the war. The failure of those talks robbed Johnson of a political win before leaving office. It also may have robbed Humphrey of an electoral win, as the race had narrowed dramatically in its final week. Although Johnson knew of Nixon's "treason," as he described it, he refused to publicize it, fearing the impact of such knowledge on the fate of the war and on Nixon's presidency.[47] In a final act of probity, Johnson worked closely with the president-elect and his aides, doing all he could to facilitate the peaceful and orderly transfer of power.

POST-PRESIDENCY

Having played his role in the presidential transition, Johnson departed Washington for his beloved ranch. He had always wanted to return to the Hill Country, though he had never really left a place that remained part of his very being. He now threw himself into its operations, assuming hands-on roles in cattle and irrigation projects until health concerns led him to focus more on management. Johnson also looked to secure his place in history through major legacy projects: the opening of his presidential library and policy school at the University of Texas and the writing of his memoirs. His reflections, however, drained the very life out of Johnson's persona.

Consistent with earlier efforts to look "presidential," Johnson smoothed out his rougher edges, obscuring much of what contributed to his political success. But aside from those endeavors, he largely shed his obsessions with the press and his image. According to Rothman, Johnson now lived "for the first time in his adult life, on personal rather than public terms." He let his hair down – quite literally – focusing on family and friends, enjoying golf and Texas football, and indulging his capacious appetites for eating, drinking, and smoking.[48] Increasingly, they took their toll.

He had never been a healthy man. Johnson had long run himself ragged, leading to repeated medical crises, particularly during moments of stress in his political life. He suffered debilitating ailments during his campaigns for the House in 1937 and the Senate in 1948 – severe stomach cramps in the former and an infected kidney stone in the latter – leaving observers to wonder how he could maintain not just his frenetic pace but any pace at all. The more frightening episode came in 1955 when he suffered his heart attack. Though he tried to pare back his consumption of food, alcohol, and cigarettes, the trials of his vice presidency, full of disappointment and depression, led him to abandon that self-control. While he took better care of himself in the White House, he still endured several health challenges, including pneumonia in January 1965, gall bladder surgery that October, and dual operations to repair a hernia and remove a throat polyp in 1966. Even when ostensibly healthy, he seemed frequently under the weather. LBJ's White House tapes capture his frequent snorts, sneezes, and belches, conveying not just his crudeness but also his overall countenance.[49]

Once in retirement, he released the reins that held his more destructive habits in check. His health deteriorated, and after a final public appearance at his library in late 1972, a call to arms to finish the work of securing civil rights, LBJ returned to his ranch. He died there on January 22, 1973, reaching for the telephone – and, as he feared, alone.

LEGACY

The juxtaposition of Johnson's passing and the Vietnam peace accords – Washington signed an agreement with Hanoi, Saigon, and South Vietnamese communists that same week – was impossible to miss.

Reflections on LBJ would never have minimized his escalation of the war, but the proximity of his death and America's withdrawal from Vietnam ensured that both would be considered in the same breath. Indeed, Johnson's name had become sufficiently toxic for Democrats that they excluded his picture from those of party stalwarts displayed at their 1972 National Convention.[50] Republicans, on the other hand, sought to invoke LBJ as an object lesson during the country's rightward political shift. "The Federal Government declared war on poverty," mocked President Ronald Reagan in 1988, "and poverty won."[51] By the 1990s, the Democrats had subtly resurrected Johnson, if only to distance themselves from his perceived excesses and the liberalism he represented. President Bill Clinton, stung by his own failure to expand the social safety net, declared in 1996 that "the era of big government is over."[52] State-based social programs with the sweep and ambition of LBJ's approach were clearly a thing of the past.

In that moment, Johnson's wars at home and abroad came in for harsh treatment. Critics bashed his handling of both from all points on the political spectrum. Hawks on Vietnam found him insufficiently aggressive and overly concerned with domestic politics, while doves condemned him for personalizing and persisting in an unwinnable conflict; indeed, Vietnam will forever stain Johnson's record, compromising his good works for those on the left, while compounding his misdeeds for those on the right. As for his self-declared War on Poverty, conservatives fault him for a misplaced faith in government to solve deep-seated social problems, while liberals held that he shortchanged his own programs and failed to do more to level the playing field. Following the economic ills and geopolitical hesitations of the 1970s, both of which became linked to the overreach of the 1960s, a more conservative America seemed to have rendered its verdict on LBJ. The subsequent economic recovery and assertive foreign policy associated with Reagan cast Johnson's image in further relief, as both seemed to indicate the triumph of conservative principles over liberal ones, with liberalism itself becoming something of a political dirty word.

The Johnson legacy also had to contend with the specter of JFK, a shadow that hung over LBJ's presidency but now haunted him in death as in life. Confronting the Kennedy mystique was one of Johnson's signal challenges following Dallas – competing with the memory of Jack, while managing the political challenge of Bobby – but renewed interest in JFK cast LBJ in even less favorable light.[53] Repeated praise of Kennedy for his handling of the Cuban missile crisis continued to lift Jack's profile, while speculation that he would have withdrawn from Vietnam or significantly de-Americanized the war further raised his stature. Johnson's reputation paled by comparison.[54]

The emergence of LBJ's White House tapes, however, changed the terms of debate. These materials, which became accessible in the late 1990s, provide more candid views of Johnson than were available through the oral histories and first-person accounts of his many aides. Comprising roughly 650 hours of telephone conversations and 150 hours of Cabinet-Room meetings, the tapes provide a unique window into Johnson's persona, political genius, and legislative strategy. While they have yet to fundamentally reshape perspectives on the Johnson presidency, they nevertheless have altered our understanding of discreet policy positions and political developments. One can no longer argue, for instance, that Johnson was eager for war in Vietnam, even if his dissembling on the war is now more evident, or that he was largely posturing in pursuit of civil rights, even if he retained a racialized view of social dynamics. Most usefully, the tapes have contextualized the written memoranda and personal reflections of aides, allowing audiences to experience LBJ in ways that approximate the more intimate, personal contact of contemporaries.[55]

The tapes, therefore, have been a boon to observers chronicling Johnson's life and career. Aided by the texture and authenticity these materials provide, biographers Robert Caro, Robert Dallek, and Randall Woods, among others, have used Johnson's presidential recordings to provide more rounded portraits of the man and his times. The Johnson they recount is consumed by ambition as well as animated by faith, a parochial politician eager to bring his region into the national mainstream, a compassionate champion of the downtrodden, and a paternalist at heart, with all that those postures imply for his programs at home and his actions abroad. Even for Caro, whose epic four volumes have thus far stretched into 1964, the darkness he has long seen in Johnson's *machtgier* – his lust for power – has now been lightened by LBJ's manifest commitment to social justice. Those attributes are also evident in several popular podcasts, including "LBJ's War" and "LBJ and the Great Society," which sustain the image of Johnson as a beleaguered and unsuccessful war president, as well as a committed though challenged social reformer.[56] The tapes, therefore, have added much greater complexity to the Johnson story, yielding works that neither avoid Johnson's foibles nor dilute his principles.

This more compassionate Johnson has also been the one that audiences have come to know through plays and films. *All the Way*, which premiered on stage and screen in 2012 and 2016, respectively, and which covers LBJ's caretaker presidency, is likely truest to the man himself. Concluding with Johnson's electoral victory in November 1964, it depicts the exercise of power and the constant tension between ethics and expediency. But Johnson's commitment to social justice rings clear throughout, a verdict less obvious in *Selma* (2014), which subordinates Johnson's principles to his pragmatism. While the bloody crackdown on civil rights activists by Alabama troopers surely affected the timing of voting rights legislation – the film captures the messy politics and ugly realities of effecting social change – Johnson had been angling for such a bill months before the events in question. Least accurate, but perhaps most sympathetic, is *LBJ* (2016), a film that begins Johnson's story with the 1960 presidential race and concludes with his speech to Congress following JFK's burial.

These and other films about Johnson, as historian Julian Zelizer observes, underplay or overlook LBJ's handling of Vietnam, perhaps the result of biases among their producers to rescue Johnson's liberal leanings and achievements from his more belligerent instincts and actions.[57] Even *All the Way*, the most celebrated of these works, fails to address Vietnam until roughly an hour into the film, and even then barely at all. But Vietnam lies at the center of *Path to War* (2004), the most comprehensive of Johnson biopics, which best reveals the intersection of foreign and domestic concerns. Michael Gambon's LBJ, like Bryan Cranston's in *All the Way*, captures Johnson's insecurities, his explosive temper, and his demanding nature. Yet Gambon also exudes a deer-in-the-headlights quality; his Johnson is a captive of events and a creature of advisers, highly reactive and beholden to fears of appeasement and falling dominoes. Although the film presents LBJ sympathetically as a reluctant warrior, his bitterness and reflex toward blaming others for his own misfortune likely leaves viewers questioning whether Johnson ever had the temperament for the job.

Despite Johnson's consistent standing in the presidential rankings – hovering around tenth in C-SPAN polling of presidential historians and around fifteenth in Siena College studies – Johnson's legacy will remain contested.[58] It could hardly be otherwise, given the drama attending his time in office. Ascending to the presidency after the murder of the charismatic and then-revered JFK; launching the most ambitious program of social welfare in the nation's history; expanding a ruinous war that for years was the most calamitous the country had endured; presiding over the crack-up of American civic life – part of the great "unraveling," in the words of historian Allen Matusow – those developments are among the most significant in modern US history.[59] The availability of LBJ's White House tapes and, in time, the release of his vice-presidential tapes and the full complement of his meeting tapes from 1968 will further shape his legacy. Indeed, the vast majority of Johnson's telephone tapes have yet to factor into published work, and their contents will likely imbue the Johnson story with new layers of subtlety in the years to come.

Regardless, Johnson himself will remain a focal point for America in the twenty-first century. His reemergence in the national consciousness since the 1990s has resulted not only from the availability of his tapes and the many works incorporating them but also from the times themselves. In the wake of not one but two military quagmires – Iraq and Afghanistan – Johnson's troubles in Vietnam may come to look increasingly like national and institutional failures rather than a more personal one. In fact, with policy in both eras suffering from conceits about counterinsurgency and nation-building, the distance between them, as historian Bruce Shulman observes, suggests that more deeply rooted dynamics are at work.[60] In addition, the COVID pandemic has refocused public attention on the virtues of an activist government, making the

Johnson experience a touchpoint in the debate over federal responses to urgent national needs. Moreover, many of the issues LBJ sought to tackle, including race, poverty, education, immigration, voting rights, public health, and the environment, remain high on the social policy agenda, and will likely remain so.

LBJ's approach to these matters, as well as our understanding of the man himself, thus remain relevant in our day and age. Warrior, dove, pragmatist, romantic, revolutionary, institutionalist – Johnson inhabited a range of personas, each of which expressed his hopes, fears, vision, and philosophy, the sum of which combined in this most confounding individual. Johnson's presidency expressed itself in those contradictions, securing extraordinary gains on behalf of those marginalized at home while unleashing bloodshed on millions living abroad. His lifelong desire for recognition, his powerful wish to be loved, his surpassing need to control and to dominate, his deep-seated yearning to lift up the oppressed and ennoble the downtrodden – these attributes coalesced in a roughly five-year presidential tenure that harnessed the power of the state to effect fundamental change. We will continue to explore these conundrums and contradictions. How, for instance did this opponent of civil rights in his younger days become an ardent proponent in his autumn years, and how did his misgivings about war dissolve into a belief in its necessity? In addressing such questions, we will grapple with the challenges LBJ faced in pursuit of sweeping reform, the conditions necessary for its success, and the circumstances under which it may fail. His experience, therefore, serves as a valuable model for how an American president, and even Washington itself, might guide the country toward a better tomorrow.

CHAPTER 2

LBJ and the Contours of American Liberalism

Julian E. Zelizer

LYNDON BAINES JOHNSON, A SOUTHERN DEMOCRAT FROM rural Texas, was a product of twentieth-century American liberalism. The political tradition that had taken root in national politics between the early 1900s and 1930s – revolving around a commitment to expanding the federal government and using public policy to alleviate social and economic hardship – shaped his entire career. Johnson's evolution as legislator, vice president, and president of the United States was profoundly influenced by the dynamics and evolution of liberal politics.[1] Yet he came of political age in an era when the deep institutional and political limitations of liberalism to roll back militarism and address racism ultimately became constraints on his vision, putting into place dynamics that would result in irreparable harm to his legacy.

THE NEW DEAL BARGAIN

President Franklin Roosevelt's New Deal, the domestic program aimed at alleviating and ending the Great Depression, was a formative period for the young Texan after he arrived in Washington in 1931. Born in 1908, Johnson had grown up in a rural community where economic hardship always surrounded him. As a young man, Johnson observed as his father, Sam, a member of the Texas state legislature, fought for an eight-hour day in the railroad industry and challenged the Ku Klux Klan. When Johnson finished his undergraduate studies at Southwest Texas State Teachers College, he decided to teach at a school in Cotulla where many of the students were the children of impoverished Mexican American farmworkers.

Johnson was deeply impacted by the fact that they barely had food to eat, living in horrendous circumstances. Later in life, he often recalled how the local white residents treated the students and their families like third-class citizens, at best. "We had no school buses," he said. "We had very little money for educating people of this community. We did not have money to buy our playground equipment, our volleyballs, our softball bat."[2]

Johnson cut his political teeth in politics by taking a job as secretary for Congressman Richard Kleberg, who was elected in 1931. He moved to Washington right at the cusp of Roosevelt's presidency, gaining the attention of key members of the Texas delegation, including economic populists like Maury Maverick and Wright Patman, as well as Sam Rayburn, who would later become Speaker. When Roosevelt was in the White House, Johnson worked behind the scenes to persuade his boss to support programs like the Agricultural Adjustment Act. The president learned of Johnson through Rayburn, who recommended the young congressional aide to serve as the Texas state director of the National Youth Administration (NYA), a program that aimed to assist unemployed young Americans with education and jobs. "I'd like that job," Johnson said upon hearing of the position.[3] The head of the NYA, Aubrey Williams, praised LBJ's efforts, which included his work to bring federal monies to Mexican Americans and Black Americans through informal channels.

In 1937, Johnson decided to campaign for elected office. An opportunity arose with a special election for the Tenth District of Texas. Much of Johnson's campaign emphasized his experiences with poverty, often exaggerated, and his solid support of FDR (see Figure 2.1). "He would fling down some kind of mortgage on his mother's or father's house and say he was a poor boy from Blanco County and you should vote for him and F.D.R.," one voter recalled.[4] During a radio address, the candidate directly aligned himself with FDR's work.

> If the administration program [the New Deal] were a temporary thing the situation would be different. But it is not for a day or for a year, but for an age. It must be worked out through time, and long after Roosevelt leaves

2.1. As a candidate for the US House of Representatives in 1937, the 28-year-old Lyndon Johnson voiced fervent support for President Franklin D. Roosevelt's New Deal. The two men met aboard FDR's yacht at Galveston on May 13, just a month after LBJ's victory. Texas Governor James Allred stands between them.
Credit: Getty Images

the White House, it will still be developing, expanding.... The man who goes to Congress this year, or next year, must be prepared to meet this condition. He must be capable of growing and progressing with it.[5]

Johnson won the seat just at the time when FDR started to find himself under fire for a proposal to increase the number of justices on the Supreme Court ("court-packing," as opponents called it). Frustrated with Supreme Court decisions knocking down key components of his New Deal, Roosevelt proposed expanding the number of justices in order to dilute the power of his opponents. Johnson supported the plan, making it a central part of his platform during the congressional race, despite its unpopularity. The effort triggered a fierce backlash. Opponents warned that this expansion of executive power was dangerous, comparing it to developments taking place in Europe. While the pressure stemming from the plan ultimately helped the court to move in a direction more favorable to the New Deal, the plan itself failed.

The battle helped give rise to a conservative coalition of Southern Democratic committee chairs and Midwestern Republicans in Congress who were determined to block the president's domestic agenda. The legislative branch quickly became a bastion of conservative power. FDR campaigned against several of the Southern legislators during the race of 1938, seeking to reverse this development. "The Democratic Party is . . . engaged in a great struggle against reaction within the party as well as without the party," noted Secretary of the Interior Harold Ickes.[6] FDR was unsuccessful, which made the situation even worse. Four of the five conservatives whom FDR campaigned against were victorious. Republicans achieved gains on Capitol Hill while conservatives replaced New Deal liberal legislators in a number of Southern states. All in all, the conservative coalition was emboldened. There was little love left for Roosevelt. "There was a time when I would have bled and died for him," said Montana Senator James Murray, a Democrat, "but in view of the way he has been acting I don't want to have any more dealings with him and I just intend to stay away from him and he can do as he pleases."[7] Worse still, from the administration's perspective, opponents were determined to block progress on matters relating to race and unions.

But Johnson's support for the administration in the middle of a campaign won him the attention and appreciation of FDR. At this fraught moment, Johnson stood firm against regional peers who were starting to take on the president. He broke with his Southern colleagues and proved to be, in the words of one FDR adviser, a "perfect Roosevelt man."[8] The administration could still count on Johnson to vote for most of the president's domestic agenda, even if it caused trouble in the district. Benefitting from the financial support of wealthy Texas businessmen, Johnson helped FDR raise money and supported allied congressional candidates in the 1940 election. "The Democrats' unknown hero was Representative Lyndon Baines Johnson," noted prominent columnists Drew Pearson and Robert S. Allen in "The Washington Merry-Go-Round." LBJ was, they wrote, "a rangy, 32-year-old ... who ... has political magic at his fingertips."[9]

None of this meant that Johnson was some sort of radical. After the 1938 elections, he remarked in candid fashion: "I can go [only] so far in Texas ... my people won't take it."[10] The New Deal form of liberalism entailed a bargain between the Roosevelt administration and Southern committee chairmen in the House and Senate over race and unionization. The implicit deal was essential to making sense of how a Southerner such as Johnson could partake in the New Deal Coalition. The founding architecture of New Deal liberalism was anchored in the continuation and preservation of white supremacy in the South. Most of the social safety net, such as Social Security and the minimum wage, was constructed as federal programs that excluded large swaths of workers, namely, domestic employees and farmers, where large numbers of Black Americans worked. When federal funds flowed into states such as Mississippi, Black communities would usually not see much of the money, which local officials made sure were directed into the hands of white constituents.

Unions, the target of the conservative coalition, were cut off at the knees when attempting to organize in the South in "Operation Dixie." Southern leaders were desperate to prevent organized labor from taking hold in the region. Not only could unions potentially reach out to Black Americans as allies, but they could also force businesses to raise wages and undermine one of the only advantages the region might count on to grow – a cheap labor force. As Roosevelt was legitimating unions through the 1935 Wagner Act, Southern Democrats worked hard to make sure that this would remain a Northern issue.

This was the deal that senior Southern committee chairs and Midwestern Republicans had insisted on if FDR wanted to grow the welfare state, which, as the political scientist Ira Katznelson argued, was an American form of apartheid.[11] Because of Johnson's ability to please the administration while retaining the trust of senior Southern Democrats through his opposition to civil rights bills, fellow Texan Sam Rayburn, who became Speaker of the House in 1940, invited Johnson into his "Board of Education," where top members met over bourbon and cigars.

"MASTER OF THE SENATE"

After a failed run for the Senate in 1941 and a brief stint on active duty in the Navy during World War II, Johnson won a Senate seat in 1948 by defeating veteran politician Coke Stevenson. This infamous contest revolved around charges of stolen votes in an extraordinarily narrow victory that earned LBJ the ironic nickname "Landslide Lyndon."[12]

Early in his Senate career, Johnson was haunted by fears that the New Deal Coalition was susceptible to attack from the right on the issue of national security – a concern that haunted many of his generation. A formative event for him took place with the 1952 elections. The GOP ran on a series of national security issues, attacking President Truman's administration for letting China fall to communism in 1949 and criticizing Truman for getting the nation into a stalemate in Korea. Republicans, led by Wisconsin Senator Joseph McCarthy, also alleged that Democrats were weak against communists lurking in the US government. Republican Senator William Jenner of Indiana claimed that "every Fair Deal dollar" was "dripping with warm blood" of the American troops who were wounded or had died in Korea. "A lot of the Republicans right up to the top," noted Truman's assistant, Stephen Spingarn, "found out for themselves about the vicious effectiveness of McCarthy's tactics."[13] Their party's presidential candidate was Dwight Eisenhower, a nonpartisan military hero whose mere presence at the top of the ticket aimed to highlight the difference between the parties.

After Truman decided that he would not run for reelection, Democrats ended up nominating Illinois Governor Adlai Stevenson, a favorite with the intellectual set but not someone who brought shining military credentials to the table. Eisenhower won, and so too did Republicans in the House and Senate. Not long after FDR's triumphant moments in depression and war, LBJ saw that Democrats would suffer defeats if they were perceived as weak on national security. The good news for Democrats was that Republican control of the House and Senate lasted only two years. The bad news was that it happened at all, and for the second time since the end of World War II. (Republicans had also gained control of Congress from 1947 to 1949.)

Notwithstanding his growing fears of the right, Johnson's rise to power within the Senate was extraordinarily quick. In 1953, only a few years after LBJ entered the chamber, Georgia Senator Richard Russell, the leader of the Southern Caucus, orchestrated Johnson's election to become Senate Minority Leader. After Democrats retook control of Congress in the 1954 midterms, they elected Johnson as Majority Leader, believing that the Texan stood the best chance to hold his party together and capitalize on divisions within the GOP that would enable them to cause trouble for the popular president. Russell also believed that Johnson was the Southerner who stood the best chance of winning the White House. "Lyndon Johnson could be president, and would make a good one," Russell said.[14] When eighty-two representatives and nineteen senators from the South signed the "Southern Manifesto" in 1956 denouncing the Supreme Court's *Brown v. Board of Education* decision prohibiting segregation in schools, Russell didn't demand that Johnson sign it, realizing that doing so would hurt his chances in a presidential campaign down the line.

As Majority Leader between 1955 and 1961, Johnson had to contend with a liberal coalition of legislators and interest groups who came together during this same period and began pushing for a much bolder domestic agenda than FDR had been willing to embrace. In certain respects, they responded to the emerging civil rights movement and wanted to test the durability of the informal agreements that had structured the New Deal on race and unionization. This effort to expand liberalism did not result inevitably from an ideological embrace of this philosophy but from a generation of legislators, interest group representatives, policy experts, and activists who believed that the government needed to intervene in new areas of domestic life, such as civil rights, health care, and urban development. Facing the power of the entrenched conservative coalition in Congress, which primarily wanted to cut down what was already in place, this liberal coalition organized and fought to move Washington in a different direction.

With the economy booming as a result of the manufacturing sector and a growing suburban middle class that spent its disposable cash on the consumer economy, this young generation of liberals believed that the time had come for the party to do much more. Their goal was to create policies that would help a greater number of citizens join this middle class while using the strong economy of the moment to finally tackle structural problems such as poor health care, racism, and poverty. Democrats such as Paul Douglas of Illinois, Herbert Lehman of New York, and Hubert Humphrey of Minnesota were no longer willing to be obedient to the Southerners who had checked them in these policy areas. Humphrey had made a splash at the 1948 Democratic Convention when, as a candidate for the Senate, he demanded that his party embrace civil rights and leave behind the Southern conservatives who opposed this agenda. "To those who say that this civil rights program is an infringe- ment on states' rights, I say this – the time has arrived in America for the Democratic Party to get out of the shadows of states' rights and to walk forthrightly into the bright sunshine of human rights."[15]

LBJ found himself during much of his term as Senate Majority Leader trying to balance the competing needs of Southern Democrats who still controlled the committee system and the liberals, who had at their command mass-membership interest groups capable of swaying the media and mobilizing pressure. This vast network of organizations such as the AFL-CIO (American Federation of Labor and Congress of Industrial Organizations) and NAACP (National Association for the Advancement of Colored People) had become a formidable presence in the halls of Capitol Hill and used its organizational muscle – as well as its membership bases – to pressure members to vote in favor of its positions. As liberal numbers kept growing throughout the 1950s, Johnson relied on his relationship with Humphrey to broker deals with his left flank that ultimately failed to satisfy either side. Johnson warned Humphrey that he had to be more pragmatic if he didn't want to "suffer the fate of those crazies, those bomb-thrower types like Paul Douglas, Wayne Morse, Herbert Lehman. You'll be ignored, and get nothing accomplished." In 1955, Johnson introduced a "Program with a Heart," which contained a thirteen-point reform agenda.[16]

Depending on Humphrey to serve as a liaison to the broader liberal coalition, Johnson's most lasting accomplishment came with the Civil Rights Act of 1957, when he used his muscle to move through the upper chamber the first major civil rights bill since Reconstruction.[17] Many liberals were not pleased with the 1957 bill, seeing it as a watered-down measure that fell short of substantive reform. Oregon Democrat Wayne Morse complained, "I am fed up with the argument that the civil rights bill the Congress passed is better than no bill at all. I deny that premise."[18]

But the relationship between the liberal coalition and Johnson endured. Because of his leadership position in the Senate, Johnson had a growing familiarity with the demands and personalities of this coalition. He knew the key players and the issues that mattered to them. The relationship changed him as he became increasingly sensitive to the rationale of their agenda and the ways it was necessary to fulfill FDR's legacy, rather than perceiving them primarily as problems that needed to be dealt with.

His evolution on the key domestic issues of the time was opportunistic and ideological. With Johnson, it was usually difficult to separate the two. Johnson started to see the ways in which responding to the demands of liberals on matters such as race or health care could strengthen his position as a party leader, allowing him to bridge the two wings of his party in a way that few others could do. Like many other Americans, however, Johnson was also personally impacted by watching battles play out on the ground over questions such as civil rights. As his time at the NYA revealed, he always understood the genuine need to provide federal assistance to disadvantaged groups. By the late 1950s, LBJ was starting to see from his perspective as Majority Leader how good policy could also be good politics.

During much of President Eisenhower's second term, Johnson was deeply influenced by another core element of liberalism in these decades – liberal internationalism. Haunted by the loss of Congress in the 1952 election, as well as Eisenhower's presidency, numerous prominent Democrats helped forge a new form of Cold War liberalism that embraced a muscular vision of foreign policy. With President Truman having spearheaded the Cold War national security state, legislators like Johnson doubled down by going after isolationist elements in the Republican Party who resisted federal authority even in this area, as well as his own party's left. Mainstream Democrats sought to expand the national security state and strengthen America's standing overseas, working through international institutions such as NATO and the UN.

Their inclinations grew partly from that political obsession with the right that led many Democrats such as Johnson to be perpetually scared of appearing dovish. When the French pulled out of South Vietnam in 1954, allowing Ho Chi Minh to rule the North, then–Senate Minority Leader Johnson said: "Tomorrow Asia may be in flames. And the day after, the Western alliance, which the Democrats so painstakingly built up brick by brick, will be in ruins." When Democrats like Senator Stuart Symington of Missouri started to go after the Eisenhower administration for spending too little on missiles, Johnson joined in without reservation. Johnson's staff, such as George Reedy, saw an opportunity for Democrats. "The issue is one which, if properly handled, would blast the Republicans out of the water, unify the Democratic party, and elect you President . . . . You should plan to plunge heavily into this one."[19] Being tough on defense was good for liberalism and promised a path to reclaiming the White House for Democrats.

The importance of national security greatly intensified when the Soviets launched the satellite Sputnik into outer space in 1957. Under the direction of LBJ, Senate Democrats pushed for a massive acceleration of research and education spending related to the Cold War, including money for intercontinental missiles. The Sputnik launch had been a disaster, Johnson said, "comparable to Pearl Harbor."[20] President Eisenhower, committed to balancing the budget and achieving efficiencies in defense spending, pushed back. Much of his second term revolved around his budget battles with the Democrats, as the administration found itself defending restrained military spending while the Democrats called for a substantial increase in the federal commitment to national security.

By 1960, his final full year in Congress, LBJ had firmly identified himself with the hawkish wing of the Democratic Party that refused to cede ground to Republicans on national security questions. Even as the isolationist wing of the Republican Party faded, Johnson strove to out-hawk the Republican hawks. The political pressure of the Cold War pointed toward increased national security spending. The drive by Democrats to flex their militaristic muscle culminated when Kennedy used the argument that there was a "missile gap" with the Soviet Union, placing the United States at a distinct disadvantage, as a centerpiece of his 1960 presidential campaign against Richard Nixon. While the argument was incorrect, it turned out to be a potent tool against Nixon.

MAKING SOMETHING OUT OF NOTHING

Johnson served as vice president under Kennedy as the liberal coalition intensified its pressure on the political system. The 1958 midterm elections had increased the number of liberal Democrats in the House and Senate, offering them a sounder political base upon which to fight for their domestic programs. In 1959, House Democrats had formed the Democratic Study Group, a caucus of like-minded liberals who whipped up votes, disseminated information about vote counts and conservative parliamentary strategy, and conducted public relations efforts to promote their programs. In the Senate, the expanded caucus of liberal Democrats doubled down on its efforts to counteract the procedural tactics of the South, namely, the filibuster.

By the early 1960s, the grassroots civil rights movement had become the main force driving domestic political debate. The movement had taken form during the previous two decades, with a large number of organizations and leaders committed to pushing for voting rights, the dismantling of legal segregation, and an end to police violence. President Kennedy was reluctant to push too far on racial questions, fearing that the conservative coalition in Congress would stifle the proposals and every other measure that he hoped to achieve, including health care for elderly Americans. The racial accord that liberals had agreed to in the 1930s under FDR, which ceded to powerful Southern Democrats decisions over local race relations, placed the Kennedy administration in an extraordinarily difficult bind.

As the administration stalled, movement activists proved skillful at organizing protests that captured media attention by exposing the violence and brutality Black Americans faced in the South. One highpoint came in Birmingham, Alabama, in May 1963, when police violence against peaceful Black protesters, including children, shocked the nation as Americans saw images on their television screens. Kennedy sent Johnson to make a speech at Gettysburg about civil rights on May 30, one of the strongest declarations of support for the cause, which came just before Kennedy sent a civil rights bill to the House in June. Although Johnson had initially been reluctant to give the speech, it turned out to be one of the most important moments in his vice presidency. The address directly responded to King's "Letter from a Birmingham Jail" by stating: "The Negro today asks justice. We do not answer him – we do not answer those who lie beneath this soil – when we reply to the Negro by asking, 'Patience.' It is empty to plead that the solution to the dilemmas of the present rests on the hands of the clock . . . . Until justice is blind to color, until education is unaware of race, until opportunity is unconcerned with the color of men's skins," Johnson declared, "emancipation will be a proclamation but not a fact. To the extent that the proclamation of emancipation is not fulfilled in fact, to that extent we shall have fallen short of assuring freedom to the free."

FROM CIVIL RIGHTS TO REELECTION, 1964

The movement's pressure on liberal Democrats only intensified when LBJ became president in November 1963 following Kennedy's assassination. The president understood that civil rights would have to be at the top of his agenda, and, as a result of the movement, he had come to support this cause. Most important, Johnson had come to believe that robust civil rights legislation was necessary to end legal segregation as well as Jim Crow laws that restricted the right to vote. As soon as he took office, Johnson moved forward with the bill that JFK had proposed in June, working with liberals to wrestle the legislation out of the House Rules Committee and then break the filibuster in the Senate. Hubert Humphrey, who had been Johnson's bridge to the liberal coalition since the early 1950s, helped maneuver the bill to Johnson's desk for signature. Johnson had a hand in the struggle as he worked with Democrats to threaten using a "discharge petition" against House Rules Committee Chairman Howard Smith to make sure the bill did not get stuck, and offering insight into how Southern senators could be worn down during their filibuster. The president did not take the moment lightly. He went on a campaign-style barnstorming trip, giving thirty speeches in ten states, where he urged support for civil rights. "We don't want any Democratic label on it. We want it to be an American bill," he said. The Civil Rights Act of 1964 constituted a huge victory of liberalism, ending legally sanctioned discrimination, and amounted to the strongest measure to protect Black American rights since Reconstruction.

His effort to expand the liberal agenda did not end with civil rights legislation. From the moment he took over the presidency, Johnson's thoughts were consumed with ideas about how he could build on FDR's legacy by advancing proposals that had been gestating among liberals for years (see Figure 2.2). On the evening of Kennedy's death,

2.2. The stage at the 1964 Democratic National Convention in Atlantic City, New Jersey, demonstrated the party's goal of tying Lyndon Johnson and his vice-presidential nominee, Hubert Humphrey, to three liberals who had preceded them in the White House. John F. Kennedy's portrait looms above center stage, flanked by those of Franklin Roosevelt on the left and Harry Truman on the right.
Credit: LBJ Presidential Library photo by Yoichi Okamoto

Johnson told one of his advisers, Bill Moyers, that "I really intend to finish Franklin Roosevelt's revolution."[21] Hoping to make a policy mark that was distinct from what President Kennedy had achieved during his term, Johnson immediately built support for the Economic Opportunity Act, a "war on poverty" that provided funding to local initiatives to help impoverished citizens to become self-sufficient. The measure even included the novel approach of allowing for the "maximum feasible participation" of local citizens who were not government officials in the construction of these programs.

The 1964 election was notable for the way President Johnson and his vice-presidential pick, Hubert Humphrey, embraced liberalism. Once Republicans selected Arizona Senator Barry Goldwater, a right-wing conservative who did not shy away from the label of extremism, Johnson's advisers decided to make the campaign a defense of the liberal agenda against conservative attack. Goldwater's recent vote against the Civil Rights Act as well as his opposition to Medicare made it relatively easy for Johnson to run as the candidate of the liberal center of the political spectrum. After Senate Republican Minority Leader Everett Dirksen, quoting Victor Hugo, had called civil rights an idea whose time had come, Goldwater appeared to have placed himself on the wrong side of history.

But the structural limitations of liberalism and the political fears that it evoked were evident even at this high point of Johnson's career. In early August, as Goldwater attacked Johnson for being weak on defense, the president asked Congress to pass a resolution granting him authority to use force in Southeast Asia if necessary. He justified the resolution based on two alleged North Vietnamese attacks against US Navy ships in the Gulf of Tonkin. Although LBJ understood that the attacks were not militarily significant, he said he was determined to make a show of force. "That's what all the country wants," he told Secretary of Defense Robert McNamara, "because Goldwater's raising so much hell about how he's going to blow 'em off the moon. And they say that we oughtn't to do anything that the national interest doesn't require. But we sure ought to always leave the impression that if you shoot at us, you're going to get hit."[22]

Then, at the Democratic convention, the pervasive nature of institutional racism was front and center, reminding Black Americans of the constrained possibilities for change within the existing political system. The Mississippi Freedom Democratic Party (MFDP) was a group of largely Black delegates who had organized during the 1964 voter-registration campaign known as Freedom Summer as an alternative to the "regular" party delegation, whose power depended on the disenfranchisement of Black voters. Led by Bob Moses, Aaron Henry, Fannie Lou Hamer, and others, the MFDP delegates arrived at Atlantic City demanding that they should be seated at the convention instead of the regulars, who would not give assurances of their loyalty to Johnson in the election. Governor John Connally of Texas warned Johnson not to accept their demands. "If you seat those black jigaboos," he said, "the whole South will walk out."[23]

During televised hearings of the Credentials Committee, viewers watched dramatic testimony by Fannie Lou Hamer, a sharecropper who had been brutally beaten in jail for her civil rights activism. Hamer asked, "Is this America, the land of the free and the home of the brave, where we have to sleep with our telephones off the hooks because our lives be threatened daily, because we want to live as decent human beings, in America?" Johnson mobilized top liberal leaders, including Humphrey and United Auto Workers (UAW) President Walter Reuther, to force a "compromise" that gave the MFDP two "at large" seats with no authority and the promise of integrated delegations in 1968, while allowing the regular delegation to be seated.

MFDP leaders, who had not been consulted when this final plan was made, were furious. If the Democratic Party, which had just committed itself to the cause of civil rights by supporting the Civil Rights Act of 1964, still did not recognize the centrality of independent Black political power, then neither party could be counted on. "As far as I'm concerned," recalled John Lewis of the Student Nonviolent Coordinating Committee (SNCC):

> this was the turning point of the civil rights movement. I'm absolutely
> convinced of that. Until then, despite every setback and disappointment

and obstacle we had faced over the years, the belief still prevailed that the system would work, the system would listen, the system would respond. Now, for the first time, we had made our way to the very center of the system. We had played by the rules, done everything we were supposed to do, had played the game exactly as required, had arrived at the doorstep and found the door slammed in our face.

The battle inspired SNCC's Stokely Carmichael to champion the concept of Black Power that centered on the notion that the institutions of American politics had to be remade.[24]

For the time being, Johnson could live with the tensions that had unfolded with civil rights activists. He had pushed beyond the convention controversy, limiting how much space there was for Black Americans to obtain a greater role in the political process – with the goal of achieving independent political power – and to shape the terms of the debate over race relations. The MFDP walked away without regular seats at the convention; the all-white delegation won out with the promise of integration in 1968, though that meant little without voting rights. Johnson's comfort straddling this line was not surprising, given that he had been figuring out how to maneuver through the structural dynamics of racism within liberalism since FDR's era.

During his acceptance speech, the president came back to the liberal themes that he was most comfortable with. He told the delegates who were gathered:

> Most Americans want medical care for older citizens. And so do I. Most Americans want fair and stable prices and decent incomes for our farmers. And so do I. Most Americans want a decent home in a decent neighborhood for all. And so do I. Most Americans want an education for every child to the limit of his ability. And so do I ... Most Americans want victory in our war against poverty. And so do I.

The television spots produced for the president's reelection campaign highlighted the administration's record in expanding government programs. Johnson promised that much more was to come as long as Goldwater was not elected. He also described Goldwater as a threat to core policies that had already been put into place since the 1930s. In one ad, viewers watched two hands holding a Social Security card and ripping it in two. Johnson is working to "strengthen Social Security," the announcer said. In another ad, viewers were told that the conditions of those without means was a result of "circumstances," not "character."[25] The War on Poverty was an effort to change those circumstances. In speech after speech and spot after spot, Johnson ran as an unabashed twentieth-century liberal, even if he emphasized to voters that the choice they faced was between "the center and the fringe."[26]

The liberal strategy, with all of its limitations, worked for the moment. Johnson defeated Goldwater in a landslide. Democrats increased their majorities in the House and Senate. There were so many Democrats on Capitol Hill, a young Republican from Illinois named Donald Rumsfeld noted, that they had to sit on the Republican side of the aisle. The election created a rare window of opportunity for liberal policymaking.[27] The results finally broke the back of the conservative coalition, at least temporarily, allowing the president to move forward with his agenda in bold fashion. Democrats enjoyed a 295-seat majority in the House and held 68 seats in the Senate, enough to defeat a filibuster. Equally important, the balance within the Democratic Party had shifted decisively toward the liberals. Southern Democratic committee chairmen would no longer be able to bottle bills up. A huge number of victorious Democrats in the freshman class had run promising to vote for Medicare and other measures that had languished on Capitol Hill.

The election also put Republicans in a defensive position. Most members of the party were terrified of being connected to Goldwater. Despite what Goldwater had told his party at their convention in San Francisco, it seemed that extremism *was* a vice – and a big one when it came to partisan power. More members of the GOP were willing to cut deals on issues like Medicare since liberals had the support that they needed in the House and Senate to move bills. Even Southern Democrats like Wilbur Mills, chairman of the powerful House Ways and Means Committee, could read the political tea leaves and had no interest in putting up roadblocks for a losing cause. One administration official said that conditions were so good that the administration stopped using the term

"Southern Democratic Republican coalition." Another observer said he could not remember when "Southern influence in Congress was at this low point" before. The 89th Congress, quipped a columnist, should be called the "Goldwater Congress," since the backlash against his radical conservatism had set up the conditions needed to accomplish exactly what he was against.[28]

BUILDING A GREAT SOCIETY

President Johnson used the first year of his full term to push his agenda forward. Once he had demonstrated through an overwhelming victory that his administration commanded the support of the public, Johnson moved to write his own chapter in the liberal tradition. After spending years negotiating with and often frustrating the liberal coalition in Washington and at the grassroots level, he now seized the opportunity that the election had provided to tackle problems FDR had failed to address. In March 1965, following the brutal attacks on peaceful civil rights activists in Selma, Alabama, on "Bloody Sunday" (March 7), Johnson sent legislation to Congress giving the federal government a major role in protecting voting rights. The bill prohibited the use of literacy tests and required states and local governments with records of discrimination to obtain "preclearance" from the Department of Justice for any changes to their voting laws. It also established a formula for how jurisdictions subject to preclearance would be identified.

The Voting Rights Act (VRA) of 1965 constituted milestone legislation. Until the Supreme Court issued a ruling in 2013 that dismantled key provisions in the law, the measure had a dramatic effect in terms of increasing the number of Black Americans registered to vote and altering who served in elected positions. In Mississippi, the state with the worst track record of race-based voting suppression, the percentage of Blacks registered to vote jumped from 7 percent in 1964 to more than 59 percent by 1969. The number of Black elected officials in states where the federal government stepped in to enforce the VRA increased from about 72 in 1965 to over 1,000 by the mid 1970s.[29]

Johnson also tackled health care, one of the most intractable issues in national politics. As his colleagues in Congress understood, popular support for providing hospital care to the aged, paid for through Social Security taxes, was clear. For the first time since Truman's presidency, when the administration suffered a stinging defeat after the American Medical Association (AMA) and conservative coalition defeated his proposal to provide national health insurance for all Americans, a majority of Democrats was willing to take up this issue. Surging liberal sentiment in Congress dramatically changed the political landscape. Liberal Democrats in the late 1950s shifted their strategy by focusing on health care for the aged, a social group that commanded sympathy from Americans, and offering hospital insurance paid for through the Social Security system. The idea behind this plan, which the media called "Medicare," was that through a narrower agenda the chances of passage would be much greater. Nonetheless, until 1964, the conservative coalition had blocked this measure as well. Even with Kennedy's assassination looming over the electorate, the conservative coalition tied Medicare up in committee in the spring of 1964.

But the 1964 election changed everything. Many members of the freshman class had campaigned on the promise that they would vote for Medicare. Republicans, terrified of being associated with Goldwater, came forth with two health-care proposals of their own: one would offer voluntary physician's insurance paid for through federal taxes and contributions from beneficiaries, and a second would provide means-tested medical assistance, administered by the states, to the poor. Wilbur Mills, who had been a top opponent of the plan, understood that the political winds had shifted. He surprised Johnson by putting together a package more grandiose than the administration had originally envisioned. The Social Security Amendments of 1965 wrapped all of these proposals into one giant bill, providing hospital insurance (Medicare Part A) and physician's insurance (Medicare Part B), as well as a means-tested program that would be called Medicaid.

Nor did Johnson stop with voting rights or health care. Determined to use the window for liberal advances that had opened, the president moved to tackle another major policy area where previous presidents had failed: federal aid for elementary and secondary education. For decades, liberals had been unable to address the clear need for federal support of schools. The needs became especially acute as the children of the Baby Boom in the 1950s and early 1960s started to overcrowd these institutions. Every effort by congressional liberals to expand the federal role for education ran into two obstacles: Southern Democratic opponents who feared that such funds would provide an opening wedge to racial integration, and Northern Democrats whose Irish Catholic constituents feared that parochial schools would not receive funding. Johnson, whose memories from teaching Mexican students remained strong, attempted to use the moment to overcome these roadblocks.

To avoid the problems that previous plans had encountered, Johnson packaged the measure as an anti-poverty program. Money was allocated to school districts where a certain number of children fell below the poverty line. Since the funds went to kids, rather than schools, the program circumvented concerns about parochial institutions. Congress passed the Elementary and Secondary Education Act. Title I provided federal assistance to "educationally deprived children," increasing federal aid for grades K12 from 3 percent of total education spending in 1958 to 10 percent by 1968. The bill authorized the government to provide aid to local school districts with high concentrations of low-income families. State education agencies could dispense the money they received from the US commissioner of education as grants to districts. Title II provided money for libraries and textbooks, while Title III offered $100 million for supplementary educational services, including labs, language programs, vocational classes, and other educational services, while Title IV offered money for research and teaching. Title V funneled dollars to state departments of education. "By passing this bill," Johnson said at the signing, as he stood near one of his former teachers, "we bridge the gap between helplessness and hope for more than 5 million educationally deprived children." In a separate but related bill, Congress created Head Start, which directed $150 million in poverty funds toward pre-school programs. And there was more. The Higher Education Act provided federal funding for university libraries, Black colleges, and community service programs, as well as low-interest loans for students. Federal funding, though controversial, has remained a central element of education policy.

Other initiatives during 1964 and 1965 similarly directed federal policy toward improving the quality of life. The Great Society, as

Johnson called it, encompassed clean water, funding for culture and arts institutions, highway beautification, consumer safety, and more. The window that the electorate had opened with the 1964 election, combined with the continued pressure that emanated from the grassroots activists and liberal interest groups, offered a president with the skills of Johnson a real chance to change the nation's policy infrastructure.[30]

RUNNING INTO WALLS, DIVING INTO A QUAGMIRE, 1966–69

But even at the height of his legislative success, when Johnson was working with the Democratic Congress at a rapid pace to transform the architecture of liberalism by connecting the tradition to issues such as race relations, education, the environment, and health care, which FDR had downplayed, the political vulnerabilities and limitations of this tradition started to overwhelm him. Foremost, the architecture of liberal internationalism was politically grounded on the determination of its proponents to avoid being seen as weak on national security. This logic had pushed Johnson deeper and deeper into the quagmire of Vietnam. Like many liberal Democrats from this period, Johnson had exited the early years of the Cold War believing that the only way he could protect his legislative coalition was to avoid being tagged as weak on defense by the Republican right. Along with the Domino Theory, which stipulated that if one country fell to communism others around it would soon follow, political fears had pushed Johnson away from any negotiated settlement and toward increasing the number of ground troops in the conflict.[31] As the president told Senator Russell during a private conversation in which they ruminated over the war, Democrats in a state like Georgia would "forgive you for everything except being weak."[32] Johnson could never get over the political trauma from the 1952 election when Democrats lost the presidency and Congress as a result of national security issues.

The political costs of expanding the war, however, turned out to be extremely high. Vietnam was not World War II, but by the 1966 midterm elections, Republicans were attacking Johnson for failing to use enough bombing force against North Vietnam and failing to achieve decisive results despite deploying tens of thousands of ground troops. As the death toll kept rising, a left-wing anti-war movement simultaneously took hold on the college campuses. Even mainstream liberals such as Senator J. William Fulbright, chair of the Senate Foreign Relations Committee, started to question the president's decisions. Fulbright convened televised hearings where his committee grilled administration officials about the logic of its Vietnam policy. Like Truman in Korea, but at a much more dramatic level, the war bogged down Johnson's domestic agenda. The escalating budgetary costs also forced Johnson into a confrontation with budget-conscious Southern Democrats and Republicans, who after the 1966 midterms insisted that he choose between "guns or butter." Guns won. The kind of marquee bills that animated 1964 and 1965 were fleeting; much of the president's energy went to protecting the gains that had already been made.

The limits of how far liberals could go on race relations, particularly when dealing with the ways that racism was inscribed into institutions such as real estate or the criminal justice system, also proved to be overwhelming when Johnson proposed the third leg of his civil rights agenda in 1966: open housing. After tackling segregation and voting rights in 1964 and 1965, the administration attempted to end discrimination in the sale or rental of housing, which Rev. Martin Luther King Jr. had decided to focus on by moving to the slums in Chicago. This leg of the administration's civil rights agenda moved deeper than the earlier bills into the problem of institutional racism. The proposed legislation was premised on the notion that an entire sector of the economy – in this case real estate – could perpetuate racism whether or not individuals in the industry intentionally endorsed white supremacy. In 1966, Johnson sent Congress a measure that prohibited discrimination in the sale or rental of all housing. After making the proposal, Johnson watched as the short window of liberal policymaking started to close and the structural power of racism within his own party took hold. While the civil rights movement had been able to break down some of the congressional resistance to legislation in 1964 and 1965, the midterm elections of 1966 bolstered conservatives in the middle of this fight; the fair housing proposal elicited a fierce response from them as well as Northern ethnic workers in cities like Chicago who did not want to see their communities integrated. The national real estate lobby supported them, mounting an expensive blitz against the bill that was unlike almost anything since the AMA's fierce lobbying against Truman's health-care plan and Medicare.[33]

The battle over the measure consumed much of the final two years of Johnson's presidency along with Vietnam. "Your home is your castle," real estate lobbyists proclaimed in their public relations campaign. The midterm elections cost some liberal lions, such as Senator Paul Douglas of Illinois, their seats. "The pro-civil rights coalition which had operated so effectively in previous years," the *Congressional Quarterly* concluded, "Republicans and Northern Democrats in Congress and civil rights, labor and church groups outside Congress – fell apart in 1966." Ray Bliss, the Republican National Committee chairman, told a room full of reporters at a Washington hotel, "This press conference will be a little different from my first one, when you were asking me if the Republican Party would survive. It looks to me like we have a very live elephant." Richard Nixon, who had tried to remake his political career by campaigning all across the country, yelled into the phone at his Fifth Avenue apartment, "We've beaten the hell out of them and we're going to kill them in '68!"[34]

Tensions about the housing bill intensified in the summer of 1967 following urban unrest that took place in major cities stemming from police brutality against Black Americans. Opponents used the upheavals as further evidence to highlight why Great Society measures did not work and why efforts to regulate housing would only cause more turbulence. "Every white man," Johnson told his friend Abe Fortas, a justice on the Supreme Court, "just says by God, he don't [sic] want his car turned over and don't want some negro to [be] throwing a brick at him." Congress did finally pass the Civil Rights Act of 1968, but only after the violence that ensued following the assassination of Martin Luther King Jr. in April and only after the bill had been watered down by removing any substantial enforcement mechanism. Johnson still promised that fair housing would "in our time, become the unchallenged law of this land. And, indeed, this bill has had a long and stormy trip."[35]

By the time that the Kerner Commission, a group of prominent officials organized by Johnson to investigate the cause of the 1967 urban unrest, produced a landmark report in February 1968, the fight against institutional racism by the administration and, to a certain extent, Congress was over. The commission offered dramatic findings, calling "white racism" the cause of the urban unrest. It pointed as well to problems with policing and unemployment as the causes of the violence rather than "agitators" and "outsiders." The commission, headed by former Illinois Governor Otto Kerner, called for a new Marshall Plan focused on revitalizing the economy of the inner cities and addressing police violence. But Johnson believed that there was no chance of an increasingly conservative Congress moving on these ideas, and he did everything in his power to drop the report upon its release. Instead, he moved in a very different direction, increasing funding for policing and criminal justice institutions.[36] Whether he should have fought to promote the reforms remains a subject of debate. But his political assessment was not wrong. Without a new window of legislating opportunity, there was almost no chance to move new proposals through Capitol Hill.[37]

There were other clashes unfolding within the Democratic coalition. Northern machine politicians in big cities were fighting with Black activists, empowered to participate in decision-making over policy through the War on Poverty, about the way that monies were bring allocated in areas outside the South. The more broadly the civil rights agenda expanded, both in terms of region and tackling institutional racism, the bigger the fissures that opened up within the party.

Meanwhile, the war in Vietnam kept intensifying as Johnson's domestic troubles grew. With over 11,000 American soldiers having died by the end of 1967 and almost 500,000 troops in the theater, Vietnam severely undercut the president's standing within his own party even as conservatives regained power. The war that Johnson had entered largely to avoid harming his political coalition at home did exactly what he feared most. By the Democratic Convention of 1968, after Johnson had announced he would not run for reelection, it was evident to Americans that the Democratic Party was crumbling under the weight of an anti-war movement that had gained strength and was bound to oppose any party leader who had endorsed the decision to commit troops to this disastrous effort. The Democratic candidate, Hubert Humphrey, struggled to survive without totally separating himself from the president. Many of the Democrats who had supported Senator Robert Kennedy's campaign, before his assassination in June, or that of Senator Eugene McCarthy could not muster enthusiasm for one of the leaders in the Johnson administration who had pushed the war despite private reservations. Richard Nixon capitalized on the divisions within the Democratic Party, the rage over Vietnam, and the backlash to civil rights to win the presidency.

The history of twentieth-century American liberalism and the Johnson presidency are deeply intertwined. Johnson devoted much of his political career to building on the infrastructure put into place by Presidents Roosevelt and Truman. When political and legislative conditions shifted in a favorable direction in 1965 and 1966, the president moved on the ideas that the liberal coalition had been pushing for over a decade.

In many respects Johnson's investment was successful. Even if the political coalition he put together was fragile and the Vietnam War devastated his legacy, many of the programs that were part of the Great Society have endured. He burned his political capital by going big on legislation, but much of the legislation that emerged from his term lasts through today – so much so, that they aren't considered controversial; they are just part of our political landscape. It was no surprise when Tea Party conservatives in 2010 attacked President Barack Obama's proposed health-care plan.

At the same time, the president was trapped by limitations and weaknesses of that very tradition. For some scholars, these failures were the most defining element of his legacy. As the historian Michael Kazin wrote, "The great musical satirist Tom Lehrer once remarked that awarding the Nobel Peace Prize to Henry Kissinger made political satire obsolete. The same might be said for those who would turn the President most responsible for ravaging Vietnam into a great liberal hero."[38]

While it is important to understand how Johnson's own agency led to his downfall, it is equally relevant to understand how the nature of American liberalism pushed Johnson into these positions.

The president was caught in the basic contradictions of the agenda that he inherited and championed. The same tradition that strengthened his resolve to grow the government to tackle new areas of domestic life also pushed him toward the decisions that drowned his legacy for decades to come. This is not just the story of Lyndon Johnson – it's the story of American liberalism in the twentieth century.

CHAPTER 3

Lyndon Johnson and the Transformation of Cold War Conservatism

Nicole Hemmer

The editors of *National Review* regretfully announce that their patience with President Lyndon B. Johnson is exhausted.[1]

That was the opening sentiment of the December 17, 1963, issue of *National Review*, the first one published after John F. Kennedy's assassination. The magazine's short fuse made sense: it was a conservative magazine at the dawn of one of the most liberal administrations of the twentieth century. Yet prior to his ascension to the presidency, Johnson's ideological bent had been more difficult to discern. The same issue of *National Review* was stuffed with writers puzzling over his politics, pointing out that he had often been called a conservative (which they found laughable) or a moderate (which they mused over a bit longer). "It will not do," contributor John Chamberlin wrote, "to make too much of Lyndon Johnson's New Deal political origins," noting that he was a pro-property, pro-South politician. Conservatives did not expect an ally in Johnson, but they did not necessarily anticipate in that moment that he would become one of the defining foes of Cold War conservatism.[2]

Born in opposition to the New Deal in the 1930s and Dwight Eisenhower's moderate Republicanism in the 1950s, Cold War conservatism had been sharpening its claws on Kennedy when, in a flash of muzzle fire, his presidency ended and Lyndon Johnson became president. At the time, conservatives largely viewed Johnson as an old-school pol, whose blend of backslapping and backroom deals suggested a politics free of ideology. But as president, Johnson used those political tactics to expand the liberal state and pursue a vision of rights and equity that catalyzed the conservative movement to reorient itself in opposition to Johnson and the Great Society.

This reorientation remade Cold War conservatism, which in the 1950s had centered on opposition to labor unions, desegregation, and communism. Those remained important targets, but during the Johnson years, the right shifted its focus to law-and-order politics, populism, and a neoconservative critique of the popular programs of the Great Society. While Johnson was president, conservatives cemented their attachment to the Republican Party – something that had been tenuous prior to the 1964 campaign – and began to work out a political strategy that would keep the more extreme elements of the movement politically engaged while shedding the extremist image that had plagued conservatives throughout the 1950s and early 1960s.

The Johnson administration, though spanning only five years, gave birth to a new era of liberalism in the United States – and, unintentionally, a revitalized left-wing movement. But it also transformed the American right, which emerged from the Johnson years savvier, more politically effective, and more ideologically complex. Those transformations would pave the way for the crowning achievement of Cold War conservatism: the presidency of Ronald Reagan.

CREATING THE CONSERVATIVE COALITION

No presidential campaign looms larger in the history of conservatism than the 1964 race between Barry Goldwater and Lyndon Johnson. For the right, it was a moment of both immense triumph and searing defeat: they had successfully captured, at least for a moment, one of the two major political parties, but they then watched as their candidate lost in one of the most lopsided defeats in US history. That loss marked the end of one phase of the conservative movement, one defined by Goldwater, and the start of another, one defined by Johnson.

The conservative movement that Goldwater represented had taken shape during the late 1940s and 1950s in response to two major political shifts: the rise of New Deal liberalism and the emergence of the Cold War between the US and the Soviet Union. The two events were linked in the conservative mind, though how closely linked depended on where you sat on the conservative spectrum. If you believed Presidents Harry Truman and Dwight Eisenhower were dupes who tragically underestimated the communist threat, you landed in the more respectable *National Review*-style camp; if you believed instead that they were willing agents of the communist conspiracy, leading a federal government honeycombed with spies and subversives, then you were more fringe. But this was often more a difference of degree than of kind.[3]

What *National Review* brought to the table was not a more level-headed conservatism but a conservative philosophy that would dominate the movement during the Cold War, a fusion of small-government libertarianism, social and racial regulation, and an anticommunism that was as concerned about domestic threats as international ones. That project of "fusionism" imbued Cold War conservative thought with a sense of consistency and coherence that it often lacked in practice, while also offering a number of avenues for the conservative movement. Such an approach was necessary in the 1940s and 1950s when the movement was small and scattered, lacking a majority in either of the two major parties. In the years before the 1964 campaign, in fact, the main goal of the movement was to bring together those disparate threads and far-flung activists under the banner of conservatism and to use that newly united group as the base for a new wave of conservative political activism.[4]

In the 1950s, conservative leaders focused on two things: institution-building and high-profile political fights, both of which laid the groundwork for the broader national battles of the 1960s. Institution-building was a necessary step, conservative activists believed, because they had lost their hold on the two major parties. They rejected the New Dealism of the Democrats as well as the moderate Republicanism of Dwight Eisenhower, the popular president who held the reins of the party for most of the 1950s. Their antipathy toward Eisenhower started early: when he defeated conservatives' favored candidate, Senator Robert Taft, in the 1952 primaries, the right believed it had not just been defeated – it had been betrayed. That sense of betrayal motivated the conservatives who founded *National Review*. Since the two parties had abandoned conservatism, it was necessary to take a step back and start changing hearts and minds in the hope that a shift in voting habits would follow.

Over the next several years, conservative activists founded a variety of organizations, media outlets, and even political parties to begin disciplining right-leaning Americans into a cohesive national movement. There were organizations like the conspiratorial John Birch Society and Young Americans for Freedom, a group aimed at students and younger activists. There were conservative magazines like *National Review* and conservative book publishers like Regnery Publishing. Conservatives even dabbled in presidential politics, most notably with the 1956 third-party candidacy of T. Coleman Andrews, a segregationist whose evolution from head of the Internal Revenue Service under Eisenhower to anti-tax crusader made him the ideal fit for the right's nascent fusion of small government and social conservatism.[5]

This institution-building happened alongside a number of political battles the right undertook in the 1950s. The most high-profile of these were the congressional investigations into internal communist subversion. Though these lasted only a few years and ended with their greatest champion, Senator Joseph McCarthy, censured and disgraced, the anticommunist cause remained a political touchstone on the right. *National Review* founder William F. Buckley Jr. and his brother-in-law Brent Bozell Jr. published *McCarthy and His Enemies* in 1954, a book that secured McCarthy's place in the pantheon of conservative saints. The right waged a more sustained battle in the 1950s over labor, fighting to roll back protections for labor unions and paint those unions as unworkably corrupt and ultimately bad for workers.[6]

Just as important in the 1950s were the battles over integration, which most on the right opposed. The 1954 decision in *Brown v. Board of Education* that declared segregated schools to be unconstitutional turned the right against Chief Justice Earl Warren and his court. The decision to send federal troops to Little Rock, Arkansas, to enforce school desegregation solidified the right's antipathy for Eisenhower. The John Birch Society regularly equated the civil rights movement with communism, describing a Black–Red alliance seeking to destabilize the United States with disruptive protests. *National Review* took that line as well, insisting that white people be allowed to disenfranchise and rule over Black people in the South, because, as Buckley put it, whites were "the advanced race."[7]

These battles over domestic communism, labor unions, and Black civil rights explain why the Cold War conservative movement was not committed to either the Republican or Democratic Party. The parties were ideologically scrambled, each containing liberal, moderate, and conservative factions. But the ideologies were scrambled as well: white Southern Democrats might support segregation and oppose labor unions, while also advocating federal spending that helped their white constituents. Conservative Republicans could oppose federal programs and economic regulation, while also chafing at the kind of social regulation – segregation laws, birth control restrictions, mandatory school prayer – that some in the movement demanded. And neither party had promoted a candidate for president who met the desires of conservative activists. So they pursued third-party candidates while they puzzled over how best to find a toehold in one of the two parties.

The structures of the US political system assured that such third-party candidacies would be quixotic affairs. Andrews, for instance, scraped together just 100,000 votes in his 1956 campaign, out of 62 million cast. Activists like organizer and radio host Clarence Manion, who spearheaded Andrews's campaign, came up with increasingly byzantine plans for putting a conservative in the White House. (Most versions involved a conservative third-party candidate somehow winning enough electoral college votes to kick the election to the House of Representatives and then somehow convincing a majority of members to choose the conservative candidate.)[8]

Manion was still toying with this plan when the 1960 election rolled around. He and other conservative activists had seized on Barry Goldwater, then a second-term senator from Arizona, to be their standard-bearer. Elected to the Senate in 1952, Goldwater blended libertarianism and contrarianism in a way that appealed to activists in the Cold War conservative movement. His strong opposition to labor unions and unflinching rejection of even the most popular New Deal programs convinced many on the right that he was a true believer. He also took the movement seriously, appearing on conservative radio programs and sitting for interviews with publications like *Human Events*, a popular newsweekly, and *National Review*. When it came time for Goldwater to write his political manifesto, he chose his speechwriter Brent Bozell to ghostwrite it and Manion's hastily assembled printing service to publish it. The resulting bestseller, *The Conscience of a Conservative*, marked Goldwater as the leading voice of the Cold War conservative movement.[9]

Manion tried to leverage the success of that book into a presidential nomination for Goldwater, launching a Draft Goldwater drive in 1960. He hoped that if Goldwater did not win the nomination, he could be lured into running as a third-party candidate. But Goldwater had no interesting in abandoning the GOP, which meant that when he finally did win the nomination in 1964, he brought the conservative movement into the party with him.

A CHANCE FOR A CHOICE

Conservative activists saw the 1964 election as their first "chance for a choice" between conservatism and liberalism. That meant that any Democratic nominee would likely have become the pure distillation of liberalism – and all its ills – in the conservative mind. But the rise of Lyndon Johnson made that a much easier task.

Johnson's ascendance to the presidency a year before the election set the tone for the campaign that followed. In his State of the Union address in January 1964, the new president declared a War on Poverty, painting a utopian vision of a federal government that would not just whittle away at poverty but do away with it altogether. A few months later, he broadened that agenda under the banner of the Great Society, a comprehensive plan to tackle not just poverty but also education, civil rights, health care, and support for the arts. Those legislative skills that tempted some conservatives to see him as a dealmaker rather than an ideologue would now be put to use to pursue one of the most expansive liberal agendas in US history. And in July 1964, Johnson showed just how effective he could be in pursuit of that agenda, signing the Civil Rights Act of 1964 and showing that the federal government could be used to dismantle Jim Crow and pursue the goal of racial equality.[10]

The first few months of the Johnson presidency had an electrifying effect on the right. Johnson's commitment to passing an expansive Civil Rights Act catalyzed the racist, segregationist right to move not just against Johnson but also against the Democratic Party as a whole. And here the combination of Johnson's presidency and Goldwater's nomination was particularly consequential. Had Republicans chosen a different nominee – Nelson Rockefeller and George Romney, two moderate-to-liberal governors, were the main alternatives during the primary season – the contrast between the two parties would have been less stark. Both governors were strong supporters of the Civil Rights Act, and Rockefeller had been unveiling his own mini-version of the Great Society in New York, where he had begun expanding spending on education, health care, public parks, and the environment.

With Goldwater, though, there was a bright line between the two candidates. Though the senator generally avoided direct racist appeals, he strongly opposed the Civil Rights Act, laying out a libertarian argument about government overreach and the need to change hearts and minds before legislating on the issue. That position made him, and the Republican Party, a viable alternative to white Southerners appalled by Johnson's support for Black civil rights – a reality borne out by Goldwater's eventual victory in five Deep South states, many of which had opted for segregationist Dixiecrats in previous elections (see Figure 3.1).

With segregationists flocking to the Republican ticket, the Goldwater campaign developed a reputation for extremism. The conservative movement struck many Americans as radical, not only because the bulk of its policy preferences were outside the mainstream but also because of far-right groups like the Birch Society, which journalists had exhaustively profiled during the early 1960s. Even Kennedy's assassination played into those narratives, as Dallas, the city where he was killed, had a reputation as a hotbed of far-right radicals. Goldwater tried to distance himself from these groups throughout the general election – anyone with known Birch Society ties was barred from the campaign – but his prickliness about the charges of extremism also led him to strike back in ways that cemented the charge. That was especially true at the raucous Republican convention, where Goldwater seemed to embrace radicalism in his insistence that

3.1. President Johnson encounters supporters of Republican nominee Barry Goldwater during a campaign stop in Orlando, Florida, on October 26, 1964, one week before the general election. Goldwater ultimately won five Southern states, though Johnson held on to Florida.
Credit: LBJ Presidential Library photo by Cecil Stoughton

"extremism in the defense of liberty is no vice" and "moderation in the pursuit of justice is no virtue."[11]

Thanks to moments like these, Goldwater never shook his reputation for extremism. It took root in popular culture and political commentary, and it remains a central part of his historical legacy. That legacy, though, has obscured the other parts of his campaign that prefigured the transformations that the conservative movement would undergo in the years that followed.

Goldwater framed his campaign as an appeal not only to the amped-up conservatives who had been thirsting for his candidacy for years, but also to the "forgotten American," a phrase popularized by Franklin Roosevelt as he promoted the New Deal in the 1930s. A few months after Kennedy won the 1960 election, ending eight years of Republican rule, Goldwater drew up an outline of Republican Party principles called "The Forgotten American," which he published in the newsweekly *Human Events*. The text itself was unremarkable, rehashing his arguments from *The Conscience of a Conservative*. But the framework was distinctly different. He argued that the Republican Party needed to become the party of the forgotten American: the American harmed by inflation and the high cost of college, swindled by labor unions and federal spending. As such, "The Forgotten American" gave a populist cast to a set of conservative politics that were often unpopular and overtly minoritarian.[12]

The piece also underscored the bland libertarianism that Goldwater brought to many of the most pressing issues of the day, a rhetorical moderation distinct from the attitude of far-right groups like the Birch Society and white Southern politicians like Alabama Governor George Wallace. He opened "The Forgotten American" with the assertion that the individual had been swamped by the organizational – "labor unions, racial groups, civil liberties groups, consumer groups, nationality groups," and so on. That trend toward the group over the individual, he argued, was a reversal of the core individualist philosophy of the United States. It was a bloodless formulation that would be used to counter civil rights activism throughout the 1960s and beyond: that group rights were being elevated above individual rights, even as individual rights were being systematically denied in the existing political order.

Goldwater also introduced his calls for "law and order" in "The Forgotten American," a theme that would become a key part of his attacks on Johnson and liberalism during the campaign. In 1961, he wrote about it in a pre-Johnson context, arguing that labor unions were the predominant threat to law and order. "One of the firmest pillars upon which American society rests is the proposition that law and order are an absolute essential for the preservation and improvement of our democratic way of life," he wrote. But there was one part of American life in which its absence was "so widespread, so persistent, and so ignored that it constitutes a genuinely serious menace to the preservation of our free institutions": labor activism.[13]

Labor unions, he argued, were violent, corrupt, and lawless organizations, qualities on full display during strikes. Neither local law enforcement nor the public were suitably alarmed by this lawbreaking because they were "completely misled and brainwashed into dangerous apathy" by the notion that labor unions represented the underdogs in society. And while Goldwater insisted that he preferred that state or local governments bring unions to heel, their unwillingness to do so meant the federal government would need to be empowered too. (He remained mostly silent on the lawlessness and violence of the Jim Crow regime.)

By the 1964 race, Goldwater had reworked his "law and order" arguments into their more familiar form. In the same convention speech in which he rolled out his infamous "extremism" line, Goldwater laid out a template for the law-and-order politics that would work so successfully for the right in the coming decade. Drawing from concerns in the 1950s over juvenile delinquency and civil disobedience, Goldwater warned that freedom should "not become the license of the mob and of the jungle." While he argued that government should be small and restrained, he told the crowd of delegates that the maintenance of law and order was one of its few "inherent responsibilities."[14]

The language of law and order would become even more important in the days that followed. Goldwater's convention speech came on the same night when the Harlem uprising, a six-day protest against police brutality, began in New York, the first major urban rebellion of the 1960s. And while Goldwater's invocations of law and order would not catch fire during the campaign – an agreement with Johnson to avoid the issues of civil rights and Vietnam made it difficult to fan the flames as much as his successors would – the Johnson administration immediately recognized the effectiveness of that line of attack combined with the urban uprisings. As unrest mounted in New York, the White House quickly arranged a summit on racial violence and urged civil rights activists behind the scenes to pause protests until after the election.[15]

It was a sign of things to come. But in the 1964 election, the association between Goldwater and extremism was too strong for the Republicans to overcome. Despite his efforts to distance himself from some of the more radical and conspiratorial parts of the conservative movement, a good number of his most ardent supporters came from exactly those parts. Millions of copies of conspiratorial tracts about Lyndon Johnson – including one called *A Texan Looks at Lyndon*, which not only painted

Johnson as unspeakably corrupt but attributed more than a dozen deaths to him – circulated during the election. Goldwater contributed to the sense that his campaign was slightly unhinged. His musings about using nuclear weapons in Vietnam terrified a wide swath of Americans, especially after the Gulf of Tonkin incident in August 1964 resulted in Congress giving Johnson the greenlight to ramp up military action there. The prospect of a trigger-happy commander-in-chief heading up a movement of wild-eyed radicals held little appeal for most Americans, already unmoored by the shocking assassination of John Kennedy just a year earlier.[16]

By the time Election Day arrived, the question was less one of who would win and more one of how wide Johnson's margin of victory would be. And for Goldwater supporters, it turned out to be devastatingly wide: 13 points, with Johnson winning 43 million votes to Goldwater's 27 million. The electoral college was even more lopsided, with Johnson securing 486 of the 538 votes.

The scale of Goldwater's defeat had lasting consequences for the conservative movement and the Republican Party. It meant that, for the foreseeable future, the conservative movement would mold itself not around Barry Goldwater but in opposition to Lyndon Johnson.

LYNDON JOHNSON AND THE RISE OF CONSERVATIVE POPULISM

Lyndon Johnson didn't just win the presidency. Armed with a massive mandate and large congressional majorities, he continued to pursue the legislative agenda of his Great Society at a head-spinning pace. In 1965 alone, Congress passed legislation to remake the immigration system, restore voting rights to millions of Black Americans, provide federal aid for higher education, establish Medicare and Medicaid, set aside millions of acres of wilderness, and create a new cabinet-level agency, the Department of Housing and Urban Development. It was an agenda few presidents could dream of enacting over the course of two terms in office, and Johnson secured it in just one year.

That muscular policymaking had a profound effect on the conservative movement, providing not only a new enemy but a new political reality to navigate. Cold War liberalism in the early years of the Johnson presidency was popular and effective, and its successes, perhaps unexpectedly, generated new grassroots movements on the right and the left. On the left, activists mobilized because they felt the programs of the Great Society did not go far enough to achieve equality and justice, and were bound up in the same utopian ideas of American exceptionalism that also fueled Johnson's rapid escalation in Vietnam. On the right, activists recoiled at the rapid dismantling of Jim Crow segregation and disenfranchisement, and were appalled, at least in some circles, by the expansion of the federal government in health care, higher education, and housing.

This reaction gave rise to a conservative movement with an increasingly active and occasionally radical base, combined with a political leadership concerned that extremism had cost them a shot at the presidency in 1964. These sentiments led conservatives to experiment with two sometimes-incompatible approaches: attempts to draft off the popularity of the Great Society by coming up with conservative alternatives, and efforts to harness the growing populist backlash against the Johnson administration to the political ideology of Cold War conservatism.

In the aftermath of Goldwater's loss, conservatives suffered from a sense of disorientation. Despite their insistence that "27 million Americans can't be wrong!" – a reference to the number of votes for Goldwater in the election – they also understood on some level that 27 million votes were substantially fewer than Johnson's 43 million. To compete with the Great Society, they would either need to mimic it or find a way to strip it of its broad support.

Attempts to compete with the Johnson administration on the level of government services made very little headway. In 1965, radio host Clarence Manion spent several shows advocating for Eldercare. Pitched as an alternative to Medicare, it was designed by the American Medical Association as a voluntary program for low-income seniors to obtain federal subsidies to purchase private health insurance. Conservatives in Congress used that plan to introduce legislation in early 1965, and Manion quickly came out in support. He invited representatives from Eldercare's primary proponents, the

American Medical Association and the House Republican caucus, to speak on his show, and regularly promoted it as an alternative to "socialized medicine."[17]

Yet when Eldercare failed to gain traction, Manion admitted that it had not been in line with his conservative principles, that he had been spooked by Johnson's successes into supporting the measure. "I am not proud of our go at Eldercare," he wrote a donor in late 1965, "but the doctors were convinced that they had to offer something positive if they were to get anywhere with L.B.J.'s Congress. The A.M.A. requested our help and we went along, but all we harvested was – as you say – a compromise of principle."[18]

That tension between pragmatism and principles revealed a core fault line for conservatives during the Johnson administration. It was hard to ignore that charges of extremism had been an effective political weapon against Goldwater. The ease with which the Johnson campaign and commentators could draw connections between the senator and the wildest and most dangerous sectors of the US right had been major drags on his campaign. If conservatives wanted to rule, they would have to find a way to create distance from those parts of the movement.

That was the conclusion of people like Buckley, who had personally had enough of the Birch Society and similar groups long before Goldwater's loss. But the 1964 election proved a powerful tool in convincing the other editors at *National Review* that the magazine needed to break decisively from the Birch Society if conservatives were ever to have a hope of winning the presidency. Even then, some editors were wary, noting that openly attacking the Birch Society meant openly attacking a core part of the conservative movement – including a sizable chunk of *National Review* readers. But the political calculations won the day, and on October 19, 1965, an editorial declared that no one who retained ties with the Birch Society could be considered a part of the mainstream conservative movement.[19]

The dissenters at *National Review* were right. The outcry that followed, not only from Birch Society members but also from other conservative media outlets, was one of the most consequential that the magazine had ever triggered. Not only did cancellations roll in, but other movement leaders saw a tactical advantage in coming to the Birch Society's defense. Clarence Manion, for instance, welcomed Birch Society members, assuring them that the organization "is being smeared precisely because it is effective." But while the *National Review*'s policy did not bolster the magazine's standing within the movement, that search for a path to enough respectability to compete in national elections was a defining feature of Johnson-era conservatism.[20]

The extremism–respectability split, however, was only one of the fault lines in conservatism in the Johnson era. Another, often overlooked by historians, may have been even more consequential: the tension between conservatism and populism.

The Cold War conservative movement of the 1950s and early 1960s was a decidedly minoritarian one. Though conservatives at times claimed to speak for a hidden majority, more often they recognized that they had for a long time been a remnant, neither well represented in either party nor embraced by the public. That public, they more often argued, had been seduced by liberal policymakers offering handouts, creating a generation of complacent Americans too comfortable being hand-fed by the government. That ostensible generosity made Johnson's Great Society all the more dangerous: a new raft of programs that would lash Americans even more tightly to the federal government. Conservatives' hesitation about majoritarianism also echoed in a phrase common among Goldwater supporters: "We're a republic, not a democracy." The saying had been around as a political slogan since the 1930s and 1940s in anti–New Deal circles, but it took on renewed popularity as inclusive voting rights became a core part of liberal politics.

The Goldwater campaign revealed the limits of minoritarian politics and the need to appeal to what a few years later would be called the "silent majority." That shift required a two-pronged approach: making liberalism less appealing and finding the right combination of policies, rhetoric, and ideas to tempt more Americans into the conservative camp.

The key to making liberalism less attractive could be found in the Goldwater campaign's powerful appeal to law and order. The years of the Great Society were also the years of considerable unrest. The free-speech and anti-war movements on college campuses came into full flower after the 1964 election, and in 1965, less than a week after the Voting Rights

Act was signed into law, the neighborhood of Watts in Los Angeles exploded in a week of protests and unrest over police brutality. A wave of similar urban rebellions followed in 1967 and 1968. The mid 1960s also saw the beginnings of a decades-long rise in crime rates.[21]

There was no reason to believe that the liberal policies of the Great Society were causing the unrest of the 1960s. Some Great Society programs, like the Civil Rights and Voting Rights Acts, were in direct response to segregationist violence and anti-racist protests. For others, there was no clear causal relationship between, say, Supreme Court rulings protecting the rights of the accused and the rising murder rate, or new poverty programs and urban uprisings. Connecting the Great Society to disorder, a line of thinking that Goldwater had previewed in his campaign, was a political project aimed at broadening the conservative coalition and kickstarting the career of a new conservative star.

THE GREAT SOCIETY AND THE INVENTION OF REAGANISM

Tying the unrest of the 1960s to Johnson's domestic policies was one of the main projects of neoconservatism, a new political movement that began during his presidency. The neoconservatives emerged in reaction to two developments of the Johnson years: a robust anti-war movement on the left that was highly critical of both the Vietnam War and US conduct of the Cold War more generally, and the social and economic programs of the Great Society. Neoconservatives like social scientists Daniel Bell and Nathan Glazer and journalist Norman Podhoretz were liberal supporters of the New Deal who soured on the poverty programs of the Johnson administration, arguing that government spending helped sustain a culture of dependency in the United States. That argument had clear racial implications, visible in publications like "The Negro Family: The Case for National Action," a government report written in 1965 by Assistant Secretary for Labor (and later US Senator) Daniel Patrick Moynihan. Known more commonly as the Moynihan Report, it argued that dysfunctions within the Black community were responsible for high poverty and crime rates.[22]

The neoconservative argument that Great Society programs had actually worsened the state of poverty, crime, and dependency in the United

States was a perfect fit for a conservative movement looking for a new line of attack against liberal Democrats. And neoconservatives were the ideal messengers for that argument: refugees from liberalism, they not only infused their analysis with a kind of empathy and understanding often absent from conservative tracts but also wrapped their ideas in a social-scientific intellectualism that appealed to an electorate that still put its trust in intellectual authorities.

Perhaps no politician used such arguments to greater effect than Ronald Reagan. A household name thanks to his career as an actor and television star, Reagan had emerged as a player in Republican politics during the 1964 Goldwater campaign, delivering a nationally televised 30-minute speech on behalf of the Republican ticket in the week before the election. That speech, formally entitled "A Time for Choosing," would become known as The Speech, a tightly written, well-rehearsed statement of the conservative creed, brimming with memorable anecdotes and poetic turns of phrase. And while delivered in support of Goldwater, it also served as a preview of the political framework Reagan would adopt a year later, when he announced his bid to become governor of California.[23]

The Cold War had defined much of Reagan's politics. When he became president sixteen years after The Speech, he set about reheating the conflict that had eased during the 1970s, tagging the Soviet Union as the Evil Empire and kicking off a new arms race between the two countries. The high stakes of the Cold War were present in The Speech, with Reagan warning that Americans would either "preserve for our children this, the last best hope of man on earth, or we'll sentence them to take the last step into a thousand years of darkness." But while the Cold War was the context for Reagan's speech, he was equally interested in domestic affairs. He began the speech talking about national debt, not national security, and spoke as often about Social Security as he did socialism. This was a Cold War speech, but it was one that began to shift the balance from fears of external threats and internal subversion to the idea that government programs, even well-intentioned ones, impinged on Americans' freedoms and weakened their commitment to liberty.

When Reagan announced his gubernatorial run in January 1966, nearly all the Cold War signifiers had been stripped from his analysis, as his focus tightened on domestic themes. So too had some of the absolutism of his earlier speeches. Having learned from Goldwater's loss, Reagan softened his approach, introducing notes of pragmatism. Calling for a "creative society" to counter Johnson's Great Society, he centered his speech on downsizing government. But he took care not to suggest anything too radical: he suggested that taxes be "looked at" rather than slashed and that the government, rather than being the enemy, should be a junior partner to the businesses and people of California.[24]

Reagan also gained appeal by vilifying a new enemy: universities. His famous 1964 speech had nothing to say about education or the protests that had begun at Berkeley during the summer of 1964. But a year later, with campus protests mounting, Reagan found a prime target in the "noisy dissident minority" now disrupting California's campuses. After invoking the need for "law and order," Reagan transformed his past calls to stand firm against the Soviets into a pledge to stand tall against student protesters and spineless administrators. Californians had a choice, he said. They could meet the protestors with "vacillation and weakness" or they could demand administrators put an end to the unrest – and "settle for nothing less." That same spirit fueled his conflicts with universities during his time as governor: Reagan sought to confront administrators just as he once pledged (and would pledge again) to do with the Soviets.[25]

During his gubernatorial run and his two terms as governor, Reagan modeled a shift other conservative activists would adopt. He allowed the Cold War to fade into the background while he focused on economic and cultural issues at home. Phyllis Schlafly, for instance, followed suit. She spent the 1950s and early 1960s focusing on military matters, writing books about missile systems and nuclear threats. But after writing *A Choice, Not an Echo*, a Goldwater campaign book making the case for a conservative candidate, she turned her attention to attacking the Great Society. Her 1967 book *Safe – Not Sorry* argued that workers in the poverty programs of the Johnson administration were in fact responsible for the uprisings in cities across America. The book offered something neoconservative attacks on the Great Society could not: neoconservatives argued that disorder was a nebulous consequence of the programs, while Schlafly argued it was the very people administering the programs who were personally responsible.[26]

Attacking the Great Society by linking it to disorder helped make those programs more unpopular. But they did not automatically make conservatism *more* popular. Even if Americans rejected Johnson, there was no reason to think they would embrace a figure like Goldwater. So the right had to find a way to attract moderates into its coalition while directing activists at the grass roots away from radicalism and toward a more palatable set of programs. In other words, conservative activists had to find a way to navigate right-wing populism.

Reagan, elected as governor of California in 1966, embodied one form of that populism. Part of his appeal was rhetorical. He explained that he was fighting for ordinary Californians in a warm, avuncular tone, making common cause with white Californians through carefully coded racial language about "the jungle" and "the mob." He also focused on a particular type of pocketbook issue: easing people's tax rates – a subject of growing concern in California in the late 1960s – and loosening regulations to allow Californians' entrepreneurial spirits to soar. He tweaked experts and intellectuals, a popular pastime on the right that fit neatly into their opposition to the Great Society. Johnson's programs had been developed by intellectuals, and the right believed they had badly failed.

This was a populism that squared neatly with the intellectual fusionism of early Cold War conservatism, that blend of economic libertarianism, social regulation, and conservative anticommunism so central to publications like *National Review* (see Figure 3.2). But it was not the only populist message on the table in the Johnson years. The right also had to contend with the candidacy of George Wallace, the Alabama governor who once stood on the steps of a school that was ordered to admit Black students and vowed "Segregation today, segregation tomorrow, segregation forever!" But rather than representing a segregationist rump unable to come to terms with the end of Jim Crow, Wallace developed a robust right-wing populism rooted in white racial identity while offering far more liberal economic policies. Rather than reject the Great Society, he embraced some of the new economic entitlements, promising to offer more generous benefits for recipients of Social Security and Medicare. He also embraced pro-union politics, opposing the anti-organizing laws that governed his home state of Alabama.[27]

3.2. Four iconic figures of the modern right review the program at festivities in 1975 marking the twentieth anniversary of the *National Review*, a leading conservative publication. At right is *National Review* founder William F. Buckley. The others are (left to right): William's brother, New York Senator James L. Buckley; former California Governor Ronald Reagan; and Arizona Senator Barry Goldwater.
Credit: Getty Images

That was an intoxicating combination for many white working-class voters, particularly men who liked both Wallace's policies and his pugilistic style. Running for president as a third-party candidate in 1968, he quickly made inroads well outside the South in states like Wisconsin, Illinois, and New Jersey. And plenty of Goldwater conservatives were eyeing Wallace, too, drawn by his hardline positions against civil rights and protestors. (On the campaign trail he vowed to run over any protestor who laid down in front of his vehicle and mocked the left as dirty, lazy hippies.)

Wallace's popularity posed a problem for traditional Cold War conservatives like the writers at *National Review*, who understood Wallace's appeal but were appalled at his liberal economic policies. Aware of how many on the right were tempted by Wallace, *National Review* writers argued that the 1968 election, like the one four years earlier, represented an opportunity for genuine choice – a choice between conservatism and populism.

For conservatives, the 1968 election was an opportunity to secure their hold on the Republican Party while moderating just enough to find a viable candidate. A sizable contingent on the right landed on the Republican frontrunner, former Vice President Richard Nixon, who had been making inroads into the conservative movement by hiring the fiery writer Pat Buchanan and wooing the editors of the *National Review*. There were plenty of detractors, including the publishers of the two main right-wing journals, *National Review* and *Human Events*, which led to a brief Reagan boomlet during the race for the GOP nomination. But Reagan was a recent convert to conservatism with only a year as governor under his belt, and Nixon easily sailed to the nomination.

Battling Reagan was far easier than containing the threat of a third-party candidate. Early in the campaign, it became clear that the biggest threat to Nixon's ability to build an electoral majority was George Wallace and his white-populist campaign.

In May 1967, a year and a half before the election, *National Review* writer Frank S. Meyer opened the salvo against Wallace and populism. "George Wallace, like every demagogue in our history, is a populist," he wrote. "Populism is the radical opposite of conservatism." True, both were aligned against liberalism, but Meyer argued that populism contradicted conservatism. Like liberalism, it subsumed the individual, binding the individual not to the state but to "the tyranny of the majority." Meyer wrote: "It is in its own way as alien to the American conservative conception of constitutional republican government as is liberalism."[28]

As the 1968 election grew closer, the attacks on Wallace escalated. That's because, while Nixon had captured the Republican nomination fairly easily, the presidential primaries had roiled the Democratic Party. In March 1968, President Johnson, having swept into office with massive majorities and a popular agenda, broke under the weight of domestic unrest and the growing unpopularity of the Vietnam War. Facing serious challenges from his left in the Democratic nomination race, he announced that he would not be seeking reelection. Once his vice president, Hubert Humphrey, locked up the Democratic nomination after the assassination of Robert Kennedy and a divisive and violent convention, Nixon had a much clearer path to victory than he had held at the start of the year. At least, he would have had, if it had not been for Wallace. The Wallace campaign was attracting disaffected Southern Democrats and conservative Republicans, precisely the base Nixon needed to build his majority.

So in October, *National Review* pulled out all the stops. The publication brought in Goldwater and John Ashbrook, an Ohio representative with a large following on the right, to join Buckley in a series of anti-Wallace columns. Goldwater started by listing all the reasons Wallace appealed to the right: his calls for "law and order," along with his rage at protestors, intellectuals, and the press. Wallace was a talented orator and showman, Goldwater noted, nodding to Wallace's infamous anti-integration stand (without mentioning the racist substance of that moment). Yet for all that, he argued that a vote for Wallace would only benefit Humphrey and that Nixon was conservative enough. It was a tepid endorsement but a necessary one heading into the election.[29]

Ashbrook was more hard-hitting. Wallace, he argued, was a liberal to his core: a big spender, a longtime Democrat, and a proponent of centralized government power. "American conservatives should make no mistake about it," Ashbrook wrote. "The only thing Wallace has against Washington is its racial policy. In all his other attitudes he is the biggest centralizer of them all."[30]

In the end, Wallace did keep the election perilously close, at least in the popular vote. Only around 500,000 votes separated Nixon and Humphrey, while Wallace racked up nearly 10 million votes. He also won five Deep-South states, four of which had gone for Goldwater in 1964 (and all of which would vote for Nixon in 1972, when he won an eye-popping forty-nine states).

But the election signaled something important for conservatives: they could win national majorities and break the Democratic coalition, but it would take some form of compromise to expand their base. That compromise could mean someone like Nixon, a more standard-issue Republican candidate open to adopting some conservative ideas, but it could also mean a white populist like Wallace. And in the late 1960s, the heart of the conservative base was with

Wallace. While the Wallace vote faded in 1972, the 1970s would show just how strong white-racial and populist-conservative politics would be for the right, as a new wave of grassroots movements – against school integration, feminism, gay rights, and taxation – became the core of conservative activism. Those movements sparked the rise of the New Right, a group of activists and institutions devoted to bringing together populism and conservatism and challenging the conservative elites – including those who had spearheaded the Goldwater campaign – who had led the movement in the 1950s and 1960s. This was exactly the blend of issues that would lift Reagan to victory in 1980.

Populism may have been intellectual conservatism's "radical opposite," but during the Johnson years, it became clear that in the broader right-wing coalition, the two political movements would have to coexist – and, eventually, merge.

THE TRIUMPH OF GREAT SOCIETY CONSERVATISM

The Johnson administration triggered a reorientation of Cold War conservatism. Goldwater conservatives found themselves forging new alliances, pioneering new arguments, and developing new political strategies, all aimed at building a new conservative movement capable of winning national majorities. Those innovations led to a wave of grassroots movements oriented around a wide array of domestic policies: opposition to taxation, the Equal Rights Amendment, school desegregation, and gay rights. Those movements not only helped bring new activists into conservative politics, but also helped refine and popularize a populist rhetoric that would become a mainstay of post–Cold War conservatism.

While Lyndon Johnson was the catalyst for this change, he was not responsible for the direction it took. The popularity of the liberal president and his agenda could have drawn conservatives toward more moderate positions. That was certainly the idea behind Eldercare and even, to some extent, conservative support for Richard Nixon, who was willing to make more space for conservatives in the Republican coalition but not cede the party to them entirely.

But the Cold War conservative movement emerged in opposition to that sort of "me-too" politics; those times they attempted to compromise, they would either disguise or eventually abandon the effort. For instance, when Ronald Reagan raised taxes in 1982, he signed the law at his ranch out in California where journalists were not allowed to attend. And when conservative think tanks dreamed up market-driven alternatives to health care – successfully, in the case of the Heritage Foundation's plan, instituted by Mitt Romney when he was governor of Massachusetts – conservatives quickly disavowed any knowledge of those efforts when health-care debates got underway during the Obama administration. Those compromise efforts, it turned out, were *strategic* rather than *transformative*: a temporary workaround at times and in places where conservatism was particularly unpopular, not a rethinking of the fundamental direction of the movement.[31]

What emerged, then, from the Johnson era was a conservative movement that was far nimbler than its early Cold War iteration. That was in part because of strategic moves but also in part due to a changing relationship to populism. If populism made the writers at *National Review* nervous in the late 1960s, by the 1970s the movement had learned to stop worrying and love populism as a political strategy and rhetoric. That was particularly true for the grassroots movements of that era, often peopled with activists drawn from white evangelical churches and suburbs who had never been active in protest politics before. These activists, drawn into politics through single-issue campaigns against abortion or property taxes or desegregation, would become part of the landslide victory that brought Ronald Reagan to power in the 1980s.

But conservatives soon learned that populist politics did not need a mass movement to be effective. In the early 1990s, the Cold War ended, and with it, the Cold War conservative movement. In that moment, a populist attack on the Great Society and its consequences became the organizing principle that held the American right together. With the communist enemy gone, conservatives latched on to a broad anti-liberalism as the core of their movement. And the liberalism that they opposed was not the liberalism of Franklin Roosevelt or Bill Clinton, but of Lyndon Johnson.

In particular, conservatives in the 1990s attacked the racial liberalism of the Great Society. When they wrote about multiculturalism and warned about the "balkanization" of the United States, they blamed the immigration reforms of 1965. When they wrote about affirmative action as an attack on the economic and social standing of white men, they blamed the Civil Rights Act and the Equal Economic Opportunity Commission it created. When they wrote about crime, they blamed what they saw as Johnson's capitulation to the lawlessness of Black protestors. As such, they used Johnson's presidency to nationalize the Southern strategy.

The Johnson administration also helped reorient the conservative movement because of the role it played in changing material and social conditions in the United States. Inflation began creeping up during the Johnson years, only to spike during the 1970s, feeding an anti-tax movement based in California that quickly spread across the country. Deindustrialization worsened the downward trend in unionization, eroding the institutional connections between the white working class and the Democratic Party at the same moment that the right was perfecting coded racial appeals to attract those same voters. The US population became far more diverse as immigrants from the Global South gained new opportunities to relocate to the US under Johnson's immigration reforms, population changes that fueled the new nativism of the 1990s and enabled conservatives to bring immigration into their suite of racist politics. And the 1964 Civil Rights Act, which had played an enormous role in beginning to dismantle Jim Crow discrimination, also created new protections for women, who in the decades that followed took advantage of new economic, educational, and reproductive opportunities to assert autonomy over their lives.

Conservatives were able to take advantage of those changes in the last third of the twentieth century precisely because they had adapted their ideology and rhetoric to counter Lyndon Johnson and the Great Society. His 1964 victory forced them to reconsider their commitment to minoritarian politics and begin to incorporate populism into the movement. While that made the American right less coherent, it also made it far more politically agile. The movement that began the Johnson era by losing in a devastating electoral landslide learned enough from that defeat to serve up some of the most impressive landslide victories in modern US history in the years that followed.

The Great Society and the Beloved Community: Lyndon Johnson, Martin Luther King Jr., and the Partnership That Transformed a Nation

Peniel E. Joseph

LYNDON JOHNSON AND MARTIN LUTHER KING JR. ARE ARGUABLY the two most impactful political figures of the 1960s, a decade that fundamentally transformed America at home and abroad. The twists and turns of the relationship between the two men offer a fascinating entrée into the hopes and shortcomings, successes and failures, of the Great Society, the Johnson presidency, and the civil rights era. At the height of their alliance, Johnson and King rode history's wave into immortality, working in creative tension with one another to produce legislative breakthroughs that resonate well into the twenty-first century.[1] At his best, President Johnson treated King with the respect due a fellow statesman. He sought the civil rights leader's advice, invited him to private White House meetings, regaled him in phone conversations with his efforts to combat racism and poverty, and offered public praise after King won the Nobel Peace Prize. On October 16, 1964, two days after the announcement of King as the youngest ever recipient of the prize, LBJ dictated a memo from Air Force One. "It signals," Johnson said of the award, "the world's recognition that Americans committed to a course of justice for all our people and the role that you have played in that effort." The president stressed that King's civil rights leadership – and its international recognition – reflected glory on the entire country. "The Award is not only a tribute to you but to the Nation as well," Johnson asserted.[2]

Yet there was another side to Johnson's attitude toward King. The president's personal sensitivity to criticism, racial blind spots, and competitive streak at times overwhelmed the instincts that led him, when their outlooks aligned, toward partnership and even friendship. Johnson allowed FBI Director J. Edgar Hoover, perhaps King's most formidable and vengeful opponent in government, to curdle his views of King. Over time, the Johnson–King relationship gave way to mutual recriminations, hurt feelings, and missed opportunities. In retrospect, we can see King as one of the key architects – no less important than LBJ and surely more important as a global symbol of racial justice and the power of American democracy – of the Second Reconstruction. In this sense, King can be seen retrospectively as Johnson's equal, an unelected prime minister of Black America who negotiated the path to citizenship with a sitting president. But Johnson did not see things that way as time passed. Partisan divisions and racial tensions drove wedges between the two men, as did LBJ's sense of economic pragmatism and his dedication to plain old political horse-trading of a kind that King found unseemly but Johnson considered the cost of doing good in the world. Contrasting temperaments and different understandings of the power and limits of racial progress and democracy meant that the partnership was perhaps bound to fail.

The complexity of the Johnson–King relationship and what it reflects about both men and the times that shaped them is key to gaining a more comprehensive understanding of the 1960s. Amid renewed political, legislative, and legal battles over voting rights in the twenty-first century, King's legacy continues to swell, augmented by an annual federal holiday, a memorial in Washington, DC, and a cultural resonance that has only grown in the aftermath of revelations about his personal life that exposed his all-too-human frailties.[3] Meanwhile, Johnson's reputation, so long burdened by the tragedy of Vietnam and the ferocity of the white backlash that forced Democrats to retreat from the ambitions of the Great Society, has made a comeback. The rise of Barack Obama, the passage of the Affordable Care Act, the massive federal intervention that followed the Great Recession of 2008, and the global pandemic in 2020 demonstrate the federal government's power to act boldly with both policy force and moral authority. In many ways, the third decade of the twenty-first century is the perfect moment to examine the nuances and subtle shades of the interaction between Johnson and King.[4] In an age of racial, political, and ideological divisions that both recall the 1960s and, in certain ways, appear sharper and less resolvable, the Johnson–King partnership takes us back to a moment in postwar American history when great crises produced unprecedented opportunities. Both Johnson and King, in different ways, seized the moment with unmatched boldness and clarity of purpose, even if their cooperation had clear limits.

PARTNERS OF A SORT

In the arena of racial justice, Lyndon Johnson is the most consequential president of the twentieth century. His vision of a Great Society centered the struggle for Black citizenship as the beating heart of an imperfect but aspirational democracy. Cumulatively, Johnson's civil rights agenda helped make America a more prosperous, integrated, educated, safe, and environmentally healthy place for tens of millions of Americans. In doing so, LBJ became one of the architects of the Second Reconstruction era stretching from the Supreme Court's *Brown v. Board of Education* decision in 1954 to the assassination of King in 1968, a period that might also be called the heroic phase of the civil rights movement. America's Second Reconstruction sought to complete the unfinished business of the first. The modern civil rights struggle represented a sequel to the nation's attempt after the Civil War to remake the nation as a true democracy. These efforts ended in the heartbreak of massive anti-Black violence, lynching, imprisonment, and land dispossession. By the end of the nineteenth century, the United States had indeed been remade, not as a racially integrated democracy but via an apartheid system euphemistically referred to as Jim Crow.

A year teaching Mexican American students as a young teacher in tiny Cotulla, Texas, helped LBJ identify with underdogs of all stripes. But Johnson's views on racial justice evolved over time and were never perfect. As a young boy coming of age in racially segregated Texas, Johnson at times engaged in the ordinary racist practices of the era. Yet by the time he ran for Congress, he displayed genuine instances of respect for Black Americans, defying the cultural rules of the era by shaking hands with African Americans who stood at the edge of his campaign rallies.

Johnson's compassion unquestionably bowed to harsh political realities as his career advanced. He voted alongside Dixiecrats in Congress to oppose legislation aimed at securing voting rights, assuring equal employment opportunities, and ending lynching.[5] As a senator and eventual Majority Leader with close ties to some of the nation's most powerful Dixiecrats, Johnson proved shrewdly pragmatic. He cultivated the loyalty of leading Southern Democrats such as Georgia Senator Richard Russell even as he publicly supported the passage of the 1957 Civil Rights Act. The first civil rights bill since Reconstruction was a largely symbolic measure that lacked enforcement powers but boosted LBJ's presidential aspirations by giving him the appearance of a moderate. Over the course of his career, Johnson at times used crude racial stereotypes and slurs when referring to Black Americans, Mexicans, and Mexican Americans. Depending on his audience, he could come across as a racially enlightened borderline Southern progressive or a conservative and hidebound Dixiecrat.[6]

As vice president, no longer politically bound just to his home state of Texas, Johnson headed the President's Committee on Equal Employment Opportunity (CEEO), a position he took seriously. Although often entangled in bitter battles with Attorney General Robert F. Kennedy, the president's younger brother and closest political confidante, LBJ left no doubt of his evolution on matters of race. Johnson tapped Hobart Taylor Jr., a Texas transplant practicing law in Detroit, to be his point person at the CEEO, which took important steps to counter racism in government and corporate employment across the nation. By 1963, in the wake of racial violence in Birmingham, Alabama, and the centennial of the Emancipation Proclamation, Johnson emerged as a steady voice advocating bold steps in the civil rights arena just as the Kennedy administration was beginning to focus on the issue. But the issue was deeply personal for Johnson, who increasingly cited the hardships that his Black cook, Zephyr Wright, endured as she and her family shuttled between Washington and Texas to care for the vice president's family. LBJ was mortified by the fact that Wright, a college graduate, could not sleep at hotels, eat at restaurants, or use restrooms during her travels through the South and told stories of her travails as he promoted civil rights bills in 1963 and 1964.

Johnson found not just his political but also his moral bearings on the subject of racial equality during his visit to Gettysburg on the hundredth anniversary of Abraham Lincoln's historic address. In his own impassioned speech, Johnson declared that until equality touched every facet of American life "emancipation will be a proclamation but not a fact" – the sort of rhetoric that many Americans longed to hear from President Kennedy.[7] LBJ told Kennedy as much, suggesting the president visit the South and show solidarity with oppressed Blacks on an issue that threatened his presidency. There could be little doubt that, well before his sudden ascension to the Oval Office, Johnson's views of Black Americans' struggles for dignity and citizenship had evolved in substantive ways from his days as a boy living in the Texas Hill Country.

King, perhaps the most important Black political leader of the twentieth century, would become LBJ's sometimes cooperative, sometimes combative partner in pursuing an array of domestic reforms that LBJ dubbed the Great Society. King's vision of a Beloved Community free of racial discrimination, economic injustice, and violence initially aligned with Johnson's goals, which the civil rights leader saw as the practical application of a social movement aimed at nothing less than the fundamental transformation of American democracy. King's genius lay in his ability to synthesize disparate parts of the nation's panoramic histories, traditions, and cultures into a coherent story that promised to heal its racially scarred soul. He linked the Black social gospel tradition that interpreted the Bible as a story of social justice against oppression to mainstream Christianity, Gandhian nonviolence, and the sacred documents written by America's founders. King found hope for radical Black citizenship in America's "great wells of democracy," the taproot of his belief that the nation could become not just a great country, but also a good one.[8]

These beliefs contained the seeds of discord with LBJ since King's vision of citizenship meant more than the extension of rights. King characterized citizenship in terms of access to decent housing, health care, food, a living wage, and communities free from violence. King's vision of a Beloved Community imagined an America not only free from racism, poverty, and violence but also aggressively committed to expanding human rights at home and internationally. He loved America enough to criticize the nation publicly, a stance that left him open to charges of being unpatriotic or worse. Yet King's stirring example of patriotism found him expressing public faith in a democracy that radical critics such as Malcolm X decried as a sham.[9]

LBJ IN THE PRESIDENCY

To his credit, LBJ recognized that the grassroots insurgency for Black dignity and citizenship that had roiled the Kennedy presidency and threatened the nation's democratic foundation required bold leadership that rose above partisanship. President Johnson met with King on December 3, 1963, just eleven days after the Kennedy assassination, a meeting that signaled LBJ's understanding of the important role that civil rights would play in the nation's, as well as his own, future. They found common ground in a shared wish to honor the Kennedy legacy primarily through the passage of the Civil Rights Act that Kennedy had proposed, yet was unable to enact. The two men also found a shared affinity for their beloved South – Georgia for King and Texas for Johnson. Each spoke in a distinctly Southern drawl and expressed love for the South's cooking, music, and folkways.

During their meeting, Johnson and King sized each other up literally and figuratively. King, who stood 5' 7" , privately expressed surprise that the 6' 3" Johnson appeared much bigger in person than on television. King still smarted from the fact that he had not been invited to the JFK funeral and adopted a distantly professional demeanor with the president.[10] Still, King appreciated the loquacious new president's sincerity. Johnson asserted that he intended to surpass the Kennedy administration's legislative record, if not the myth already enveloping his legacy, by signing major civil rights legislation before the next year's presidential election. The two men spent 45 minutes going over strategy for defeating a Dixiecrat filibuster and passing a bill through Congress. King took note of Johnson's tremendous energy, his knack for reeling off esoteric Senate rules from memory, and his impulsiveness. Johnson took phone calls during the meeting and at one point put King on the line with the president of the United Steelworkers.[11]

King emerged cautiously optimistic that the momentum that the movement had gathered since the March on Washington would not vanish with Kennedy's death. "I was very impressed by the president's awareness of the need of civil rights and the depth of his concern," King told reporters as he left the Oval Office. "As a Southerner, I am happy to know that a fellow Southerner is in the White House who is concerned about civil rights," King added. Privately, he confided to two of his closest advisers that the president possessed "great ego and great power" as well as "pragmatic compassion" that signaled a new day. "It just may be that he's going to go where John Kennedy couldn't," King speculated.[12]

King found it curious that Johnson failed to press him about alleged communist ties as Kennedy had done, but King should not have felt safer. FBI Director J. Edgar Hoover's efforts to poison the relationship between Johnson and King began immediately after the Kennedy assassination. Johnson showed little overt enthusiasm for Hoover's sordidly granular distillation of FBI wiretaps documenting all aspects of King's private life, but the president did nothing until mid 1965 to stop the surveillance. The president kept this information close, just in case the tenor of their new political friendship changed. Johnson's treatment of King exhibited all the Janus-faced tendencies of the man, the politician, and the president. These complexities, containing the contradictions that make Johnson so achingly human, help explain – or at least contextualize – how a president who passed some of the most progressive social legislation in American history also supported policies that would punish the very communities aided by the Great Society through intensification of policing of Black urban areas.

The Johnson–King relationship evolved in the context of enormously high stakes. They needed each other and assisted each other when their interests aligned, as they often did in the early phase of the LBJ presidency. The relationship was inherently political, transactional even, which is not to say that each man did not admire parts of the other. The alliance thrived above all in the first two years of Johnson's presidency. King took an active role in the presidential campaign of 1964, which earned Johnson the presidency in his own right, encouraging Black voter turnout and helping Johnson by halting civil rights demonstrations as the election drew near.

But even in the best of times, there were signs of trouble, not least Johnson's backroom maneuvering to prevent the Mississippi Freedom Democratic Party (MFDP) from being seated at the Democratic National Convention in Atlantic City. Led by the brilliant sharecropper-turned-organizer Fannie Lou Hamer and activist Aaron Henry, the MFDP sought to unseat the white-supremacist Mississippi "regulars" who excluded Blacks from the convention. Hamer's televised August 22, 1964, testimony before the party's credentials committee shocked viewers. "Is this America?" she asked. Watching the hearings from the White House, Johnson cut short a meeting with Democratic governors to hold a press conference that knocked Hamer off the air. The White House received more than 400 telegrams in support of seating the MFDP delegation.[13] But such advocacy proved in vain. Johnson authorized Minnesota Senator Hubert Humphrey, his future running mate, to end what he perceived as an unseemly public skirmish in the larger war for civil rights. MFDP representatives flatly rejected Humphrey's offer of two non-voting seats as unofficial observers at the convention. Hamer retained an effervescent dignity in defeat, while young Student Nonviolent Coordinating Committee (SNCC) activists such as Stokely Carmichael, who sang freedom songs alongside Hamer while waving posters emblazoned with portraits of three slain civil rights martyrs, would never again attend a major party convention. Instead, they would seek unfettered Black Power as an antidote to white supremacy.

Still, King stayed on the Johnson team, reasoning that the rough-and-tumble world of politics required the kinds of private humiliations endured by the MFDP in the service of freedom's larger purpose. For King, the broader goal was voting rights, a cause that President Kennedy had urged Black student activists to pursue in the early 1960s and that Johnson prioritized following the passage of the Civil Rights Act in 1964.

Johnson's finest political moments came with his back against the wall during the voting rights struggle. He strategized with King as the latter's Southern Christian Leadership Conference (SCLC) turned its focus to voting rights with a direct-action campaign in Selma, Alabama. Urging that Black activists highlight the most egregious voter-suppression practices and assure wide coverage of injustice, Johnson suggested that King pursue a strategy that the SCLC had in fact been practicing since the Albany, Georgia, desegregation campaign four years earlier. The national breakthrough had come not in Albany, as King had initially hoped, but in Birmingham, Alabama, where vivid photographs captured local police turning dogs and firehouses against defenseless protesters. But Selma, King and his aides decided, would be the crucible through which voting rights for all Americans would be secured.[14] On March 7, 1965, soon dubbed "Bloody Sunday," white Alabama state troopers, some on horseback and armed with electrified cattle prods, bludgeoned peaceful Black demonstrators on the Edmund Pettus Bridge. The images on America's airwaves and front pages evoked gruesome scenes of subjugation from America's era of antebellum slavery. John Lewis, the brave and earnest chairman of the SNCC, suffered a brutal beating at the hands of lawmen that left him with a fractured skull. The death of James Reeb, a Boston minister and married father of five, a few days later at the hands of white thugs, further pressed Johnson to act decisively. Thousands of white supporters and allies flocked to Selma to participate in a voting rights movement that was quickly transformed into a moral referendum on the national soul.

LBJ's nationally televised address to a joint session of Congress on March 15 showcased the brutality of Jim Crow for all the world to see. Inspired by King's example at the 1963 March on Washington and rhetorical elegance in his "Letter from Birmingham Jail," the president embraced racial justice as a core principle of American democracy with words that moved King and other civil rights leaders to tears. "I speak tonight for the dignity of man and the destiny of democracy," Johnson began. The courageous quest for freedom playing out in Selma, LBJ declared, had placed Black demonstrators in an unbroken chain of patriots going back to the American Revolution. Selma, he correctly predicted, would now take its place alongside Lexington and Concord as sites of democratic transformation and renewal. The president urged passage of a voting rights bill designed to extend "the rights of citizenship to every citizen of this land."[15]

He then went further. "There is only the struggle for human rights," observed LBJ, challenging those who viewed Black citizenship and dignity as regional or sectional issues. "The real hero of this struggle is the American Negro," he declared, briefly cataloging how the courage on display in Selma held the power to strengthen and extend the democratic experiment to all people. The speech proved to be Johnson's finest as president. It centered on the struggle for Black freedom as a core expression of American democracy. He challenged Americans to face their long history of racial injustice and praised Black folk as the avatars of a new American founding that promised to enrich the lives of all.

The most extraordinary part of LBJ's speech is the way his words amplified the goals of the Black freedom struggle. Memorably championed by Malcolm X, Black dignity proved indispensable to the quest for citizenship personified by King. Malcolm defined dignity as the recognition of Black humanity from the inside out. Until African Americans recognized their inherent value, traditions, and history, Malcolm argued, no one else would. Similarly, King defined Black citizenship as more than just the right to vote and the end to racial oppression. He came to define citizenship as decent housing, safe neighborhoods, a living wage, guaranteed income, and the end of state-sanctioned violence, systemic racism, and structural inequality. Johnson's speech buttressed both perspectives. "Open your polling places to all your people," Johnson demanded of areas of the country that loathed the idea of federal intervention in local politics. "There is no moral issue," LBJ stated. "It is wrong – deadly wrong – to deny any of your fellow Americans the right to vote in this country."

The president spoke of his plans to present a robust voting rights bill. "But even if we pass this bill," he conceded, "the battle will not be over." Selma was a metaphor for the grandeur and travails of American democracy. In his speech, Johnson came closer than ever to baring his soul on race matters, as a Southerner, a politician, and human being who understood "how agonizing racial feelings are." He then pivoted to the boomerang effect of white supremacy on the health of the nation's democracy. "How many white children have gone uneducated, how many white families have lived in stark poverty, how many white lives have been scarred by fear, because we have wasted our energy and our substance to maintain the barriers of hatred and fear?" This was bold, prophetic leadership that echoed, however unknowingly, Malcolm X's notion, following President Kennedy's assassination, of "chickens coming home to roost." Malcolm was pilloried by journalists who mistook his analysis as glee about the death of a president. Johnson's description of the effects of systemic racism on white Americans elicited no such controversy but was nonetheless remarkable. "This great, rich, restless country can offer opportunity and education and hope to all," Johnson promised. He extolled Black Americans' "faith in American democracy" as an example to the nation as a whole.

Speaking less than a year after urban rebellions had engulfed parts of Harlem, Bedford-Stuyvesant, Brooklyn, and other urban centers, LBJ spoke of the need for national unity. "But we will not accept the peace of stifled rights, or the order imposed by fear, or the unity that stifles protest," added Johnson, noting "peace cannot be purchased at the cost of liberty." These words amplified King's sentiments in "Letter from Birmingham Jail." In that essay, King identified the white moderate "who prefers a negative peace which is the absence of tension to a positive peace which is the presence of justice" as a greater threat than overt white supremacy.[16] Johnson culminated his speech by embracing the unofficial anthem of the civil rights struggle: "We shall overcome."

Less than three months later, Johnson used a commencement speech at Howard University to lay the groundwork for turning words into deeds. At the nation's most important historically Black university, the president discussed the need for more than equal opportunity – equality of outcomes. Before an audience of 5,000, LBJ outlined a "more profound stage" of political conflict facing the United States. He sought nothing less than "equality as a fact and a result," a definition that went beyond "equality as a right and a theory" into the realm of concrete reality. Johnson described the impact of structural racism on the Black community through metaphor. It would not be fair to "take a person who, for years, has been hobbled by chains, and liberate him, bring him to the starting line of a race" and declare that equality had now been achieved. The badge of racial slavery and a century of American apartheid meant that "Negro poverty is not white poverty." The generational nature of racial subordination, with its intimate ties to corporate, political, eco-nomic, and cultural institutions, social norms, and personal attitudes required nothing less than revolutionary policy innovations that, as Johnson suggested, would inspire the national embrace of "the glorious opportunity of this generation to end the one huge wrong of the American nation."

Along with the voting rights speech, the Howard University address cemented LBJ's legacy as a champion of racial justice and helped to institutionalize a consensus that conceived of Black citizenship and dig-nity as moral and political goods. The speeches also raised expectations in the minds of Johnson's allies, none more so than King, who fervently hoped that the president would commit to ending racism, poverty, violence, and injustices previously unrecognized by many Americans.

DIVERGENCE

A week of urban rioting in the Watts neighborhood of Los Angeles from August 11 to 18, 1965, strained the relationship between Johnson and King (see Figure 4.1). The uprising, which began five days after LBJ's signing of the Voting Rights Act, shocked much of the country. On August 20, against the backdrop of a crisis that would leave thirty-four people dead, cause millions of dollars in property damage, and shake faith in the promise of the Great Society, Johnson and King conferred by telephone about what could be done. As usual, LBJ talked more than King. "We've got so much to do that I don't know how we'll ever do it, but we've got to get ahead with it," said Johnson. "If they could get ... this poverty program going in Los Angeles, I believe that it would help a great deal," King replied, responding to LBJ's plea for ideas with an appeal for quick action to alleviate poverty. Johnson listed his efforts to get more anti-poverty funding, and King praised LBJ's Howard University speech, while calling for emergency funds for Watts. But Johnson also lobbed a warning shot. "They all got the impression that you're against me on Vietnam," he told King.[17]

Johnson and King managed to paper over their differences about federal investment in eradicating Black urban poverty and the presi-dent's commitment to military intervention in Vietnam. On the heels

4.1. Police arrest a young man on August 13, 1965, during unrest in the Watts neighborhood of Los Angeles, the first major outbreak of urban turmoil that would torment the Johnson administration and strain the president's relationship with Martin Luther King Jr.
Credit: Getty Images

of the Voting Rights Act, the two men still needed each other. This feeling unquestionably flowed from political calculation, but there was something more. They both wanted to believe that they could work with each other toward shared goals of citizenship and dignity for all Americans (see Figure 4.2). Unbeknownst to King and Johnson, however, the Watts episode was a crossroads in their political and personal relationship. If the first half of their story included the victories of the Civil Rights Act of 1964 and the Voting Rights Act of 1965, the final chapters would play out against the backdrop of world-historical events that tested the personal sincerity, political integrity, and moral compass of an American president and an American prophet.

4.2. President Johnson confers with civil rights leaders in the Cabinet Room of the White House on March 18, 1966. Rev. Dr. Martin Luther King Jr. sits in the foreground and Attorney General Nicolas Katzenbach on LBJ's right.
Credit: LBJ Presidential Library photo by Yoichi Okamoto

The curdling of Johnson's relationship with King took place at the gap between the Great Society's soaring rhetoric of justice and expanded rights, on the one hand, and a much harsher reality, on the other. The War on Poverty's efforts to allow citizens to become architects of their economic and political liberation through the Community Action Program faltered over bureaucratic turf wars, patronage battles, and old-fashioned racism that stirred fears of Black urban militants using government assistance to plot violent revolution. The Great Society meshed poorly with King's pushes for redistributive justice in the form of guaranteed income, an end to the Vietnam War, and reimagined citizenship that touched the spirit of the universal through the everyday struggles of poor Black share-croppers in the South and residents of segregated projects in the North.

The long-planned White House conference on civil rights, ambitiously titled "To Fulfill These Rights," in the first days of June 1966 illustrated the subtle but growing distance between Johnson and King.

The event, planned in the aftermath of the Voting Rights Act, came to fruition amid growing militancy within the civil rights movement. Stokely Carmichael, the 24-year-old Howard University graduate who had shared a Mississippi jail with John Lewis when he was a teenager, revered Malcolm X and King, and possessed a bracing combination of intellectual precocity and personal charisma, replaced Lewis as SNCC chairman in late May. Carmichael promptly decided to boycott the conference, branding the event a publicity stunt orchestrated by LBJ.

By all rights, King should have been a featured speaker at the conference and indeed wanted to be asked. But Johnson felt more rapport by this time with the Urban League's Whitney Young, Roy Wilkins of the National Association for the Advancement of Colored People (NAACP), and especially Thurgood Marshall, the nation's first Black solicitor general and soon to be associate justice of the US Supreme Court. King spoke at one session, unattended by the president and largely overlooked by a press corps more interested in a photo op featuring President Johnson and Boston Celtics basketball star Bill Russell. Hurt by LBJ's snub, King sulked in his hotel room and attended a conference dinner only because the White House had previously arranged for his wife, Coretta Scott King, to sing the national anthem.[18] Amid the pomp and circumstance of more than 2,000 delegates representing secular, religious, and civic communities, the Johnson–King political collaboration and personal friendship faded. King's marginalization at the conference helped to radicalize him. Johnson, still accessing Hoover's surveillance of King, grew increasingly wary of the civil rights leader as reports revealed his most intimate thoughts about Vietnam and his criticisms of the shortcomings of the Great Society. The president, meanwhile, lavished attention on Marshall, whom he called "one of the greatest Americans of our time."[19]

The White House packed the conference line-up with prowar civil rights leaders who effusively praised LBJ's record amid growing storm clouds of white backlash and urban rebellion. Carmichael unleashed the phrase "Black Power!" two weeks later in Greenwood, Mississippi, during the Meredith March Against Fear, an almost three-week-long demonstration in which King participated, taking time away from his campaign for racial justice in Chicago. The appearance of King clasping hands with, and marching alongside, Black Power leader Carmichael must have been unsettling for Johnson and his allies.[20]

On April 4, 1967, King delivered one of the most important – and divisive – speeches of his life. At Riverside Church in New York City, he called for a halt to America's bombing in Vietnam. Arguing that political turmoil unleashed by the war made political silence tantamount to betrayal, King characterized the United States as "the greatest purveyor of violence in the world." He delivered an epic sermon imploring America to grow into a political maturity capable of recognizing the connection between domestic urban rebellions and global wars against communism as parts of an imperial trajectory that threatened the very core of the American democratic project. Side by side, Black and white soldiers were committing grievous acts of violence in Vietnam, King observed, but they still could not live in the same neighborhood of Detroit owing to the nation's unresolved history of racism. King's speech linked the limitations of the Great Society's efforts to eradicate poverty directly to the massive expenditures in Vietnam, resources of blood and treasure that prevented the nation and its president from more forcefully committing to the War on Poverty.

By this time, King and LBJ were sharply at odds with one another. Egged on by his old friend J. Edgar Hoover, Johnson proved receptive to the FBI director's increasingly vociferous efforts to discredit King publicly as some kind of communist subversive and hypocrite. Hoover, with Johnson's tacit approval, leaked damaging reports about King based on illegal FBI wiretaps to directors of government agencies, the military, intelligence services, and the press. King and Johnson were, in a sense, speaking past each other. The president viewed Black Power radicalism and King's contribution to it through his anti-war activism as a political dead end that risked provoking an even greater backlash than the one Johnson himself predicted after signing the Voting Rights Act in 1965.

King's Riverside Church address sent shockwaves through the White House. Harry McPherson, a close adviser to Johnson, declared that King now sided "with the commies." Another aide reported to Johnson that King's speech grew from a toxic combination of "ambition" and stupidity. Black allies loyal to Johnson, ranging from Carl Rowan to Nobel laureate Ralph Bunche, publicly repudiated King. Bunche's criticism even generated coverage in the *New York Times* a week later. Meanwhile, Johnson obtained the text of King's speech via inquiries to Hoover.[21] On April 15, the same day King led a demonstration of 400,000 people against the war, Johnson revealed publicly that he was being regularly briefed by the FBI on the anti-war movement. That revelation triggered further condemnation of King in the press, reports that were filled with details supplied to the White House by Hoover.

The Vietnam War crippled the scope, ambition, and effectiveness of the Great Society, LBJ's slate of programs encompassing civil rights, voting, immigration reform, health care, education, the environment, and criminal justice, to name a few areas of focus. By the second half of LBJ's presidency, with urban rebellion erupting in Newark and Detroit, the Great Society was in trouble, burdened by the gap between its promise and the actual investments made in some of the most impoverished parts of the nation. Johnson increasingly looked to Congress to approve higher military spending. Vietnam robbed the president of his political and moral authority to demand new domestic spending on anti-poverty efforts. The more LBJ denied this link, the angrier King became. In essence the Vietnam War – along with the anger, debate, anguish, and protest it inspired – created political divisions within American society that profoundly limited the Great Society agenda. Following King's break from the president in 1967, more apostates followed, including Minnesota Senator Eugene McCarthy, whose presidential campaign attracted youthful long-haired Americans who promised to "Get Clean for Gene" and oust Johnson as a liberal pretender more committed to waging war in Southeast Asia than bolstering peace.

Johnson privately railed against what he viewed as political betrayals by civil rights leaders, especially King, and chafed against the release of the Kerner Commission report on civil disorders that he believed ignored the herculean legislative achievements of the Great Society in favor of fantastical recommendations for tens of billions of dollars in aid that Congress would never approve. The report documented the social, political, and economic roots of the violent civil disturbances – invariably described as riots by politicians and rebellions by activists – that had rocked the nation since the 1963 uprising in Birmingham. Chaired by Illinois Governor Otto Kerner, the commission's eleven members included New York City's Republican mayor, John V. Lindsay; Edward Brooke, the Massachusetts Republican who became the first Black person elected to the Senate in the twentieth century; and Republican Congressman William McCulloch of Ohio. Democrats on the commission included Senator Fred R. Harris of Oklahoma and California Congressman James Corman. NAACP Executive Secretary Wilkins was, along with Brooke, one of the two Black members of the commission. Commerce Secretary Katherine Peden of Kentucky was the lone woman.[22]

The commission's report, published to great acclaim in March 1968, proved to be a blockbuster analysis of the structural inequalities, systemic racism, and poverty that led to the "long hot summers" of the 1960s, when police interactions with racially segregated and economically impoverished communities became tinderboxes that allowed long-simmering tensions to explode. The commission visited numerous cities where violence had broken out, interviewed a cross-section of stakeholders, and held public hearings to investigate the origins of the growing pandemic of violence in major, mid-size, and small cities, towns, and communities.[23] The report contended that the chaotic explosions of unrest – on the east and west coasts, Down South, and Up North – were rooted in racial prejudice. "White racism is essentially responsible for the explosive mixture which has been accumulating in our cities since the end of World War II," the commission observed. High rates of Black unemployment, unequal schools, substandard housing conditions, and police brutality resulted in pervasive "hostility and cynicism" among Black residents against police, law enforcement, and other ostensible structures of government that were viewed as almost inherently oppressive.[24]

The commission's recommendations were, for the time, nothing short of revolutionary. "Only a commitment to national action on an unprecedented scale can shape a future compatible with the historic ideals of American society," the report stated. It went on to call for economic investment in full employment, housing, education, and social welfare that would surpass the Great Society as well as the New Deal.[25] Johnson did not publicly address the report until a March 22, 1968, press conference, three weeks after its release. The president privately informed cabinet officials that the commission's recommendations, which would cost between $75 and $100 billion over several years, were too costly at a time when he was recommending spending cuts to parts of the budget unrelated to the Vietnam War. To the press, he characterized the report as "very thorough" and "very comprehensive" but made no effort to use it as a basis for new legislative initiatives.

LBJ achieved new legislative victories a few weeks after King's assassination in Memphis on April 4, 1968. Johnson praised King as "an outstanding leader" who deeply loved his country and, as with Kennedy's assassination in 1963, used the tragedy to muster congressional majorities to pass a third civil rights bill, this time focused on fair housing.[26] In June, Johnson signed another bill, the 1968 Omnibus Crime Control and Safe Streets Act, one of the lesser-known but most impactful bills of the entire Great Society. But the law, far from addressing conditions in Black communities, helped lay the foundations for the era of mass incarceration as the War on Poverty was transformed into a War on Crime that disproportionately punished, imprisoned, and marginalized Black America. LBJ's crime-control initiatives created Youth Services Bureaus that comingled law enforcement with social welfare programs to control the so-called "hard core" Black youth perceived to be active participants in the rioting of the 1960s. The bureaus were tasked with "identifying future criminals" and became sources for states and municipal governments looking for social welfare funds that could be channeled into law enforcement.[27]

For his part, Johnson signed the crime bill because, as he put it, "it responds to one of the most urgent problems in America today – the problem of fighting crime in the local neighborhood and on the city street."[28] The act provided $400 million in federal funds to expand training, recruitment, and equipment for police officers nationwide. The bill also expanded the surveillance powers of local, state, and federal agencies to wiretap citizens, a decision the president characterized as "an unwise and potentially dangerous step" that might endanger civil liberties.[29] But Johnson had political, pragmatic, and personal reasons for supporting the legislation, which had been sixteen months in the making. Politically, he did not want to be outflanked on issues of law and order by any potential Republican opponent in 1968 if he decided to run. Pragmatically, he felt such a bill would help the Democratic Party stem the tide of white backlash. Personally, LBJ clung to a feeling that the urban rebellions of the 1960s had been part of a conspiracy, with Black Power revolutionaries such as Stokely Carmichael serving as mere fronts for even more sinister communist influence.

LBJ's decision not to run for a second full term robbed the nation of perhaps the one man who might have been able to stem the decline of full-throated liberalism exemplified by the New Deal and Great Society. But Johnson remained an intractable hawk about the Vietnam War even in the face of advice about the damage that the war was causing to the nation. The roots of public skepticism about the integrity of elected leaders and political institutions in the late twentieth and early twenty-first centuries can be traced to the "credibility gap" between the White House's optimistic narrative of the Vietnam War and the unvarnished truths being uncovered and disseminated by returning soldiers, reporters, and officials. As the Johnson White House's reputation for veracity and integrity declined due to Vietnam, so too did chances to pass more expansive civil rights legislation. King turned out to be correct when, during his Riverside Church address, he linked the fates of the Great Society and the Vietnam War. The two were – and remain – inextricably linked. Failure in Vietnam propelled growing disaffection with the War on Poverty and the promise of the Great Society. Both showcased the grand ambitions and humbling limits of government intervention. King's argument that only one war – the domestic one against racism and poverty – deserved to be fought and could actually be won resonates as much as ever in the twenty-first century, a time of limited national resources and burgeoning international problems.

LEGACIES

Richard Nixon's campaign and subsequent election opened a Pandora's Box of racially motivated resentment against economic justice, civil rights, and deep democracy, and also echoes half a century later. Johnson did not produce the Watergate scandal, but his exit from the national stage helped unleash political forces from which the nation has struggled to recover. The hyper-partisan political divides, rooted in racial antagonisms that predate the republic, festered and flourished in pernicious and at times unprecedented ways once Johnson left office. LBJ's presidency helped to achieve a new consensus on the struggle for Black citizenship and dignity in a manner previously unseen. His absence from national life, where he so often told a story of America's strength as a multiracial nation, left a space that went unfilled.

A second full LBJ term might have produced a negotiated withdrawal from Vietnam while simultaneously pivoting back to the domestic programs that remain Johnson's enduring legacy. In resounding ways that too often go unappreciated, Johnson's decision not to run set the stage for a half-century of debate, division, and discussion of the role of government in America's constitutional democracy. Whereas Johnson's domestic vision played out in bold strokes, subsequent presidents hemmed and hawed over the role of the state as a transformative force for good, with such notable exceptions as Barack Obama's Affordable Care Act.

To his lasting credit, Johnson endorsed a robust vision of American liberalism in service of social justice. He cared about racial justice, poverty, clean water, quality education, safe schools, and the health of children and the elderly. To the nation's lasting regret, Johnson's stubborn support of war hastened the decline of a potentially greater society that some Americans were still trying to create half a century later. Of course, the political divisions that sparked backlash against the Great Society transcended the Vietnam War. Hostility to racial progress was deeply rooted in the original sin of racial slavery and structures of anti-Black racism that disfigured important aspects of American democracy. Efforts to build the Great Society and achieve King's Beloved Community ran afoul of the stubborn hierarchies of race, class, gender, and other aspects of identity, not to mention economic problems that led many white Americans to question their support of expensive social programs. White backlash set the boundaries for racial justice during the Johnson administration. Still, formal equality before the law, with the passage of the 1964 Civil Rights Act and the 1965 Voting Rights Act, produced a sea change in American democracy. Johnson helped to institutionalize a half-century-long consensus on racial justice bookended by John F. Kennedy's civil rights speech on June 11, 1963, and the June 25,

2013, decision by the Supreme Court in *Shelby v. Holder*, which gutted many of the enforcement powers of the Voting Rights Act that Johnson and King had helped to secure.[30]

King's search for racial justice and Black citizenship found him consistently decrying the yawning gap between the lofty rhetoric of American democracy and the brutal reality of oppression. At his best, King painted a picture of American society poised at a historical crossroads that would decide both the destiny of democracy and the limits of human potential around the world. In the "Letter from Birmingham Jail," he declared that "the goal of America is freedom." American politics in the twenty-first century, featuring debates over building walls, legislation designed to suppress voting rights, and widespread racial and economic inequality, betray King's legacy even as national historical markers and civil rights museums celebrate the man.

Celebrations of King cleave him in two. The "good King" delivered a sermon for the ages at the 1963 March on Washington, promoted nonviolence as the key to achieving racial justice, and served as a friend and adviser to Presidents Kennedy and Johnson, making possible the passage of major legislation. The "bad King," criticized at the time by major newspapers, clergy, and politicians, boldly denounced the Vietnam War as immoral, linked the shortcomings of the Great Society to global war and domestic riots, and called for a notion of American citizenship expansive enough to guarantee jobs, housing, food, and justice to the poor living in a vast sea of wealth. The Martin Luther King Day holiday, signed into law by President Reagan on November 2, 1983, at once elevated the martyred civil rights leader and limited the radical parts of his legacy by encasing him in the amber glow of the most revered parts of American history. Reagan, a Cold War hawk who opposed major aspects of King's call for radical Black citizenship, signed the law under duress, pressured by a coalition that included Republicans as well as Democrats. Fifteen years earlier, speaking to a California audience the day after King's assassination, then-Governor Reagan linked King's murder to the refusal by social movement leaders and ordinary Americans to "compromise with the laws of the land."[31] For Reagan, civil disobedience in defiance of white supremacy crossed a Rubicon that led to social disorder, urban chaos, and cultural drift.

The federal holiday amplified King's celebrity at the expense of his revolutionary politics. King's nonviolence compelled local, regional, national, and global social movements to use the weapon of peaceful disobedience to compel powerful interests to change. King proved to be far more than an American Gandhi. He challenged the most powerful nation on earth to uphold a morally transcendent vision of democracy that centered on the faces at the bottom of the well. King's personal reputation took a hit after biographers discovered that he plagiarized parts of his Boston University dissertation and uncovered his extramarital affairs, which were recorded in some cases on declassified FBI wiretaps. But King's personal frailties have made him an earthier, less distant, and more humane figure to subsequent generations.[32]

The radical King's influence is best seen in the political actions of a new generation of activists, organizers, and young people who honor his legacy with deeds that push the nation toward his Beloved Community. King defined that community not only as a world free of racism, war, and poverty. He argued that justice was what love looked like in public and that all citizens could achieve greatness through a purpose-driven life of service. King offered an example to all Americans that a life dedicated to social justice and human rights was the greatest vocation. He inspired American citizens, presidents, and the nation to take moral stands that entailed political consequences, something sorely missing from public and civic discourse in the twenty-first century. The problems of racism, poverty, voter suppression, housing inequality, unemployment, violence, and war that plagued King's era remained half a century later. A key difference was the evolution of the civil rights struggle from a movement dominated by a singular voice to a later landscape featuring multiple leaders who, in the best tradition of King, stirred debate over the meaning of freedom, democracy, justice, and citizenship.

King's radical legacy continues to be overwhelmed by his iconography in the early twenty-first century at exactly the time the nation needed it most. King is presented to schoolchildren and the general public as an advocate of nonviolence who quietly pushed for racial and political reforms that achieved Black citizenship before his assassination. Nothing could be further from the truth. King wielded the specter of nonviolent civil disobedience as both sword and shield in his unrelenting quest for Black citizenship. Inspired by the Watts uprising, he questioned the fundamental structure of American capitalism, and he openly wept after witnessing barefoot children in Marks, Mississippi, accompanied by parents who went without heat and blankets in winter and food year-round. The radical King spoke truth to power to sitting American presidents, questioned the fundamental unfairness of capitalism, blasted the Vietnam War, and railed against militarism, racism, and materialism. He marched alongside Black Power activists, accused the US Congress of being unapologetically racist, and planned a campaign of massive civil disobedience in Washington, DC, in the name of poor people across the racial spectrum.

We have also cleaved President Johnson's legacy in two. The "good" LBJ is a towering portrait of presidential ambition in service to the larger public good. Johnson's Great Society fundamentally altered America's democratic institutions. LBJ's achievements in civil rights alone stand out as landmark policymaking victories. But there was much more. Johnson's Great Society created new standards for clean air and water, transformed infrastructure in the rural South and urban North, opened new pathways to citizenship through immigration reform, and promoted other measures with profound implications for Black America. In this way, the Johnson administration expanded the boundaries of citizenship in ways that went beyond strictly racial metrics. The "good" Johnson rivaled his idol, Franklin D. Roosevelt, by updating and amplifying the idealism and activism that undergirded the New Deal in the 1930s.

The Johnson who forged an effective and friendly working relationship with King and risked political capital for civil rights stands as perhaps the most important president in American history, after Abraham Lincoln, with respect to racial justice. LBJ's support for Thurgood Marshall as the first Black solicitor general and Supreme Court justice proved to be one of many such racial firsts orchestrated by an administration that at times anticipated the changing arc of the times with bold proposals for racial justice. This part of Johnson's legacy, forged in no small part through his relationship with King, deserved celebration in later eras of backlash and racial injustice. The good Johnson displayed a profoundly humane understanding of, and solidarity with, the long struggle for Black dignity and citizenship. His most acclaimed speeches said as much, and his best, most daringly provocative legislative proposals aimed to secure equality of outcomes, not mere opportunity, for Black Americans marginalized by more than a century of racism, terror, violence, and poverty.

The "bad" Johnson faltered in pursuit of racial justice by pivoting toward the Vietnam War. This Johnson grew impatient with the rising demands of Black radicals, the growing pattern of Black rebellion in major cities and smaller hamlets, and King's increasingly harsh criticism of the war and the deficits of the Great Society. The bad Johnson could be vindictive; he did not approve FBI wiretaps on King – Attorney General Robert F. Kennedy did that in October 1963 – but he did little to stop it until 1965 and after that probably knew of ongoing FBI harassment flowing from Hoover's obsession with the civil rights leader. LBJ listened to FBI Director Hoover's increasingly agitated vendetta against King. Over time, Johnson grew distrustful of King, and by 1967 the two no longer enjoyed the easy rapport that marked their earlier relationship. Johnson's shifting views of Black activism culminated in the 1968 crime bill that empowered law enforcement and laid the foundation for the carceral state that would take shape in subsequent decades.

Johnson and King defy Manichean portrayals. Individually and together, they represent a complicated tapestry of strengths and weaknesses, successes and failures, too complex to be reduced to two dimensions. The two men presided over one of the most important epics in American history. Johnson served as commander-in-chief during crucial parts of America's Second Reconstruction, a period of convulsive racial violence and historic advances for Black Americans. Johnson's leadership as a statesman during the era of desegregation helped forge a broad consensus on racial justice that led to the presidency of Barack Obama. At key moments, such as the aftermath of the Kennedy assassination, Johnson rose to the occasion by meeting crises with bold policy proposals. Johnson's stewardship both impressed and surprised civil rights leaders who feared that a Southern president might be a bulwark against dreams of upending the status quo. LBJ's soaring rhetoric in support of civil rights peaked in 1965, the year the movement triumphantly captivated the national and global imagination through the voting rights campaign that fully revealed the reality of white-supremacist violence on a bridge in Selma named for a Confederate general and Ku Klux Klan grand dragon.

Ironically, Martin Luther King Jr. was in Atlanta during Bloody Sunday, an accident of history that became less consequential as the days passed, the movement regrouped, and King stepped to the fore by leading the march of 30,000 activists to Montgomery, Alabama, between March 21 and 25, 1965. Six days before the march began, Lyndon Johnson had delivered his finest speech as president. In an eloquent call for multiracial democracy that might have made the great abolitionist Frederick Douglas proud and surely resonated with King, LBJ placed the civil rights movement – and by extension King – in the pantheon of revolutionary American heroes who forged expansive visions of democracy bequeathed to subsequent generations. Johnson's words echoed across time and space to place racial justice at the center of American democracy. The president upheld the quest for Black citizenship and dignity as part of a universal search for freedom whose success would reflect the best aspirations of the nation. If Johnson worked from the heights of political power to enact transformative legislation, King inspired the president and the entire nation from below. King's efforts to challenge America's moral and political imagination helped to humanize the Black experience in innovative and unprecedented ways. For a time, it seemed as if King's dreams of a Beloved Community free from racial and economic injustice could be manifested in the sprawling agenda of the Great Society. By the end of their relationship, both Johnson (privately) and King (publicly) expressed disappointment in one another. Yet their enduring legacy remains indelibly captured in the flowering of a productive relationship, forged in creative tension, that helped move the nation closer to their shared dreams.

CHAPTER 5

Lyndon Johnson, Mexican Americans, and the Border

Geraldo Cadava

O N NOVEMBER 7, 1966, PRESIDENT LYNDON JOHNSON visited the so-called Mexican school in Cotulla, Texas, where he had taught decades earlier when he was a college student. The purpose of his visit was to emphasize the importance of education for all children in the United States and to promote his administration's investment of "billions of new dollars to help improve your school and schools all over America." For Johnson, the school where he had taught in 1928 and 1929 – the Welhausen school – was an example of what could be accomplished in a community that cared about education. The residents of Cotulla, many of whom were Mexican and Mexican American ranchers and farmers, had, Johnson said, built a "beautiful brick building," given children free textbooks, and hired "generally good teachers." Johnson was proud that the Cotullans he had taught – and occasionally paddled – were on hand to hear him talk that day. They had come with their own children who, at the time of Johnson's speech, were part of a new generation of students. "You set the example," he told his one-time pupils, "and you gave the inspiration."[1]

Johnson would not rest, he said, until all Mexican American students in the United States, and all students generally, had the same opportunities that the Mexican American kids in Cotulla had gotten. "We say to all the Nation," Johnson remarked, "that we have not yet done enough." Until "every Mexican-American child has the right to go through grade school and high school and college," he said, "I shall not be satisfied." He would not be satisfied, he continued, "until the day comes when we no longer hear the hum of the motor before daylight hauling the kids off in a truck to a beet patch or a cotton patch in the middle of the school year." Three out of four Mexican American children in Texas would drop out of school before the eighth grade, Johnson noted. One out of three Mexican Americans who were older than 14 had less than five years of school. Half of all schoolchildren in one district were Mexican American, but "Anglo" students would make up two of every three graduates.[2]

Johnson thought and talked about his time in Cotulla much more than he visited. It was an important part of his *Bildungsroman*, a story about the development of his moral and political compass that he often returned to after his election to office – first to Congress, then to the presidency. To Johnson, his memories of Cotulla highlighted his concern for Mexican Americans in particular and the priority he placed on eradicating poverty more broadly. In doing so, Johnson became the first US president to claim that, from the time he was a young man, his relationship with Mexican Americans had shaped the president he became. Later presidents said the same, especially the Republicans Richard Nixon and George W. Bush. But Johnson was the first. He had taught Mexican students in Cotulla. He relied on their votes when he ran for national elected office. His interactions with Mexican Americans, he said, caused him to empathize with and admire them. They led him, he claimed, to keep their concerns in mind and to advocate for them when he had the opportunity.

But Johnson's concern for Mexican Americans also flowed from profound shifts within the Mexican American community and Latino communities broadly, developments that dwarfed the significance of his personal experiences. In short, Latinos began to play a bigger role in US politics and society as their population grew from the mid twentieth century onward. More particularly, Latinos played a growing role in Democratic Party (and Republican Party) politics in the 1960s, since they were concentrated in areas of the United States with increasing electoral influence. They also played an important role in the conduct of US–Latin American relations, both as cultural brokers and diplomats – individuals with knowledge and experience in the region, who spoke its languages – and as part of the calculus policy-makers used to make decisions that affected them, as immigrants, citizens with immigrant family members, and potential voters. Johnson was the catalyst for some, but hardly all, changes for Latinos in the 1960s.

Lyndon Johnson's near-decade in power as vice president and president unfolded alongside and intersected with national and international changes that shaped Latino history: the shifting place of Texas in national politics, the growing importance of Latino voters to both national parties, Cold War tensions that influenced US–Mexican diplomatic relations, and the evolving politics of immigration. Johnson's rise to national power was both cause and effect of these changes. His concern for advancing the civil rights of Mexican Americans was genuine and stemmed from his interactions with them since he was a young adult. He also rose to power, though, both despite and because of the fact that he was a representative of Texas at a time of shifting racial politics. Even though many Americans questioned whether a Southerner like Johnson would ever rise to national power, the state's influence in national and international politics, precisely because of Latinos and the issues that affected them, was surging in ways that few at the time recognized.

Overshadowed by the African American civil rights struggle and the Vietnam War, Johnson's navigation through an extremely significant period in the history of Latinos in the United States, the US–Mexico borderlands, and US–Latin American relations during the Cold War are underappreciated aspects of his administration. Johnson was caught at the center of these changes, and as he tried to find his way through all of them successfully, his actions appeased the Latinos with whom he was closest while leading others to conclude that his efforts were not sincere or were not enough. Johnson was both more and less than the tales that he told about himself and the tales that were told about him, including the one about how his time at Cotulla had sparked a lifetime of care for Mexican Americans and Latinos. This contradictory reality makes the former president like many Americans in the United States in the late twentieth century, who proclaimed their sympathies with Latinos but whose commitments to meaningful change went only so far.

"HE LIKES MEXICAN PEOPLE"

Throughout his political career, Johnson credited the relationships he developed with Mexicans and Mexican Americans as a young man for his lifelong concern with their wellbeing. He attended the Southwest Texas State Teachers College (now Texas State University) in San Marcos, Texas, between Austin and San Antonio, in the late 1920s. There was a *colonia*, or Mexican neighborhood, in San Marcos that had open sewers and segregated schools. Many of the town's restaurants and drug stores refused service to Mexicans. This was typical of many Texas cities in the first decades of the twentieth century. When Johnson was a student at Southwest Texas, he did not interact much with the Mexicans and Mexican Americans in San Marcos. He really came to know them, he said, when, in 1928, during the summer after his first year in college, he accepted a teaching position at the Welhausen school in Cotulla, a small ranching and farming town in the Rio Grande Valley. The majority of his students were of Mexican descent (see Figure 5.1).[3]

Towns like Cotulla in the early twentieth century were basically farm "labor camps," notes historian David Montejano.[4] At the time Johnson taught in Cotulla, it was a deeply unequal society, defined by segregation, racial violence, and rampant Ku Klux Klan activity. Johnson came to empathize with his students because of the inequality and discrimination

5.1. In 1928 and 1929, Lyndon Johnson earned money to support his studies at Southwest Texas State Teachers College by working as a teacher and principal in tiny Cotulla, Texas. Pictured here with some of his students, LBJ later said the experience helped sensitize him to the injustices of discrimination and poverty.
Credit: LBJ Presidential Library photo, photographer unknown

that shaped their lives. He earned a salary of $125 a month for teaching seventh- and eighth-grade history. According to historian Robert Caro's description of Johnson's time in Cotulla, he was rather strict and required his students to participate in debate competitions, spelling bees, and physical education classes, none of which they had ever done before.[5] Before returning to San Marcos to finish his degree, Johnson served for a brief period as the Welhausen school's principal. After he became president of the United States, when close acquaintances were asked what Johnson was like as a young man, they regularly said his time in Cotulla had played an important role in shaping his persona.[6]

Johnson had the opportunity to show how his experience with Mexicans and Mexican Americans in Cotulla had shaped his thinking not long after he was elected in 1948 to his first term as a US senator. That same year, three years after the end of World War II, the remains of a Mexican American soldier named Felix Longoria were recovered in the Philippines, where Longoria had been killed at the very end of the war. His body was shipped back to his hometown, Three Rivers, Texas, between San Antonio and Corpus Christi, in the Rio Grande Valley. The owner of the Rice Funeral Home in Three Rivers informed Longoria's widow that Longoria would get buried in the town's segregated "Mexican cemetery." He also told her that the family could not hold the wake at the funeral home because the "whites would not like it."[7]

Dismayed, Longoria's widow reported the refusal to Dr. Hector García, the founder of the American GI Forum, a civil rights organization that advocated for Mexican American veterans. García had been a doctor in the military. He was from the Rio Grande Valley and was inspired to form the GI Forum after observing the poverty and poor health outcomes for Mexicans and Mexican Americans in the region. He took up Longoria's cause, hoping to secure for the deceased veteran a proper burial.

García discussed the situation with "Forumeers" – the nickname for GI Forum members – in the Corpus Christi chapter, which was the organization's first. He called the funeral director at the Three Rivers cemetery himself but was told no, just as Longoria's wife had been told. He also sent letters and telegrams to Texas congressmen, including Lyndon Johnson. García had never met Johnson, but he had served in World War II, in Italy, with Congressman John E. Lyle, who was good friends with Johnson.

García talked with his friend Lyle, who put him in touch with Johnson and assured him that Johnson would help, as García recalled in a 1969 interview that's now part of the LBJ Presidential Library's collection, because "he's a fair man, and he likes Mexican people."[8]

Senator Johnson did help, perhaps because he liked Mexican people but also because it was an early opportunity to show his Mexican American constituents in Texas that he could get things done for them. He arranged for Longoria to be buried in Arlington National Cemetery, giving him an honored resting place in the same hallowed ground as other military heroes and government leaders. The funeral took place on February 16, 1949. The Longoria family, Senator Johnson, and a representative of President Harry Truman were in attendance.

Johnson's collaboration with García on what has become known as the "Felix Longoria Affair" marked the beginning of a relationship that lasted for more than two decades, until Johnson's death in 1972. Hector García did not always endorse Senator Johnson's positions. Sometimes he opposed them. Even though Johnson would become the president who signed landmark civil rights legislation in the 1960s, he had opposed the federal civil rights bills proposed during the 1940s and 1950s, despite the fact that most Mexican Americans supported them. Johnson also opposed laws proposed by the Fair Employment Practices Committee (FEPC).

Johnson's opposition to some of the civil rights initiatives that Mexican Americans supported led even his closest Mexican American allies to question his commitment to them. Johnson said he worked within the constraints of national politics, and it was certainly true that he faced political pressures from Texans who supported segregation and opposed civil rights. But Mexican Americans took his inaction on some of the things they cared about as a sign that they were not a priority for him. It did not stop allies like García and other GI Forum members from endorsing Johnson, though, in all of his Senate reelection and presidential campaigns.

"VIVA KENNEDY"

By the time John F. Kennedy selected Johnson as his vice president, Johnson had spent decades forming relationships with Mexican Americans in Texas. Most were his former students in Cotulla and the leaders of two Mexican American civil rights organizations, the GI Forum and the League of United Latin American Citizens (LULAC), such as García and J. T. Canales, the founders of the groups. He frequently consulted them on matters related to Mexican Americans, even if he ended up not doing what they recommended.

Johnson's success among Mexican Americans in Texas was part of the reason that Kennedy chose him to be his running mate in his presidential campaign in 1960. Texas was critical both because it had the third largest number of electoral votes, behind New York and California, and because it was a state that had swung back and forth between Democrats and Republicans in recent election cycles.

For the first time in the 1960s, the two major parties in the United States were beginning to take Latinos seriously as a distinct group of voters that could swing closely contested elections. Democrats like Thomas Dewey and Republicans like Dwight Eisenhower had made minimal efforts to appeal to Latino voters in the 1940s and 1950s. But before those decades, the Latino population was tiny and largely concentrated in areas of the country that were not as contested as they became in the 1960s. Politicians also did not consider Latinos to be independent political actors but rather the wards of machine bosses who paid their poll taxes in exchange for their political loyalty.[9]

All of this changed by the early 1960s. As the population and economic importance of the American Sunbelt boomed after World War II, states like Florida, Texas, and California grew in electoral importance. Slowly, they began to overshadow Eastern states like New York. These Sunbelt states were also where the vast majority of Latinos in the United States lived, and they were more up for grabs than at any point in the previous century; Texas had mostly gone for Democrats, while California had mostly gone for Republicans, for example, but the reverse was about to become true.[10]

To support Kennedy's presidential campaign, Mexican Americans in Texas formed "Viva Kennedy" clubs that set a new bar for campaign outreach to Latinos. Its founding organizers were members of the League of United Latin American Citizens and the GI Forum. After the GI Forum's national conference in Los Angeles in 1959, Kennedy sent the Forumeers a congratulatory note that paved the way for them to officially endorse him in 1960. At the 1960 Democratic National Convention, also held in Los Angeles, Kennedy endorsed civil rights, school desegregation, fair housing, and voting rights. He also supported legislation that would protect the rights of migrant workers, and he promised to appoint a Mexican American to an ambassadorship in Latin America. Liking what they were hearing from Kennedy, García and Carlos McCormick, a member of Senator Johnson's staff, decided to start Viva Kennedy clubs to officially support Kennedy's campaign for president.

Viva Kennedy clubs formed in nine states with sizable Latino populations, but Texas was very much the center of their activity. The clubs organized groups of Latino voters and helped them register to vote. They got prominent Mexican American politicians, like Senator Dennis Chávez of New Mexico, to endorse Kennedy and pose for photos with him. They printed campaign pamphlets that depicted Kennedy riding a burro into the White House. The result of their efforts was that Kennedy received 85 percent of the Latino vote nationally and 91 percent in Texas.[11]

The clubs stayed open after the 1960 election, when they became an effective vehicle for pressuring the Kennedy administration to follow through on its promises. Kennedy did follow through when he appointed Raymond Telles, the first Mexican American mayor of El Paso, as the ambassador to Costa Rica. Telles had served in World War II, headed Lend-Lease programs in Latin America, assisted Latin American leaders during their visits to the United States, and assisted US presidents when they visited Latin America. He epitomized the idea that Mexican American leaders could serve the United States as cultural brokers, especially during the Cold War, because they spoke Spanish and were familiar with the region's history and politics.[12]

In the fall of 1963, organizers of the Viva Kennedy clubs began to talk about how they could aid Kennedy's reelection campaign in 1964. When the president visited Texas that November, the former head of LULAC, John Herrera, invited him to be the honored guest at the group's State Director's Ball at the Rice Hotel in Houston. In the invitation, Herrera told Kennedy that Viva Kennedy clubs had formed throughout the state in Corpus Christi, Dallas, San Antonio, Galveston, El Paso, and other places. Kennedy accepted LULAC's invitation, even though he had been invited to attend many other events in Houston. A musical ensemble called *Trío Internacional* serenaded Kennedy. The LULAC Ball was held on November 21, 1963. Kennedy was killed the next day in Dallas.[13]

The most important legacy of the Viva Kennedy clubs was to show that groups of Latinos – mainly Mexican Americans in 1960, but a more diverse group as well – could come together to influence electoral politics. Johnson learned the lesson immediately. In some ways, he knew it already, since he had organized Mexican American voters to support him in his Senate campaigns. Johnson assumed the presidency after Kennedy's assassination and then ran for reelection in 1964. His Mexican American supporters used the same playbook they had used in 1960 and launched Viva Johnson clubs across the country (see Figure 5.2). The former president of LULAC, Oscar Laurel from Laredo, Texas, was the Texas chairman of the Viva Johnson clubs. Women, including Clotilde García, sister of GI Forum founder Hector, formed the "State Ladies Viva Johnson Club" to register Mexican American women to vote. In future years, Viva Nixon, Viva Carter, Viva Reagan, and Viva Bush campaigns formed to support the presidential campaigns of nominees from the Republican and Democratic Parties.

5.2. Imitating an approach that had helped John F. Kennedy in 1960, Mexican Americans formed Viva Johnson clubs across the United States during the 1964 election. The clubs issued pins and posters, registered Latino voters, and encouraged turnout on election day. Credit: LBJ Presidential Library photo by Jay Godwin

They all took their cues from the pathbreaking Viva Kennedy–Viva Johnson movements.

"VIVA JOHNSON"

Many books have been written about the 1964 election, in which Johnson defeated Arizona Senator Barry Goldwater by a wide margin. Johnson headed into the campaign with a large degree of sympathy from the American electorate, having taken over the duties of president from his slain predecessor and promising to honor Kennedy's legacy by carrying out his agenda. Goldwater did himself in with his own extremism. An underappreciated aspect of the 1964 race, though, is how both candidates competed for the Latino vote.

Johnson and Goldwater were both Westerners. Goldwater was the first in a string of Republican Westerners to run for president, including Richard Nixon and Ronald Reagan from California, and George H. W. Bush and George W. Bush from Texas. The fact of their candidacies demonstrated the shifting power center of US politics. But the efforts their campaigns made to recruit Latino voters also highlighted the growing importance of the Latino vote. Johnson told stories about his experience at the Mexican school in Cotulla. Goldwater told Mexican Americans that he was practically born along the US–Mexico border, and that, as a child, he spoke Spanish nearly as well as he spoke English.[14]

Goldwater also hung Kennedy's debacle at the Bay of Pigs around Johnson's neck, saying that Johnson would be soft on communism and would betray Cuban exiles, just like his predecessor. This strategy was aimed, in part, at the small number of exiles who had been naturalized and were therefore able to vote. But it also targeted all conservative Latinos, be they Mexican Americans or Puerto Ricans living on the mainland, whose anticommunism stemmed from the particular experiences of their nationality groups. It did not work; Goldwater still won only single-digit support from Latinos. But Republican leaders believed in the strategy nevertheless, because they were worried that Black voters were fleeing the party in droves and were convinced that the party needed to do more in future elections.[15]

As many historians, including those with essays in this volume, have demonstrated, Johnson's first full term in office saw a bonanza of domestic programs and legislative accomplishments: War on Poverty programs, the Civil Rights Act of 1964, the Voting Rights Act of 1965, and Medicare and Medicaid, among others. He benefited mightily from Democratic majorities in both chambers of Congress. Most of his efforts helped Latinos just as they helped other groups of US citizens.

All of Johnson's civil rights initiatives had widespread support among Mexican Americans. The leaders of civil rights and advocacy groups such as LULAC and the GI Forum had great hopes that Title VII of the Civil Rights Act, which prohibited "employment discrimination based on race, color, religion, sex and national origin" – and established the Equal Employment Opportunity Commission (EEOC) to ensure that employers complied – would increase the representation of Mexican Americans and other Latinos in federal jobs.[16] The prohibition against sex and gender discrimination also gave Mexican American women hope that Title VII would help them combat what historian Julie Pycior describes as "double discrimination on the job," as both women and Mexican Americans.[17]

Mexican Americans criticized Johnson's signature Civil Rights Act, though, on the grounds that it aimed to ameliorate discrimination against African Americans more than discrimination against Mexican Americans. Their criticism of the Civil Rights Act was echoed in the larger criticism that some Latinos had of the Democratic Party in general: that Democrats cared more about African Americans than Mexican Americans. Hispanic Republicans and the Republican Party, deeply concerned about the fact that African Americans were leaving the GOP, used this idea to recruit Latinos away from the Democratic Party, by telling them that the Democratic Party was for African Americans while the Republican Party was for them.[18]

Evidence that the Democratic Party seemed to care more about African Americans came shortly after the passage of the Civil Rights Act. In 1964, the White House held a conference, "To Secure These Rights," to celebrate the landmark legislation. But no Latinos were in attendance. A report that same year – the "Status Report on Efforts of the Department of Commerce to Improve Employment Opportunities for

Members of Minority Groups" – dealt only with African Americans. A civil rights advocate from Texas named George I. Sánchez, along with GI Forum members, attended the State Department's "Conference on Equal Employment." They were dismayed to find that this conference, too, focused exclusively on the concerns of African Americans. They complained to the State Department, which responded by meeting with Mexican American and Puerto Rican leaders and establishing a summer internship program for Latinos. The complaints by Latinos put pressure on the Johnson administration to hire more of them to work in the White House. The GI Forum wanted someone who would serve "in a position [where] he would be able to influence policy."[19] It became a common strategy for Latino leaders to use these perceived slights to increase their access to, and representation within, the federal government.

Another monumental piece of legislation, the Voting Rights Act of 1965, had the same impact for English-speaking Latinos that it had for African American voters, but it did not do much for Latinos who spoke Spanish. Spanish-speaking Latinos and other "language minorities" had to wait for the relief provided by the 1975 Extension of the Voting Rights Act, signed into law by Republican President Gerald Ford. In areas of the country where a minority group that spoke a language other than English constituted more than 5 percent of the population, election materials had to be made available in that language. For Latinos who spoke only Spanish, the ability to receive election materials, including registration documents and ballots, in that language dramatically increased their participation. But during the Johnson administration, deliberations over the 1975 Extension of the Voting Rights Act had not even begun.

GOOD NEIGHBORS

As much as domestic politics, Inter-American relations underwent important shifts after World War II, mainly as a result of the Cold War between the United States and the Soviet Union. These shifts were global in scale, but the Cold War in Latin America was a major ideological and military battleground. In its effort to curb the spread of communism and, conversely, promote the benefits of free enterprise and global capitalism, the

United States intervened militarily in nations and territories such as Uruguay, Puerto Rico, Guatemala, Panama, and Cuba. As the United States placed a heavy thumb on the scale of Latin American affairs, the US government needed Mexico as an ally more than ever before. This was a delicate matter considering that the annexation by the United States of more than half of Mexican territory in 1848 remained a live issue for many Mexicans, who witnessed with apprehension US imperial expansion into other Latin American nations.[20]

The Johnson administration presided over at least two negotiations between the United States and Mexico that required considerable diplomatic tact. The first was the winding down of the Bracero Program – a binational migration agreement that had facilitated the movement of millions of Mexicans to the United States to work in fields, on ranches, and on railroad tracks for a fixed period of time. The program had facilitated the migration of more than 4 million Mexicans to work in the United States between 1942 and 1964, when Johnson ended the program. The second, at around the same time, was the negotiation of the Chamizal Treaty, which led the United States and Mexico to trade about 200 acres of land after the Rio Grande shifted course. Johnson was a central player in both negotiations. In some ways, the Cold War context gave Mexico leverage in each, so long as Mexico promised to remain neutral or take the side of the United States in conflicts throughout the Americas.

Economic changes in Mexico and a new immigration law in the United States also defined cross-border relationships during the Johnson administration. In the early 1960s, the Mexican government announced the Programa Nacional Fronterizo (PRONAF), which aimed to modernize the economy of the Mexican border region. As part of PRONAF, Mexico also established the Programa de Industrialización Fronteriza (PIF), or the Border Industrialization Program, which created the Mexican factories known as *maquiladoras*. The overall result of both initiatives was improved living standards in northern Mexico, as well as a dramatic shift in Mexico's internal migration patterns, from south to north, as the *maquiladoras*, owned by international companies, offered higher salaries than other industries in southern and central Mexico. Once Mexicans moved north to take *maquiladora* jobs, many moved further north to the United States, with and without authorization.[21]

These shifts in the Mexican economy that pushed Mexicans northward happened just as Johnson signed the Immigration and Naturalization Act of 1965. This new law ended the national origins quotas that had been in place since the 1924 Johnson–Reed Act, which restricted the number of immigrants who could enter the United States from southern and eastern Europe in particular. The 1924 law did not restrict the migration of Mexicans or any other Western Hemisphere migrants. Johnson's new immigration law was anti-discriminatory in the sense that it lifted the national origins quotas, but, for the first time in US history, it set caps on the number of migrants who could come to the United States from Latin America.[22] The termination of the Bracero Program, the northward migration of Mexicans, and new caps on the number of Mexican migrants who could enter the United States each year had the effect of increasing the number of unauthorized migrants.

When it came to the issue of undocumented immigration, the 1960s was a decade of transition for the Democratic Party. It was a time of party realignment on many issues, especially on matters related to race. As many historians have observed, the Republican Party's opposition to civil rights, especially in the South, drove African Americans to the Democrats, even though the civil rights records of Democrats, including Johnson, had been mixed at best before the mid 1960s.[23] There was an analogous situation with immigration. Republican politicians were beholden to business interests that did not support what we would call today immigrants' rights, but they did have a need for cheap, exploitable laborers, so they lobbied for the continued renewal of the Bracero Program, which ensured the steady stream of Mexicans into the United States. Johnson had relationships with businessmen in Texas who wanted him to continue the Bracero Program, but he was also accountable to Mexican American unionists and civil rights organizers, such as César Chávez, who wanted to end the Bracero Program because Mexican migrants competed for jobs with the Mexican Americans who were their core constituents. In later decades, of course, the Republican Party would seek to restrict immigration, whereas the Democratic Party, at least nominally, would become the party of immigrants' rights. But in the 1960s, the politics of immigration were in transition.[24]

The period when it became a priority for the United States to establish neighborly relations with Mexico began in the 1930s. When Franklin Delano Roosevelt took office, which came after two decades of US military interventions in Central America and the Caribbean, he announced what historians have called the "good neighbor policy." In his inaugural address on March 4, 1933, Roosevelt said, "In the field of world policy I would dedicate this nation to the policy of the good neighbor – the neighbor who resolutely respects himself and, because he does so, respects the rights of others." Backing up Roosevelt's words, his secretary of state, Cordell Hull, traveled to a gathering of Inter-American leaders at Montevideo, Uruguay, where he committed the United States to an agreement that "No state has the right to intervene in the internal or external affairs of another."[25] This would be the official policy of the United States through the Johnson administration, even though Dwight Eisenhower and John F. Kennedy used the Central Intelligence Agency to attempt coups in Guatemala and Cuba in 1954 and 1961, respectively. Especially after the Cuban Revolution, when US leaders were desperately worried about Fidel Castro's effort to export communism to other Latin American nations, the United States needed Western Hemisphere allies, which affirmed Johnson's desire for friendly relations with Mexico.

As president, Johnson continued the good neighbor policy when he met with Mexican President Adolfo López Mateos in Palm Springs, California, on February 21, 1964, almost three months to the day after Kennedy's assassination. Johnson told López Mateos that, in his opinion, "relations between the United States and Mexico had never been better." The two governments had recently solved a thorny diplomatic issue that had troubled the United States and Mexico for almost 100 years, since 1864, when a massive flood changed the course of the Rio Grande at Chamizal in El Paso, Texas. Because of the flood, land that had been in Mexico became part of the United States. The Treaty of Guadalupe Hidalgo, signed in 1848, established the path of the border, but did not make clear what would happen if the river shifted course. Earlier US and Mexican presidents had discussed the Chamizal issue, but without resolution. Following Kennedy's visit to Mexico in June 1962, when the matter of Chamizal again came up in his meeting with López Mateos,

US and Mexican government agencies began studying possible solutions.[26]

A year later, in July 1963, the United States and Mexico jointly announced the Chamizal Treaty: the United States would surrender 437 acres of the Chamizal, the United States would receive about 200 acres further down the Rio Grande, and Cordova island would be divided in two, with a new concrete channel cutting right through the middle of it. Local residents whose homes were razed protested the Chamizal Treaty, but the US and Mexican governments called it a huge victory. When the two presidents met in Palm Springs, Johnson told López Mateos that he wanted to plan an event at Chamizal that would be a tribute to the Mexican president. According to a notetaker present at the meeting, López Mateos responded that the "Chamizal solution should not be credited to him personally but rather to the rule of law and the goodwill evidenced by the two countries."[27] Johnson and López Mateos did meet at Chamizal on September 25, 1964. They placed a shiny new monument to peace between the two countries in front of El Paso's Bowie High School, named after James Bowie, a Texas rebel killed at the Battle of the Alamo.

The twenty-year-old accord known as the Bracero Program also came up in the meeting between Johnson and López Mateos. In some ways, the Bracero Program was more complicated than the Chamizal matter. Since its establishment in 1942, the Bracero Program had been a boon to both the United States and Mexico. Growers, ranchers, and railroad companies gained access to a steady supply of cheap laborers. Because they would be in the United States only temporarily – at least in theory, since many Braceros skipped out on their contracts and stayed in the United States permanently – the United States did not have to grant citizenship or other rights. For Mexico, the Bracero Program employed millions of Mexicans for whom Mexico did not have to provide jobs. Mexican leaders believed that Braceros would acquire important skills in the United States that they could bring home with them. But by the time Johnson and López Mateos met, the US Congress had decided to let the Bracero Program expire, and Johnson wanted to know what López Mateos thought about that prospect.

Many members of Congress, like President Johnson himself, had plenty of constituents who were businessmen interested in maintaining the steady flow of cheap laborers. But Democrats in particular sided with labor unions in the United States, including César Chávez's United Farm Workers Union, which argued that Braceros competed with Mexican Americans and other US citizens for jobs. López Mateos told Johnson that it was always his understanding that the Bracero Program "was a matter of mutual convenience rather than an obligation on the part of the United States." Yet he did say that Mexico would probably have to undertake some sort of "public works program" that would create jobs for Braceros when they returned to Mexico. He also said he was worried about the inevitable uptick in undocumented immigration, which would happen because Mexicans would still want to work in the United States, and because US employers would still want to hire them. The so-called "wetback" problem – a derogatory term for migrants who had crossed the Rio Grande River – had been an issue for more than a decade when the Immigration and Naturalization Service (INS), headed by Commissioner General Joseph Swing, announced the commencement of "Operation Wetback" in 1954. The initiative deported more than a million Mexicans in barely more than a year.[28] But undocumented immigration was not the focus for Johnson that it would become for later US presidents. The numbers of undocumented Mexicans in the United States began to climb during Johnson's final years in office, but they increased dramatically from the 1970s through the end of the twentieth century under both Democratic and Republican presidents.

Johnson's main accomplishment when it came to immigration was not a solution to the problem of undocumented immigration but the passage of the sweeping Immigration and Nationality Act, signed at the foot of the Statue of Liberty on October 3, 1965. Overall, the new law led some 60 million immigrants to come to the United States and greatly increased the number of immigrants arriving from Latin America, Africa, and Asia.

For Mexicans, the law was consequential for two reasons. First, it capped the number of Mexicans who could enter the United States at 120,000 a year. It was the first time that a numerical restriction had been placed on Mexican immigrants or immigrants from any Western Hemisphere country.[29] Because the number of Mexicans wanting to move to the United States each year was greater than the number allowed to move, this law, like the end of the Bracero Program, contributed to the growth of the undocumented population. Second, the Immigration and Nationality Act prioritized "family reunification" instead of employment-based immigration, which meant that, once naturalized, Mexicans could help their family members settle in the United States with them.[30] Family members, moreover, would not count toward the 120,000-immigrant quota, so many more Mexicans were able to enter legally than the number intended by the law.

Conservatives immediately railed against Johnson's immigration law, wondering how it was possible that he and fellow Democrats could not have anticipated that this would be the outcome. Dreading the "browning" of the nation, they also lamented that the law led to the demographic transformation of the United States. But for Johnson, it was a way to "repair a very deep and painful flaw in the fabric of American justice" because it brought fairness to an immigration law that had discriminated against immigrants from certain countries. His immigration law, he stated, said "simply that from this day forth those wishing to immigrate to America shall be admitted on the basis of their skills and their close relationship to those already here."[31] Despite the new numerical cap, this was welcome news to Mexican immigrants who sought security and opportunity as well as a chance to improve life for their families by bringing them to the United States.

Johnson's Great Society programs, the heart of his domestic policy agenda, also had international dimensions. Johnson continued to work with López Mateos's successor as president of Mexico, Gustavo Díaz Ordaz, to eradicate poverty and develop the economies of the US–Mexico borderlands. In 1966, they established a "bilateral planning agency," as the historian Sean Parulian Harvey describes it, called the Commission for Border Development and Friendship (CODAF). As the head of CODAF for the United States, Johnson appointed Raymond Telles, the ambassador to Costa Rica who had previously served as the mayor of El Paso. Telles was charged with solving problems related to poverty in the border region, especially the paucity of educational opportunities, the unavailability of housing, and the scarcity of employment options.[32]

Telles turned to Mexico as the model for solutions to poverty and economic development in the border region. In the years before Johnson and Díaz Ordaz established CODAF, Mexico had established PRONAF and PIF, which led to the construction of *maquiladoras*.

For US-owned, Chinese, or European companies that produced cars, electronics, and other goods, the benefit of the *maquiladoras* lay in access to Mexican laborers who worked for less than the workers in their own countries. The factories paid for labor and material, which they could import into Mexico duty-free, and paid taxes only on the profits they earned. So, for example, if the labor and parts to build a car cost $5,000, and the car sold for $10,000, the company would only pay taxes on the $5,000 profit. Over time, the arrangement would have grave social and political consequences in the United States, because the establishment of *maquiladoras* was tied to the deindustrialization of US regions like the Upper Midwest, complaints that US companies were killing jobs in the United States and sending them abroad, and the idea that Mexican workers were stealing jobs from US citizens.[33]

For Mexico, meanwhile, the *maquiladoras* led to the dramatic social and economic transformation of the border region. Jobs in the *maquiladoras*, even if they paid less than jobs in the United States, paid higher wages than jobs in southern and central Mexico. As a result, millions of Mexicans migrated to near-northern cities such as: Tijuana, Baja California; Nogales, Sonora; Ciudad Juárez, Chihuahua; or Nuevo Laredo, Tamaulipas. In a region that economic planners had long seen as devoid of natural resources, industrialization held out the promise of modernization. The modernization of the borderlands in this way certainly had a cost – labor exploitation, sexual violence, and pollution, among other problems – but the governments of Mexico and the United States mainly saw upside.

Upside is what Telles saw when, as head of CODAF, he argued for the construction of *maquiladoras* on the US side of the border as well. It did not make a lot of sense, since factories north of the border would have to adhere to US labor and environmental regulations and would have to pay wages that were competitive in the United States. But Telles nevertheless maintained that Mexico-style factories would bring jobs to border communities in the United States and would therefore lead to modernization, which, in turn, would lead to improvements in health and education. Telles's plan met stiff resistance from the labor movement in the United States, especially the AFL-CIO (American Federation of Labor and Congress of Industrial Organizations). The AFL-CIO eventually killed the idea of *maquiladora*-style factories for the US side of the border, but Telles's proposal nevertheless offered a glimpse of a Democratic Party in transition: still committed to Johnson's Great Society and building on Roosevelt's New Deal government interventions, but increasingly willing to embrace what critics would come to regard as neoliberal solutions.[34]

Johnson himself remained far removed from the day-to-day planning, but when he met with Díaz Ordaz to come up with the framework and announce their plans for CODAF, he again returned to his time in Cotulla. It was there, he said in a speech, that he first became acquainted with the problems of poverty within the border region's Mexican and Mexican American communities. Cotulla was the source of his commitment throughout his political career, he claimed, to making sure that Mexicans and Mexican Americans had the same opportunities as all other US citizens.

THE CHICANOS AND JOHNSON'S "PERFUMED SELLOUTS"

Latino history during the Johnson administration is not, however, only the story of Latinos benefiting from the slew of civil rights legislation or the president's efforts to build peaceful relationships with Mexico. Civil rights leaders and youth activists in particular still protested the continued injustices experienced by their communities. In 1965, César Chávez of the United Farm Workers led the effort by almost a thousand Mexican American and Filipino agricultural workers to boycott grape growers across the country. The next year, in March 1966, Chávez led about a hundred Mexican American and Filipino workers from Delano, in California's Central Valley, to the state capitol in Sacramento, to put pressure on growers and forced them to the negotiating table to discuss working conditions. The march led to the first contract for the union. Just a couple of months after Chávez's march to Sacramento, in June 1966, Chicago police shot a Puerto Rican man on Division Street near Damen Avenue, and a police dog bit another in the leg. This all took place in the evening, after the first-ever Puerto Rican parade in the city. Puerto Ricans responded by hurling rocks, bottles, and cans at police and smashing the windows of police cars. The violence that broke out night after night, for three nights in a row, has been called the Division Street Riots.

Then, in 1967, the Pentecostal preacher Reies Lopez Tijerina led an armed raid of the courthouse in Tierra Amarilla, in northwestern New Mexico, just a couple of hours from Albuquerque by car. Tijerina was the head of La Alianza Federal de Mercedes, which sought to reclaim federal land that the group argued had been stolen from Mexicans and Indigenous peoples. They entered the courthouse to demand the arrest of New Mexico District Attorney Alfonso Sanchez for not allowing members of La Alianza to protest peacefully a couple of days earlier. Tijerina's group fired shots, including one that hit a prison guard. The Aliancistas fled into the surrounding forests, and the lieutenant governor of New Mexico ordered the National Guard to pursue them in tanks.

In Texas, Chicanos, as Mexican American youth called themselves during the civil rights era, formed their own political party: El Partido de La Raza Unida. They felt that neither the Democratic nor the Republican Party represented them. Further west, in East Los Angeles, Mexican American high school students walked out of their classes in 1968 to fight for a more inclusive curriculum and a greater number of Mexican American teachers. They also drew attention to the appallingly high drop-out rate for Chicanos. Finally, college-age Chicanos, who were dramatically underrepresented in higher education, held conferences, formed student groups such as El Movimiento Estudiantil Chicano de Aztlán (MEChA), and issued manifestos calling for pride in their Indigenous roots and for an end to the "brutal 'gringo' invasion of our territories," by which they meant the lands annexed from Mexico after the Mexican-American War of 1846 to 1848.

All these episodes demonstrated how many Latinos, despite Johnson's historic accomplishments, took an oppositional stance toward his administration and felt like he still was not doing enough for them. What he had done, they charged, was offer rhetoric instead of action, performance instead of commitment to real change. Latino communities still suffered injustices including over-policing, educational discrimination, health disparities, and higher rates of unemployment, among others.

Johnson seemed like he was listening to the criticisms of his administration when, in June 1967, he established the Inter-Agency Committee on Mexican American Affairs (ICMAA). As its head, he chose his long-time acquaintance, Vicente Ximenes, a World War II veteran who had served the Kennedy administration in the US Agency for International Development in Ecuador and Panama. Ximenes's father had also known Johnson for decades, and during Johnson's campaign for president in 1964 Ximenes headed up the Viva Johnson campaign in Texas.

As head of the ICMAA, Ximenes coordinated the efforts of cabinet-level federal officials, including the heads of the Departments of Labor, Agriculture, and Health, Education, and Welfare, to make sure they paid sufficient attention to the concerns of Latinos, and to make sure that their agencies hired more of them. It was all part of LBJ's War on Poverty agenda. As Johnson wrote in a letter, Ximenes's responsibility as head of the ICMAA would be to "assure that Federal programs are reaching the Mexican Americans." In addition to making sure that existing agencies were doing a good job for Latinos, Ximenes would "seek out new programs that may be necessary to handle problems that are unique to the Mexican American community."[35]

On the same day Johnson made Ximenes the head of the ICMAA, he also appointed him to be the first-ever Latino Commissioner of the Equal Employment Opportunity Commission (EEOC). Johnson heaped praise upon Ximenes, saying that his life was "a very vivid story of what we call American opportunity. He is a distinguished public servant, a teacher, a war hero, a leader of the Mexican American community."[36]

One of the first things Ximenes did as head of the ICMAA was to plan workshops and listening sessions in El Paso. Mexican American leaders had wanted a meeting at the White House, but Johnson instructed Ximenes to hold the gathering in Texas instead. Ximenes extended invitations to older civil rights organizations such as LULAC and the GI Forum – two groups to which he himself belonged – but he also invited academics and Chicano Movement leaders such as César Chávez, president of the United Farm Workers, and Rodolfo "Corky" Gonzáles, head of the Crusade for Justice, a Chicano rights organization based in Denver. Gonzáles had just written a manifesto for the Chicano movement, a poem called "Yo Soy Joaquín," which included the lines, "My land is lost / And stolen. My culture has been raped."[37] Both Chicano leaders chose not to attend Ximenes's meeting. Chávez said he was still waiting for the Johnson administration to support farmworkers' rights. Gonzáles declined the invitation as well, but he traveled to El Paso nonetheless.

The Chicano leaders who were in El Paso but not at Ximenes's meeting held their own "rump conference," as the sociologist G. Cristina Mora has described it, at a nearby hotel. Chávez wrote a message to be delivered at the gathering, congratulating Chicanos for standing their ground against the "perfumed sellouts" that Ximenes had gathered together. According to Mora, the rump conference "provided members of different Chicano organizations ... with an opportunity to convene and unite against the Johnson administration."[38]

Suggesting his frustration with the Chicanos who had organized their own gathering to oppose his, Ximenes said he was glad that "solutions-oriented" Mexican Americans had decided to attend. Mora has described the difference between the "integrationist" Mexican Americans attending Ximenes's meeting and the Chicano movement activists who gathered elsewhere as the difference between those interested in developing "viable policy solutions" and those focused only on the "problems facing Mexican Americans." By the end of Johnson's presidency, Ximenes believed that the ICMAA had indeed made a difference through the usual policy channels. The Department of Labor started employment programs in Mexican American communities. The Department of Agriculture started programs for migrant farmworkers. Other government agencies committed to hiring more Latinos.[39]

Johnson's advisers had been telling him that he risked losing the votes of Mexican Americans and, to a lesser degree, Puerto Ricans, if he did not follow through on some of their demands. Unwilling to heed their advice, the president delivered a sharp message to his aides, writing on a memorandum they had written to warn him that there could be consequences if he did not meet with Latinos. "Keep this trash out of the White House," Johnson scrawled.[40] Certainly, the Johnson administration took different approaches to the civil rights activists who needled him and insiders from groups like LULAC and the GI Forum, which were more willing to work with the White House. Still, these harsh words hardly sounded like the sentiments of a president whose sense of self had been forged through his relationships with Mexican Americans back in Texas. But in early 1968 – before he announced in March that he would not run for reelection – he still needed their votes, so he established the committees, made the appointments, and held the ceremonies that he needed to in order to win their support.

LEGACIES

One less generous interpretation of Johnson's legacy for Mexican Americans, immigration, and the US–Mexico borderlands is that he ushered in an extended period – one that maybe even endures today – when politicians feigned care about Latinos in order to win their votes, even though their inaction proved that their expressions of concern and commitment were just rhetoric; when both legal and illegal immigration, and the backlash against it by conservatives, became a lightning rod in national politics that deepened the nation's political divisions; and when the United States began its turn toward neoliberal solutions to poverty and environmental degradation.

But there are more generous interpretations as well. Even after Johnson decided not to run for reelection, when there was less incentive for him to do the patronage-based politicking for which he was famous, he established National Hispanic Heritage Week. On September 17, 1968, Johnson said in his remarks inaugurating the celebration that "It is with special pride that I call the attention of my fellow citizens to the great contribution to our national heritage made by our people of Hispanic descent."[41] If one beginning of Johnson's political career was his expression of admiration for his Mexican and Mexican American students in Cotulla, one ending could be his statement marking the beginning of the first Hispanic Heritage Week. His Civil Rights Act had prohibited discrimination against Latinos in government jobs. His Voting Rights Act, even if it did not address the difficulties of political participation faced by Spanish-speaking Latinos, made it illegal to bar Latinos from voting based on their race. He had done more than earlier presidents to include Latinos in government. Perhaps as important, he included Latinos in conversations about racial justice.

Johnson had formed lasting relationships with many Mexican Americans in Texas and across the country. Civil rights activists like

César Chávez and Corky Gonzáles were critical of him, but he was also critical of them and the direction they would take the Democratic Party if its leaders listened to them. During the 1972 presidential race, Johnson said he believed that Nixon could be defeated "if only the Democrats don't go too far left."[42] But the GI Forum's Hector García and Vicente Ximenes, on the other hand, were steadfast supporters who trusted Johnson to do what he was able to do for Mexican Americans, when he could do it. In doing so, he, like his predecessor in office, understood that Mexican Americans would help shape the future of the United States. Both the less and more generous interpretations of Johnson's legacy are, of course, valid. They depend on multiple perspectives within extremely diverse communities that are to this day debating their political identities. The views that Mexican Americans and other Latinos had of Johnson revealed as much about them as they did about the president himself.

In the decades since Johnson's presidency, and in part because of it, Latinos have held more elected and appointed offices than ever before. They have become cabinet-level secretaries, attorneys general, and Supreme Court justices. Presidents from Richard Nixon to Joseph Biden have said that Latinos are key to the future of the United States. By the beginning of the twenty-first century, about one in five Americans was Latino. They were no longer a regional population, confined to the US Southwest, Florida, and pockets of the Northeastern and Midwestern United States. They had spread across the United States and could influence the outcome of elections in Iowa, Wisconsin, Michigan, Pennsylvania, and North Carolina, for example. Americans, even if they did not like it, grew accustomed to hearing Spanish in grocery stores, when they called help centers, and in the kitchens of their favorite restaurants. Yet many Americans still did not appreciate how long they had lived on the lands that made up the United States – since before there was a United States. They still saw the racial history of the United States in black and white, and believed that racial discrimination had been conquered in a nation that had elected a Black president. Latinos still earned less, attended college less, and had poorer health outcomes than non-Latino white Americans. They were still treated as poor and dangerous foreigners, even though they were economically diverse and committed crimes at lower rates than non-Latino white Americans, and a significant majority had been born in the United States. Progress and its limitations for Latinos characterized Johnson's times, and our own.

CHAPTER 6

The War on Poverty:
How Qualitative Liberalism Prevailed

Joshua Zeitz

Y EARS AFTER THE FACT, WALTER HELLER, THE CHAIRMAN OF
the Council of Economic Advisers, vividly recalled the prevailing
sense of unease when he first learned of John F. Kennedy's death on
November 22, 1963. Along with several other members of the president's
cabinet, Heller was aboard an Air Force plane bound for Japan when the
news came over the wire. As the aircraft turned back toward the United
States, he huddled in the back of the cabin with Orville Freeman (secretary of agriculture), Luther Hodges (secretary of commerce), Stuart
Udall (secretary of the interior), and W. William Wirtz (secretary of
labor). "The five of us had a long, long seminar, so to speak, on
Lyndon Johnson," Heller remembered, "everybody tossing in his impres-
sions. We went back to the events of 1960, going back to the relationships
they had had one way or another over the years, what kind of man was
this, so and forth." The cabinet members were divided in their assessment
of Johnson's worldview. Some envisaged a deeply conservative Johnson
presidency: LBJ was, after all, a former member in good standing with the
Senate's Southern Caucus and had racked up a checkered legislative
history that gave cold comfort to liberals. Others wondered if he were
not more of a Southwestern populist and pointed to his formative years as
a young, New Deal congressman as evidence that he perhaps hailed from
a more progressive tradition.[1]

For Heller, the stakes seemed particularly high. As the president's top
economic adviser, he had struggled for several months to obtain Kennedy's
support for a comprehensive federal initiative to combat poverty. It had

proved difficult enough to convince JFK. How could he possibly hope to win over LBJ?

After a day of nonstop travel, Heller arrived back in Washington and promptly secured an appointment with Johnson early on Saturday evening – Johnson's first full day in office. He briefed the new president on a range of pressing economic issues and then raised the question of the poverty program. Leaning in close, LBJ gave a surprising response. "Now, I want to say something about all this talk that I'm a conservative who is likely to go back to the Eisenhower ways or give in to the economy bloc in Congress," he began. "It's not so, and I want you to tell your friends – Arthur Schlesinger, Galbraith and other liberals – that it is not so . . . . If you looked at my record, you would know that I am a Roosevelt New Dealer. As a matter of fact, to tell you the truth, John F. Kennedy was a little too conservative to suit my taste."[2] As he later recalled, Johnson ended the meeting by affirming that the anti-poverty initiative was "my kind of program. I'll find money for it one way or another."[3] After consulting with Heller and Budget Director Kermit Gordon at the LBJ Ranch over the winter holidays, on January 8, 1964 he delivered his first State of the Union address before Congress, in which he boldly declared an "unconditional war on poverty." The "chief weapons" in this attack would include "better schools, and better health, and better homes, and better training, and better job opportunities to help more Americans, especially young Americans, escape from squalor and misery and unemployment rolls where other citizens help to carry them." (See Figure 6.1.)

It was an audacious proclamation – one that critics then and later would condemn for its overstated promise.[4] After all, what did it mean to fight an unconditional War on Poverty? What instruments would the government bring to bear in this fight, and how would it define victory?

The War on Poverty was in many ways a political slogan rather than a concrete set of policy initiatives. Often invoked interchangeably with "the Great Society," it included anti-poverty programs that contributed to America's patchwork safety net and other initiatives intended to maximize the individual citizen's ability to realize his or her fullest potential. Conservatives then and later derided the War on Poverty as a failed attempt at economic redistribution that led millions of Americans into a state of permanent dependency on the government, but in truth, LBJ

6.1. Accompanied by members of his staff, President Johnson poses on June 6, 1964, with tenant farmer William David Marlow and his family on the front porch of their house in Rocky Mount, North Carolina. LBJ visited the area during a tour of Appalachia to build support for his War on Poverty.
Credit: Getty Images

and his aides never seriously contemplated policies that would enforce equality of income, wealth, or condition. They did not broadly support quantitative measures like a guaranteed minimum income or employment. Instead, they believed that qualitative measures like education, workforce training, and access to health care and food security would level the playing field and help poor people realize their share of a growing economy. When economic growth sputtered in the early 1970s, the limitations of these policy decisions became immediately evident. But considered by its own terms, the War on Poverty proved a lasting and important component of the nation's response to poverty.

THE POSTWAR CONTEXT

Lyndon Johnson and his aides were audacious in their ambition because they lived in an era without parallel in American history. In the quarter-decade following World War II, the United States experienced an economic boom unprecedented in scope and size. Median family income grew by a stunning 30 percent in the 1950s,[5] driving the typical American's transition from renter to homeowner,[6] from blue-collar to white-collar worker,[7] and from a culture of Depression-era scarcity and wartime rationing to postwar consumer abundance.[8] Abundance transformed the way that liberals thought about public policy. In the darkest days of the Great Depression, most liberal intellectuals agreed that capitalism was foundationally broken. Franklin Roosevelt's aide, Harry Hopkins, expected permanently high levels of unemployment "even in future 'prosperity' periods," while Alvin Hansen, an economist at Harvard University, warned of a future marked by "sick recoveries which die in their infancy and depressions which feed on themselves and leave a hard and seemingly immovable core of unemployment."[9]

Many reformers assumed that this permanent state of affairs would require radical changes to the very structure of capitalism – changes as wide-ranging as public ownership of utilities and factories, a guaranteed family income, the breakup of monopolies or, conversely, the establishment of industrial cartels invested with sweeping power to set uniform wages and prices. But World War II forced a swift reevaluation of these assumptions. The federal government built ships, airplanes, and tanks by the thousands. It raised, supplied, and deployed a military force of 16 million men. It defeated fascism in Europe and the Pacific. In so doing, the government lifted the country out of Depression and proved that, through skilled planning and management, policymakers could provide, as labor leader Walter Reuther described it, "full production, full employment and full distribution in a society which has achieved economic democracy within the framework of political democracy."[10]

Thinking back on the New Deal era, Chester Bowles, who led the Office of Price Administration during the war, recalled that people of his generation previously assumed that they "must learn to live with a certain amount of scarcity in the midst of plenty." Now, America was growing – and its "population isn't going to stop growing, technology isn't going to stop growing, and all these new plans and machines ... will steadily increase our ability to produce."[11]

This new faith in expert management and growth changed the way that many liberals thought about the world. Richard Hofstadter, an influential historian and public intellectual, observed that "the jobless, distracted and bewildered men of 1933 have in the course of the years found substantial places in society for themselves, have become home-owners, suburbanites, and solid citizens."[12] During the Depression, many liberals had advanced radical reforms to break up banking and industrial interests and redistribute wealth; now, they envisioned a consensus culture that was essentially classless in nature. Unbounded growth extended the promise of unlimited prosperity. Importantly, the new liberal world-view assumed that a rising economic tide would lift all boats.

POVERTY IN A PROSPEROUS SOCIETY

This was not to say that liberals denied the existence of poverty in the United States. Under the chairmanship of Senator Paul Douglas of Illinois, the Joint Committee on Economics issued a report in 1959, *Low-Income Population and Economic Growth*, that found poverty remained a persistent challenge and that wealth and income distribution had grown *more* unequal in recent years. In 1962 the writer and socialist organizer Michael Harrington published a book on American poverty that gripped the public's attention. Entitled *The Other America*, it argued that upwards of 50 million people – over a quarter of the population – lived in a "system designed to be impervious to hope." The "other America" was "populated by failures, by those driven from the land and bewildered by the city, by old people suddenly confronted with the torments of loneliness and poverty, and by minorities facing a wall of prejudice." Largely "invisible" to members of the prosperous middle class, other Americans were trapped in a national "ghetto, a modern poor farm for the rejects of society and of the economy."[13]

Very few people read Harrington's book, but many, including JFK, absorbed Dwight Macdonald's long and engaging review, which appeared in the *New Yorker* in January 1963. It shocked the liberal con-science to learn that even by the government's tight definition, 34 million Americans – more than one out of six – lived beneath the poverty line, and that three-quarters of these individuals were children and senior citizens.[14] Many, including Kennedy, also read a series of vivid articles in the *New York Times* by the veteran reporter Homer Bigart, who chronicled the trenchant social decay of communities in West Virginia, where the steady decline of the coal economy was already taking a heavy toll on individuals and families.[15] Perceiving an opening, in the last months of the Kennedy administration Heller convened interagency meetings each Saturday afternoon at the Executive Office Building, where officials from the Council of Economic Advisers (CEA) and Budget Bureau, as well as the departments of Labor, Agriculture, Justice, and Health, Education, and Welfare, ruminated on the problem. "We would get into discussions about the definition of poverty," one participant remembered.

> Some people would say poverty obviously means a lack of money income. . ... But other people said that's not what poverty really means. . ... It's a spiritual concept, or a participation-in-government concept or it's a lack of some kind of self-esteem, sort of a psychological or image problem that people had . . .. Still others would say it really has to do with lack of opportunity. It has to do with lack of public facilities like school and so on. That's what makes people really poor.[16]

While some participants, particularly those representing the Department of Labor, argued that what poor people needed most was income, and that the government should resolve this need by creating public-sector relief jobs in the spirit of the New Deal, most officials identified broad-based ideas like a "culture of poverty" and lack of "opportunity" as the real cause of poverty. Such thinking made sense in the context of 1963. The economy was strong, and those who had been left behind only needed to be equipped with the means to claim their fair share of an ever-growing pie.

Not everyone agreed. W. Willard Wirtz, the secretary of labor, took a more straightforward view of the problem. Poor people, he believed, were poor because they did not have enough money. To make money, they needed jobs, and, for a multitude of reasons, there were pockets of the country where good jobs were simply not to be had. "Without question," he urged, "the biggest single immediate change which the poverty program could bring about in the lives of most of the poor would be to provide the family head with a regular, decently paid job." Wilbur Cohen, the assistant secretary of health, education, and welfare, agreed that poor people needed money, not "opportunity." But Cohen was skeptical that even a New Deal–style program of mass public-works jobs would reduce poverty, given how ill-equipped many poor people were to thrive in the workforce.

However much they differed on the efficacy of qualitative measures to unlock "opportunity," most participants agreed that income redistribution was neither politically viable nor necessary. As the columnist Walter Lippmann argued,

> [a] generation ago, it would have been taken for granted that a war on poverty meant taking money away from the haves and turning it over to the have-nots .... But in this generation a revolutionary idea has taken hold. The size of the pie can be increased by intention, by organized fiscal policy and then a whole society, not just one part of it, will grow richer.[17]

It was this thinking that informed the Johnson administration's War on Poverty – a collection of qualitative measures intended to help poor people help themselves, rather than a negative income tax or jobs program.

QUALITATIVE LIBERALISM AT WORK

Perhaps the most enduringly popular of Johnson's Great Society programs, Operation Head Start, an early childhood education initiative, was a textbook example of qualitative liberalism at work – the idea that what poor people needed were education, training, and other measures to help them help themselves, rather than cash transfers or a guaranteed income. Launched as a pilot program that served 560,000 low-income children in the summer of 1965,[18] it soon grew into a permanent, full-year program that some thirty years later served 900,000 poor children annually and enjoyed the approval of over 90 percent of respondents to public opinion polls. As early as 1969, critics questioned the lasting value of early child-hood education generally and Head Start specifically. Some studies concluded that whatever educational gains poor children made through the program quickly eroded by the time that they reached grade school and middle school. Though other studies challenge this finding, in the decades after Head Start's launch some consensus emerged that early intervention was not powerful enough in and of itself to reverse the combined challenges of single-parent households, persistent income and wealth inequality, neighborhood crime and deterioration, and failing public schools. Such criticisms implicitly call into question the underlying logic behind the War on Poverty – namely, that what was needed to break the cycle of poverty was opportunity, not cash transfers or income assistance.

But these criticisms understated the program's broad intent. Closing the educational achievement gap was just one of its mandates. Head Start also sought to provide poor children with hot, nutritious meals; medical and dental care; and a stable and nurturing environment where their parents could act as full partners in their care and development. A government study found that among Head Start pupils in 1969, roughly one-third had not received their complete diphtheria, pertussis, and tetanus immunizations, nearly 40 percent had not been vaccinated against polio, and very few had received dental or eye exams. In Jacksonville, Florida, 52 percent of Head Start children were anemic, 31 percent suffered from hearing defects, and 25 percent had eye problems. In South Carolina's Beaufort County, 90 percent of pre-school-aged children had hookworm or roundworm. In Boston, 31 percent of eligible students endured major physical or psychological issues. More than just an early education program, Head Start provided its students services that materially narrowed the wellness gap between poor and nonpoor youngsters, including free medical care and breakfast, lunch, and supper each day. It was more than just an early education program. It did not permanently erase child poverty, but it did materially change the circumstances of poor children and, in the parlance of qualitative liberalism, set poor kids up to achieve their share of prosperity as students.[19]

In line with the War on Poverty's ethos of helping poor people help themselves, parents and paraprofessionals from the community played an outsized role in staffing and maintaining local programs. Based on both first-hand knowledge and program data, Head Start's first director believed that "the non-professionals bring a different quality to the program than a program that's purely professionally run ... it brings a dimension of sensitivity and concern that's better than you have in a purely professionally run program."[20]

The same ethos of qualitative liberalism informed the administration's approach to health care. As early as 1934, when Franklin

Roosevelt's Committee on Economic Security first contemplated but ultimately rejected including health insurance in the original Social Security Act, liberals aspired to make access to affordable health care a fundamental right of citizenship. In the 1940s Senator Robert Wagner and Congressmen John Dingell Sr. and Reid Murray introduced legislation that would have established a national program for hospital and medical insurance. It went nowhere, as was also the case with Harry Truman's efforts after 1949 to achieve the same result.[21] At every turn, powerful opposition from the American Medical Association (AMA) and its Republican supporters in Congress stymied progressive efforts. The AMA alone showered $1.5 million on lobbyists and public relations professionals to defeat Truman's program – a staggering sum in its day. In 1952, when the GOP platform roundly denounced "federal compulsory health insurance, with its crushing cost, wasteful inefficiency, bureaucratic dead weight, and debased standards of medical care," Dwight Eisenhower – the very model of moderation – blasted Democrats who would foist "socialized medicine" on an unsuspecting public. There was little room for bipartisan compromise.[22]

If Republicans were steadfast in their opposition to national health care, increasing numbers of working-class voters who might have been inclined to support it no longer needed it. In an era of unmatched economic growth, universal, government-provided health care seemed as radical and unnecessary as a guaranteed family income. After World War II, major employers had begun extending unprecedented benefits to workers, including paid vacations, annual cost-of-living adjustments to wages, defined-benefits pensions, and *private* health insurance. Liberal industrial unions endorsed this new model for labor–management relations. What many liberals once assumed government would need to do for its working-class citizens, private industry now offered on a contingent basis. Only people who, by definition, could not avail themselves of these benefits – senior citizens, who were not employed, and the very poor, who were also presumed to be unemployable or permanently disabled – needed access to help. Or so the thinking went.

Certainly, the need was real. At a hearing in 1959, a retired blue-collar worker from Tampa told a Senate subcommittee that he and his wife got by on just $1,500 each year. "Well, we are old people and we don't require much," he offered. "But I want to ask you … what do we do if we need medical care … I will have to seek some charity institution and submit to the humiliation of what they call a necessity, and pronounce to the whole world that I am only a pauper, a beggar." A 75-year-old woman from Boston shocked the panel with her tale of waiting "in line like a lot of cattle" at a charitable clinic, because she and her husband could not afford to spend $7 to visit a private doctor. "We pay $1.75 or $2 for a ticket to get in," she complained. "Then they write out a prescription … $11 prescription. How in the world can I pay $11 for a prescription?"[23] As a Senate aide to Lyndon Johnson, George Reedy, who later served in Johnson's White House, had urged LBJ to take up the cause of health care for the elderly. The "problem of aging amounts to a collective responsibility," he insisted. "America is no longer a nation of simpler pioneer folk in which grandmother and grandfather can spend their declining years in a log cabin doing odd jobs and taking care of the grandchildren."[24]

That was precisely what Medicare (and Medicaid, aimed at disabled workers and widows and children) intended from the start to do. Medicare entitled senior citizens to ninety days of hospitalization coverage a year, per illness, and access to voluntary medical insurance to cover physician visits. The administration also established Medicaid insurance for indigent Americans of all ages, including dependent children; states would administer the program, with a sliding-scale match from Washington, DC.[25] The program fell far short of universal, single-payer health insurance, which many liberals had vocally supported in the 1930s and 1940s. But in 1965 it represented the perfect embodiment of liberal thinking: a growing economy would secure private health care for the vast majority of workers and their families; the government would fill in as a stopgap for seniors, the disabled, and widows and their children.

Federal aid to education also aligned well with the predominant thinking in the 1960s. In the early 1960s universities and colleges were under mounting strain to accommodate millions of Baby Boomers who arrived on their campuses. Moreover, few poor students could afford tuition, resulting in a disparity between the portion of middle-class

(78 percent) and working-class (33 percent) high school graduates who attended college. More than one-fifth of students who began post-secondary studies had to drop out because of financial difficulty. For many Black families, whose median income was little more than half that of white families, postsecondary education was entirely out of reach.[26] Believing that access to a quality education would help poor people achieve their share of American prosperity, the Johnson White House secured passage in 1965 of the Higher Education Act, which supported library expansion at private and public universities; established work study programs; and extended reduced-interest loans to make tuition and fees affordable for poor and working-class students.[27]

The same thinking – that access to education would help poor people achieve their share of the growing economic pie – influenced the administration's Elementary and Secondary Education Act (ESEA). Since the 1930s federal aid to public education had been a signature aspiration of American liberals. It was "shocking," Harry Truman told Congress in 1949, that "millions of our children are not receiving a good education. Millions of them are in overcrowded, obsolete buildings. We are short of teachers, because teachers' salaries are too low to attract new teachers, or to hold the ones we have." Truman requested direct federal appropriations to assist local schools in upgrading their facilities and paying their teachers and proposed that the various government agencies responsible for administering federal health, education, and welfare programs be accorded cabinet-level status.[28] Congress responded by creating the Department of Health, Education, and Welfare in 1953, but in the absence of a more sweeping mandate, the tiny and toothless Office of Education remained a stodgy resting place for government bureaucrats with no discernable connection to presidential power or authority. As had been the case for most of the nation's history, state and local governments bore the primary responsibility for funding and administering elementary and secondary schools, resulting in disparities between wealthy and poor districts, segregated and nonsegregated jurisdictions, and rural and urban areas. As the Baby-Boom generation swelled America's schools, creating massive teacher and classroom shortages, efforts to pass a bill providing for federal aid to local education stalled repeatedly.

Liberals persisted in their argument that the country was in dire need of additional education funding. The argument was of a piece with opportunity theory, which held that poor people needed help unlocking economic opportunities that a prosperous nation inherently held out for them. In the case of education, if the nation's poorest students did not have access to a quality education, how could they expect to capture their share of a growing economy? The numbers supported this concern. In any given year American schoolchildren suffered a shortage of 304,000 classrooms. Many schools in poor areas lacked gymnasia, lunchrooms, or libraries. To double up on space, administrators shifted fifth and sixth graders into middle schools and ran double-shift days. In Kentucky, more than half of all pupils attended overcrowded classes – many with over sixty children per room – and, according to the state superintendent of instruction, more than 40 percent of facilities were "outmoded or unfit or should be abandoned."[29] Unsurprisingly, student achievement reflected these broad disparities in resources and facilities. In 1960, the high school completion rate for young adults in the wealthiest five states and five poorest states in the country differed by 20 percentage points. For African Americans, who were substantially less likely than their white peers to finish secondary school, the disparity between residents of wealthy and poor states was 27 percent. It was precisely this fundamental opportunity deficit that enabled LBJ and his administration to untie the Gordian knot that was federal education policy.[30]

It was a knotty issue. Some Republicans supported the idea, including conservative Senator Robert Taft and President Dwight Eisenhower. "We have helped the states build highways and local farm-to-market roads," the former general offered. "We have provided federal funds to help the states build hospitals and mental institutions." Why not classrooms?[31] But most GOP leaders agreed with Barry Goldwater that "if the camel once gets his nose in the tent, his body will soon follow." The moment that local government became reliant on Washington, "supervision, and ultimately control of education" would fall into the hands of "federal authorities." House Minority Leader Gerald Ford warned of "[f]ederalized schools, text books, and teachers, federalized libraries, laboratories, auditoriums, and theaters," while even Richard Nixon, a relative moderate, predicted in 1960 that when "the federal government gets the power to pay teachers, inevitably, in my opinion, it will acquire the power to set standards and to tell the teachers what to teach."[32]

In addition to conservative opposition, efforts to secure federal funding for K-12 education met with the pointed resistance of Catholic political and religious leaders, who insisted that any aid bill must include the vast network of diocesan and parish schools that the church had meticulously constructed and nurtured over the better part of a century. In the early postwar era, many white ethnic communities remained tightly bound and organized around a sweeping array of separate institutions – youth clubs, sports teams, fraternal organizations, newspapers – that all led back to the neighborhood church. Primary and secondary schools, which educated 5 million Catholic children each year, formed a mainstay of this sweeping religious network.[33] Catholic Democrats were disinclined to support legislation that might create wider disparities in classroom funding and teacher salaries than already existed between parochial and public institutions. For their part, liberal Protestants steadfastly agreed with the National Council of Churches it was neither "just" nor "lawful that public funds should be assigned to support the elementary or secondary schools of any church."[34] The religious question constituted a major impediment to progress.

Finally, the issue of race proved a stumbling block for advocates of federal aid. Whenever the issue of aid to education came to the House floor, liberals of both parties routinely supported efforts by Adam Clayton Powell, a Black clergyman and lawmaker from Harlem, to bar funds to school districts that were out of compliance with the Supreme Court's decision in *Brown v. Board of Education*. Without the amendment, liberals could not vote for the broader legislation; with it, Southerners would not support it.

The bill that LBJ ultimately signed provided school districts with compensatory education dollars based on the number of children in households earning less than $2,000 annually. Title I provided aid to public schools to support supplemental programs that would benefit poor students (including those who attended private institutions). Title II funded textbooks and libraries in public and private schools, alike. Title III underwrote supplemental programs in music, science, remedial skills, and physical education for poor children.[35] Francis Keppel, who served as commissioner of education under LBJ, spoke for most liberals when he argued that "income correlates highly with the number of years of schooling completed." He sincerely believed, as did most of the War on Poverty's architects, that additional funds "could interrupt the cycle of poverty where we have a fighting chance."[36] At the time of the bill's passage, it was still an article of liberal faith that more education funding generated better educational outcomes, and that better educational outcomes would lift children out of poverty. The very logic behind this thinking lay at the heart of opportunity theory.

There was something to the argument. In big cities especially, federal assistance proved critical, and officials could make the case that even offsets of ordinary course expenditures benefited poor children. As Benjamin Willis, the Superintendent of Schools in Chicago, explained to Congress, urban centers had in recent years attracted "large families from the rural South" – white and Black, alike – who "have little education and limited vocational skills." Their children "require specialized programs of education if they are to overcome the disadvantages imposed upon them by their limited background." More so than small towns and suburbs, "a large portion of the tax dollar in the great cities is required for non-school governmental services," including public transportation, police and sanitation, and public welfare. "Site and construction costs are considerably higher in the large cities than in smaller communities." Metropolises like Chicago could spend more on educating disadvantaged youth if they had more money.[37]

Education experts continue to debate whether more funding results in better educational outcomes, but on balance, federal funding for K-12 education closed massive gaps between wealthier and poorer regions and addressed a clear deficiency in resources that states would otherwise have been ill-equipped to remedy. Between 1958 and 1968, federal spending on primary and secondary education rose from less than 3 percent to more than 10 percent of total education funding. As LBJ predicted, once in place, the program became popular and grew. By 1985 the federal government's share of all K-12 school spending rose to 16 percent, the percentage provided by state governments rose from 41 percent to 55 percent, and the portion funded by local governments fell from 51 percent to 31 percent. Because many local and state governments

rely heavily on regressive property and sales taxes, the growing importance of federal and state funds shifted some of the burden for funding
schools from working-class and poor families to middle-class and wealthy
taxpayers. As the federal government gradually tightened restrictions
governing the use of Title I money, state authorities centralized and
professionalized their education departments and school systems to
ensure ease of compliance and the continued flow of federal dollars.
All of these developments represented a practical application of opportunity theory.[38]

The War on Poverty also turned to job training programs to help
unlock opportunity for poor people. A primary example of this priority
was the Job Corps, modeled in part after the New Deal–era Civilian
Conservation Corps and National Youth Administration. Its mandate
was to relocate, socialize, and train tens of thousands of young men
who were otherwise outside the labor force and lacking the basic skills
to become gainfully employed.

As well, it included controversial measures like legal aid for the poor
and community action programs – CAPs, as they were known – that
empowered poor people to organize, and in some cases politically
mobilize against, local elected officials, many of them Democrats, to
demand improved infrastructure, policing, sanitation, and education
resources. By the end of the decade, more than 1,000 community action
agencies participated in the initiative. These programs opened a rift
with mayors and governors who resented that the federal government
was using tax dollars to encourage organizing in opposition to local
political machines. "Many mayors assert that the CAP is setting up
a *competing political organization* in their own backyards," an aide confided to Johnson. (Indeed, in 1965 the US Conference of Mayors
pressed the administration to turn control of community action programs over to local political authorities.) He urged that "*we ought not to
be in the business of organizing the poor politically.*"[39] James Rowe,
a prominent attorney, former White House staff member to Harry
Truman, and longtime friend of LBJ and his wife, warned that "high
minded ... innocents" within the Office of Economic Opportunity
(OEO) were arming radicals with resources to upend local government.
"The *political implications* of using public funds to *instruct* people how to

protest are obvious," he told Johnson.[40] Of course this approach was precisely how many of the OEO's framers understood the strategic value of community action. It empowered poor people to help themselves by demanding their fair share of public resources. Hence, the grant to Syracuse University for a program that trained local poor people in the political organizing tactics of Saul Alinsky. In turn, they used their newly acquired skills to agitate for better sanitation services, rent subsidies, tenant rights, and parks, and – in a move that raised the ire of the city's mayor – to register voters. "We are experiencing a class struggle in the traditional Karl Marx style," the mayor complained, "and I do not like it."[41] Architects of the War on Poverty would have disagreed. In a thriving and prosperous, and capitalist, society, everyone had a right to work through political channels to hold their elected officials accountable.

When a CAP in Albuquerque organized pickets outside City Hall to demand greater services for poor neighborhoods, Senator Clinton Anderson, a Democrat, called the White House to complain. "The demonstration is being led by an ex-Peace Corps volunteer who's working in the Community Action Program now," he said with bewilderment.[42] Community programs in Newark, San Francisco, and other cities drew sharp scrutiny for their radicalism, financial irregularities, and palpable animosity toward established institutions, be they public or private. On the Lower East Side of Manhattan, Mobilization for Youth – one of the first products of the Ford Foundation's Gray Areas Project – sued the New York Police Department and clamored for the establishment of a civilian review board. When a police shooting of a Black teenager prompted riots in Harlem, conservative critics scored Mobilization as a radical and incendiary organization.

In Chicago, where the OEO insisted that the city government comply with the requirement that its program include "maximum feasible participation" on the part of local poor people, Mayor Richard Daley grew enraged. "What in the hell are you people doing?" he berated Bill Moyers, a top aide to LBJ. "Does the president know he's putting M-O-N-E-Y in the hands of subversives? To poor people that aren't a part of the organization? Didn't the president know they'd take that money to bring him down?"[43] Daley was an indispensable ally whose complaints reverberated loudly within the West Wing, as was also the case with Sam Yorty and John Shelley, the Democratic mayors of Los Angeles and San Francisco, respectively. "Mayors all over the United States are being harassed by agitation prompted by Sargent Shriver's speeches urging those he calls 'poor' to insist upon control of local poverty programs," Yorty complained in mid 1965. Though in many instances the administration interceded on behalf of elected officials – including in Syracuse, where Shriver folded the controversial action program under an umbrella organization governed by municipal officials and old-line welfare agencies – there was no clear consensus about the definition of "maximum feasible participation" or even its very purpose. Vice President Hubert Humphrey, who often served as a mediator with local officials after his election to the vice presidency in 1964, saw "no conflict between full involvement of local government officials and 'maximum feasible participation' of the poor. What disturbs the Mayors is their belief that OEO is building and funding in the community action committees opposition elements to the city administration."[44]

It was easy for critics to latch onto CAPs as the embodiment of all that was wrong with the War on Poverty, but several lasting and popular initiatives – notably, Head Start – began life as community action programs. Tying these disparate programs together was the conviction that poor people needed opportunity, resources, and training – not income support or money.

BACKLASH

Politically, race and economics were inseparable. Johnson's Council of Economic Advisers cited hard facts and figures that established a positive correlation between both lack of education and discrimination – by which it meant *racial* discrimination – and income. Though 78 percent of poor families were white, the poverty rate among nonwhites was much higher. More than 50 percent of poor people lived in cities, but 40 percent of all farm families – and 80 percent of nonwhite farm families – were poor. Though only 25 percent of poor families were headed by single mothers, among female-headed households roughly half were poor. Buried in these statistics were several landmines that the Johnson administration did not immediately perceive but later tripped. Most of the beneficiaries of the Great Society were white, but because its programs disproportionately aided nonwhites – and because conservative critics associated anti-poverty initiatives with civil rights – backlash politicians were easily able to harness racial fears and resentments to scale back LBJ's legacy. Equally, though patterns of family dissolution had long been in evidence among white communities in Appalachia, the administration's focus on Black poverty led many white Americans to assume that the rise of single-parent households and welfare dependency was unique to the Black urban ghetto."[45]

Backlash began to build as early as 1964, when Alabama Governor George Wallace stunned political observers by performing well against LBJ in that year's presidential primaries. In Berkeley, California, where voters had recently defeated an open housing referendum, he reminded the crowd that "they voted just like the people in Alabama." After launching his campaign in Appleton, Wisconsin, home to the late GOP Senator Joseph McCarthy, Wallace canvassed the state's blue-collar wards. In Milwaukee, over 700 white working-class voters packed the local Serb Memorial Hall to hear Wallace warn that the civil rights bill then still pending in Congress would imperil their jobs, neighborhoods, and safety. "A vote for this little governor will let people in Washington know that we want them to leave our houses, schools, jobs, businesses, and farms alone," he roared to thunderous applause. The statute would "destroy the union seniority system and impose racial quotas." It would be "impossible for a home owner to sell his home to whomever he chooses." The crowd had in recent years watched with guarded caution as the city's Black neighborhood pushed up against its insular community of small, tidy bungalows, community schools, and ethnic churches. Wallace's message resonated with them.[46]

Initial polling had Wallace running at a negligible 5 percent, but on primary day, he won 265,000 votes, or one-quarter of those cast. He carried the governor's own district and took 30 percent of the vote in Milwaukee and 47 percent in the newly created ninth congressional district, which included some of the region's most prosperous suburbs. "We won without winning!" he boasted, a deed that he replicated weeks later in Indiana, where he took 30 percent, and again in Maryland, where

43 percent of the state's primary voters backed the outspoken segregationist. Disenchanted voters marched to the polls "with big grins on their
faces," a newspaper editor observed. "I never saw anything like it."
Governor Daniel Brewster, Johnson's proxy on the ballot in Maryland,
fumed that Wallace's supporters had been hoodwinked by a "pack of
mindless thugs," but there was little doubting that something was darkly
amiss in the nation's heartland.[47]

Much was at work behind Wallace's political success. During the
previous five decades, more than 4 million African Americans had left
the South, swelling the population of Northern, Midwestern, and
Western cities. Though leaving Dixie presented them with comparatively
greater freedom, including the unqualified right to vote, discriminatory
employment practices limited Black residents to some of the lowest-
paying jobs (and highest rates of unemployment). Racially restrictive
housing laws – some enforced by a complex web of regulations handed
down by federal mortgage agencies – consigned them to the worst, most
cramped, yet paradoxically most overpriced, housing stock. An absence
of basic public services like reliable garbage removal, building inspec-
tion, and quality schools made them second-class citizens in most places
where they lived.[48] Discrimination created a vicious cycle. Since African
Americans faced rampant job discrimination, they tended to earn less
cash income than their white neighbors and rely more heavily on welfare.
Because discriminatory rental and mortgage practices sharply limited
their residential options, Black residents had little recourse when landlords in transitional neighborhoods consolidated and subdivided their
properties, creating more cramped and rundown housing stock. As
a result, many urban Black neighborhoods came gradually to resemble
wastelands – at least in the eyes of working-class white residents whose
own neighborhoods stood in close proximity. Boarded-up, abandoned
buildings seemed to dot every block, as landlords often found it more
advantageous to pack more tenants in one property than to pay property
taxes and maintenance on two. Such decay inevitably attracted drug
dealers, vagrants, prostitutes, and vandals. In short, when residents of
white ethnic enclaves in Gary, Indiana, or Milwaukee, Wisconsin, pointed
to surrounding Black neighborhoods with fear, they were reacting from
genuine experience. In their assumption that ghetto residents *chose* to

live in such impoverished circumstances, they spoke from a position of ignorance – ignorance of the privilege they derived from the GI Bill's housing and educational opportunities, ignorance of their advantaged position in unionized industries, and ignorance of their superior access to public services.

Richard Scammon, an influential political scientist whom JFK had installed as Director of the Census, warned the White House of a deep undercurrent of disaffection. "The American white majority's view of civil rights and race can only be labeled as confused, contradictory, and apprehensive." Most Northern white respondents supported federal protection of civil rights activists, but they also believed that "mass Negro demonstrations are harmful." A commanding majority supported the Civil Rights Act, but

> it is in such areas as street violence, the busing of school children, the right of a home owner not to sell to a Negro, the movement of Negro families "onto this block," and the movement of Negro workers "into my job," that the deep, gut-level apprehension bites into a super-structure of white tolerance and liberalism. While almost no whites would deny the Negro the right to vote, the majority would say: "I'll be Goddamned if my kid has to ride a bus across this city to go to school in a Negro slum."

Scammon found this sentiment increasingly evident among "lower middle class and working class families, many of them life-long Democrats."[49]

By 1967 a combination of conservative Democrats and Republicans, who now enjoyed renewed influence – particularly in the House – created a check against further expansion of programs associated with the War on Poverty. That year, the White House hammered out a compromise set of amendments to the Social Security Act that raised the payroll tax (much to the chagrin of liberals, who viewed this measure as a means to obscure and offset the war's drain on the regular budget) to fund a 13 percent increase in retirement benefits. This measure helped lift many elderly Americans above the poverty line. But the White House had to swallow caps on Medicaid, an opening volley in a decades-long effort by conservatives to constrain the program's growth, as well as new work training requirements for recipients of assistance through the Aid to

Families with Dependent Children (AFDC) program.[50] The administration was even less successful that year in convincing Congress to approve a modest appropriation of $40 million to help cities pay for rodent control in urban ghettos. "The knowledge that many children in the world's most affluent nation are attacked, maimed, and even killed by rats should fill every American with shame," the president told House and Senate members. The initiative quickly foundered as Newark erupted in flames. Conservatives seized upon urban riots as confirmation that Black ghetto residents were beyond redemption. "Let's buy a lot of cats and turn them loose," a Southern Democrat cackled from the House floor. "Civil rats!" another member catcalled from the rear of the chamber. Martha Griffiths, a liberal congresswoman from Michigan, was appalled by her colleagues' insensitivity. "If you're going to spend seventy-nine billion dollars to kill off a few Vietcong," she intoned, "I'd spend forty million dollars to kill off the most devastating enemy that man has ever had." Her plea fell on deaf ears; the House rejected LBJ's proposal by a wide majority.[51] For the balance of his presidency, LBJ worked to preserve the anti-poverty programs he had already put in place, recognizing that he lacked the political capital to expand them.

THE WAR ON POVERTY RECONSIDERED

George Reedy, who served as Johnson's White House press secretary and special assistant, later offered that the sweeping promises associated with the War on Poverty and the Great Society "may have had a negative impact on the willingness of Americans to trust such efforts."[52] When those measures did not meet the expansive expectations that liberals established in the prosperous days of 1964, many Americans came to view government itself as the disease, not the cure.

Some of the apparent failure was the product of Johnson's own decisions. The Vietnam War did much to undermine LBJ's credibility and standing with the American public. More fundamentally, it catalyzed economic and social trends that would erode the very intellectual foundation of the Great Society. Johnson and his aides knowingly dissembled with the American public, failing to disclose the real cost of the war effort and promising that it would not lead to inflationary pressure on the economy. In 1965 he buried Vietnam expenditures in the Pentagon budget. It would shock members of Congress when, six months later, in the middle of the fiscal year, the administration was forced to request a sizable supplementary appropriations package to cover the swiftly mounting costs of the war. It was a pattern that continued through Johnson's presidency. "The old C&O canal which runs north from Georgetown is bounded by the Cumberland Gap at one end and the Credibility Gap at the other," one satirist noted.[53] But the facts spoke for themselves. With the economy overheated by wartime spending, the unemployment rate dipped from a high of 5.7 percent when LBJ took office to below 3.5 percent in mid 1968 – well below full employment. Inflation, which hovered around 1 percent throughout most of JFK's term in office, cracked 5 percent as Johnson left the White House in 1969 – nowhere near the heights of the "Great Inflation" of the 1970s, but still very high in recent context.[54] One of Johnson's aides worried that the administration's public dissemblance on the hard and soft costs of the war – most notably, LBJ's resistance to request a tax increase – "was taking a toll on his credibility. Many economists were beginning to wonder whether he was serious about reining in inflation.... Rising war costs and funds for Great Society programs were stretching the outer limits of the President's ability to manipulate the federal budget."[55]

The idea of the "credibility gap" became a fixture of opposition to the administration. As it became clear by 1967 that the country could not afford guns *and* butter – that permanent growth without inflation was in fact an elusive dream and that equal opportunity often fails to deliver equal results – Johnson's War on Poverty stalled. The administration could not ask for additional programs or spending, and even if it had, Congress would have met the request with skepticism. For some fifty years, Johnson would be known, at best, as a "flawed giant" who, in his own words, "left the woman I love – the Great Society – in order to fight that bitch of a war." At worst, he was the exemplar of runaway liberalism.

Conservatives then and later were quick to declare the War on Poverty a disastrous experiment in central planning. In a blistering address some two decades later, Ronald Reagan denounced the Great Society as a collection of expensive and failed initiatives that exacerbated, rather than alleviated, poverty. LBJ's legacy reinforced the "central political error of our time," the flawed notion that "government and bureaucracy" were the "primary vehicle for social change."[56]

Reagan's view, shared by many right-leaning politicians and writers, judges the Great Society by what it did not achieve – the end of poverty – rather than what it did achieve. The government normally measures poverty on the basis of pre-tax cash income; but when economists take into account noncash assistance including the Supplemental Nutrition Assistance Program (SNAP), a New Frontier/Great Society program formerly known as food stamps, Medicare, Medicaid and housing subsidies (also a legacy of the War on Poverty), and tax adjustments like the Earned Income Tax Credit (a product of the Nixon administration), the poverty rate fell by 26 percent between 1960 and 2010, with two-thirds of the decline occurring before 1980.[57] Some groups, like African Americans and the elderly, experienced an especially steep drop in poverty. Others, including children, did not. LBJ's domestic programs assumed that economic output and wages would continue to grow in perpetuity; they were not designed to combat trends that neither the president nor his staff anticipated, including the rise of single-parent households, stagflation, supply shocks, globalization, and – most importantly – stagnant wages in the 1970s and beyond. Even toward the end of Johnson's term in office, leading administration officials began to question the efficacy of qualitative measures. In 1966, Shriver underwent a change of mind. He now argued that to "end poverty in the United States, as we know it today, within a generation," the government should institute a "negative income tax" that would effectively provide poor Americans with a guaranteed income. (As president, Richard Nixon proposed a similar measure that died in Congress.)[58] But instituting a negative income tax would cost at least $7.5 billion in new spending – something the administration could not fathom amid rising inflation and spending on the Vietnam War.[59]

The social and economic reality that informed the Johnson administration's strategy in fighting poverty no longer held in the decades that followed. As the unwritten contract between employers and employees broke down, companies moved the risk burden back onto individuals, eliminating or watering down employer-based health coverage and replacing defined-benefits pensions with market-based retirement products.[60] Now, Great Society programs had to provide a safety net for more people than they were originally designed to assist.

A few examples make the point. SNAP originally provided 500,000 people with food security when it launched in 1965; in 2020 some 40 million relied on it for food security. Medicaid, the Children's Health Insurance Program (CHIP), and Medicare today provide 147 million Americans – or 45 percent of all the country's population – with health care. Originally, they were intended to cover those who could not, because of age or disability, enjoy employer-based health insurance.[61] In effect, over the years, the War on Poverty has proven more, not less, necessary, even if its individual provisions are inadequate to the twenty-first-century economy.

In other ways, some War on Poverty initiatives have evolved in a manner Johnson never intended. In constant (2010) dollars, the federal government's support of postsecondary student expenses rose from $1.64 billion in 1963 to $169 billion in 2010.[62] When LBJ signed the Higher Education Act (HEA) into law, he intended its benefits to flow primarily to poor people. "The important role of the federal government is somehow to do something for the people who are down and out," he declared, "and that's where its major energy in education ought to go."[63] Despite this original intent, as tuition and fees at both public and private institutions climbed sharply in the 1980s and since, successive Congresses and administrations expanded eligibility to include more middle-income students. Upon signing a reauthorization of HEA in 1992, President George H. W. Bush proudly asserted that it "gives a hand up to lower-income students who need help the most. But it also reaches out into the middle-income families, the ones who skipped a vacation and drove the old clunker so that their kids could go to college." Through subtle means – including the exemption of home equity in calculating a family's eligibility for assistance, and the shift from grants (which accounted for about half of all student aid in 1965 but today account for less than 30 percent) to loans – the program morphed into a middle-class subsidy that also happened to help those poor families in a position to capture its benefits.[64]

None of this negates the importance of the War on Poverty or detracts from its lasting importance. It strains credibility to imagine a country without Medicare and Medicaid, federal aid to primary and secondary schools, federally guaranteed college loans, Head Start, or SNAP – programs that continue to inspire wide support and cover increasing numbers of people and communities. The economic history of the last fifty years has armed Johnson's critics on both the left and right with ammunition to dismiss the War on Poverty. For many conservatives, it was a failed experiment in European-style socialism; it generated a culture of dependency that held millions of families in an intergenerational cycle of privation. For progressive critics, the Great Society's preference for qualitative rather than quantitative measures doomed the project from the start. Each of these critiques has some merit, but each also grossly understates the central role that the Great Society programs have played in reducing poverty and alleviating the suffering of those who live in it. They also judge the War on Poverty by the economic and social reality today, rather than the context in which it was born – an earlier era, when American liberals genuinely believed in the boundless capacity for economic growth and shared prosperity. The War on Poverty was a child of its times, even if those times proved painfully short-lived.

CHAPTER 7

LBJ's Supreme Court

Laura Kalman

J UST AS WE LIVE IN JOHNSON'S AMERICA, SO WE LIVE WITH HIS
Supreme Court. It is often said that Ronald Reagan's 1987 nomination of Robert Bork to the court rang in the modern era of partisanship
in the confirmation of justices. In fact, the pivotal events occurred twenty
years earlier. Johnson's presidency saw two successful Supreme Court
nominations and two failed ones. His quest to enlist the court in consoli-
dating presidential power caused battles that had lasting consequences
for the court and the selection and confirmation of Supreme Court
justices. As LBJ, the Senate, nominees, interest groups, and the public
mobilized, they created and politicized the confirmation process, and
Republicans realized what a powerful tool the threat of an "activist
Supreme Court" could be in shaping and uniting the GOP.[1]

LBJ'S COURT

The 1930s cast a long shadow over Lyndon Johnson. Because he had
boldly backed FDR's controversial effort to pack the Supreme Court with
additional justices in 1937, he thought in terms of a president's need to
dominate not just the executive branch but the legislature and judiciary
as well. Just as he feared that the public would compare withdrawal from
Vietnam to appeasement, so he recalled Roosevelt's struggle with a court
that repeatedly struck down New Deal legislation. When Congress
rejected FDR's proposal to remedy the problem by increasing the court's
size, the president sustained his first big domestic policy loss, and
emboldened conservative Southern Democrats abandoned him. They
joined Republicans in constructing a coalition that blocked all civil rights

and social reform legislation for the next quarter-century until LBJ became president. So it was not surprising that when Johnson was fretting that the House might reject his 1964 poverty bill, he would tell one person after another, as he successfully lobbied for its passage, that he had not been "beat yet" and that if he suffered defeat now, he would become as impotent as FDR after the Senate shelved his court bill: "They're gonna say the King's dead." The crisis that moved Roosevelt to battle the court also reminded LBJ of the need for judicial approval of Great Society legislation.[2]

The court he inherited made favorable decisions likely. Chief Justice Earl Warren presided over it genially, forcefully, and effectively. The one-time Republican governor of California, appointed chief justice by Eisenhower to pay off a political debt, had surprised everyone by embracing legal liberalism, and displaying faith in using the federal courts and the Constitution to improve the lives of the disadvantaged. The Warren Court established its reputation as a liberal bastion in 1954 when it declared school segregation unconstitutional in *Brown v. Board of Education.* "It was the Court, not any other branch of government that for the first time gave meaning to the phrase 'with liberty and justice for all,'" a judge stressed. Ironically, *Brown* also triggered "massive resistance" in the South even as the court's decree implementing it mandated only that desegregation need occur with "all deliberate speed," thus legitimating token efforts. Never mind: with *Brown*, the Warren Court launched a rights revolution that expanded civil rights and civil liberties and made it the darling of liberals.[3]

Liberals dominated law school faculties when Johnson became president. Virtually all then worshipped at the shrine of *Brown* and sympathized with other Warren Court decisions, even if they quibbled over their reasoning. "Legal realists" celebrated Warren and like-minded judges for understanding the law's place as one of the social sciences and its potential as an instrument of social policy. But at Harvard, "legal process" scholars fretted that the court that they had condemned for undemocratically functioning as a "superlegislature" when conservatives controlled it in the 1930s had become one for liberals a quarter-century later. They charged that Warren Court opinions too often proved unsupported by legal principle or precedent and, one alumnus recalled, chided the chief justice "for often asking from the bench whether a particular legal position was 'just.' Sophisticated legal scholars did not speak that way." The leader of this pack of sophisticates and the patron saint of the legal process, judicial restraint, and deference to the executive and legislative branches was the court's Jewish justice, Felix Frankfurter, who managed the bloc opposing what he darkly called "the Four" – Warren, William Brennan, Hugo Black, and William O. Douglas.[4]

Outside the law-school world, some on the right were even more critical. They concluded that "politicians" like Warren lacked respect for precedent, were too liberal, and made bad judges. By the time the John Birch Society paid for its first "Impeach Earl Warren" billboard in the late 1950s, Senate conservatives were unsuccessfully introducing bills in Congress that required court nominees to possess prior judicial experience.[5]

Yet that was blather. Criticism of the court barely affected the nomination and confirmation of justices when LBJ took office. The Senate had rejected nearly one in four Supreme Court nominations during the nineteenth century. But during the first two-thirds of the twentieth century, an era of good feelings for the confirmation process, it treated "advise and consent" as "advise and approve" and confirmed all but one Supreme Court nomination, typically by voice vote or overwhelming majority. Nominees easily dodged senators' questions in their short hearings by claiming that controversial issues might come before the court and citing the principle of separation of powers. When Kennedy nominated another Jew, Secretary of Labor Arthur Goldberg, to succeed Frankfurter in 1962, the Senate Judiciary Committee threw him softballs, even though it was chaired by segregationist James Eastland of Mississippi, no fan of the Warren Court. Predictably, Senator Sam Ervin (D-North Carolina), a former state Supreme Court justice and another court detractor, griped about Goldberg's lack of judicial experience and asked him whether he was "aware of the fact that many informed, intellectual, and honest and sincere persons" had concluded that "the Supreme Court has usurped and exercised the power of Congress and the States to amend the Constitution, while professing to interpret it." But Ervin's inquiries, like those of his colleagues were formulaic, and on the Senate floor, only Strom Thurmond (R-South Carolina) voted against Goldberg. Conservative Senator Barry Goldwater wired JFK that he was an "excellent" choice.[6]

With Goldberg's arrival, the Warren Court became more liberal than ever as "the Four" acquired the crucial fifth vote. Beyond declaring compulsory reading of the Bible in public schools to be unconstitutional, the court in 1963 struck down legislation designed to stop the NAACP (National Association for the Advancement of Colored People) from litigating segregation and discrimination cases. It proclaimed indigents' right to counsel in state felony cases in *Gideon v. Wainwright.* It gave teeth to the prohibition against unreasonable search and seizure, and declared the right of those convicted in state courts to habeas corpus. It announced the principle of "one person, one vote" for legislative districting. In 1964, it invalidated unequally populated state legislative districts because they violated the principle of "one person, one vote." It held that counties could not dodge integration by closing their public schools. It supported civil rights activists who mounted marches and sit-ins, and sustained the constitutionality of the 1964 Civil Rights Act. It declared that the values of free speech and press required the protection of all statements about public figures and officials, including those portrayed as segregationists, except those made with the knowledge that they were false or with "reckless disregard" for the truth. It expanded protection for obscenity. It voided legislation that denied passports to US citizens with communist connections. It announced that the privilege against self-incrimination was applicable in state, as well as federal, court proceedings and that self-incriminating statements made in the absence of counsel after suspects' indictment were inadmissible. As one enthusiast acknowledged in celebrating the court's tenth anniversary, "its display of judicial force and authority, coming as the culmination of a decade of constitutional change that began with the school-desegregation decision of 1954" was hardly popular everywhere.[7]

Barry Goldwater, LBJ's Republican presidential opponent in 1964, was no longer ready to roll over. He attacked the court's decisions on criminal procedure, reapportionment, and school prayer. Of government's three branches, "today's Supreme Court is least faithful to the constitutional tradition of limited government and to the principle of legitimacy in the exercise of power," Goldwater contended. At the Mormon Tabernacle, he urged adoption of a constitutional amendment to permit school prayer, and, in the South, he promised to appoint federal judges who would "redress constitutional interpretations in favor of the public."[8]

His polarizing rhetoric damaged him. A bipartisan coalition of the nation's leading lawyers issued a widely publicized statement rebuking Goldwater for relying on "catch phrases and slogans" in attacking "the ultimate guardian of American liberty." The chair of the House Judiciary Committee compared him to Hitler and Mussolini, and Drew Pearson reported that the candidate planned "to pack the Supreme Court with pro-segregationist judges." Although Goldwater fatefully moved the issues of judicial activism and law and order to the center of political discourse, Richard Nixon played a far greater role in making criticism of the court respectable four years later. Like LBJ, the Warren Court seemed invulnerable in 1963–65, a time in which *Brown v. Board of Education*, its most famous decision, was headed toward canonization.[9]

"I doubt if there ever has been or will be again a judicial bench better than ... the Warren Court," the president told reporters in 1965. "There has never been less friction between the executive, legislative, and judicial branches." The bickering among liberal academics did not interest him. What concerned LBJ was what decisions did and how Congress and the public reacted to them. The Kennedys viewed judges and justices as "passive spectators"; he saw them as partners in making law a tool of social policy.[10]

THE FIRST SUPREME COURT VACANCY

What Johnson apparently decided he needed that year, writes historian Robert Dallek, was "a mole" at the court to protect his interests. The Warren Court would handily uphold all Great Society legislation while he was in office, but Johnson's memories of the confrontation between court and president during the 1930s made his anxiety understandable. Further, as his shrewdest political adviser, Lady Bird Johnson, said, her husband had "a Harding complex" and feared that administration corruption might taint his presidency, just as it had scarred Warren Harding's. A grand jury was investigating LBJ's disgraced former aide, Bobby Baker, who would soon be indicted for income tax evasion. Issues involving Baker and his associates might well reach the court, for which inside knowledge of its members' thinking would prove useful.[11]

By tradition, dating back to the first chief justice, John Jay, it was appropriate for justices to advise presidents on political and policy matters. The American Bar Association's Canon of Judicial Ethics, adopted in 1924, vaguely exhorting judges to maintain "official conduct ... free from impropriety and the appearance of impropriety," made them guardians of their own virtue. It was acceptable for presidents or their emissaries to consult justices about political matters or draft them for extra-judicial assignments, as LBJ had done when he tapped Warren to chair the commission investigating Kennedy's assassination. But if by the 1960s the president wanted to know about the court's work, he was supposed to read its opinions or newspaper accounts of them. Then, as now, no one thought that justices should keep anyone outside the court apprised of its deliberations as it took and resolved cases. That President-elect James Buchanan had helped shaped the contours of the proslavery *Dred Scott* decision in 1857 by privately lobbying his friends on the court, and had known what it would hold before its announcement, was considered almost as shameful as the opinion itself. "Today such collaboration between the president and members of the Supreme Court would be a Nation-rocking scandal," historian Merlo Pusey had written in 1957. No president, much less one who feared scandal as much as Johnson did, was supposed to consult a member of the court about its internal workings. While issues of propriety rarely bothered LBJ and some justices were his longtime allies, he would have known that none of them would do for the job.[12]

The obvious candidate would be his intimate adviser, a brilliant Washington super-lawyer. Abe Fortas's roots in the South as a lower-middle-class Jew made him an outsider, but he had reinvented himself as the quintessential insider. He was one of the proverbial New Dealers who had come to Washington in the 1930s to do good and stayed after World War II to do well. Establishing a celebrated DC law firm, Fortas went to work guiding corporations through the very regulations he had once drafted to stymie them. At the same time, he won praise from liberals by doing plenty of *pro bono* work, such as defending victims of McCarthyism and successfully arguing for indigent criminal defendants' right to counsel before the Warren Court in *Gideon v. Wainwright*. In 1948, when his Senate election victory was disputed, LBJ had turned to Fortas, who saved the seat for his friend, and he proved his usefulness repeatedly afterward. Following the assassination, when Johnson was saddled with Robert Kennedy as attorney general, Fortas, though still a private practitioner, functioned as shadow attorney general. The president chose Nicholas Katzenbach as attorney general in 1964 only after Fortas refused the position. Johnson thought Fortas was "the ablest lawyer in the country" and admired his style. He once told a reporter that Fortas "could cut a fellow's pecker off . . . but he'll do it clean and neat and wrap it up nice and tie it with a ribbon and pour perfume all over it."[13]

If Johnson replaced any justice but Goldberg with Fortas, though, two Jews would occupy the bench. The president realized that the public expected a "representative" Supreme Court. He should have recalled that during the 1930s, the court had included two Jews. Since then, however, there had been just one "Jewish seat." Johnson, who always worried about "overdoing" minority appointments, would have reasoned that Goldberg must leave the court so Fortas could join it.[14]

Opportunity appeared in 1965 when United Nations Ambassador Adlai Stevenson suddenly dropped dead. Since Stevenson was a "dove," Johnson knew that his successor must question the wisdom of escalation in Vietnam and embody the president's commitment to a negotiated settlement. Eager to prevent Johnson from considering one John Kenneth Galbraith, Galbraith had told him that Goldberg was "a little bored on the Court," something Goldberg would spend the rest of his life denying. But the call to the UN was hard to resist. As Goldberg would subsequently admit, the position proved enticing because he feared that "we were going to get enmeshed in Vietnam," and he had the "egotistical feeling . . . that I could influence the President to not get overly involved." While Goldberg pondered his options, LBJ sold him to Congress. He wanted Goldberg, he explained to Senator Richard Russell (D-Georgia), because his excellence as an extemporaneous speaker would make him effective with the Russians. "He's a bulldog, and he is pretty abrasive," said LBJ, adding that Goldberg "looks like he is power." The appointment would show that the United

States did not discriminate and boost Johnson's standing with liberals: "I think this Jew thing would take the *New York Times* and all this crowd that gives us hell all the time" by storm and yield "a Johnson man" in the UN. "I guess the lawyers would cuss me for taking him off the Court," the president continued, "but I'm going to put Abe Fortas on."[15]

LBJ was so sure that Goldberg would take the ambassador's job that before Goldberg officially accepted it, Johnson offered his seat on the court to Fortas. But Fortas initially demurred. A justice would earn less than a quarter of his income, he thought his firm needed him, and, Fortas told Mrs. Johnson, "I would just dread if the President was faced with any real troubles, his emotional reaction. For instance, if Bobby Baker were indicted then I would want to be around to help him. And if I were on the Court, I could not." But Johnson insisted. Calling his friend to the White House, he said, "Abe, I'm sending fifty thousand boys to Vietnam today, and I'm sending you to the Supreme Court" in a tone that made it evident that he would install Fortas there, regardless of his wishes, just as he had dispatched Goldberg to the United Nations. It was another example of how LBJ always got his man (see Figure 7.1).[16]

The 1965 Fortas nomination was the last one that the Senate treated as pro forma. Fortas was a well-known liberal whom Arthur Goldberg judged a jurisprudential "clone" of himself. Though conservative Southern Democrats and Republicans dominated the Senate Judiciary Committee hearings, all committee members apparently welcomed the nomination. One Republican asked whether Fortas's friendship with the president would affect his ability to function as a judge. "[L]et me take this opportunity to say to you that there are two things that have been vastly exaggerated with respect to me," the nominee puckishly replied. "One is the extent to which I am a Presidential adviser, and the other is the extent to which I am a proficient violinist." No relationship he had "with the President would in any way bear upon the discharge of my functions in the Court," Fortas continued. "It could not be." And after Senator Ervin made a chummy comparison between the Senate and mules that didn't kick according to the rules, the committee adjourned less than three hours after it had come to order. Confirmation became preordained. In part that camaraderie reflected the sense, then current, that the only fair grounds of objection to a nominee related to his

7.1. In a classic image of the "Johnson Treatment," President Johnson looms over attorney Abe Fortas on July 29, 1965, one day after nominating him for a seat on the US Supreme Court. Fortas won confirmation the following month.
Credit: LBJ Presidential Library photo by Yoichi Okamoto

credentials or character; in part, it reflected a fear of challenging the liberal consensus and the president who embodied it. For the last time ever, the Senate approved a court nominee by voice vote.[17]

It turned out that Goldberg was right about Fortas's jurisprudence. One of the new justice's early opinions upheld civil rights workers' First Amendment rights to protest segregation by sitting in at a Southern library. So, too, did Fortas join the bare majority that handed down the decision in *Miranda v. Arizona* (1966) mandating that the police must advise all criminal suspects in custody of their right to remain silent and to court-appointed counsel. That decision, supported by Warren, Fortas, Black, Douglas, and Brennan, sparked dissent from Justice Tom Clark, who complained that it went "too far too fast."[18]

It also turned out that that Fortas's relationship with the president had not been exaggerated and that it affected his discharge of his judicial obligations. The closeness made some of his court colleagues "uncomfortable," one recalled, though like most others they were unaware of its extent. Had they known, they would have worried more. As LBJ's aide, Joe Califano, revealed in his 1992 memoir, Justice Fortas had counseled LBJ "on the constitutionality of limits on the president's authority to close military bases and of the 1966 D.C. crime bill," evaluated "the Supreme Court's likely response should the President unilaterally impose wage and price controls," immersed himself "in shaping Vietnam and economic policies and in advising the president on a variety of crises, ranging from the Detroit riots to the 1967 railroad strike," and conferred with Johnson "on the Penn-Central case when it was pending before the Supreme Court and then written the court's final opinion."[19]

And when LBJ's telephone recordings became available, such activities seemed like the tip of the iceberg. Some White House telephone calls made work for Fortas at the court. When the justices considered the criminal conviction of Bobby Baker's associate, Fred Black, for example, Justice Fortas became involved in a squeeze play to use the case to embarrass Senator Robert Kennedy by exposing his illegal wiretapping as attorney general. Others involved listening to Johnson vent. "Now are you all going to do anything on law and order this session and tell these fellows that they got to quit turning over cars and stuff?" the president queried Fortas just before the 1966 midterm elections turned Congress more conservative. Law-and-order problems hurt the president more than inflation, Vietnam, and everything else "put together," Johnson insisted. "Every white man just says, by God, he don't want his car turned over and he don't want some n— throwing a brick at him. . . . And we've got to do something to shake them up like convict that damn [Stokely] Carmichael."[20]

Why would Johnson have thought that the justices in the Warren Court majority should care about his poll ratings? He saw the Warren

Court as part and parcel of the Great Society. He worried that some blamed the court for the breakdown of law and order at the same time he remained proud of and identified with its confident liberalism.

THE SECOND SUPREME COURT VACANCY

Consequently, LBJ seized the chance to name Thurgood Marshall as the first African American justice (see Figure 7.2). As head of the NAACP Legal Defense and Educational Fund for more than twenty years, the great-grandson of a slave had one of the century's most significant legal careers. Marshall braved threats of violence as he took his traveling civil rights law office through the South. To millions, he embodied the struggle for racial equality and justice, and he won twenty-nine of the thirty-two cases he argued before the Supreme Court. "He brought us the Constitution as a document like Moses brought the people the Ten Commandments," said one NAACP official. Of his most famous victory, *Brown v. Board of Education*, Marshall said, "We hit the jackpot." When

7.2. After being told by President Johnson that he had been nominated for a seat on the Supreme Court, Solicitor General Thurgood Marshall calls his wife from the Oval Office on June 13, 1967. Marshall would go on to become the high court's first Black justice.
Credit: LBJ Presidential Library photo by Yoichi Okamoto

Johnson asked Marshall to leave the Court of Appeals and take a pay cut to become solicitor general in 1965, the president hinted that he might harbor even larger plans for him. "I'm going to appoint Thurgood Marshall to the Court," LBJ confided to Galbraith that year, noting that service as solicitor general would ensure "no one can say that he's not one of the best qualified men that has ever [been] appointed."[21]

But Johnson realized that goal would require another game of musical chairs. By 1967, LBJ wanted to get rid of Attorney General Katzenbach, whom he considered too close to Robert Kennedy. First, the president moved Katzenbach to the State Department. Then, through Fortas, he let his old Texas friend, Justice Tom Clark, know that LBJ wanted to make Tom's son, Ramsey, attorney general, but that nepotism concerns would prevent it unless Ramsey's daddy quit. That reasoning was ridiculous: Ramsey Clark was already deputy attorney general, and senators in both parties had told LBJ that they were untroubled by the idea of one Clark at the court and another as attorney general. LBJ was replacing Katzenbach with a loyalist and getting a second Supreme Court vacancy in the process.[22]

In creating the "black seat," LBJ acted partly from political calculation. That Congress had become a more uncertain ally on civil rights made a Supreme Court seat that the president could use to demonstrate his sincere commitment to equality more valuable than ever. With inner cities exploding, Johnson hoped the appointment "might kind of rock the Negroes and put them in a position where they wouldn't be mean to me." To be sure, he fretted that, with Marshall's addition, liberals on the court "wouldn't send a man to the penitentiary for raping a woman if you had a photograph of him doing it." Yet for all his anxiety about the court's record on crime and law and order, he remained devoted to legal liberalism. Fortas had told LBJ that he, Warren, Brennan, and Douglas could no longer count on Hugo Black, who was carving out his own path on civil rights. Marshall would give them a fifth vote.[23]

The era of good feelings in Supreme Court nominations ended abruptly when Thurgood Marshall came before the Judiciary Committee in 1967. Senate scrutiny of Supreme Court nominees became more intense and partisan. Nominees who had routinely been approved by voice vote now routinely faced roll call votes that required senators to stand up and be counted. Nomination hearings became longer, more substantive, and confrontational as participants used them to mobilize public opinion. Where most had taken no more than a few hours, Marshall's consumed five days.

That was not because his opponents had any hope of prevailing. Segregationists realized that they looked like history's losers. For all their antipathy toward *Brown v. Board of Education*, they knew it had become a sacred icon of America's hesitant march toward equality. That's why they did not allude to it when they confronted its chief strategist or overtly play the race card. That LBJ had outfoxed beleaguered Southerners seemed clear when they initially responded to the nomination with "silence." Any strategy they developed, they acknowledged, had little promise, Senator Herman Talmadge (D-Georgia) told a constituent, because "the liberal majority" in Congress always overwhelmed "the small bloc of Southern Senators" who contended that "we should have Judges on the Supreme Court bench who will interpret the Constitution as it is written, and not in accordance with their own sociological philosophy." A Supreme Court nomination was still considered the stuff of presidential prerogative. Though he had less power over Congress after November 1966 than he had between 1963 and 1965, when he was riding high, LBJ remained a force. Senators expected him to run for reelection, and they feared him. Finally, liberal Democrats and all Republicans except Senate Judiciary Committee member Strom Thurmond of South Carolina were backing Marshall.[24]

But four powerful Southerners on the Committee who understood the long game – Chairman Eastland, along with Thurmond, Ervin, and Arkansas Democrat John McClellan – realized that crime could take them where appeals to white supremacy could not. They used Marshall's hearing to transform the Warren Court into a bogeyman. For five days, they savaged its criminal procedure decisions and the nominee for refusing to discuss them. Demagoguery was out, dog whistles in, particularly when Thurmond tried to expose Marshall as an ignoramus by asking him some sixty detailed questions about the Fourteenth Amendment's history. The hearing became the first instance in modern times when senators justified their close scrutiny by predicting that the substitution of Marshall for Clark would change the balance of power on the court by liberalizing it – an argument that would echo in 1987 when liberals said Robert Bork's replacement of Lewis Powell would make the court more conservative. And while senators had quizzed prior nominees about whether the Constitution and its amendments still meant what they did at ratification, calls for adherence to the Constitution's "original intention" now became common among Warren Court foes. "Judicial activism" and "judicial activist," two phrases around since the 1940s and insignificant in prior confirmations, emerged as epithets for the Warren Court too.[25]

For the present, Southerners had the lonely task of reassuring hometown voters that they remained on the job. Marshall's nomination was acclaimed, and he was overwhelmingly confirmed by Democrats and Republicans by voice vote after Eastland, Ervin, Thurmond, and McClellan rehashed their complaints over six hours on the Senate floor. The GOP remained the party of Lincoln, and liberal Democrats were cheering.[26]

Journalists wondered what the vote meant. One hypothesized that "[t]he strong vote for Mr. Marshall," like the "relatively mild reaction to *Miranda* . . . seemed to confirm what Court observers had suspected for the past couple of years – that informed public opinion has come to accept the Supreme Court's activism and that many political leaders have concluded that it is a good thing." Others differed. "The Supreme Court as an institution was the biggest target in the wordy Senate proceedings that culminated in the confirmation of Thurgood Marshall," one journalist said. Another agreed that Marshall had become the scapegoat for the court and maintained that, although white Southerners understood that they had lost the "battle over equal rights for the Negro," they realized they could win a national majority by decrying criminals' rights.[27]

The last claim came closest to the mark. Marshall's race and extraordinary life helped him, as did his sparse judicial record, which made it impossible for his antagonists to say for certain that he would become the "activist" he did. Yet despite popular approval, his brutal interrogation revealed that the Warren Court had become a lightning rod for a minority that claimed it "coddled criminals." White supremacy had morphed into "law and order," though the transformation preserved the underlying racism. White Southern Democrats obviously realized the political potential of racializing crime. So, increasingly, did Republicans.

"IMPROVING THE DAMN COURT"

That became clear in June 1968 after Warren met with Johnson. "He came down to say that because of age, he felt he should retire from the court and he said he wanted President Johnson to appoint his successor, someone who felt as Warren did," LBJ's appointments secretary recorded. Both Warren and Johnson feared that Republican candidate Richard Nixon, who was making the Warren Court an issue in the presidential campaign by taking aim at *Miranda* and other decisions that gave a "green light" to criminals, would win the election. Nixon promised to nominate individuals to the court who believed in their mission to *interpret* the law that elected politicians enacted under the Constitution, as well as those who would strengthen law and order and "the peace forces" against the criminals. Johnson also understood, Califano stressed, "that his Great Society legislation had stepped on many powerful economic and political interests that had the resources to continue to struggle" and that "the contest would inevitably play out in the courts long after he left the White House."[28]

LBJ followed his usual practice when facing a difficult decision. He called in his two advisers, Secretary of Defense Clark Clifford and Justice Abe Fortas, and directed Clifford to arrive early. Johnson informed Clifford that he wanted to make Fortas chief justice and to name Homer Thornberry – a federal judge, politician, and old Texas friend – to replace Fortas. The news about Fortas delighted without surprising Clifford, who considered his friend's qualifications outstanding. But the prospect of Thornberry, a beloved former member of Congress no one had ever characterized as "Supreme Court material," alarmed him. The secretary of defense now saw anew that the president "really was not conscious of how much his power had diminished" since he announced that he would not seek reelection. He cautioned that the Republicans had high hopes for November, and while "[t]hey would probably accept Abe on his own," they would balk if LBJ tried "to pack the court with your friends at a very late date in the political calendar." Why not couple the

Fortas nomination with that of a prominent, nonpartisan Republican, such as American Bar Association stalwart Albert Jenner of Chicago? LBJ balked, however, at the prospect of putting "some damned Republican on the Court." When Fortas appeared, he stayed quiet while Johnson and his secretary of defense argued. Asked who was right, he predicted that with the appropriate "handling and preparation," LBJ could sell a Fortas–Thornberry package. Afterwards, Fortas told Clifford, "I don't know if the President can bring this off, but I couldn't very well sit there and disagree with him when he wants to make me Chief Justice."[29]

Johnson clung to Fortas–Thornberry. Fortas was "the most experienced, compassionate, articulate, and intelligent lawyer I knew, and . . . I was certain that he would carry on in the Court's tradition," LBJ explained in his memoir. Moreover, Fortas had no intention of leaving the court. "The only question we're talking about is whether you've got Thornberry or Warren, and I don't think I'm liberalizing the Court with Thornberry, trading him for Warren," LBJ told Senate Minority Leader Everett Dirksen. "I think I'm improving the damn Court." Johnson also anticipated that Republicans and Southerners would find Fortas and Thornberry "more acceptable than Warren" because, the president believed, they were "more moderate." Liberals who would applaud the Fortas nomination, he reasoned to Senate Majority Leader Mike Mansfield, would remember that because the president had appointed Thurgood Marshall of New York to replace Tom Clark of Texas, the next vacancy belonged to a Southerner, and Thornberry's record was "about as good a liberal [record] as you can get from that part of the country." The appointments would enable LBJ, a president who delighted in breaking barriers for Jews and other minorities, to name the first Jewish chief justice, to reward devotion, and to sustain the Warren Court's mission of fostering equality.[30]

At the same time, he believed the new justices might rein in judicial protection of criminals and demonstrators, two groups with which Fortas was signaling some fatigue. He had recently joined the majority holding that it was not unconstitutional for police to "stop and frisk" individuals they reasonably suspected were armed and involved in a crime. And he had just published a pamphlet insisting that civil disobedience was immoral, impolitic, and illegal when it involved violation of constitutional, valid laws just to dramatize disagreement and that the principle of selective conscientious objection that led some young people to say they would take up arms against Hitler but not Ho Chi Minh was no good, either. Johnson's package responded to his own misgivings about the Warren Court and enabled him to save what he considered its best part when law and order was becoming the rallying cry.[31]

It also, LBJ believed, would sell. In Fortas and Thornberry, as he saw it, he was not overreaching but playing a shrewd game rooted in the mores of the Senate. He believed that he had successfully bargained for the support of his powerful friend, Richard Russell, who would take Fortas to get Thornberry and get rid of Warren, and he thought that enough Southerners would follow the Georgian's lead to preclude a filibuster. LBJ clung to the hope, fostered by the Senate Minority Leader, that Dirksen could deliver plenty of Republicans and dangled bait that made him agree to do so. But the Senate of 1968 was a different place from the Senate of Lyndon Johnson's heyday, when the "minnows" swum gamely behind the "whales." Neither Russell nor Dirksen carried as much weight as Johnson assumed, and in the end, both abandoned him.[32]

That, however, was later. When Johnson announced the nominations on June 26, 1968, their prospects were good. To be sure, some Southern Democrats borrowed from the Marshall playbook to assail Fortas's nomination. Sam Ervin said that "[c]onsidering what the Supreme Court has done to the Constitution, I'll have to read Fortas'[s] decisions before I can decide," and Russell Long of Louisiana numbered Fortas among "the dirty five" who took the criminals' side. Meanwhile, freshman Senator Robert Griffin of Michigan, a Republican, ignored the eight previous successful Supreme Court nominations by presidents during an election year. He argued that "lame duck" LBJ should save the appointment for the next president and contended that the Fortas–Thornberry combination was "cronyism at its worst."[33]

Yet Griffin, the leader of the anti-Fortas forces, knew he faced an uphill struggle. Even the *Wall Street Journal*, which charged LBJ with making the court "a political football" by appointing two cronies, one of them "a relatively unknown fellow-Texan," predicted that Fortas might become an "outstanding" chief justice. Other newspapers hailed the appointments, particularly Fortas's. So did the American Bar Association, Senate Majority Leader Mansfield, and Senate Minority Leader Dirksen. Although the media reported that Nixon had said the next president should name the next chief justice, few thought that would happen, and even Nixon publicly pronounced confirmation "quite likely." White House head counts in early July 1968 showed as many as seventy-three votes for Fortas. On July 4, the *Washington Post* editorialized approvingly that the "tempest" over his nomination was "subsiding" and that his opponents had found "no firm ground on which to make a fight against a nominee as well qualified for the post as is Mr. Fortas." The Washington press corps and television networks predicted both candidates' confirmation. "Do you realize that you are fighting the Supreme Court, the American Bar Association, the Democratic Leadership and the Republican Leadership as well as the President of the United States?" Griffin's wife asked. "Just who do you think you are?"[34]

The Fortas–Thornberry hearings were even longer and more contentious than Marshall's. Fortas himself appeared for four days. One target was LBJ, especially the question of whether the relationship between president and justice violated separation of powers. "[W]hat justification could be offered in the event a member of the judicial branch should actively participate on a regular, undisclosed basis in decisions of the executive branch while serving on the Bench?" Griffin asked. Presidents had long appointed "cronies" to the court, Dirksen answered. Lincoln had put his campaign manager there; John Kennedy, his deputy attorney general. And when Truman named his secretary of treasury as chief justice, "nobody got up on his hind legs and shouted cronyism." The "cronyism" charge, Dirksen erupted, was "a frivolous, diaphanous – you know what that means, don't you – gossamer – you know what that means, don't you – argument that just does not hold water." True. Nevertheless, when Fortas appeared and invoked the principle of separation of powers in referring to "the constitutional limitations" on him as he discussed the court's work, he already looked like a hypocrite.[35]

And, some of his opponents suspected, a perjurer. Asked whether he had ever recommended candidates for judgeships or other jobs, Fortas deceitfully said he had not. Whereas he said he had just attended a few meetings on Vietnam and only restated the arguments of others, the documentary record would reveal that he had gone to many and prodded the president to stand firm. Whereas he denied drafting LBJ's message sending troops into riot-torn Detroit, he had helped create it. "Fortas's testimony was so misleading and deceptive that those of us who were aware of his relationship with Johnson winced with each news report of his appearance before the Senate committee," Califano remembered.[36]

Yet the concrete evidence from White House files, the justice's papers, and recorded conversations that would have proved that Fortas probably committed perjury before the Senate Judiciary Committee surfaced only later. The media had uncovered just enough in 1968 to suggest that Fortas had not been fully candid about the depth of his involvement in White House affairs. But discretion is expected in presidential advisers. And Fortas sounded persuasive when he explained that Johnson had turned to him because of their long lawyer–client relationship, declared that he had responded out of patriotism, and echoed Dirksen's reminder that Supreme Court justices traditionally counseled presidents. Further, with one exception, senators had no way to disprove Fortas's claim that none of his interactions with Johnson affected the court. (The exception related to Vietnam: Based on what little they were told, senators might have pressed him about how he could decide cases about the constitutionality of the war or how he could rule on the constitutionality of draft-card burning.) So when Fortas lectured Senator Ervin, "I cannot conceive of any President of the United States, and certainly not this President, talking to a Supreme Court justice whether his own nominee or not, about anything that might possibly come before the Court," Ervin had to assume the justice was speaking truthfully. What else could he do when Fortas was telling him that "Presidents of the United States do not do that: Justices of the Supreme Court would not tolerate it. That is our country, Senator"? Thus, while Fortas's recklessness before the committee was remarkable, it worked to his benefit.[37]

So did his defense of the court. The Fortas–Thornberry hearings became the moment when the memory of the Warren Court as too "liberal" and "activist" was set in stone for the confirmation process. That was ironic, given how much support still existed for legal liberalism. The Warren Court had indeed attracted powerful antagonists. But to an extent that would surprise those who painted the Warren Court as outside the mainstream, the vote for Marshall, the editorials hailing the Marshall and Fortas–Thornberry confirmations, and some polls suggested that its decisions largely reflected majority will. After all, even the infamous *Miranda* decision did not go as far in limiting the police as many had feared. And though some of the same senators who tried to make the Warren Court the issue during the Marshall hostilities worked to do so in 1968, their actions initially backfired.[38]

The second ground for complaint about the nominee related to specific decisions by the Warren Court, which, Griffin acknowledged, was "the only real issue in the Fortas nomination" for "many senators." Like Fortas, the Warren Court was on trial for disregarding the Constitution, Ervin showed, as he proceeded to lay out his disagreement with more than twenty opinions. Though Ervin prudently kept quiet about *Brown*, he criticized the court's civil rights, labor law, and especially criminal law cases. The senator devoted eighteen minutes alone to *Miranda*.[39]

The attack on the court and on the nomination process that perpetuated it failed, however. It was not just that many still admired the Warren Court. It was also that, as some had insisted during the Marshall confirmation hearings, many senators believed it their duty to evaluate nominees based only on fitness and shrank from attempts to probe ideology through questions about decisions, an area where nominees had long been expected to provide evasive answers, anyway. Griffin himself tried to show that he was focused on fitness, not ideology, by professing sympathy for many Warren Court opinions and pledging to take Arthur Goldberg as chief justice. Further, Ervin's exposition of Warren Court decisions was technical, almost dull. And when he and others badgered the witness, they sounded as demagogic about crime as Joe McCarthy had about communism in the 1950s. All the while, Fortas won points for his impressive restraint. As Griffin said, by questioning the record of the Warren Court, Ervin simply increased "sympathy for the Justice" during "what was commonly referred to as his 'ordeal.'" Consider what happened when Strom Thurmond berated Fortas about the court and the 1957 case of *Mallory v. United States*, decided eight years before Fortas became a justice. As he described the case, Thurmond worked himself into a rage: "Mallory – I want that word to ring in your ears," he shouted at Fortas. "Mallory, a man who raped a woman, admitted his guilt, and the Supreme Court turned him loose on a technicality. . ... Is not that type of decision calculated to encourage more people to commit rapes and serious crimes?" Fortas said nothing for several moments, then slowly and dramatically responded, "Senator, because of my respect for you and this body and my respect for the Constitution of the United States and my position as Associate Justice of the Supreme Court of the United States, I will adhere to the limitations I believe the Constitution places upon me and will not reply to your question."[40]

Outside the committee room, there was plenty of applause for the nominee, who was obviously winning the match. Distinguished law professors, attorneys, and American Bar Association officers leapt to defend Fortas against the "vicious" and disrespectful attacks. Two-thirds of the Judiciary Committee membership still approved the nomination, and the pubic backed the nomination by nearly 2:1. Officials at the White House still believed they had the votes to prevail against a filibuster. The momentum remained with Fortas.[41]

As the Fortas controversy disappeared into the mists of time, Thurmond's attempt to make "Fortas the scapegoat for the sins of the Warren Court" was remembered as "an effective strategy." But it did *not* seem one in 1968. Thurmond's legislative aide mourned that Fortas's opponents had come across as rigid and overbearing bullies; the nominee himself, heroically self-contained. "Our strategy in the Fortas hearings has been a disastrous mistake," he admonished his boss. Thurmond should not have asked the justice about his reaction to criticism of the court or questioned him about decisions. "Obviously, he is not going to agree with attacks upon himself," and "the line of questioning did not appear to be a sincere attempt to investigate his views; rather, it appeared to be an irrational attempt to delay and harass." Thurmond had turned Fortas "into a martyr" and strengthened him. "Even though our questions were constructed upon the premise that Fortas and the Court have undermined the Constitution, Fortas managed to turn the tables and make it appear that Senator Thurmond was recklessly disregarding Constitutional principles, while he, Fortas, was patiently trying to uphold them in the face of great provocation."[42]

And Thornberry, who spent two days before the Senate Judiciary Committee, provided more of the same. When Ervin put Thornberry on the spot about one opinion, he proved as unforthcoming as Fortas. "[T]hey cannot tell us anything about the future, and they cannot tell us anything about the past, which means they cannot tell us anything," the senator griped. To Fred Graham, who described how Thornberry looked at his Senate interrogators "unblinkingly as if no answers were expected," he seemed "more at ease" than Fortas. But Thornberry's prospects for a vote alongside Fortas were dimming. If he were recalled after the Senate disposed of Fortas, there might be no time to confirm Thornberry during this congressional session.[43]

In part because of Thurmond's overkill, however, Fortas's chances still looked good enough. His opponents were not united. Griffin, the Northern Republican, Thurmond, the Southern Republican, and the Southern Democrats all violently mistrusted one another. And though candidate Nixon was egging on opposed Republicans behind the scenes, LBJ's support for Fortas was public and rock solid. Clearly, Fortas's opponents required a game-changer.[44]

They finally got it, thanks to the growing concern about "family values," the Democratic convention, and Fortas's indiscreet behavior. The Citizens for Decent Literature belatedly zeroed in on Fortas's and the Warren Court's obscenity decisions and its constitutionally protected "dirty movies." When the Senate Judiciary Committee recessed for the party conventions without reporting out the nominations, the battle moved to the press. After viewing one film, syndicated columnist James Kilpatrick wrote that "if this filthy little peep-show" qualified for First Amendment protection, something was "fearfully wrong." Such outrage meant lots of constituent mail. "The nomination of Abe Fortas as US Supreme Court Justice has run into unexpected trouble," Thurmond crowed. Fortas's antagonists encouraged undecided senators to see the film themselves. In the following weeks, senators lined up for porn, and the movies were shown repeatedly. Now that the first round of hearings had ended in July and the Senate was in recess, the momentum was belatedly shifting toward Fortas's opponents. Then there was the chaotic Democratic convention in August. "The violent clashes in Chicago between club-swinging police and youthful anti-war, anti-Humphrey demonstrators" would affect the Fortas fight by "strengthening the hands of those in Congress who have long deplored the breakdown in law and order," one reporter predicted.[45]

Then there was the late-breaking September revelation of Fortas's honorarium for teaching a course for a huge payout ($15,000, equal to about $100,000 today) raised by Fortas's former law partner from former clients, as hostile senators repeatedly observed. Fortas had put the last nail in his own coffin. The lecture fees became yet another excuse for senators to jump ship. Richard Russell cited them, along with the fact that "at least 99%" of his constituent mail about Fortas was negative, when he wrote LBJ to say that he could not support the nomination. In explaining his change of heart, Dirksen alluded to the lecture fees too. Dirksen and Mansfield agreed "that the 'dirty movies' issue has taken its toll on Fortas, and that the $15,000 fee ... has been hurtful." They warned that the "floor debate on pornography will be dirty, that Thurmond tastes blood now ... and that the movies were what the opposition needed to make their positions jell." Griffin announced that the fee raised "serious questions of judicial ethics." Of course, he urged LBJ to withdraw the nomination.[46]

"I won't do that to Abe," LBJ loyally told Califano. The situation was hopeless, and the White House lacked the votes for cloture to end the filibuster that had begun, but LBJ believed most senators would at least vote to cut off debate. "With a majority on the floor for Abe, he'll be able to stay on the Court with his head up," the president said. Ultimately, forty-six of eighty-nine senators, a bare majority, voted for cloture in October 1968. Fortas then asked LBJ to withdraw his name. For the first time, a filibuster had prevented the Senate from confirming a judicial nomination.[47]

Arthur Goldberg soon began sending envoys to the White House to say that he was available for the chief justice nomination, and LBJ met with him so he could make his case. No one would have labeled Goldberg a crony: he had recently resigned from the UN, and his disagreements with the president over Vietnam were well known. "Goldberg just talks *all* the time," LBJ complained to Mansfield in mid October. "He wants to be Chief Justice of the Supreme Court and says you've got to be for him, and Dirksen's got to be for him, and everybody up there is going to be for him if I just got guts enough to name him." The following day, Goldberg breakfasted with Fortas. "Arthur's a remarkable fella," Fortas told the president, "a combination of self-assurance and ambition that's seldom been seen," and had insisted in "a long monologue" that he could win confirmation. Fortas then spoke with Earl Warren and reported that the chief justice "hopes that this will be done." Warren was "ready to resign tomorrow" and wanted only to ensure the survival of legal liberalism. But Johnson doubted that Goldberg could win confirmation. His advisers concluded that the Senate Judiciary Committee might well reject the Goldberg nomination and that if it did not, the Senate would. Turning down another Jew, particularly one for whom Griffin had said he would vote, "might prove slightly embarrassing for the Republicans but to be repudiated again by the Senate on a Chief Justice nomination would also be embarrassing to the President." So after all the noise about the "Warren Court," Warren would stay on for another term, Nixon would win the vacancy he coveted at its end, and Thornberry would remain in Texas.

For LBJ to determine whether the Goldberg nomination would succeed, he had to understand the reason for Fortas's defeat. "The truth is that Abe Fortas was too progressive for the Republicans and the Southern conservatives in the Senate, all of whom were horrified at the thought of the continuation of the philosophy of the Warren Court," he wrote in his memoir. That was one explanation: Some Republicans and Southern Democrats who knew how to run down the clock disliked the Warren Court's approach to criminal law and civil rights.[48]

There is something to be said for the argument that ideology lay behind Senate voting patterns. But if LBJ had been thinking only in terms of ideological compatibility, instead of ideological compatibility and friendship, he could have chosen a legal liberal who would have survived the heat. Given the likelihood of Fortas's confirmation at first, it is difficult to imagine the Senate girding itself to defeat someone without Fortas's baggage, like Goldberg, Justice Brennan, or popular liberal Senator Phil Hart. Had the nomination failed because Johnson was too willful? Yes. There was something pathetic about the president's end-game consideration of Goldberg, whom he had forced off the court. If LBJ had kept Goldberg there and nominated Fortas in 1968 from private practice, no one could have claimed Fortas had violated separation of powers, he probably would have had no time to teach a summer course, and he would have had no paper trail linking him to the Warren Court. Because of timing, changes in Senate mores, and LBJ's status as a "lame duck" who no longer bestrode the Senate like the proverbial colossus? Of course. Because LBJ's growing unpopularity had tainted Fortas, the justice-cum-presidential adviser? Certainly. Because Johnson had over-reached by naming not just one, but two, "cronies" and Fortas was suspected of obfuscating about his role in White House affairs? Definitely. Because the Warren Court's controversial opinions handed the right a great political issue and its friends had made the colossal blunder of allowing its foes to frame a narrative contending that the court was more out of step with public opinion than it was? Positively. Because of the "dirty movies"? Absolutely. Because of the lecture fees? Without a doubt.

The riddle of the Fortas defeat was that this protean causation stew could signify anything its interpreters wished. Thus, Griffin told the press that lecture fees felled Fortas. Phyllis Schlafly portrayed the battle as a seminal moment that marked the arrival of a "New Right" that fought for family values. For Pat Buchanan, it marked the beginning of "the culture war." Lady Bird Johnson treated it as evidence of "the rising anger against Lyndon and mostly the rising anger against liberalism." Fortas saw it as confirmation of "the fragmentation of liberalism" and the unpopularity of the Warren Court. Goldberg, however, argued that despite his own identification with political and legal liberalism, he could win confirmation because he lacked Fortas's negatives.[49]

HAUNTED BY THE 1960S

Whatever the reason for its failure, the Fortas fight, coming on the heels of the Marshall confirmation, transformed nomination and confirmation politics. Almost as if he foresaw the Bork battle, Yale's Alexander Bickel told a reporter in 1968 that "20 years from now the Fortas controversy 'may seem a precursor of what was in the offing.'" The Marshall and Fortas nominations set the prototype for our modern confirmation battles. The Senate Judiciary Committee hearings on nominees were not carried live on radio and TV until Reagan nominated Sandra Day O'Connor in 1981. But especially in Fortas's case, there was intense media scrutiny of nominees and page-one stories about the struggle day after day. There was anger at nominee elusiveness. There was a focus on nominee ethics, character, and private life because of senators' squeamishness about directly addressing nominee ideology. There was interest-group mobilization: The Citizens for Decent Literature proved crucial to the nomination's defeat. There was anxiety about the "politicization" of the court amid awareness that it had become the arbiter of vital national questions and had become vital to presidential politics.[50]

The Marshall and Fortas struggles also helped define the way the Warren Court is remembered. In the decades since Warren stepped down, it's become common to say his court epitomized "liberal judicial activism." Law professors, however, have recently confirmed the important point that political scientists recognized long ago. Most Warren Court decisions, even those involving criminal procedure, were popular, and the court was widely accepted. Liberalism retained considerable public support into the late 1970s, and liberals dominated the Senate until 1978. Recall Marshall's popularity in 1967 and the backing for Fortas until the last-minute revelations about obscenity and lecture fees in 1968. It is ahistorical to say the Warren Court did not reflect public opinion and majority will. For most of the 1960s, its liberalism was mainstream.[51]

Yet today even Democrats often run away from the Warren Court because they accept the cartoonish image of it promoted by its opponents *with relatively little success* during the 1960s. Presidents Clinton and Obama tried to respect and reject the Warren Court by relegating it to history and touting their nominees as nonideological and moderate. Think of the 1990s announcement by one liberal columnist that in nominating Justices Ruth Bader Ginsburg and Stephen Breyer, Clinton broke free of "the excesses of the Warren Court" and ended "[t]he age of judicial heroics." Or consider that when candidate Obama called for justices with "empathy," conservatives argued that was Obama's code for Warren Court–types. Not so, said Obama, who maintained that 1960s judicial "activists . . . ignored" congressional will and "democratic processes."[52]

Thus, even as confirmation hearings feature nominees ritualistically swearing loyalty to *Brown v. Board of Education,* they underline the bipartisan acceptance of a caricature of the Warren Court its opponents advanced in the 1960s. Southern Democrats showed the potential of "dog-whistle politics" in the Marshall battle when they touted the need for a Supreme Court to stress "law and order." Many of their descendants have become Republicans, attracted in part by the promises of Nixon and his successors of a less "activist," more "conservative" court that focused more on crime and less on civil rights. The Warren Court has molded the contemporary Republican Party, just as Republicans have shaped it into an invaluable whipping boy that appealed to its disparate factions. No wonder Clinton and Obama proceeded cautiously. Notably, they nominated judges. Since 1975, judicial experience has become a prerequisite for every candidate but Elena Kagan. "Perceptions of the Warren Court's activism fueled a debate about the judiciary; critics wanted the Court to stop legislating from the bench," one law professor said. "Picking candidates with judicial (as opposed to political) experience may be seen as a way of pursuing this end" – as if judges were incapable of using law politically.[53]

Moreover, besides creating a bias against election year confirmations and making "original intention" and "judicial activism" household phrases in confirmation battles, the Marshall and Fortas battles probably also made a difference to the court's opinions. By the late 1960s, for example, some thought that the Warren Court was on the verge of singling out wealth as a suspect classification. Perhaps a Fortas, Goldberg, Brennan, or Hart Court might have subjected laws that sustained economic, as well as gender and racial, inequality to strict scrutiny. Perhaps it would have required regional busing to achieve racial balance in the schools, announced indigent women's right to government-funded abortions, and forced Americans to focus more on how class, like race and gender, divides us.[54]

Historians should not dwell on counterfactuals, but we do know that Fortas's defeat in 1968 ultimately yielded two seats at the court for Richard Nixon. The first was the chief justiceship; the second, the slot cleared by Fortas's own resignation in 1969. In an attempt to move the court in a more conservative law-and-order direction, the Nixon administration launched a smear campaign against Fortas, who had given it plenty of grist for its mill by becoming involved with a charitable foundation headed by a former client who was an indicted stock manipulator. In pressing him to quit, the administration publicized an FBI file saying that Fortas had sex with an under-aged boy and threatened to indict two of his former partners, one of whom was his wife.[55]

That Fortas would cast a long shadow over the court became clear soon after he became the only justice ever to resign in disgrace when Nixon nominated as chief justice Judge Warren Burger, a prominent critic of the Warren Court's criminal procedure decisions. He could not appoint his own Fortas. Nixon told reporters that the Fortas hubbub had shown he must avoid "a political friend or ... [in[the Washington vernacular, 'crony.'" After the Senate had defeated two of his nominees in further bitter fights, Nixon chose Burger's crony, Harry Blackmun, for Fortas's spot.[56]

Constitutional experts in the 1980s portrayed the Burger Court as the "counter-revolution that wasn't" because they believed that Chief Justice Burger and his colleagues did not roll back Warren-era jurisprudence. Equally distinguished ones today, however, emphasize its erosion of the equality that underlay Warren Court opinions. They show that the Burger Court chomped, rather than nibbled, on its predecessor's desegregation and criminal procedure decisions and lay the foundation for the Roberts Court's transformation of the electoral process in the next century by protecting corporate speech.[57]

And ever since the Burger nomination, the possibility of placing a presidential intimate at the court has withered. "Any friend of the President's who can be painted as a 'crony' will be torn to pieces," one Republican warned Reagan. When President George W. Bush nominated White House counsel Harriet Miers, *Slate Magazine* rehashed Fortas's chief justice fight and concluded, "The practice of naming presidential pals began to wane decades ago, and ... [t]he wisdom of avoiding cronyism is now ... settled." This "wisdom" is mystifying. While many might agree that justices should be less involved with presidents than Fortas was, distinguished cronies such as Louis Brandeis and Robert Jackson have populated the bench from John Jay's time through Fortas's. The ban may finally be ending: It's noteworthy that in nominating Elena Kagan, Obama selected someone whom he explicitly called a "friend" – a quasi-crony, perhaps.[58]

Without a doubt, though, Kagan's confirmation reminded Americans of the long shadow the 1960s still cast. She had clerked for Justice Thurgood Marshall, and Republicans mentioned Marshall repeatedly on day one. Would she use the law to help the disadvantaged as Marshall had done, a Republican asked on day two? "[Y]ou'll get Justice Kagan, you won't get Justice Marshall, and that's an important thing," she responded. That didn't answer his question, the senator complained. A *Washington Post* op-ed semi-facetiously entitled "Kagan May Get Confirmed, But Thurgood Marshall Can Forget It," put it this way: "Did Republicans think it would help their cause to criticize the first African American on the Supreme Court, a revered figure who has been celebrated with an airport, a postage stamp and a Broadway show?" Yes, they did. The ghosts of Lyndon Johnson's 1960s still haunt the way Supreme Court justices are selected and confirmed.[59]

CHAPTER 8

"If I Cannot Get a Whole Loaf, I Will Get What Bread I Can": LBJ and the Hart–Celler Immigration Act of 1965

Madeline Y. Hsu

LYNDON BAINES JOHNSON SHEPHERDED THE MOST RECENT overhaul of general immigration policy more than fifty-five years ago. The Hart–Celler Immigration Act of 1965 receives credit for the transformation of the US into a richly multiracial and multicultural nation whose primary immigrant flows now originate from Asia and Latin America through its replacement of the racist national origins quota system. Despite this enduring accomplishment, Johnson had not been considered an active proponent of immigration reform until he assumed the presidency. The issue had been a priority for the late John F. Kennedy, and Johnson was persuaded to adopt immigration reform as complementing his civil rights agendas.[1] Johnson's shallow commitment to immigration reform is sometimes blamed for the most serious problems resulting from the 1965 Act, which imposed the first numeric limits on immigration within the Western Hemisphere, making illegal the migrations of millions originating from the closest US neighbors.[2] This highly visible and deeply divisive stratum of permanent residents performs economically necessary labor while receiving, as immigrants outside the law, lesser rights and legal protections.[3] In this chapter, I situate Johnson's significant legislative achievement, and its shortcomings, in the long history of the particular difficulties of enacting systemic immigration policy in the institutional maze of the US legislative process. The prolonged and constantly thwarted struggles to remove overt racial discrimination from immigration policy conditioned Johnson and even the most liberal and committed of immigration reformers to accept compromises as the necessary price to abolish the "iniquitous" national origins system.[4] As expressed by Johnson's friend and occasional congressional ally, Everett Dirksen (R-Illinois), when it came to immigration reform, sometimes part of a loaf of bread was all that could be had.[5]

BARRIERS TO LEGISLATING IMMIGRATION POLICY

Significant shifts in immigration policy have almost always required decades to legislate because immigration laws affect so many stakeholders with sharply divergent, deeply entrenched interests. It is the most direct mechanism available to the federal government to shape the US population's size and various demographic attributes such as race, socioeconomic class, educational attainment, and political beliefs. National economic competitiveness depends on a ready supply of different kinds of worker, but how immigrants participate in the US labor market sharply divides major interest groups such as organized labor, which seeks to protect the livelihoods of its membership, from that of major employment sectors such as corporate and finance conglomerates, factories, research centers, agribusinesses, construction, and service industries. Congress and the White House have frequently clashed because the former tends to prioritize domestic anxieties about excluding unwanted foreigners while the latter focuses more on the international relations implications of maintaining open doors to aligned nations. Immigration regulation inherently discriminates and in its criteria for legal admission clearly reveals core national priorities about the kinds of people who are welcomed to become citizens and share neighborhoods and resources. It also reveals who are excluded and allotted lesser rights and standing.

For these reasons, the stakes of restricting immigration are higher in democratic countries where immigrants gain equal political rights when they become citizens. Immigration regulation enacts the most heartfelt philosophies about what it means to be an American when the American people disagree bitterly about what kinds of and how many persons may immigrate and share their privileges as citizens. Geography shapes localized priorities as well, as different regions receive varying immigrant flows from areas physically most proximate to them. As an illustration, in 1803 the Haitian revolution led slave-owners in lower South states to fear that freed Blacks would enter and challenge their racist institutions and successfully requested that Congress ban the "importation" of "any negro, mulatto, or other person of color."[6] Although this particular law was not actively enforced, race and national origins were the dominant criteria emphasized in immigration regulation until 1965, an ugly history that underscores the magnitude of Johnson's accomplishment in securing passage of the Hart–Celler Act.

Regional migration influxes produced the earliest attempts to restrict immigration, even though, as a matter related to international commerce, immigration regulation is constitutionally a matter of federal authority. During the 1840s, the arrivals of hundreds of thousands of famine-driven Irish led the states of Massachusetts and New York to adapt poverty laws into policies and institutional practices developed to expel poor immigrants.[7] In 1852, California passed laws restricting immigration by Chinese who had arrived seeking gold and continued coming for the abundant opportunities accompanying the dramatic agricultural and infrastructural development of the Western United States. California's laws were challenged and set aside as unconstitutional violations of federal authority that remained preoccupied with the issue of slavery dividing North and South. Not until after the Civil War and the retreat from Reconstruction in 1876 did Congress take up immigration regulation systematically.

Its first targets were easily identifiable as different, unassimilable, and unwelcome. Moreover, California's importance as a swing state during the 1870s made the anti-Chinese platform politically expedient for both the Democratic and Republican Parties. Chinese immigrants were already legally barred from gaining citizenship since the 1790 Nationality Act and offered no electorate to court.[8] Even with such bipartisan consensus, however, Chinese restriction required half a dozen years to become law as the White House vetoed congressional efforts, seeking to avoid an open breach with China while assessing US authority under international law to enact immigration regulation. Only after the US compelled the Chinese government to sign a treaty acknowledging US rights to "limit, suspend ... but not absolutely prohibit" Chinese immigration did the 1882 "Act to Execute Certain Treaty

Stipulations Relating to Chinese," now known as Chinese Exclusion, become law.[9] A few months later, Congress addressed the concerns of New York and Massachusetts with the 1882 Immigration Act, barring entry to the poor, who were labeled "likely to become public charges" (LPC). Subsequently, immigration regulation targeted an expanding array of unwanted groups, accompanied by a growing enforcement bureaucracy. Race and national origins were the primary criteria determining immigrant desirability, with a consensus that Asians were unassimilable and unable to become Americans, although the legal strategies used to limit their immigration depended on US relations with their home countries. Restriction of Japanese, for example, ensued from the diplomatically negotiated "Gentlemen's Agreement" (1907–08) whereby the Japanese government agreed to prevent emigration by unwelcome laborers in exchange for the continued rights of Japanese American children to attend integrated schools with white children.

The goal of reducing overall immigration also required targeting Europeans. By the 1880s, immigration had reached unprecedented peaks and increasingly comprised arrivals from eastern, Mediterranean, and southern Europe of non-Protestant religions (see Figure 8.1). Associated with urban ghettos and industrial manual labor, Italians, Jews, Poles, Czechs, Slovaks, and Greeks were considered to be of questionable whiteness, or of assimilability into the American civilization developed by the western and northern Europeans who had migrated earlier, such as English, Germans, Dutch, Swedes, Finns, and French. The Immigration Restriction League (IRL), founded in 1894, campaigned to significantly reduce overall immigration levels by excluding poorer and less educated eastern and southern Europeans identified by imposing a literacy standard. Senator Henry Cabot Lodge (R-Massachusetts) first introduced such legislation in 1896, which passed through Congress only to meet with Grover Cleveland's veto on the grounds that restricting European immigration was a "radical departure" for the US, that testing literacy did not assess the true potential for aspiring immigrants, and that it would have a negative impact on "friendly intercourse" with aligned nations.[10] The literacy standard required two decades to enact, despite increasing peaks of

8.1. At a ceremony on Liberty Island in New York Harbor, President Johnson signs the Immigration and Nationality Act of 1965, also known as the Hart–Celler Act, which vastly expanded immigration from areas outside of Europe. Over LBJ's right shoulder, Lady Bird Johnson and Vice President Hubert Humphrey look on. Prominent over LBJ's left shoulder are Senators Edward M. Kennedy and Robert F. Kennedy.
Credit: LBJ Presidential Library photo by Yoichi Okamoto

immigration and the findings of the forty-one-volume, congressionally funded Dillingham Report (1911) that documented America's "immigration problem."[11] Repeatedly, Congress passed legislation only to meet with presidential vetoes from William Howard Taft and Woodrow Wilson. Not until 1917 did the literacy standard gain passage when Congress mustered two-thirds majorities in both houses to override Wilson's veto.

Despite this decades-long struggle, the literacy standard barely made a dent in overall numbers. The fervor for effective immigration restriction raged unabated and led Congress to adopt the severest measures in US history by imposing quantitative limits on legal immigration. This radical experiment, the 1921 Emergency Quota Act, was initially a temporary constraint but pioneered a system of quotas allocated by national origins and race that have remained a dominant principle of US immigration regulation. It worked so effectively in lowering immigration severalfold, from over 1 million a year to 350,000, and reducing eastern and southern European immigration, that Congress made the system permanent with the 1924 Johnson–Reed Act.

The national origins quota system set aside *qualitative* considerations of individual worthiness to immigrate and prioritized the *quantitative* numbers of immigrants deemed acceptable by Congress. Applying flat percentages, the law allocated each nation an annual quota of legal immigrants so that every year the proportion of immigrants matched that of the nationalities identified in the 1890 census count. The quotas limited the absolute numbers of immigrants while conserving the US's ethnic and racial composition. Only just over 150,000 persons could legally immigrate, with 85 percent of visas reserved for Great Britain, Germany, and Ireland. Italians were the worst impacted, with their immigration reduced from more than 100,000 annually to a quota of just 5,306. From the outset, community leaders of impacted groups expressed their objections, with newly elected Representative Emmanuel Celler making his opposition the topic of his maiden speech in Congress. The 1924 law summarily excluded all "aliens ineligible for citizenship," ending Asian immigration and openly offending the Japanese government. Despite some pressures, the Johnson–Reed Act held back from restricting migration within the Americas in order to maintain "good neighbor" relations and cater to agricultural and industrial employers seeking to retain their access to nearby workers.

Since 1921, the spine of immigration regulation has been quantitative restriction.[12] Numeric quotas allow immigration authorities to reject visa applicants simply because quotas had been depleted and sometimes even when they had not. During the 1930s, British and German quotas were never used up, and yet US consular personnel denied visas to Jews fleeing Nazism. The Johnson–Reed Act plunged immigration to levels unseen since the early nineteenth century, but its effectiveness relied on quantifying and rendering obvious US racial and national prejudices against most peoples of the world. The domestic triumph of US restrictionism presented an intractable problem for American foreign relations.

THE PENDULUM SWINGS:
FROM ISOLATIONISM TO COLD WAR GLOBAL LEADERSHIP

Not until World War II did the United States plunge back into world affairs and cultivate international alliances, a transformation of priorities that required reforming its immigration laws. The global war against the spread of authoritarianism led the United States to reopen its door to once-excluded races and nationalities of peoples, starting with the repeal of the Chinese exclusion laws through the granting of citizenship and a token immigration quota, followed by similar treatment for other Asian allies. In 1944, the coalition of immigration reform organizations that supported repeal, including the American Jewish Council, the Hebrew Immigrant Aid Society, B'nai B'rith, the National Catholic Welfare Conference, the Federal Council of Churches, the American Committee for Christian Refugees, the American Civil Liberties Union (ACLU), and the Young Men's Christian Association (YMCA), formed the Committee on Postwar Immigration Policy to apply domestic pressures for greater admission of nationalities with low quotas. International affairs abetted their efforts as the US engaged the Soviet bloc for economic, military, and moral leadership of the world even as decolonization produced the emergence of scores of new nations navigating the competing political and economic ideologies of communism and capitalism. In asserting itself as the world's leading democracy, the US sought to woo the "hearts and minds" of newly independent Africans and Asians, in part by addressing its domestic history of racism and segregation while mitigating the discrimination embedded in its immigration laws.[13] The "diverse coalition of ethnic, religious, and civic organizations" that formed in 1950 to press for "comprehensive immigration reform" confronted the same steep challenges to changing immigration policy as had restrictionists a half-century before.[14]

The campaign to reduce racism in immigration laws required decades. Restrictionists staunchly defended the national origins quotas as necessary to protecting the United States from disastrous changes. Driven to address Europe's refugee crisis in 1945, President Truman worked within the quota system to admit about 39,000 displaced persons by reallocating unused visas from the previous three years. His 1947 Presidential Committee on Civil Rights included calls for immigration reform describing the national origins quotas as racist and damaging to foreign relations and economic efficiency. The 1948 Displaced Persons Act authorized 200,000 admissions but only by mortgaging years into the future the immigration quotas of sending countries. The logic of quantitative restriction remained firmly in place, regardless of the millions of persons uprooted by global conflicts, decolonization, and the onset of the Cold War.

The national origins quotas strained to accommodate these changing priorities. From 1949 through 1952, more than 600,000 quota immigrants had arrived, 335,000 of whom were mortgaged against the future quotas of unfavored countries, even as preferred countries such as Britain and Ireland often did not use up their visa allocations, underscoring the inequalities of the national origins system.[15]

Immigration restrictionists sought to entrench the national origins quotas. One influential political broker, Senator Pat McCarran (D-Nevada), codified various "scattered" and divergent immigration and naturalization acts into a new federal law, the McCarran–Walter Act.[16] McCarran's tremendous clout over immigration policy stemmed from his position as chair of the Judiciary Committee, which controlled the immigration bills that made it to the Senate floor. He coordinated closely with Francis E. Walter (D-Pennsylvania), who chaired the House Subcommittee for Immigration. McCarran and Walter shared powerful anticommunist antipathies and often invoked national security to justify restrictive immigration regulations. As this chapter describes, control of these key subcommittees would enable the shrinking ranks of restrictionists to block growing demands for immigration reforms until 1965.

McCarran's consolidation of immigration policies retained the national origins quotas with the 1920 census as the baseline for setting limits while gesturing to Truman's call to abolish racial preferences by removing race as a criterion for citizenship and allocating immigration quotas to all nations. The 1920 baseline ensured that the overall cap remained low, at 154,206, and that most of the newly established, postcolonial nations in Asia, Africa, the Pacific, and the Caribbean received nominal quotas of 100 each. Meanwhile, 71 percent of visas remained committed to Britain, Ireland, and Germany, while all of Asia received just 1.2 percent and all of Africa under 1 percent. Although Asians gained citizenship rights and immigration quotas, they continued to face racial discrimination due to policies that tracked Asians by ancestry, not nationality or place of birth, and capped their total immigration at 2,000 annually. The McCarran–Walter Act added a system of preferences, so that 50 percent of each quota went to first-preference immigrants defined as those with "high education, technical training, specialized experiences, or exceptional ability" and the other 50 percent to relatives of US citizens and permanent residents. The 1952 McCarran–Walter Act addressed refugee migration by authorizing the attorney general to parole refugees into the US temporarily.

Seeking more genuine reform with extensive support from the White House and a plethora of community interest groups, Senators Hubert Humphrey (D-Minnesota) and Herbert H. Lehman (D-New York) had introduced a competing bill that changed the base year for quotas to 1950 (thereby increasing the overall numbers of visas allocated), added flexibility by authorizing redistribution of unused visas, and removed the mortgages on quotas resulting from the Displaced Persons Act.[17] Despite its widespread support, the Humphrey–Lehman bill did not even reach the floor of Congress because Senator McCarran, from his strategic position as chair of the Judiciary Committee, blocked it at the subcommittee level, claiming that it would open the door to "subversives, the criminals, and the undesirables." McCarran's bill was voted on, passed easily, and met with Truman's expected veto. The next day, the House voted 278 to 113 to override. The Senate margin was tighter but also overcame Truman's veto with both Senators Richard M. Nixon and Lyndon B. Johnson voting for the discriminatory national origins quotas. Over the next decade, despite shrinking support for the national origins system, McCarran and his allies would successfully manipulate legislative processes to strangle reform efforts.

Truman's veto message pointed out the flaws of the McCarran–Walter Act and the unmet needs for genuine changes. The overall cap of 154,000 was too low, lower even than that of the 1924 Act, which admitted about 0.014 percent of the 1920 population, while the new cap consisted of only about 0.010 percent of the 1950 population. Actual quota immigration ran even lower, because the countries with the largest quotas never exhausted them, so that only one-half or one-third of allocated visas were used. Truman's veto asserted: "This system ... [is] a constant handicap in the conduct of our foreign relations ... that ... discriminates, deliberately and intentionally, against many of the peoples of the world."[18]

Truman established a Commission on Immigration and Naturalization, whose report, *Whom We Shall Welcome*, recommended measures for immigration reform that eventually shaped the 1965 Immigration Act. *Whom We Shall Welcome* recommended abolishing the national origins system, enacting a "unified quota system ... without regard to national origin, race, creed, or color," setting the overall cap at one-sixth of 1 percent of the most recent census count (the 1950 census produced an overall annual limit of 251,162), and ensuring distribution of "the maximum annual quota of visas" based on five priorities: right of asylum, family reunion, "Needs in the United States," "Special Needs in the Free World," and "General Immigration." A Commission on Immigration and Naturalization would be formed to revisit visa quotas every three years, subject to review by the president and Congress.[19] *Whom We Shall Welcome* became one of many thwarted efforts by immigration reformers from both sides of the aisle, and Truman's successors in the White House, to abolish the discriminatory national origins quotas.

Unlike the battle lines leading up to enactment of the literacy standard and quota restrictions of 1917 and the 1920s, which pitted Congress against the White House, during the 1950s changes in immigration policy were defeated at the level of the House and Senate Judiciary Committees, and particularly by the House subcommittee on immigration chaired by the formidable Francis Walter until his death in 1962. Even after McCarran passed away in 1954, Walter ably worked with a coalition of segregationist Southern Democrats. Through his control of this key subcommittee, Walter fought his reform-seeking colleagues, the shifting tides of public opinion, international exigencies, and economic development to baffle and block bills and proposals that sought to dilute or replace the national origins system he viewed as crucial to protecting the United States. In McCarran's words:

America is ... a joining together of many streams which go to form a mighty river which we call the American way. However, we have in the United States today hard-core, indigestible blocs which have not become integrated into the American way of life, but which, on the contrary are its deadly enemies. Today ... untold millions are storming our gates for admission and those gates are cracking under the strain ... if the enemies of this legislation succeed in riddling it to pieces, or in amending it beyond recognition, they will have contributed more to promote this nation's downfall than any other group since we achieved our independence as a nation.[20]

As Immigration Subcommittee chair, Walter modified or simply did not forward immigration bills that he opposed, among other strategies. The reporter Meg Greenfield described Walter's "two most effective weapons – a superior knowledge of the technicalities of the law and an unparalleled canniness in parliamentary maneuver ... Half the time ... his colleagues are not quite sure what it is Walter is introducing or repealing or amending."[21]

Walter's dire warnings did not stop immigration reform from gaining momentum and supporters in Congress. After having voted to overturn Truman's veto in 1952, Johnson voted for the Refugee Relief Act of 1953, which authorized 209,000 nonquota visas, despite Walter's objections that it would "destroy the national origins system."[22]

SENATOR JOHNSON'S RECORD ON IMMIGRATION POLICY

Johnson was more informed about immigration policy than has been described by many immigration historians. For example, he was conversant with the scope and problems attending the Bracero Program which regulated temporary Mexican workers in the United States. As early as the 1910s, Southwestern US agricultural and construction businesses increasingly recruited workers from Mexico. The severe labor shortages of World War II led the federal government to enact the Bracero

Program, working with the Mexican government. This program made poorly paid, exploitable Mexican workers readily available for employment by major Anglo agricultural interests, both inside and outside the law, depending on employer needs. Mexican Americans in Texas lobbied the federal government, and Johnson specifically, to improve working conditions for Braceros or eliminate the program altogether, because they found that poor treatment of Braceros damaged their own working situations. According to Robert Caro, Johnson consistently sided with white employer interests, knowing that Mexican Americans had no other option but to back him as the most powerful Democrat in Texas. Anglo *patrons* wanted a surplus labor supply, which Johnson protected because he needed their support. As Democratic whip, Johnson supported legislation to renew the Bracero Program, opposed bills increasing penalties for hiring unauthorized workers, and fought increasing funding for the Immigration Service to police the illegal importation of workers.[23] Johnson's awareness of, and indifference to, the dire situations of exploited temporary Mexican workers and their high levels of circular migrations presaged the most difficult problems resulting from the 1965 Immigration Act.

Johnson was not a member of the entrenched restrictionist bloc of Southern representatives. On behalf of the Northeastern moderate John F. Kennedy, who was positioning himself as a major Senate proponent of immigration reform, Senate Majority Leader Johnson introduced a bill in June 1955 "to establish a Hoover-type Commission on Immigration and Naturalization Policy."[24] This bill guttered, as did so many other attempts to shift immigration policy. This long-standing logjam perhaps fueled Johnson's ire at the veteran journalist John Chadwick at a July 2, 1955 press conference. Chadwick questioned Johnson as to why there would be no amendment of the McCarran–Walter Act in the current session. Irked by Johnson's reply that he could do nothing about a bill not yet reported out by the Judiciary Committee, Chadwick persisted with his question, commenting that Johnson was willing to predict passage for other bills also still in committee and challenging Johnson's commitment to immigration reform. Johnson then "exploded with invective, tongue-lashing Chadwick so severely that his colleagues defended him." Embarrassed at this loss of control, Johnson quickly ended the press conference.[25]

Johnson directly experienced the frustration of constructing a careful campaign for immigration reform only to be thwarted by Walter's control of the Immigration Subcommittee. President Eisenhower called for major immigration reforms in his 1956 State of the Union address reiterating the recommendations of *Whom We Shall Welcome.*[26] Johnson undertook Eisenhower's charge and worked out a complicated strategy with Senator Dirksen and in negotiation with influential leaders, including Francis Walter. After soliciting a wide array of input and developing multiple drafts, Johnson and Dirksen produced a thirteen-point plan that cannily contained "a little something for everyone,"[27] including redistribution of 18,500 unused quotas to countries with low quotas, the cancelling of mortgages stemming from the 1948 Displaced Persons Act, admission of about 40,000 more refugees from communism using visas remaining from the 1953 Refugee Relief Program, expansion of refugee orphan programs, admission of 1,200 tubercular immigrants to rejoin families, and enhanced finger printing security requirements.[28] Late in the session, Johnson attached this amendment to a Senate bill guaranteed for passage – extension of a program to admit Basque shepherds to work in Western states that originated with the late Senator McCarran.

Despite Senate Judiciary chair James O. Eastland's (D-Mississippi) "bitter" objection that his committee had neither considered nor approved the amendment, it reached the Senate floor, where it passed, to Eastland's lament that it would "do away with the basis of our natural culture."[29] Murrey Marder of the *Washington Post* reported less hyperbolically that "For the first time in thirty-two years, a serious dent in the substantive basis of national origins had been made in the Senate." Johnson's campaign collapsed in the House, however, where Representative Walter refused to report out the bill from the Immigration Subcommittee despite feeling "'sick' over losing his own revisions." Walter refused repeated appeals that ran late into the night until the session expired.[30] Johnson's concerted attempt at immigration reform, forged with all his wiles and legendary deal-making prowess, failed in the face of Walter's determination and strategic control at the subcommittee level. Apart from a brief mention in the *Congressional Record*, Johnson's archive contains no records of the Johnson–Dirksen Amendment, leaving historians in the dark about what Johnson thought and felt about his most ambitious effort at immigration reform before 1965.

Immigration reform remained a pressing, unresolved issue, and some of the terms sought in the Johnson–Dirksen amendment reemerged two years later in what became Kennedy's greatest accomplishment in immigration reform as a senator, Public Law 85–316. This endeavor succeeded primarily because Kennedy bent over backwards to work with Representative Walter. In 1957, Kennedy sponsored Senate bill S2222 to provide for reuniting families, greater refugee settlement, and making permanent the residency of paroled immigrants – measures that admitted about 90,000 new immigrants. However, Walter had introduced a narrower bill in the House, and Kennedy realized "the only chance for change that year was the Walter bill." He conferred with Walter and Majority Leader Johnson and "concluded that a combination of bills embracing the best features of all of them was the best solution," promptly withdrew S2222, and presented S2410, with Walter's assurance "that the major provisions of the bill are in accord with his thinking on the subject and that it has his strong support."[31] In backing these limited reforms, Walter was acknowledging the severity of pressures to abolish the national origins system altogether by introducing more limited changes. His bill erased mortgages on eastern and southern European countries from the 1948 Displaced Persons Act and authorized distribution of 60,000 visas left unused from the 1953 Refugee Relief Act while admitting already approved refugees otherwise inadmissable by existing law.[32] This measure passed and became the "first major bill modifying the [McCarran–Walter] act," although "President Eisenhower signed with 'disappointment'"[33] because it still did not go far enough in abolishing the national origins system.

Eisenhower was not the only frustrated and exhausted proponent of genuine immigration reform. As reported by Greenfield in 1961, after enactment of the 1952 Act reformers had vowed "in every session to abolish what is usually referred to as the 'iniquitous national-origins system' on which the law is based, proposals that have a way of disappearing into committee never to be heard of again." On top of many efforts to change policies to admit additional categories of deserving immigrants – such as refugees, close family members of US citizens and permanent residents, and strategically skilled persons such as scientists, medical personnel, and technicians – Congress had to deliberate on thousands of private immigration and nationality bills introduced by individual members on behalf of deserving constituents seeking adjustment of status. These private bills, submitted on behalf of worthy individuals, consumed time and energy, even as they underscored the inadequacies of the national origins system, which imposed long waits or no legal immigration pathway at all for persons with excellent justifications to immigrate. Kennedy's aide, Myer Feldman, conducted a study of such cases in 1961 and found that, between the 80th and 86th Congresses, there was a peak of 4,797 such bills introduced during the 83rd Congress, with only 753 cases approved. During the 84th Congress, members proposed 4,474 independent bills, with only 1,227 meeting success; the 85th Congress 4,364, with 927 enacted; and the 86th Congress 3,069, with 488 enacted.[34] Dirksen's resigned response to the 1960 bill for token US participation in the World Refugee Year provides the title for this chapter. Greenfield reported use of the "partial loaf" metaphor by several other legislators frustrated at superficial reforms. On the eve of yet another such vote on September 15, 1961, Senators John Pastore (D-Rhode Island) and Arthur Watkins (R-Utah) "ruefully" made "the sacrifice of taking half a loaf," and Kenneth B. Keating (R-New York) did so with "anger as well as sorrow," while Jacob Javits (R-New York) refused to vote for the bill at all.[35]

While Walters and other restrictionists blocked significant reform efforts, dysfunction and injustices continued to roil immigration policy. Immigration levels rose to about 2.5 million for the 1950s, reaching its highest level since the early 1920s. However, less than one-half occurred within the quotas (1,098,790), with about 1.4 million immigrants from nationalities that did not meet "traditionalist identity criteria" who arrived through legal "alternative entry gates" outside the national origins quotas, while only 71 percent of 1,547,500 quota slots were used. These contradictions in actual immigration demonstrated that "while demand from the less favored countries remained very high, the favored northwest Europeans used only 566,218 out of the 1,251,650 slots reserved on their behalf (about 45 percent)."[36] Italy, for example, had a decennial quota of 56,660 but actually sent 185,491 immigrants between 1951 and 1960. Greece had a decennial quota of about 3,080 and sent 47,608 immigrants, while China sent 9,657, despite a quota of just over 1,000 for the decade.[37] The increasing irrelevance and symbolic damage of the national origins system mandated reforms.

IMMIGRATION REFORM FROM THE WHITE HOUSE

The 1960 presidential election sent Kennedy to the White House with Johnson as his vice president. Although Kennedy had pledged immigration reform during his campaign, he forwarded only modest proposals to Congress during his first two years as president, including an act to make international adoptions permanently a form of nonquota immigration and Public Law PL 87–885 "To facilitate the entry of skilled alien specialists and certain relatives of US Citizens," which lifted quota restrictions on first-preference, skilled workers already in the United States. Not until July 23, 1963, two months after the death of Francis Walter, did Kennedy send a message to Congress supporting a major reform bill sponsored by Senator Philip Hart (D-Michigan). Emanuel Celler, the long-serving representative whose maiden speech had criticized the 1924 Johnson–Reed Act, sponsored the House counterpart. Nonetheless, as described by contemporary observer Jethro Lieberman, "In all but its repeal of national origins, the bill was a conservative measure,"[38] because it raised the overall cap by only about 7,000. The Hart–Celler bill proposed a five-year transition away from quotas attached to specified nations to a worldwide quota with admissions based on a first-come, first-served system. It abolished the Asia-Pacific Triangle and replaced the fixed national quotas with a flexible system whereby countries sending many immigrants would be capped at 10 percent of the total annual limit. Exceptionally skilled immigrants would receive 50 percent of admissions visas and the other 50 percent would go to relatives of US citizens and permanent residents. Within this scheme, Britain, Germany, and Ireland would be the only countries to have their national quotas reduced, while immigrants from all other countries would gain immigration access. The Hart–Celler system removed discrimination on the basis of national origin, adapted to actual immigration levels to ensure use of all visas each year, and prioritized immigrants on the basis of employment skills and family reunification. Within the Americas, migration would be regulated but quantitatively unrestricted for flexibility. The Hart–Celler bill had broad support, with twenty-seven co-sponsors in the Senate and fifty-five representatives introducing bills identical to Celler's in the House.

This bill did not even make it to the floor of Congress in 1963. The late Representative Walter's seat as chair of the Immigration Subcommittee in the House Judiciary Committee had been taken by Michael A. Feighan (D-Ohio), who took up the banner of preserving the national origins system. Kennedy died in Dallas without realizing his long-held commitment to democratizing US immigration regulation.

That challenge fell to Johnson, who had to be persuaded to take up immigration reform. According to political scientist Daniel J. Tichenor, who interviewed several key players, Johnson was unwilling at first to undertake immigration reform because he saw it as a battle not worth waging on behalf of an issue unpopular with the US public. However, Myer Feldman and other Kennedy staffers such as Abba Schwartz persuaded Jack Valenti, Johnson's close adviser, to change Johnson's mind. Valenti recalled that "The President eventually recognized that existing immigration law, and in particular, national origins quotas created many decades before on racist grounds, as inconsistent with civil rights and racial injustice."[39] Nine years after his unsuccessful first attempt, Johnson once again took up the cause of immigration reform, knowing the legislative obstacle course that lay ahead.

On January 13, 1964, Johnson launched his immigration reform campaign with the messaging that would feature constantly in the nearly two-year struggle ahead. Before Congress and "Representatives of Organizations Interested in Immigration and the Problems of Refugees," Johnson called for immigration policy that was "reasonable and fair and right" that would admit immigrants by asking "What can you do for our country?" rather than "In what country were you born?"[40] Johnson's White House advanced the Hart–Celler bill proposed by Kennedy, but again, this bill did not make it out of committee. Later that year, Johnson gained advantages with his landslide election victory and Democratic gains in Congress adding liberal members for the 89th Congress, which proved the most productive legislative session for civil rights in US history. Johnson accomplished immigration reform with the support of supermajorities in both chambers of Congress.[41] Even with these advantages, Johnson had to thread the needle of subcommittee dynamics, because the key congressional Judicial and Immigration Committees remained chaired by staunch defenders of the national origins system, Senator Eastland and Representative Feighan.

Johnson again pressed the cause of immigration reform during his State of the Union address delivered on January 4, 1965, calling upon Congress to enact laws that "open opportunity to all our people," including "Negro Americans" and "to those in other lands that are seeking the promise of America, through an immigration law based on the work a man can do and not where he was born or how he spells his name."[42] He marshalled an active cadre of immigration reformers such as Celler, Hart, Javits, both Ted and Robert Kennedy, and Kennedy's former aides Abba Schwartz and Myer Feldman, to provide wide-ranging support. Advocates for the Hart–Celler bill reiterated key platforms: that the bill would "prevent an influx of undesirables and safeguard our people against excessive or unregulated immigration" by maintaining "all of the security requirements we now have"; "No immigrants admitted under this bill could contribute to unemployment"; and "the total number of immigrants would not be substantially changed," or only 7,000 more than the 158,361 quota admissions a year. In the consistency of his messaging that immigration regulation should consider chiefly "personal qualities" and not place of origin, Johnson left room for negotiation about how such priorities would be realized in practice.[43]

In 1965, Feighan recognized that congressional numbers and committee membership were now against him and that some version of immigration reform was inevitable. As had Walter in 1957, he decided to mitigate these anticipated changes by authoring his own bill. After several meetings with Johnson, Feighan introduced his bill on June 1, 1965, which superceded the Hart–Celler bill and thereby set the terms for immigration reform.[44] During the summer of 1965, Johnson had limited energy to devote to wrangling over immigration policy. As recorded by Lady Bird Johnson, "the pressures of Vietnam saw a resurgence of Lyndon's depression and volatility," even as the showdown over Martin Luther King Jr.'s march for voting rights at the Pettus Bridge required tremendous attention. Johnson's physical health suffered, with weight gain, lack of sleep, and gallstones adding to his debilitation even as he shouldered requests for raising troop levels in Vietnam and pursued voting rights and Medicare.[45] Amid this deluge, Feighan's bill fulfilled his major goals for immigration reform by abolishing the racist national origins quotas and the Asia-Pacific Triangle despite its conservative elements.

Feighan's bill retained fixed national quotas, set at the superficially equal level of 20,000 per country, and imposed a cap of 170,000 on the Eastern Hemisphere. The preference system added a layer of restriction, with Feighan's bill reversing priorities favoring family reunification, so that 75 percent of visas were allocated for close relatives, including the parents, adult children, and siblings of US citizens and the immediate families of permanent residents. Skilled workers received only 20 percent of visas and had to undergo Department of Labor certification that they would not displace US workers. Refugees received the remaining 5 percent of visas. Although not included in Feighan's bill, Representative Clark MacGregor (R-Minnesota) proposed adding a cap on Western Hemisphere immigration in the Judicial Committee, which was voted down both in committee and again, narrowly, when MacGregor proposed an amendment on the House floor.

Feighan's bill performed the sleight of hand of satisfying both Johnson's priority that overt racial discrimination be stripped from immigration regulation while its emphasis on family reunification reassured restrictionists that immigration would not change that much. The American Legion dropped its opposition when its analysis determined that most immigrants would be closely related to US citizens, about 85 percent of whom were white in 1960, and determined that Asian immigration would remain limited but without the "sting" of prejudice. In contrast, the Japanese American Citizens League complained that preferences for family reunification privileged European immigration and limited that of Asians. In their campaigning for the bill, Celler and Robert Kennedy also argued that it would not lead to huge increases in Asian, Caribbean, or African immigration and that the greatest increases were anticipated in the immigration of southern and eastern Europeans.[46]

Senate discussions proceeded in parallel with those of the House and also took up Feighan's bill. Unlike in the House, the restrictionist chair, Eastland, chose not to participate in the Judicial Committee meetings, and Ted Kennedy presided as acting chair. Even so, Kennedy needed to win over Senators Sam Ervin and Everett Dirksen to ensure their votes to advance the bill. Ervin and Dirksen's price for supporting immigration reform was the imposition of caps on Western Hemisphere immigration, the last measure added to the bill. Without reference to racial discrimination, they pointed to rising population in the Americas to justify beginning quantitative restriction on hemispheric immigration. They also turned the discourse of civil rights on its head by arguing that continuing to treat Western Hemisphere countries as exceptions to immigration regulation was to discriminate against other countries.

Repeated experiences with the choking of immigration reform at the committee level conditioned Johnson and his fellow immigration reformers to take this deal. Speaking to reporters on August 25, 1965, Johnson expressed his support for Feighan's bill, noting that "I had put this legislation very high in our list ... I have continually urged the leadership to proceed with this consideration." But he expressed concerns about the bill's chances in the Senate Judiciary Committee.[47] Johnson reassured Ervin and Dirksen that he would not oppose a Western Hemisphere cap.

Long-term immigration reformers such as Celler and Javits also viewed the Western Hemisphere cap as the necessary price for abolishing the national origins system in the Senate.[48] Even Abba Schwartz, the liberal friend and lawyer whom Kennedy appointed to improve refugee admissions at the Bureau of Security and Consular Affairs, accepted the situation. Schwartz advised Robert Kennedy about avoiding "impairing passage of the bill" after Kennedy had spoken on television about "the undesirability of imposing a ceiling on immigration from the Western Hemisphere." Fearing that Kennedy's statement might lead Ervin and Dirksen to withdraw their support, Schwartz advised Kennedy to ameliorate his statement by attributing it to Secretary of State Dean Rusk, who remained the most outspoken opponent of the Western Hemisphere "exception," citing Washington's longstanding Good Neighbor policy and the lack of need based on current immigration levels.[49]

As a gesture to immigration reformers, Dirksen proposed formation of a "Select Commission on Western Hemisphere Immigration" to study the situation and report to Congress in three years before imposition of the Western Hemisphere limit. If new legislation was not passed, the cap would go into place on July 1, 1968. However, Dirksen also used the bill to press for his own agenda and delayed its advancement for two weeks while he bargained for an unrelated apportionment amendment. Once Dirksen got his funds, the bill passed through the Judiciary Committee, with only Eastland and McClellan opposed.[50] On the Senate floor, Dirksen "cited the four-fold increase in Latin American immigration into the US over the last ten years," an average of 110,000 a year over the past decade from nonquota countries, to persuade "his colleagues to ratify the hemisphere quota system."[51] As thus amended, Feighan's bill passed through the Senate, and in the reconciliation proceedings the Senate version prevailed, adding for the first time quantitative restrictions on immigration from the closest neighbors.

Within four days of the bill's passage through Congress, Johnson signed it into law at a grand ceremony convened at the base of the Statue of Liberty (see Figure 8.1). Johnson described it as "not a revolutionary bill" that would "reshape the structure of our daily lives, or really add importantly to either our wealth or our power." He thanked the deep list of politicians – Celler, McCormack, the three Kennedy brothers, Attorney General Nicholas Katzenbach, Feighan, Dirksen, Javits, Mansfield – who played major roles contributing to its passage. Johnson celebrated the new law for "repair[ing] a very deep and painful flaw in the fabric of American justice" and invoked the primary principle "that from this day forth those wishing to immigrate to America shall be admitted on the basis of their skills and their close relationship to those already here" as a standard of fairness "so self-evident" but that had been "twisted and … distorted by the harsh injustice of the national origins quota system." Johnson set the 1965 Hart–Celler Act alongside his other achievements in civil rights legislation because it restored to immigration regulation "the basic principle of American democracy – the principle that values and rewards each man on the basis of his merit as a man."[52]

AFTERMATHS

Despite Johnson's disavowal that the 1965 Hart–Celler Immigration Act was not "revolutionary," its conditions have literally changed the face of the United States. From historic lows between the 1930s and 1965, immigration levels have matched historic highs. In 1960, the foreign-born share of the population was just 5 percent, but the figure increased to 13.9 percent by 2015, just below the 14.8 percent reached in 1890. In 2015, the US had the world's largest immigrant population, about one in five of the international total.[53] The composition of immigrant Americans has also changed dramatically. In 1960, 67 percent were born in Europe, 3 percent in Asia, 9 percent in Latin America and the Caribbean, and 21 percent in other regions. In 2013, just 13 percent of immigrants were born in Europe, 27 percent in Asia, 52 percent in Latin American and the Caribbean, 4 percent in Africa, and 5 percent in other regions.[54]

The Pew Foundation finds that the 1965 Immigration Act significantly diversified the US population racially and ethnically. In 2015, the racial and ethnic composition of the national population was 62 percent white, 18 percent Hispanic, 12 percent Black, 6 percent Asian, and 2 percent other. Without enactment of the law, the US population would have been significantly less heterogeneous at 75 percent white, 14 percent Black, 8 percent Hispanic, less than 1 percent Asian, and 3 percent other.[55]

The legal scholar Gabriel Chin argues that "Congress understood ... that it was putting US immigration policy on a race-neutral basis, and that the chips would fall where they might," citing 1990s interviews of former House Representatives Gerald Ford and Pete Rodino Jr. and their expectations of increased and diversified immigration flows, especially from Asia. Immigration statistics during the 1950s and 1960s indicated clearly which countries experienced high pressures for immigration to the US.[56] Immigration from Italy, Greece, and China exceeded their quotas severalfold, as described earlier. Drawing on data available in 1964, the sociologist Brinley Thomas observed that PL 87–885, which removed quota restrictions from first-preference, highly skilled workers in 1962, resulted in the greatest increases in immigration from "underdeveloped regions" such as Asia, South America, Cuba, and Mexico.[57] As anticipated in Thomas's 1968 analysis, Asians used the employment preferences to initiate immigration chains to the United States as highly skilled workers, who in turn seeded the immigration of extended family chains over the coming decades. The addition of Southeast Asian refugee migrations in the 1970s further increased immigration from Asia, which since 2011 has become the major source of immigrants to the US.[58] Asians disproportionately immigrate through the employment preferences, which results in an overall population that is more highly educated, with higher average household incomes, and employment in white-collar and professional fields. In contrast, immigration from Europe and other parts of the developed world including Japan declined because, starting in the mid 1950s, these areas had reached their postindustrial stage of economic development.[59] The different trajectory of immigration from various regions of the world, with disparate conditions of economic opportunity and political stability to motivate immigration, directs attention to how the 1965 Immigration Act retained inefficient and inegalitarian quotas with the imposition of inflexible 20,000 per country immigration caps.

Historian Mae Ngai criticizes the "formal equality" of Cold War liberalism, which did not seek "to actually end racial subordination" in its civil rights agendas. On the immigration front, "liberals formulated a policy of formal equality that put all countries on the same footing and favored no national group over another. . ... But arguably that policy was substantively unequal, because it failed to consider differences in size and needs among countries or the particular historical relations between some countries and the United States."[60] For example, in 1964, annual migration from neighboring Mexico based on long-established circuits was several hundred thousand, far in excess of the 20,000 cap imposed in 1969, thereby rendering illegal most immigration within the Americas for persons who did not qualify under the family reunification, skilled employment, or refugee preferences. The majority, now considered unskilled workers, had almost no chance of receiving legal authorization under the new labor certification process.[61] As summarized by legal scholar Kevin R. Johnson:

> The hemispheric ceiling at first appeared objective, neutral, and fair.... Its application, as a practical matter, however, placed the heaviest burden on prospective migrants from Mexico, the nation with the greatest demand of any country in the hemisphere – as well as on Earth – for immigration to the United States.... At a most fundamental level, the artificially low ceiling failed to account for the huge demand in Mexico, as well as most of Latin America, for migration to the United States.[62]

The decision to impose quantitative caps within the Western Hemisphere ignored the long history of shared spaces, communities, and economies binding the United States and its closest neighbors, particularly Mexico. Since the 1910s, these relations had been institutionalized in various Bracero Programs to bring needed workers for the fields, factories, and construction projects of the United States. Immigration historian Aristide Zolberg described the special, and exploitative, US–Mexico relationship that partnered capricious immigration regulation with access to a flexible labor supply. In the 1920s, writes Zolberg, even as Congress severely restricted new immigration,

> [it] refrained from closing the country's back door, in full knowledge that it allowed for a growing stream of Mexicans who, by their own racial standards, were more objectionable than southern and eastern Europeans because they were for the most part not even "white." The emerging distinction between a main gate tightly regulated in keeping with the "national interest," ... and an informally managed "back door" where agricultural employers ruled supreme, was thus institutionalized into a long-lasting feature of American immigration policy.[63]

Before 1965, Mexican migration was regulated through "flexible enforcement" of immigration laws made possible without a fixed ceiling so that access to Mexican workers adapted with employers' demands.[64] Between 1955 and 1959, about half a million Mexicans were legally entering the US annually, about 450,000 through the Bracero Program, and about 50,000 as immigrants, alongside unauthorized migrant worker influxes. Many immigrants had experience as agricultural workers in the US, so that through the Bracero Program Mexico became, and has remained, the largest source of immigrants to the US. Mexican immigration increased across the 1950s: it was 9,600 in 1952, doubled to 18,454 in 1953, and reached 65,047 in 1956. Zolberg observed that the waning of the Bracero Program after the late 1950s led temporary worker numbers to peak at about 450,000 a year and then decline to about 200,000 in 1964.[65]

After the controversial Bracero Program expired in 1964, the hundreds of thousands of workers it had once regulated received no legal immigration pathway in the 1965 Hart–Celler Act. The preference for H-2 unskilled worker visas did not apply to the former Braceros, and the added pre-screening requirements for work-related immigration visas provided authorization for very few unskilled and semiskilled laborers.[66] The labor certification process meant that "growers in the post-1965 period in effect replaced *legal* Mexican workers with *undocumented* Mexican labor." No steps were taken to diminish "the robust demand by Mexican workers to come work in the United States. Nor did these measures in any way reduce the demand by American employers, particularly in the agricultural, construction, and service industries, for relatively inexpensive labor." In contrast, the 1965 Act accommodated most Canadian immigrants who qualified for legal immigration through the skilled worker preference, such as nurses, doctors, engineers, and technicians.[67] Legal scholar Leticia Saucedo argues that Congress's failure to incorporate provisions for Mexican temporary workers "created a huge undocumented exploitable worker population for U.S. employers." This transformation is evident in the numbers. Without guest worker visas, and just 20,000 immigrant visas available annually, illegal entries rose from around 40,000 in 1965 to hit unprecedented new levels of around 460,000 in 1977.[68] The numbers of Mexicans migrating to the United States remained the same, while the numeric limits set by Congress for those allowed to do so legally transformed the majority into unauthorized immigrants.

The approximately half-million Mexican temporary workers and immigrants arriving annually did not prevent Congress from proceeding with its plan to impose drastically lower numeric caps when it had the opportunity to reconsider in 1968. The Select Commission on Western

Hemisphere Immigration, whose fifteen members included Ted Kennedy, Dirksen, Eastland, Celler, Feighan, and Rodino, issued its report in January 1968 with a majority recommending postponement of the ceiling to July 1, 1969, to allow time for further study of its likely impact. Congress, however, chose not to act on this recommendation, and the Western Hemisphere cap went into effect July 1, 1968.[69]

Since 1965, institutional barriers to legal Mexican immigration have only increased, while the economic and social forces driving both legal and illegal migration northward remain largely unchanged. Within a decade of the 1965 Act, the severe recession of 1973–75 ended the post–World War II economic expansion, directing significant negative attention to Mexican migrants, who became associated with the nation's economic crisis.[70] In 1976, Congress voted for more severe restriction of hemispheric immigration to apply per-capita quotas of 20,000, far lower than ongoing levels of Mexican migrations. President Gerald Ford signed the amendment but expressed concern that annual legal Mexican immigration was 40,000 a year, and said he intended to raise Mexico's immigration quota. After winning the 1976 election, Jimmy Carter also aimed to increase immigration limits for Mexico and Canada to 50,000 each, but failed to persuade Congress.[71]

According to immigration historian David Reimers, most Mexican immigrants arriving after 1965 worked, but only a minority of about 10 percent received Labor Department certification. About 80 percent of employed Mexican immigrants entered through family unification or as refugees at double or more in excess of the projected 45,000 a year. By 1978, the annual average of immigration from the Western Hemisphere over the prior decade was about 90,000, passed 125,000, and reached 138,000 in 1979.[72]

Despite the surface uniformity of the quotas, the practical inequities of the 1965 Immigration Act are also visible in the lack of immigration pathways provided for African immigrants. According to legal scholar Bill Ong Hing, although each African country received 20,000 visas annually, none "has come close to reaching its ceiling," because few people qualify under the high educational bar for skilled employment or family reunification, since formerly enslaved Black Americans had their family connections severed. More African immigrants qualified after the 1990 Immigration Act modified legal requirements with the Diversity Visa

Lottery Program and employment requirements that allowed employers to hire skilled laborers, defined as high school graduates or the equivalent, with two years' work experience in fields requiring a minimum of two years' training or experience. African immigrants – primarily Nigerians, Ethiopians, Egyptians, and Ghanaians – have gained greater opportunity to immigrate legally, after which they have initiated family-chain immigration. African-born US residents have doubled every decade after 1990, rising from 363,819 to reach 881,300 in 2000 and almost 1.7 million in 2010.[73]

Prospective legal immigrants from countries with high demand, specifically Mexico, the Philippines, India, and China, face other inequitable conditions in the form of much longer waiting lines. The longest lines are for the F4 preference for siblings of adult US citizens, with the average application to US Citizenship and Immigation Services (USCIS) beginning processing in January 2021 for applications filed October 8, 2006 – a fourteen-year wait. For Mexican applicants, however, the wait is eight years longer for applications filed July 1, 1998, and for Filipinos four years longer for applications filed February 1, 2002.[74]

Hundreds of thousands more Mexicans continued to migrate, but illegally, because the 1965 Immigration Act had transformed them "from legal and temporary to permanent and undocumented."[75] Although overall immigration has been declining since 2005 and the numbers of unauthorized immigrants peaked in 2012, at about 11.8 million,[76] the contradictions between US immigration policy and the realities of immigration separating the US and its border-sharing neighbors have transformed millions of immigrants "outside the law" into a caste of largely working residents with lesser rights and protections who remain vulnerable to detention and permanent deportation because their historic immigration patterns became illegal in 1968.

Congress has responded by expanding enforcement measures rather than addressing the problem of the artificially low immigration caps for Mexico and the underlying economic relationships that mobilized so many workers to cross borders, leading to a resident population of about 3 million unauthorized immigrants in 1980. Congress sought to address the problems resulting from the 1965

Hart–Celler Act with the 1986 Immigration Restriction and Control Act (IRCA), which implemented a three-pronged approach. The IRCA provided amnesty so that unauthorized immigrants who were employed, including farmworkers, had resided in the US for a couple of years, and had clean records, could regularize their status. The IRCA also increased resources for immigration regulation agencies to prevent future unauthorized immigration and imposed greater restrictions on employers to discourage hiring unauthorized immigrants. About 2.7 million long-term residents were able to gain permanent status, but illegal immigration continued because under-lying conditions remained unchanged. Congress made another attempt by further fortifying enforcement mechanisms with the 1996 Illegal Immigration Reform and Immigrant Responsibility Act without ameliorating measures to acknowledge employed, unauthor-ized immigrants. Resources, personnel, and bureaucracy devoted to immigration enforcement have steadily increased, particularly after September 11 and the creation of the Department of Homeland Security in 2002. The year 1996 was the last time Congress acted bilaterally on immigration policy, and it has since deadlocked over resolving contradictions between economic realities and employment practices.

US democratic institutions were undermined by the presence of just over 11 million permanent residents in 2022, people trapped in a caste-like status with fewer rights and protections, and thereby perpetually vulnerable to lifetime deportation because of their illegal immigration. Rates of employment for foreign-born residents are higher than the US average, while rates of criminal activity are lower. The ongoing contra-dictions and their dire consequences are most visible in the situations of those least culpable, the so-called "Dreamers," who were brought in as children and who have lived most of their lives in the United States but remain confined in a legal prison because they lack status and are liable to removal. Regularizing their status permanently, however, requires legislative action by Congress. Unless and until this happens, their fraught lives underscore the inhumanity of quantitative limits on legal immigration, which insists that unauthorized immigrants cannot have lives within US borders because they arrived outside the quantitative limits and employment preferences of the immigration law. Congress has deadlocked on this issue since it was first introduced as a bill in 2001, leading the frustrated Obama administration to implement the Deferred Action for Childhood Arrivals (DACA) by executive order in 2012. This basic gesture of humanity enables DACA recipients, who must have strong academic records and no criminal records, to stop living half-lives and openly pursue basic necessities such as employment and drivers' licenses. Permanent acknowledgement of their claims on this country, and the ways in which their lives are already woven into the fabric of the United States, rests with Congress to take legislative action.

Fifty-five years after Johnson's milestone of immigration reform, the US remained far from a truly democratic "nation of immigrants." As this chapter has described, the final terms of the 1965 Immigration Act were hastily settled and introduced considerable strains on relations with the US's closest neighbors even as immigration became more generally available to persons who qualified as skilled employees, refugees, or close relatives of US citizens. Most significantly, the 1965 Immigration Act finally ended the overt racial discrimination that had dominated earlier immigration policies, thereby operating in parallel with the landmark Great Society and civil rights reforms realized through Johnson's vision and leadership and the exceptionally favorable conditions presented by the Democratic supermajorities in Congress. Even as he pushed through his priority policies, Johnson must also have recognized that the 89th Congress presented an unprecedented opening for finally overcoming the entrenched defenders of the problematic national origins quota systems. Johnson chose to seize his opportunity to enact, at last, the "whole loaf" of immigration reform. This bold decision continues to set the primary conditions for immigration to the US today, an accomplishment that none of Johnson's successors in either the White House or Congress have come close to matching.

CHAPTER 9

"It's Always Hard to Cut Losses": The Politics of Escalation in Vietnam

Fredrik Logevall

O N THE EVENING OF MARCH 31, 1968, PRESIDENT LYNDON B. Johnson went before the television cameras and told a stunned nation that he would not be a candidate for reelection. His poll numbers had plunged in recent weeks, in large measure because of the war in Vietnam, and he faced an increasingly formidable nomination fight within his own party. Still, even many seasoned analysts were taken aback by the announcement. The move seemed out of character for the Johnson they knew, a political fighter of the first order. And indeed, LBJ was himself torn, preparing two versions of the address, one containing the withdrawal announcement and one not. Only shortly before he went on the air did he decide which one to give.

Astonishingly, and unknown to viewers at the time, Johnson had long suspected this moment would come. From his earliest days in office, he had told his wife, Lady Bird, and various aides and associates that he felt trapped on Vietnam, that he would be crucified whatever he did, and that the struggle in far-off Southeast Asia, a commitment he never wanted, would ultimately be his undoing. As early as May 1964, almost a year before he committed the United States to major war – a war whose reverberations continue to be felt today – Johnson cast doubt on Vietnam's importance, asking National Security Adviser McGeorge Bundy, "What is Vietnam worth to me?" In late February 1965, at the start of Operation Rolling Thunder, which in due course would drop more bombs on the Democratic Republic of [North] Vietnam (DRV) than were dropped on Europe in World War II, the president was downbeat: "Now we're off to bombing these people," he told Secretary of Defense Robert McNamara. "We're over that hurdle. I don't think anything is going to be as bad as losing, and I don't see any way of winning." A week later, shortly before the first American ground forces set foot in Vietnam, Johnson glumly told Georgia Democratic Senator Richard Russell, a mentor and the chairman of the Armed Services Committee, "[A] man can fight if he can see daylight down the road somewhere. But there ain't no daylight in Vietnam. There's not a bit."[1]

True, more even than most politicians LBJ could say different things to different people; alongside these quotations could be placed others that were less despairing. Overall, though, it can be said with assurance that Lyndon Johnson was always a skeptic on Vietnam – skeptical that it could be won, even with US air power and ground troops, especially in view of the persistent and deep-seated weaknesses of the army and government of the Republic of [South] Vietnam (RVN), and skeptical that the outcome really mattered to American and Western security.

This attitude was reinforced by the opinions of people he valued. The Senate Democratic leadership on foreign policy – Majority Leader Mike Mansfield, Foreign Relations Committee chairman J. William Fulbright, and Russell – privately warned him in 1964–65 against Americanizing the war. So did his vice president, Hubert H. Humphrey, and so did leading allied leaders abroad, as well as prominent voices in the American press.[2] US military leaders, meanwhile, cautioned against believing that Americanization would bring swift victory in the struggle. Five years, 500,000 troops, was the general estimate Johnson heard from them in that fateful winter and spring of 1965. Where would that put the president in 1968, as his campaign for reelection began in earnest? Right where he now found himself as he looked in the camera and delivered his announcement: in a bloody, stalemated war, with no end in sight.

"I WILL NOT LOSE IN VIETNAM"

It all suggests that there is a mystery at the heart of Lyndon Johnson's Vietnam. His decision for war, often seen as obvious, as overdetermined, is not easy to explain. It's not, however, inexplicable. For although

Johnson may have been a doubting warrior, he was also a determined one, from his first day in office to his last. A Cold War hawk from the late 1940s onward, he never deviated from the conviction that communist expansion must be resisted; Americans, moreover, had a duty to rally behind the flag and behind the president. "It is an American, not a political foreign policy that we have in the United States," he said as a congressman in 1948. "This is a question of patriotism, not politics." A half-dozen years later, when the Eisenhower administration orchestrated a counterrevolutionary coup in Guatemala, Johnson declared, "We've got to be for America first." To the extent that in the 1950s he criticized presidential decision-making on foreign policy, it was most often for being insufficiently aggressive in fighting the Cold War. He blasted Harry Truman for failing to crush Chinese forces during the Korean War, and he faulted Dwight Eisenhower for allowing a "missile gap" with the Soviet Union.[3]

On Indochina, Johnson was similarly vigilant, backing first Eisenhower's and then John F. Kennedy's effort to build up and sustain an independent, noncommunist South Vietnam. In the spring of 1954, with France on the brink of defeat against Ho Chi Minh's revolutionary forces, he seemingly showed a different side, arguing against any unilateral US military intervention to try to save the French position at Dien Bien Phu. "We want no more Koreas with the United States furnishing 90 percent of the manpower," Johnson said at a pivotal meeting with administration officials on April 3. But that spring his concern was really with making sure that any military action be multilateral; he did not object to intervention as such. In his newsletters to his Texas constituents, Johnson indeed voiced support *for* military action. "We are at a crossroads," he wrote in the April 15 issue, warning of the need for "hard decisions – the kind that will tax our determination and willpower." The fall of Indochina, he continued, "would be disastrous to all our plans in Asia" – a phrase that echoed what senior administration officials were saying. In subsequent newsletters Johnson continued the theme, arguing that the United States must be prepared to go for broke. "We are ready to meet the President and the Administration *more* than halfway," he said in the May 15 issue, a few days after the surrender of the French garrison at Dien Bien Phu and the start of the Geneva Conference. "As responsible men, *we are ready at any time to cooperate in the preservation of our country*" (Johnson's italics).[4]

In 1961, Johnson, now vice president, visited South Vietnam at JFK's behest. While there he extoled Saigon leader Ngo Dinh Diem, and he returned from Saigon adamant about the need to annihilate the growing insurgency and warning darkly that failure to persevere could force America to retreat to California and "leave the Pacific . . . a Red Sea." He still held to that view when he assumed the presidency two and a half years later, following Kennedy's assassination in Dallas. Like many of his generation, Johnson was scarred by the Western allies' failure to stop Hitler at Munich, and often vowed he would not reward "aggression" with "appeasement." Another analogy loomed large as well: 1949 and the "loss of China," which taught Johnson that Republicans and conservative Democrats would crucify him if he allowed South Vietnam to be likewise lost. Mere hours after taking power, he vowed that he would not be the president who saw Vietnam go the way of China. As he later told author Doris Kearns Goodwin, in a dubious reading of history:

> I knew that Harry Truman and Dean Acheson had lost their effectiveness from the day the communists took over in China. I believed that the loss of China had played a large role in the rise of Joe McCarthy. And I knew that all these problems, taken together, would be chickenshit compared to what might happen if we lost Vietnam.[5]

Kennedy's top foreign policy aides stayed on under Johnson, and all of them advised maintaining the course in Southeast Asia. But it was LBJ more than his aides who set the tone for Vietnam in the early days and weeks. At his first meeting on Vietnam, on November 24, 1963, he expressed worry about the growing congressional sentiment in favor of disengagement but said the most important task was to win the war. Too much emphasis had been placed on "so-called social reforms" within South Vietnam, not enough on battling the enemy. He instructed US ambassador to Saigon Henry Cabot Lodge Jr., who was present at the meeting, to make clear to the new South Vietnamese leaders (Diem had been overthrown and killed in a US-backed coup three weeks before) that they needed to get on with the task of defeating the insurgency and that "Lyndon Johnson intends to stand by our word." He added, for good measure: "I will not lose in Vietnam."[6]

That was the presidential message throughout the early months of his administration: Win the war. According to one of the attendees at the November 24 meeting, Johnson urged people to devote "every effort" to the struggle. "Don't go to bed at night until you have asked yourself, 'Have I done everything I could to further the American effort to assist South Vietnam?'" A few days later, the president told David Nes, the new deputy chief of mission in Saigon, that failure was not an option in battle against the Vietcong insurgents. "Lyndon Johnson is not going down as the president who lost Vietnam," he said as Nes prepared to leave. "Don't you forget that."[7]

There was continuity here, but also change. Though Johnson sought to maintain his slain predecessor's Vietnam policies, there occurred a subtle but important shift on his watch, toward a greater commitment to preventing defeat in Vietnam, a greater insistence on doing whatever necessary to thwart the Hanoi-directed insurgency. Johnson's reading of history drove him forward, as did his reading of what would be best for him in the looming presidential campaign. His temperament, moreover, was of a type that avoided the kind of reexamination necessary for a change in policy direction. His possessed a formidable mind, fast and nimble, but he had little interest in, or patience for, intellectual give and take. In the words of longtime aide George Reedy, Johnson "could think but not reflect; devise ingenious schemes for achieving goals but not ponder the validity of the goals; outguess his fellow human beings in playing the game of one-upmanship without realizing that the game might not be worth playing."[8] In international affairs especially, Johnson lacked both confidence and a detached analytical perspective, which left him vulnerable to stereotypes and clichés about foreign policy matters.

But if Johnson sought victory in Vietnam, he also insisted in these early months that it come quietly – that is, without a significant expansion of the American commitment. He wanted the conflict to be kept on the backburner as long as possible, and certainly through the 1964 US presidential election. Voters would frown on a move to either extreme, LBJ felt certain – that is, toward either withdrawal or major military intervention – and he proceeded accordingly, meanwhile playing to his strengths in domestic policy. Throughout 1964, Johnson and his aides worked to reconcile these twin objectives: to turn the war around while keeping it from becoming Americanized. Unfortunately for them, the situation on the ground in

South Vietnam steadily deteriorated in the first half of the year, as the Vietcong expanded its territorial control and the Saigon leadership (now headed by Nguyen Khanh) showed greater interest in political infighting and self-dealing than in pursuing the war effort. By the spring, senior US leaders were coming to the view, privately, that a substantially deeper American involvement would be necessary before long.

Optimism was hardly the order of the day. Not only were the trendlines going in the wrong direction, but powerful voices – in Congress, in the press, in allied capitals – were counseling against an expansion of the war.[9] Worse, top policymakers conceded privately, there was logic in the skeptics' arguments. On May 27, three days after Secretary of Defense Robert McNamara told the Executive Committee of the National Security Council that "the situation is going to hell" and "we are continuing to lose," LBJ poured out his frustrations to his national security adviser, McGeorge Bundy:

> I'll tell you the more that I stayed awake last night thinking of this thing, the more I think of it, I don't know what in the hell – it looks to me like we're getting into another Korea. It just worries the hell out of me. I don't see what we can ever hope to get out of there with, once we're committed. I believe that the Chinese Communists are coming into it. I don't think we can fight them ten thousand miles away from home. . . . I just don't think it's worth fighting for and I don't think we can get out. It's just the biggest damned mess I ever saw.

I just don't think it's worth fighting for and I don't think we can get out. Is there a more stunning presidential assertion in the long history of American decision-making on Vietnam? Later in the conversation Johnson tipped his hand further: "Of course, if you start running from the Communists, they may just chase you right into your own kitchen. . . . I was reading Mansfield's stuff this morning, and it is just milquetoast as it can be. He's got no spine at all." And: "[T]his is a terrible thing we're getting ready to do."[10]

A BIGGER WAR

In early August, LBJ ordered the first direct American military attacks on North Vietnam, after two US destroyers reported coming under attack in the Gulf of Tonkin. He did so despite contradictory evidence as to what had happened in the Gulf and why. The president also pushed through Congress the Gulf of Tonkin Resolution, which gave him the authority to "take all necessary measures to repel any armed attack against the forces of the United States and to prevent further aggression." By this action, lawmakers essentially surrendered their constitutional war-making powers to the executive branch. The resolution, Robert McNamara later noted, served "to open the floodgates."[11]

Johnson, pleased with the broad authority the resolution granted him, also understood what the Gulf of Tonkin affair accomplished for his political standing. His public approval ratings went up dramatically, and his show of force effectively removed Vietnam as a campaign issue for Republican presidential nominee Barry Goldwater. On the ground in South Vietnam, however, the outlook remained grim in the final weeks of 1964, as the Vietcong made more gains. US planners responded by fine-tuning the secret plans for an escalation of American involvement.

LBJ went on to crush Goldwater in the November election, where-upon he and his aides settled on a two-phase escalation of the fighting. The first would involve "armed reconnaissance strikes" on infiltration routes in Laos – part of the so-called Ho Chi Minh Trail that carried men and materiel into the South – as well as retaliatory air attacks against North Vietnam in the event of a major Vietcong action. The second phase would involve "graduated military pressure" against the North, in the form of sustained aerial bombing, and, in all likelihood, the dispatch of American combat forces to the South. Phase one would begin as promptly as possible; phase two would come later, some time after thirty days.

In February 1965, in response to Vietcong attacks on US installations in South Vietnam that killed thirty-two Americans, Johnson ordered Operation Rolling Thunder, a bombing program that went on, more or less continuously, until October 1968. Then, on March 8, the first US ground battalions came ashore near Danang. The North Vietnamese, having determined over the previous six months that they would expand their own presence below the 17th parallel, met the challenge. They hid in shelters and rebuilt roads and bridges with a tenaciousness that frus-trated and awed American policymakers. They also increased infiltration into the South.

That July, Johnson convened a series of top-level discussions about US war policy. Though these deliberations had about them the character of a charade – Johnson wanted history to record that he agonized over a decision he had already made several months before (and many historians have obliged him) – they did confirm that the American commitment would be to a large degree open-ended. On July 28, the president publicly announced a significant troop increase, disclosing that others would follow. By the end of 1965, some 180,000 US ground troops were in South Vietnam; in the months thereafter, the figure climbed to 385,000. The Soviet Union and China responded by raising their material assistance to the DRV, though their combined amount never came close to matching American totals.

In opting for Americanization, Johnson refused to seek a declaration of war, and he rejected the plea from several top civilian and military advisers to fully prepare the nation for the struggle ahead. There would be no call-up of the reserves, no declared state of emergency, no national debate about what ought to be done in Southeast Asia. The United States would go to war on the sly – or, in George Herring's words, in "cold blood."[12] How to explain these decisions? Historians often point to LBJ's fear that a full-fledged debate on Vietnam would have jeopardized major pieces of Great Society legislation then pending on Capitol Hill, and to his belief that a more restrained, gradual escalation reduced the risk of a direct military confrontation with China and perhaps the Soviet Union. No doubt he held these beliefs (in the case of the former, with dubious justification),[13] but almost certainly he also had a third worry: that a public debate would reveal the depth of the misgivings in Congress and in the press, and thereby undermine the shaky national consensus that existed on Vietnam. Johnson knew as well as anyone that formidable players on Capitol Hill and elsewhere opposed the new measures; it was not at all certain that his side would win a debate. And so he gambled – on a short-term strategy. He gambled that, without taking exceptional measures, he could hold public support long enough to achieve his objectives.

Thus, the core explanation for the mystery of Lyndon Johnson and Vietnam: In the short run, military escalation was the path of least resistance for him. Three presidents before him, going back fifteen years, had committed American resources and personnel to the struggle for Vietnam, first in support of the French effort, then, after 1954, to building and sustaining a noncommunist bastion in the southern part of the country. At each point when a decision had to made about whether to increase or decrease American involvement, presidents had chosen to increase it. Though there is a qualitative difference between these earlier moves and the one Johnson now confronted (none was remotely as consequential, as irreversible, as risky in domestic political terms), it stands to reason that he too would give close consideration to upping the ante.

It didn't help that he and his leading advisers had backed themselves into a corner with their repeated affirmations of South Vietnam's importance to US security (in the case of top advisers McNamara, Bundy, and Secretary of State Dean Rusk, all of them holdovers from JFK, the affirmations went all the way back to 1961) and of the certainty of ultimate success; one can see why they might stand firm in the hope that the dramatic new measures would work. The concern was credibility, and the fear that it might be irreparably hurt by failure to maintain the course. This imperative is usually considered by scholars to concern the credibility of US commitments abroad – in this case, if the United States failed in its Vietnam effort, foes and friends around the world would respect it less. American power would be less credible, causing adversaries to become emboldened and allies to lose heart. But there were other dimensions to this concern as well: for Johnson and other top policymakers, it was also about domestic credibility and, even more, personal credibility. Call it *credibility³*. LBJ feared that failure in South Vietnam could harm his domestic standing; even more, he foresaw personal humiliation should he preside over a defeat (and for him, a negotiated disengagement constituted defeat). Top lieutenants, meanwhile, feared for their reputations and careers should they jettison their previous support for a stalwart commitment to South Vietnam and its survival.

Idealism also factored into the Americanization decision, though to what degree can be debated. Some part of Lyndon Johnson believed he was doing right by the Vietnamese, giving them an opportunity to achieve a better way of life. Unlike France, which had been trying vainly to prop up a decrepit colonial enterprise, the United States sought only to help an ally suffering under external aggression; it would not keep its troops in the country one day longer than necessary. Many foreign policy intellectuals thought in similar terms. They maintained that the United States could modernize Vietnam using the tools of foreign aid, development planning, and technical assistance. Vietnam, in other words, could be made more like the United States. Or, as LBJ put it, "I want to leave the footprints of America in Vietnam."[14]

He could have chosen differently, not merely in hindsight but in the context of the time. Consider in this regard his stance as compared with that of his vice president, Hubert Humphrey, a savvy political veteran steeped in the politics and ideology of the Cold War. No one needed to educate Humphrey on the risks for politicians seen as lacking sufficient toughness in foreign affairs, as being "appeasers" who were "soft on communism." Yet here we find Humphrey, in mid February 1965, a crucial point in the decision-making, telling LBJ in a carefully prepared memorandum that 1965 would be the best time to incur these risks and that the risks of escalation were far greater. A full-scale war, Humphrey warned, would gravely endanger other US foreign policies, including relations with the Soviets and with European allies, and would facilitate an end to the Sino-Soviet split. It would also cut into the funding for the Great Society. The American public, meanwhile, would soon lose patience, because the White House had not made clear why the defense of South Vietnam was a core "national interest." The public, Humphrey wrote, "can't understand why we would run grave risks to support a country which is totally unable to put its own house in order." Disengagement was therefore the only viable course and need not be politically disadvantageous:

> It is always hard to cut losses. But the Johnson administration is in a stronger position to do so now than any administration in this century. 1965 is the year of minimum political risk for the Johnson administration. Indeed, it is the first year when we can face the Vietnam problem without being preoccupied with the political repercussions from the Republican right.... The best possible outcome a year from now would be a Vietnam settlement which turns out to be better than was in the cards because the President's political talents for the first time came to grips with a fateful world crisis and so successfully. It goes without saying that the subsequent domestic political benefits of such an outcome, and such a new dimension for the President, would be enormous.

Even if a settlement proved elusive, Humphrey concluded, disengagement would still be preferable to a risky escalation. "If, on the other hand, we find ourselves leading from frustration to escalation and end up short of a war with China but embroiled deeper in fighting in Vietnam over the next few months," he wrote, "political opposition will steadily mount. It will underwrite all the negativism and disillusionment which we already have about foreign involvement generally – with direct spill-over effects politically for all the Democratic internationalist programs to which we are committed – AID, UN, disarmament, and activist world policies generally."[15]

It was a tour de force, a lucid and unsparing – and, as it turned out, utterly prescient – assessment of the choice facing the administration at that critical moment. It would have won quiet nods of approval had copies of it circulated among Humphrey's former Senate colleagues, not least among the Democratic leadership. We do not have a Humphrey-type memorandum by Mansfield, Russell, or Fulbright from this period, but we know that all three of them feared the domestic implications of a long and bloody war. Such a war, they surely understood, could put Johnson and the Democrats in serious trouble as the campaigning began for the 1968 election.

Johnson waved aside Humphrey's missive. If this seems hard to fathom in hindsight, with our knowledge of what was to come, we must ask whether a *President* Hubert Humphrey would have accepted his own advice in February 1965. Very possibly he would have. But it would not have been easy – as he himself acknowledged, "It is always hard to cut losses." Getting out would not have been the path of least resistance, especially in domestic political terms. It would have carried a cost, even if accomplished under the terms of a face-saving negotiated settlement, one ensuring a "decent interval," to borrow the later phrase, before any DRV takeover of the South. Republican hawks may have been a small group that spring and may have been reeling from the crushing defeat suffered by their party the previous November, but that would not have stopped them from going on the offensive. Charges of "Hubert the Appeaser" would have flown. If hawkish Democrats joined in the attacks, the administration's legislative agenda might be compromised at least temporarily. The temptation for Humphrey would have been considerable to head off these condemnations and to stay in, which given the grim situation in South Vietnam would have meant some form of escalation – the status quo was no longer feasible – if not necessarily as large and open-ended as that chosen by Johnson. (William Bundy, assistant secretary of state for Far Eastern Affairs, proposed a "middle way" option that argued for a modest troop commitment and for having these forces concentrate on seizing and holding certain "enclaves" in the South. Any decision about a bigger buildup would await the end of the summer monsoon season, when a comprehensive assessment would be made.)[16]

Having opted for large-scale war, Lyndon Johnson hoped to see rapid results. And indeed, the introduction of US ground troops and the initiation of the air war made an important difference. By the middle months of 1966, it seemed clear that Americanization had staved off the imminent collapse of the Saigon government. As US officials were fond of saying, "We have demonstrated to the Communists that they cannot win." Unfortunately, it was also apparent that the enemy had demonstrated the same thing to the Americans. For the North Vietnamese had matched the buildup of American forces with increased infiltration of their own troops into the South and new weapons supplied by the Soviet Union and China. The American commander, General William Westmoreland, aware of this enemy buildup, asked for and received additional forces. By mid 1966 there were about 350,000 US troops in South Vietnam. By 1967 the figure rose to 400,000, and Westmoreland was outlining plans for about 100,000 more. The air war, meanwhile, waged with a fury against Vietcong-held areas in the South and against targets in North Vietnam, caused severe hardships for communist forces but failed to break their will.

TENSIONS AT HOME

The stalemate on the ground caused growing restiveness on American college campuses and in the press. In Congress, too, there were murmurings of dissent, though many lawmakers initially were inclined to hope for the best and to back the administration's policy. (Some who had been dovish prior to the escalation, such as Richard Russell, became hawks, on the theory that the big step had been taken and now there was no option but to support the troops and hence the policy.) Of particular concern to the White House, in January 1966 Senate Foreign Relations Committee chairman Fulbright convened televised hearings on US policy in Vietnam. Eighteen months earlier, in August 1964, the Arkansan had smoothed passage of the Gulf of Tonkin Resolution through Congress, and at key points in the winter and spring of 1965 he had voiced public support for Johnson's policy. The subsequent Americanization dismayed him, and in the autumn he had grown steadily more outraged by the escalating violence. He had been deceived, he now believed, into believing that the administration sought a peaceful resolution to the conflict and would avoid dramatically stepped-up military action.

Fulbright hoped to use the hearings to ask tough questions of top administration officials, and to invite testimony from distinguished skeptics with sterling foreign policy credentials – figures such as George F. Kennan, one of the architects of America's Cold War containment strategy, and Retired General James M. Gavin, former commander of the 101st Airborne Division. Both testified that the United States had committed too many resources to the struggle and that, in Kennan's words, America's "preoccupation" with Vietnam was undermining its global obligations. Administration officials, meanwhile, including Secretary of State Dean Rusk, endured tough questioning from Fulbright and other senators about how long the war would last and what American objectives were.

Judging the impact of the hearings on congressional and public opinion is not easy. On the one hand, they appear to have caused no radical shift in thinking. When Democratic Senator Wayne Morse of Oregon in February 1966 introduced a bill to repeal the Gulf of Tonkin Resolution, it was voted down ninety-two to five. Not long thereafter, the Senate approved another $12 billion for the war. In the same way, public opinion polls in early 1966 did not show a major change as a result of the hearings. On the other hand, the hearings were in some respects the first in-depth national discussion of the US commitment in Vietnam, and they provoked Americans to think about the conflict and the nation's role in it. To an important degree, they legitimized public dissent on the conflict. And no longer could anyone doubt that there were deep divisions on Vietnam among public officials or that two of them, Lyndon Johnson and William Fulbright, had broken completely over the war. In the months that followed, Johnson privately derided the Arkansan as "Senator Halfbright" and labeled him and other critics a bunch of "Nervous Nellies" who lacked the guts to strive for victory.

At the same time, it pleased Johnson that most lawmakers remained on board in support of the war. Congressional hawks were never as visible or articulate as their dovish counterparts – and thus have never gotten as much attention in the literature on the war – but they mattered a great deal, both in keeping the congressional profile on Vietnam low throughout the period of major escalation in the Johnson years (by 1968, there were more than half a million ground troops in South Vietnam), and, in the case of Republican leaders, in subtly pressuring Johnson to pursue a military solution and resist calls for disengagement. Privately, Senate Minority Leader Everett Dirksen urged Johnson in 1965 and 1966 to maintain the course and pursue a military victory. "If we are not winning now," he told the president at the White House in January 1966, "let's do what is necessary to win. I don't believe you have any other choice. I believe the country will support you."[17]

Johnson heard the same refrain that year and in 1967 from many other Republicans as well as conservative Democrats, and he came increasingly to depend on that support as public frustration with the war mounted. From time to time, Republican hawks such as Senator John Tower of Texas and Representative E. Ross Adair of Indiana criticized the president as overly timid, as not being aggressive enough in fighting the war, but this critique gained little traction on Capitol Hill – to suggest that round-the-clock bombing and a steadily expanding troop commitment to a weak regime 10,000 miles away represented timidity on the president's part was not exactly an easy sell. Still, in their own way, these hawks, though comparatively few and lacking in influence, helped shape administration policy, if only indirectly. Johnson, telling anyone who would listen that he was getting pressure from both sides, the peaceniks and the warmongers, pointed to the congressional hawks' carping to say that he was adhering to the only sensible path: the middle of the road. It was a disingenuous claim – he always traveled much closer to the escalation side of the street than to the withdrawal side – but for a long time it worked.

THE MELANCHOLY SECRETARY

Of greater concern to Johnson in 1967 than the restiveness on Capitol Hill was the nervousness in Arlington, Virginia, in the office of the secretary of defense. Robert McNamara had always been LBJ's chief deputy on Vietnam, as he had been under JFK before him (see Figure 9.1). Johnson marveled at McNamara's authoritative manner, his way with numbers, his can-do attitude. Behind the bullish bravado, however, there existed another McNamara, introspective and sensitive; this one had long harbored private misgivings about the prospects in the

9.1. President Johnson meets with Defense Secretary Robert S. McNamara in the Oval Office on August 7, 1967. By that time, almost half a million US military personnel were committed to the defense of South Vietnam.
Credit: LBJ Presidential Library photo by Yoichi Okamoto

war, even before he emerged as a champion of Americanization. A fall 1965 visit to South Vietnam left him despondent. Upon his return he told Johnson that the North Vietnamese apparently "believe that the war will be a long one, that time is their ally and that their staying power is superior to ours," and added that he saw only a one-in-three chance – or at best a one-in-two chance – that the United States could win militarily. Consequently, he reported, more efforts should go to the negotiating track.[18] As the months passed, McNamara's gloom deepened. Influenced by Pentagon deputies Paul Warnke, Adam Yarmolinsky, and John McNaughton, whose appetite for the war had waned as well, he feared that the fighting damaged America's global credibility, as allies and adversaries questioned the administration's judgment. The conflict's destructiveness troubled him, particularly the civilian deaths. Moreover, the heavy American reliance on technological might – including carpet bombing, napalm, and crop defoliants that destroyed entire forests – alienated many South Vietnamese and brought new recruits to the Vietcong.

By early 1967, McNamara concluded that the enemy's morale had not broken and that the South Vietnamese political scene was nowhere near stable. The air war was failing – a rural society could not be pounded into submission, McNamara determined – and had cost the administration mightily in domestic and international opinion. "The picture of the world's greatest superpower killing or seriously injuring 1,000 non-combatants a week, while trying to pound a tiny, backward nation into submission on an issue whose merits are hotly disputed, is not a pretty one," he wrote Johnson in May 1967.[19]

Decades later, McNamara would rue his and others' repeated failure to question the assumptions behind the war. "I deeply regret that I did not force a probing debate about whether it would ever be possible to forge a winning military effort on a foundation of political quicksand," he wrote. "It became clear then, and I believe it is clear today, that military force – especially when wielded by an outside power – cannot bring order in a country that cannot govern itself."[20]

So why didn't he compel that debate? More important, why didn't he quit in protest? Loyalty to his commander-in-chief was one reason. McNamara served a president who had vowed from his earliest days in office that he would not be the man who lost Vietnam; McNamara sought to help fulfill that pledge. To many later critics, this was a misplaced loyalty: What about loyalty to principle, to nation, to constitution, to people's lives? Beyond loyalty, McNamara persuaded himself – as did other internal skeptics, such as Undersecretary of State George Ball – that he could better influence policy by staying in the mix. Moreover, like many other skeptics, he wasn't certain in his bleak diagnosis. Maybe, just maybe, things would turn out okay after all, or at least stabilize enough to be handed off to the next administration, sustaining not only Johnson's historical credibility but also his own. As Leslie H. Gelb, himself a veteran of McNamara's Defense Department, would in time write, "It is almost superhuman to expect one responsible for waging war" to fundamentally reevaluate its merits and then to proceed on the basis of that reevaluation. "And so doubts simply float in the air without being translated into policy."[21]

Late in life McNamara offered up another explanation for the war policy and his own role in it: ignorance. His mantra became "If only we had known" – about the determination of the enemy, about the systemic political problems in the South, about Vietnam's longstanding tradition of standing up to foreigners, especially the Chinese. The administration had no Vietnam experts, he self-servingly claimed. The assertion was spurious. McNamara and Johnson had plenty of know-how they could tap merely by picking up the telephone. More to the point, they themselves were far from ignorant about conditions in Vietnam. They needed no tutorial about the chronic problems in the war effort and in the South Vietnamese political situation, or about the dim prognosis for substantial improvements. The evidence was plain to see.

Ultimately, McNamara did leave the administration. On November 29, 1967, Johnson announced that the Pentagon chief would leave his post to run the World Bank. "I do not know to this day whether I quit or was fired," McNamara wrote decades later. "Maybe it was both."[22] It's actually pretty clear: He was fired. Johnson, fuming privately that McNamara had gone soft, also suspected him of secretly scheming to coax Robert Kennedy, then a Democratic senator from New York, to run on a peace ticket in the following year's presidential election, challenging LBJ for the Democratic nomination. In late

February 1968, McNamara exited, succeeded by Democratic Party elder statesman Clark Clifford.

McNamara did succeed in nudging Johnson away somewhat from his rigid posture on the topic of negotiations with Hanoi. In the summer of 1967, in an initiative known as PENNSYLVANIA (its public phase was known as the "San Antonio formula"), the administration backed away from its firm prior insistence on mutual deescalation. The United States would stop the bombing if given private assurances that this would lead "promptly to productive discussions," and would "assume" that the DRV would not take "military advantage." The North Vietnamese were suspicious. There had been major increases in American bombing in August and again in September, which no doubt raised doubt in their minds about how serious Johnson was about seeking a deal.[23]

Moreover, the PENNSYLVANIA initiative took place against the backdrop of Hanoi's preparations for the Tet Offensive, preparations begun in the spring of 1967. DRV leaders were not prepared to settle for anything less than an unconditional bombing halt; they may indeed have preferred to avoid all negotiations until the Tet Offensive gave them additional advantage. In August 1967, Do Phat Quang, Hanoi's ambassador to Poland, told Swedish diplomat Jean-Christophe Öberg in Warsaw that his government remained fully ready to talk to the Americans, provided there was first an unconditional end to the bombing. But Öberg detected little sense of urgency in the ambassador's voice. More than likely, North Vietnamese minds were now focused on the coming offensive.[24]

It was launched on January 31, 1968, the first day of the Vietnamese New Year (Tet). Vietcong and North Vietnamese forces struck all across South Vietnam, capturing provincial capitals. During the carefully planned offensive, Saigon airport, the presidential palace, and the ARVN headquarters came under attack. Even the American embassy compound was penetrated by Vietcong soldiers, who occupied its courtyard for six hours. US and South Vietnamese units eventually regained much of the ground they had lost, inflicting heavy casualties and devastating numerous villages.

Although the Tet Offensive did not achieve the resounding battlefield victory Hanoi strategists hoped for, the heavy fighting called into question American military leaders' confident predictions in earlier months that the war would soon be won. Had not the Vietcong and North Vietnamese demonstrated that they could strike when and where they wished? If America's airpower, dollars, and half a million troops could not now defeat the Vietcong, could they ever do so? Had the American public been deceived? In February, the highly respected CBS television anchorman Walter Cronkite went to Vietnam to find out. The military brass in Saigon assured him that "we had the enemy just where we wanted him." The newsman recalled, "Tell that to the Marines, I thought – the Marines in the body bags on that helicopter."[25]

"A HOPELESS BOG"

Top presidential advisers sounded notes of despair. Clark Clifford, the new secretary of defense, told Johnson that the war – "a sinkhole" – could not be won, even with the 206,000 additional soldiers requested by General Westmoreland. Aware that the nation was suffering a financial crisis prompted by unchecked deficit spending to sustain the war and other international commitments, they knew that taking the initiative in Vietnam would cost billions more, further disturb the budget, panic foreign owners of dollars, and undermine the economy (see Figure 9.2). Of his associates in the business community, Clifford told the president, "These men now feel we are in a hopeless bog." To "maintain public support for the war without the support of these men" was impossible.[26]

Key architects of America's early Cold War policies also chimed in. Former Secretary of State Dean Acheson, veteran diplomat W. Averell Harriman, and NSC-68 author Paul Nitze, all top Truman advisers, joined with Clifford and other dovish insiders to argue for a new course. "Our leader ought to be concerned with areas that count," Acheson acidly observed.[27] He and other so-called "Wise Men" attended a White House meeting on March 26–27, 1968, during which a dominant theme was put forth: in Vietnam the United States could "no longer do the job we have set out to do in the time we have left and we must begin to take steps to disengage." A downcast Johnson is said to have mumbled after the meeting: "The establishment bastards have bailed out."[28] Nevertheless, this incipient

9.2. Protesters offer stinging critiques of both President Johnson and the Democratic nominee to replace him, Hubert Humphrey, during a demonstration in New York in the fall of 1968. Credit: Getty Images

revolt, combined with the challenge presented in the primaries by Senators Eugene McCarthy of Minnesota and Robert F. Kennedy of New York, caused the president to give up the game and to deliver his March 31 address.

Hanoi officials hoped Johnson's withdrawal from the presidential race would spark a major reconsideration of the US commitment to South Vietnam, and they accepted his invitation to begin negotiations. In reality, however, there were deep cleavages within the American administration on how to approach the talks. On the side stood Clark Clifford, Averell Harriman, Cyrus Vance, and others, who saw Vietnam as a lost cause. On the other side were Johnson, Dean Rusk, Walt Rostow, and General Earle Wheeler, who still sought victory, or at least something other than defeat. Johnson's view was decisive, weakened though his authority might have been by the recent developments. This was made clear in a revealing argument between Ambassador Harriman, the president's official negotiator, and General Andrew Goodpaster, chosen by the Joint Chiefs of Staff (JCS) as their military representative in the negotiations, en route to Paris for the start of the talks. In Mark Perry's account, quoting an interview with Goodpaster:

> "Now it's our job to end this war," Harriman told his colleagues [on the plane to Paris] soon after their departure, "to get the best terms we can, but to end the war." Goodpaster, seated across from Harriman, shook his head. "That's not my understanding," he said, and he reviewed Johnson's instructions: the delegation was to negotiate with the North Vietnamese, but "not in any way [to] compromise the 'maximum pressure' being put on North Vietnam by American troops".... "That's not right, General," [Harriman] said politely but firmly. "I think it's clear what our position is – what the president ordered".... "No sir," Goodpaster said. "The president would not want us to endanger American lives. We have not been instructed to end the war on the 'best terms we can.'" "We're going to end this war," Harriman responded angrily. "That's what the president said we should do." Goodpaster tried to get in the last word. "Sir," he said acidly, "that is not what the president said. Those are *not* our instructions."[29]

Goodpaster had it right. Robert Dallek, in his sympathetic biography of Johnson, *Flawed Giant*, cites Clifford's view in these months that LBJ was "torn between an honorable exit and his desire not to be the first President to lose a foreign war." In Johnson's mind, Dallek goes on, "these were not mutually exclusive goals. Indeed, the key to his peace-making was to arrange a settlement that both preserved South Vietnam as an independent [non-communist] state and sped America's exit from a war the country no longer wished to fight. Contrary to Clifford's belief, Johnson knew what he wanted."[30]

And so the bombing continued in the spring and summer of 1968 – more intensely than before – below the 19th parallel and in Laos. Daniel Ellsberg, in his gripping memoir of these years, notes that among officials and military men there was a "much lower proportion" with a preference for escalation over withdrawal than among the general populace. This was true before Tet, and it was true after it:

> Even among relatively conservative military officers, a number of whom were on the Pentagon Papers task force, and especially among officers who

had served in Vietnam, there was more readiness for simple withdrawal by late 1967 than there was in the general public even after Tet. Nevertheless, the orders to bomb were still coming down, and the orders were being executed.

Thus, in the ten months after Robert McNamara left the Pentagon, "Clark Clifford, under the President, dropped a greater tonnage of bombs on Indochina than had been expended in the previous three years: 1.7 million tons compared to 1.5." The expanded bombing, Ellsberg darkly concludes, was "obediently carried out by men who, from Clifford on down to flight crews, believed it served no national purpose whatever. I have spent a lot of time in the last thirty years seeking to comprehend and, in some sense, to come to terms as an American with that phenomenon."[31]

The explanation is perhaps quite simple: Clifford and Harriman might be prepared to argue in private for a complete bombing halt without a reciprocal agreement from Hanoi to deescalate, but they were not willing to break openly with the president. And Johnson stood firm, backed to the hilt by his chief diplomat, the diplomacy skeptic Dean Rusk. When Harriman in July again pressed the White House to stop the bombing and reduce the level of American military activity while making clear that the next move was up to Hanoi, Clifford backed him. Both pointed to a recent lull in enemy actions as an encouraging sign. The military, however, argued that the lull merely presaged a coming enemy offensive and that a bombing halt would endanger US forces. An incensed Johnson dismissed Harriman's proposal and told top officials on July 30 that he wanted to "knock the hell" out of the North Vietnamese. Recalled one US diplomat of the period: "Our most difficult negotiations were with Washington and Hanoi. . . . We just couldn't convince the president that summer."[32]

Nor was it just the bombing. To strengthen its position in South Vietnam, the United States conducted huge search-and-destroy operations in the spring and summer, sending 100,000 troops against enemy forces in several provinces in the Mekong Delta. Simultaneously, US and South Vietnamese officials initiated an expanded pacification program in the South, designed to secure as much of the countryside as

possible in the event of substantive negotiations. The Vietcong, drastically weakened by the heavy fighting during the Tet Offensive, was
deemed highly vulnerable, and the pacification efforts yielded considerable success. With further American troop increases off the table, the
United States also moved forward with what would later be called
Vietnamization, an ambitious effort to expand and upgrade the South
Vietnamese armed forces so that the American troop-count could gradually come down. By the end of 1968 the ARVN was larger and better
equipped, but US officials still doubted its effectiveness and motivation.
In July, Clifford returned from a visit to Saigon chagrined by the "pervasive Americanization" of the war. The United States was still bearing the
brunt of the fighting. "Worst of all," he said, "the South Vietnamese
leaders seemed content to have it that way," enjoying what Clifford called
"the golden flow of money."[33]

All the while, the impasse in Paris continued. The North Vietnamese
negotiators refused to discuss anything but the unconditional and permanent cessation of the attacks on the North, and their US counterparts –
under orders from Johnson – said the bombing would not stop without
"reciprocation" by the DRV. This the Hanoi representatives refused, on
the grounds that the bombings had no legitimate basis and Washington
was in no position to demand anything in exchange for stopping them.

The deadlock was hardly good news for Vice President Hubert
Humphrey, who in the wake of Robert Kennedy's assassination in Los
Angeles in early June had cemented his hold on the Democratic nomination. By July he could claim a clear majority of delegates, and he cruised
from there. But Humphrey felt compelled on Vietnam to play a delicate
double-game: he needed the approval of anti-war Democrats, but he
dared not alienate his temperamental boss. Whenever Humphrey gin-
gerly expressed a desire to stake out an independent position on the war
and to shift policy even slightly in a dovish direction, Johnson denounced
him to aides as cowardly and disloyal – and, to Humphrey's face, made it
clear he disapproved. Humphrey got the message, but his servility came
at the price of respect even from Johnson. It contributed to LBJ's covert
preference for Richard Nixon as his successor, along with the fact that he
anticipated, correctly, Nixon to be more resolute than Humphrey in
pursuing an aggressive Vietnam policy. On September 24, the president

told Clifford that he doubted that "Humphrey had the ability to be President." He would have respected him more, he said, if he "showed he had had some balls."[34]

At the end of September, with his poll numbers sagging following a calamitous Democratic convention in Chicago, Humphrey at last struck an independent chord. In a speech in Salt Lake City he declared, "As president, I would stop the bombing of the North as an acceptable risk for peace." Lost in the intense press coverage was the qualifying phrase: "Now if the government of the North were to show bad faith, I would reserve the right to resume the bombing." Nor did anyone mention that the vice president said nothing about including the Vietcong in the talks. All that mattered to journalists was that he seemed to be separating himself from the White House at last. His poll numbers began inching up; dollars flowed in at campaign headquarters. The trash-talkers who had been so common at his appearances on the trail mostly disappeared. One man at a Boston rally held up a sign, "Former Heckler for Humphrey."[35]

It was not enough. Though Humphrey closed the gap dramatically in the final days, he came up short, losing by half a million votes out of 72 million cast. By one pollster's estimate, he would have won if the polling had begun just eight hours later. Would it have made a difference to Vietnam policy if he had emerged victorious? No one can know, but Ellsberg's conclusion sticks in the mind:

> In retrospect, there really *was* a great difference between the two candidates. There wasn't much difference between Nixon and Johnson in their perspectives on Vietnam, and there really was a big difference, in secret, between Johnson and his vice president. Thus, there was actually a large difference between Nixon and Humphrey in their private views on Vietnam. But neither of them made it possible for most people to guess that. Certainly I didn't, and I also didn't know anyone else who did. In hindsight, timely support from a lot of us for Humphrey, tipping a razor-thin election to him, could have made an enormous difference to Vietnam, sparing it, and America, five or six more years of war.[36]

And so it ended, the saga of Lyndon Johnson's presidency, its last act having been anticipated by him at the beginning. He was a man who dreamed big dreams for the Great Society, who believed deeply in the power of government policy to make things better for the mass of Americans, who hoped that his massive efforts on civil rights, education, voting rights, and Medicare would earn him a place alongside Lincoln and FDR, and who forecast from the start that Vietnam would destroy it all. It bears all the characteristics of tragedy, but of a certain type, more Shakespearean than Greek, more Macbeth than Agamemnon. Whereas for the Greek playwrights the cosmos is deterministic, the hero at the mercy of forces beyond his control, a mere pawn of the gods, for Shakespeare the tragedy lies in the very choices the protagonist makes – choices that are never wholly inevitable. His Macbeth is no mere victim; he has agency, he contributes to his own downfall. The same must be said of Lyndon Johnson.

Today, some six decades after Johnson made his choice, Americans continue to grapple with the consequences. The numbers are stark: more than 58,000 Americans and between 1.5 and 4 million Vietnamese killed; 8 million tons of bombs, and 19 million gallons of defoliants, dropped on Vietnam, Cambodia, and Laos; billions in tax dollars spent. Yet despite these vast expenditures, the United States ultimately could not achieve its core objective: to preserve a noncommunist, independent South Vietnam. What is more, the war contributed to troubles that continue to afflict American society to this day – resentment; alienation; mistrust of government and of fellow citizens; erosion of civic institutions and public discourse. As the disconnect grew between what leaders were saying about the war and what the news reports showed to be happening, many Americans became cynical, concluding that the president and his aides were all too willing to deceive the public to serve their short-term needs. Analysts began referring to Johnson's (and later Nixon's) "credibility gap."

For those who believe in symbolism, there is, finally, this: On January 22, 1973, Lyndon Johnson died alone in his bed, in Austin, Texas, two days after hearing Richard Nixon, in his four-more-years inaugural address, hint at cuts to the Great Society and remind Americans how far they had come from that bleak time of 1968, when they faced "the prospect of seemingly endless war abroad and of destructive conflict at home."

The following day, Nixon announced that an agreement had been reached in Paris that would end war in Vietnam and "bring peace with honor."

CHAPTER 10

Lyndon Johnson and the Shifting Global Order

Francis J. Gavin

I T IS WIDELY RECOGNIZED THAT THE PRESIDENCY OF LYNDON B. Johnson transformed the domestic political and socioeconomic landscape of the United States. In fields from education to civil rights, to health and social welfare, LBJ's policies and the deft politics to enact them are seen on par with Franklin D. Roosevelt's extraordinary New Deal legislation of the 1930s. The reason LBJ's time as president is not held in the same historical esteem as FDR, however, emanates from the perceived gap between the two in their foreign policy and grand strategic acumen. FDR is credited with smartly guiding the American people out of deep isolation to prepare them for conflict in Europe and Asia. Roosevelt is also seen as an outstanding wartime commander-in-chief, leading the "Big Three" alliance to victory over Nazi Germany, Fascist Italy, and Imperial Japan during World War II while laying the groundwork for international institutions such as the United Nations and Bretton Woods organizations that would help generate postwar peace and stability.[1] Foreign policy and grand strategy for LBJ, on the other hand, have been seen, at best, as a subject in which the Johnson administration took little interest or, at worst, as an unmitigated disaster.[2] As Randall Woods has said, more than most presidents "Lyndon Johnson would have preferred to concentrate on domestic affairs."[3]

Is this judgment fair? When assessing the legacy of President Johnson's foreign policy, scholars and commentators understandably focus on the story of America's disastrous military conflict in Southeast Asia. Johnson inherited an uneasy military and political commitment to South Vietnam from his predecessors, Democratic President John F. Kennedy and Republican President Dwight D. Eisenhower. This pledge was soon tested, as the government of South Vietnam struggled to put down a communist insurgency and win wider legitimacy in the eyes of its citizens. In his classic study, *Choosing War*, Fredrik Logevall demonstrates that President Johnson *chose* to escalate America's involvement in the war, despite harboring deep doubts about the wisdom or winnability of the clash.[4] LBJ is understandably held up to withering criticism for his pursuit and management of a conflict that ultimately led to enormous human, physical, and political destruction in Southeast Asia while generating debilitating discontent within the United States.

The passing of time has not softened this critique, and the Vietnam War is widely seen as a geopolitical blunder as well as a stain on America's standing in the world. Historical perspective does, however, offer an opportunity to revisit and reappraise what might be thought of as the *historical weight* – or long-term impact – of other global forces, events, and policies during the Johnson presidency that were perhaps not fully appreciated as they unfolded.[5] This essay reflects upon that larger set of issues. It is true that while historical perspective has provided greater insight into both the origins and unfolding of United States policies in Southeast Asia, the collective historical judgment of President Johnson's decisions has hardly been more forgiving. What has changed, however, is a recognition that President Johnson and his administration faced other international problems and forces outside of the war in Southeast Asia – some traditional and some entirely new. These forces generated keen problems and difficulties and may, in the long run, have been equally or even more consequential than the war, and resonate to this day. To fully assess the Johnson administration's foreign policy and grand strategy, we must also explore how LBJ and his advisers responded to these other challenges.

This chapter suggests that profound if unrecognized changes to global affairs were emerging during the Johnson presidency. Typically, the Johnson administration's foreign policies are viewed almost solely through a Cold War lens.[6] "The Cold War was a fact of life."[7] Yet other global challenges arose. To be sure, it can be difficult, in real time, to appreciate when the international system is undergoing important shifts. Sometimes a transformation in world order is obvious. The close of World War II in 1945, or the end of the Cold War and the collapse of the Soviet Union in the late 1980s and early 1990s, presented sharp evidence that world politics would be shaped by new forces. Other times, the shifts are less apparent, more hidden, driven by powerful underlying forces that can be fully understood only after the passage of time.

In retrospect, it is possible to recognize the 1960s as such a national and global turning point. When Lyndon Johnson inherited the presidency of the globe's most powerful nation in late 1963, he faced not one but at least three unfolding shifts in international relations: the stabilization and changing nature of the Cold War in Europe; the profound effects wrought by decolonization, ideological ferment, and rising nationalism in what was called the developing world; and the emergence of an intensifying globalization driven by new technological, cultural, and economic forces. These forces, sometimes alone but more often in combination, altered world politics in profound ways.

This chapter will focus on selected aspects of two of those three transformational systems – the changing character of the Cold War, especially in Europe, and the intensification of globalization. Globalization is, of course, a vast subject, including issues ranging from energy production to the environment to telecommunications. The focus here will fall on two aspects – international monetary relations and the global challenge of nuclear weapons technology, especially as they interacted with more traditional geopolitical and ideological concerns in Europe. While the third challenge – the consequences of decolonization and emerging nationalism – is left to the next chapter, its effects are crucial to any assessment of international relations and United States foreign policy during the 1960s.

These tectonic shifts overlapped and interconnected in important ways. In truth, it is impossible to understand the Cold War in Europe without assessing the tumult and change in former colonies. Likewise, the forces of nationalism and decolonization are better understood when paired with an analysis of emerging globalization. The war in Southeast Asia was a product of both the Cold War and nationalism. Similarly, the 1967 war between Israel and its Arab neighbors – whose consequences resonated deeply for decades after – mixed Cold War and anti-imperial forces and, with oil brandished as a new weapon, the power of economic interdependence in a globalizing world. A key feature of the era in which LBJ led was, in fact, the increasing complexity and interconnectedness of foreign policy problems that went beyond a simple state-driven, Cold War binary and, as such, demanded more sophisticated responses than simple containment. For a politician like President Johnson, whose worldview was shaped by the moral and political clarity of the war against Nazi Germany and Imperial Japan and the early Cold War confrontations with the Soviet Union, the emerging complexity of international affairs was daunting and beyond his grasp.

THE UNITED STATES AND POSTWAR EUROPEAN SECURITY

Nowhere was the changing global order more challenging than in Europe. We often think of the Cold War as a global ideological struggle, in which the United States laid down the policy of containment almost immediately after World War II. In fact, America's Cold War grand strategy was not predetermined or inevitable; its commitment was reluctant and slow, driven by specific global concerns, particularly in Europe. To understand the Johnson administration's Cold War dilemmas during the 1960s, it is important to understand American policy toward Europe in the years immediately after World War II. This history is more complex than often is recognized.[8]

The Truman administration was not eager to commit American military power or resources abroad after World War II ended. The United States rushed to dramatically demobilize its military, and the overwhelming policy concern was transitioning to a civilian economy without a return to the economic duress of the 1930s. While there were few illusions about the nature of the Soviet regime, there was hope that a combination of postwar cooperation amongst the wartime allies and the new United Nations could provide stability and manage the shift from war to peace. These hopes were soon dashed.

The war's devastation created deep political instability and economic want worldwide, nowhere more so than in Europe, where the enormous destruction and political uncertainty inhibited recovery. Yet it was difficult to come up with a positive program for the European continent until the nettlesome problem of the future of Germany was resolved. During the war, the Grand Alliance had struggled to develop a shared, permanent plan to deal with Germany's future, despite all sharing a goal of preventing the emergence of another militarized, aggressive state. What eventually emerged, less as a permanent plan than a stopgap, was a division of the defeated state into four, temporary zones of occupation: the eastern-most zone held by the Soviet Union and three zones in the west controlled by the United States, Great Britain, and France, with the city of Berlin within the Soviet zone also divided into four.

Increasing tension and distrust between the United States and the Soviet Union prevented a common policy toward Germany from emerging. Understandably, there was a desire to guarantee that Germany's power to wage world war was permanently curtailed. Perhaps, in time, Germany would be unified and neutralized. The Soviet Union's ruthless treatment of its eastern zone, as well as its political and economic demands on the western territories, gave American policymakers pause, especially as disagreements emerged in places like Poland, the Turkish Straits, and northern Iran. As the Western European economy continued to languish in 1946 and 1947, the Truman administration began to re-think policies toward Germany and Europe, concluding a European recovery would not be possible without some effort to rehabilitate the German economy. A new set of policies emerged: the Truman Doctrine, to provide support against communism; Marshall Plan aid, both to invigorate and integrate Western Europe's economy; and the fusing of the three western zones of Germany into what was to become the Federal Republic of Germany (FRG), or West Germany, as it was commonly called. While this shift in policy had, by 1949, helped revive Western Europe, it also solidified the division of Europe into Eastern and Western blocs and deepened the enmity between the Soviet Union and the United States.

This brutal division of both Germany and the continent *might* have provided a rough if cynical basis for a stable peace, except for one frighteningly complicated factor – the new, uncertain, and seemingly revolutionary role of nuclear weapons in international politics. The Soviet detonation of an atomic device in 1949, sooner than expected, coinciding with the victory of the Chinese Communist Party in its civil war and coming soon after the 1948 coup in Czechoslovakia and the Soviet blockade of Berlin to protest the creation of West Germany, induced an increasing sense of panic in Washington and other Western capitals. This panic turned to full-blown crisis after the North Korean invasion of the South in June 1950, the intervention of United Nation forces, and the People's Republic of China's decision to enter the war on the peninsula against the United States a few months later. A largely economic and political rivalry transformed into a dangerous military competition.

The United States faced a dilemma – how could a recovering but still weak Western Europe be defended if the Soviet Union, possessing massive conventional forces, decided to invade? With the atomic monopoly gone, America could not rely on its nuclear arsenal alone to deter Russia. For the second time since the end of World War II, the United States rewrote its grand strategy. These changes were reflected in NSC-68, crafted by George Kennan's successor in policy planning at the US Department of State, Paul Nitze. They were reaffirmed in the Eisenhower administration's NSC-162 and in a series of lesser-known treaties, such as the London and Paris Accords of 1954 and the North Atlantic Treaty Organization (NATO) strategy document called MC 48.

This new policy possessed several controversial strands. First, West Germany would return to something akin to political normalcy but not full sovereignty, an ally of the West rather than an occupied country, contributing to its own defense with an army but within certain limits. Second, because of the Soviet Union's proximity and overwhelming conventional superiority, the defense of Western Europe would rely on the rapid and massive use of nuclear weapons by the United States. Third, the intertwined nature of the nuclear problem and the German issue demanded a strong American military presence. No one in Europe – neither the Soviets nor America's close allies, France or Great Britain – wanted a West Germany adrift, seeking its own security. A strong US military presence on the continent was seen as vital to allowing West Germany to recover economically without destabilizing the continent.

This fragile arrangement started to unwind almost as soon as it was established. Balance of payments pressures and political frustration with European allies caused both the Eisenhower and Kennedy administrations to question America's expensive troop deployments to Europe.

West Germany – doubting America's commitment, divided, exposed to the Soviet threat, and surrounded by countries of equal economic size possessing the bomb – wondered if, over time, it should get access to its own atomic weapons. The Soviet Union was distressed by any signs of German revanchism and atomic ambitions, and Moscow waffled between wanting to chase the United States from Europe and recognizing the stabilizing impact of America's presence. All of this was made far more uncertain and dangerous by the profound and often poorly understood consequences of the nuclear revolution.

These problems were on display during the deep crisis period that began with Soviet Premier Nikita Khrushchev's ultimatum over Berlin's status in November 1958 and ended with the outcome of the Cuban missile crisis in October 1962. While it took months to work out, what Marc Trachtenberg has called a "constructed peace" was established in 1963, whereby the Soviet Union would keep its hands off West Berlin, the West Germans would not get nuclear weapons, and the United States would maintain a strong military presence in West Germany to guarantee its non-nuclear status. The basic outlines of this interconnected settlement had barely been established when President Kennedy was assassinated.

Compared to the previous decade, therefore, President Johnson inherited a relatively stable geopolitical situation versus America's key rival, the Soviet Union, and a sharply decreased threat of war on the continent. Arguably, this was a propitious situation for the new president. International politics, however, never remains motionless, and, as LBJ soon discovered, stability generates its own challenges. Several questions soon emerged.

Would President Johnson be able to build upon this settlement to craft a more peaceful, constructive relationship with the Soviet Union? The president was eager – some critics believed too eager – to achieve explicit recognition of the new stability with America's ideological and geopolitical rival. Because of its own internal and external dynamics, the Soviet Union was often less responsive than the president hoped, and over time it appeared skeptical of LBJ's view that meaningful progress could take place between the superpowers while the United States escalated in Southeast Asia. Johnson was often held back from greater outreach to the communist bloc by his own domestic ambitions, and the shadow of Vietnam hung over any effort to achieve détente.

Stability posed a crucial question. Would the United States be able to maintain its own interests and commitments to Western Europe in the face of various domestic, economic, and international pressures to reduce its military forces in Europe? With relative stability in Europe, increasing military needs in Southeast Asia, and a deteriorating international monetary situation, many questioned why the United States continued to provide hundreds of thousands of front-line forces to the NATO mission. America's historical isolationist instincts, which President Johnson understood well, were not far from the surface of American political life.

This problem was related to a second challenge brought by peace and stability – how to manage an alliance in the face of a declining threat. Deep tensions and disagreements within the Western alliance had been the norm in the Cold War. Throughout the Truman, Eisenhower, and Kennedy administrations, however, the United States and its European partners were often able to overlook their own preferences when the danger of the Soviet threat to the continent appeared overwhelming and imminent. As the threat from Russia receded, however, each partner felt less need to sacrifice its own interests and views for the greater good of the alliance. A stable and prosperous Europe in the 1960s was also one marked by divergent strategic views, and LBJ would be challenged by an increasingly fractious coalition, including a Gaullist France seeking to exclude America from the continent and a Great Britain wrestling with its own economic and strategic challenges. Most worrisome on this front was the temperament of West Germany, whose status was central to the whole arrangement. Would West Germany continue to accept its unusual status – an economic powerhouse, contributing to the defense of the West, with limits on its political sovereignty and access to military technology? The Johnson administration would often find itself vexed as it dealt with the grand strategic choices of its European partners, which were sometimes at odds with American preferences and interests.[9]

CHANGING LEADERS, SHIFTING POLICIES

Making the policy mix more combustible was the ever-changing leadership dynamic LBJ faced amongst his interlocutors. In the Soviet Union, the volatile Khrushchev involuntarily gave way to what appeared at first to

be a power-sharing arrangement with a troika of seemingly cautious bureaucrats, Premier Alexei Kosygin, Presidium Chairman Nikolai Podgorny,
and eventual leader of the pack, Leonid Brezhnev. Amongst the allies,
France was ruled by an imperious and, to Americans, often vexing Charles
de Gaulle, who appeared set on humiliating the president. Ironically,
however, President Johnson found even more challenges among the
leaders of nations with which, arguably, he shared more in common: the
United Kingdom and West Germany. Despite a political background
ostensibly aligned with the Labor Party, LBJ took a strong dislike to
Harold Wilson. In West Germany, the economist Ludwig Erhard struggled
to fill the shoes left by the country's commanding first chancellor, Konrad
Adenauer. Much of President Johnson's non-Vietnam foreign policy
agenda would be shaped by the need to manage the US–European alliance
in a time of challenge, brought on ironically by a decreased threat, and
interact with leaders whose own domestic constraints and different visions
of global politics generated deep problems.

Great Britain was the United States' closest ally during World War
II and in the postwar period. The relationship had not been without
its challenges, however. From concerns over nuclear cooperation to
the 1956 Suez fiasco, Anglo-American relations were often tested.
This was even more true during the Johnson presidency. There
were several factors at play. First was LBJ's simple dislike of Prime
Minister Wilson. This sentiment was exacerbated by Great Britain's
lack of overt support for America's policies in Southeast Asia. Larger,
structural forces also challenged the relationship. In the 1960s, Great
Britain found itself caught between roles. Its historical source of
great-power status, its colonial empire, was in the final stages of an
unraveling that had begun almost as soon as World War II was
finished. Especially challenging was the situation in Rhodesia (later
Zimbabwe). Nor had Great Britain embraced a continental role in
Europe, much to the annoyance of the United States. Britain still saw
its role as one of the Big Three powers that had won World War II,
with a special relationship with Washington, DC, and as a nation with
widespread global interests.

The most difficult aspect of the relationship, however, was Great
Britain's economic, financial, and monetary weakening. Great Britain's

currency, sterling, was overvalued for international exchanges and always under pressure. To the great frustration of the Johnson administration, the Wilson government was unwilling to reduce the domestic spending that many in the United States identified as the source of Britain's monetary weakness. Instead, Wilson sought to shrink or eliminate crucial overseas military commitments which the Johnson administration saw as vital to defense of the Western alliance. First, Great Britain brought back some of its forces stationed in West Germany. Second, it ended its strategic commitment "East of Suez," its global responsibility to contribute to Western security needs in the Middle East, South Asia, and East Asia. Both moves put unwanted pressure on US grand strategy. Facing its own balance of payments problems and seeking to reduce its military footprint in the Federal Republic of Germany, US decision-makers worried that a dramatic reduction in the British Army of the Rhine would further undermine West Germany's faith in NATO. Abandoning its commitment to the greater Middle East created a political vacuum there that worsened after the 1967 Six-Day War between Israel and its Arab neighbors, a situation the Johnson administration worried was ripe for Soviet exploitation.

Making matters worse was that even with these strategic reductions and America's own monetary woes, the Johnson administration had to come to the rescue of British sterling. Still, the Wilson government – despite promises to the contrary – was forced to devalue sterling in 1967, which unleashed forces that would put enormous pressure on the US dollar and the whole international monetary system.

For all the tensions – personal, economic, and strategic – within the US–UK relationship, they paled in comparison to the outright acrimony with President Charles de Gaulle's France (see Figure 10.1). De Gaulle had been a leader of France's government-in-exile during World War II, briefly led the nation after the end of the war, and returned to lead the new Fifth Republic in 1958. De Gaulle had always put the narrow interests of France – and hopes for a return to great-power status for his nation – above building transatlantic relations or supporting pan-European institutions. His recalcitrance throughout the Eisenhower and Kennedy administrations dramatically intensified during the Johnson presidency.

10.1. Momentarily setting aside their numerous disagreements, President Johnson and French President Charles de Gaulle shake hands on April 26, 1967, during funeral ceremonies in Bonn for former German Chancellor Konrad Adenauer. German President Heinrich Lübke stands between them.
Credit: Getty Images

De Gaulle worked actively to undermine America's policies, both in Europe and globally. On European security, he denigrated both NATO and America's commanding position in European security, while pushing against efforts to create a multilateral nuclear force and deal constructively with West Germany's nuclear aspirations. He ultimately pulled out of NATO's military apparatus and demanded American troops vacate France. While other Europeans were skeptical of the United States' war in Southeast Asia, few dared offer the kind of withering criticism that de Gaulle shared with the world. He sought to establish a relationship with Moscow independent of the Western alliance while recognizing the People's Republic of China's place as a global power. He worked actively against what he saw as the hegemony of the dollar within the Bretton Woods system, demanding gold for France's surplus dollars regardless of the potentially debilitating effects. The imperious French leader missed few opportunities to challenge America's policies and positions in the world.

Many American policymakers were furious with de Gaulle's obstreperous behavior and insisted the United States take revenge. President

Johnson, however, chose a wiser path. He understood that de Gaulle sought out clashes with the United States to burnish his own domestic standing and elevate the role of France in the world. LBJ avoided getting into what he colloquially called "pissing matches" with the French leader.

The most consequential European relationship – and in many ways the most complex during the Johnson presidency – was with the Federal Republic of Germany. During the Johnson presidency, West Germany, unlike France, did not directly challenge the United States. Nor, as a rising economic power, was it struggling with decline like Great Britain. Its unusual status in postwar Europe, however, created challenges.

The first challenge was on the leadership front. West Germany had been headed for its first fourteen years by Konrad Adenauer, a visionary statesman who helped navigate West Germany from its Nazi past to a more secure, democratic place within the Western alliance. The economist Ludwig Erhard had replaced Adenauer as chancellor in 1963 but lacked his predecessor's sure footing. Furthermore, US–German relations suffered from a variety of problems connected to the structural changes in Europe. On the security side, the Johnson administration's decisive shift to prioritizing nuclear nonproliferation meant that West Germany's ambitions for a role in NATO nuclear decision-making, if not an independent nuclear force akin to France's and Great Britain's, were pushed to the side by the United States. On the economic front, West Germany's extraordinary economic recovery had generated large balance of payments surpluses and dollar and gold holdings. The United States believed these surpluses both reflected the cost of America's security commitment and, if not managed, threatened the Bretton Woods monetary arrangements. The Johnson administration put enormous pressure on West Germany to "offset" these monetary costs through military purchases and a policy of not exchanging dollars for American gold. These security and economic tensions took place in a political environment where the Johnson administration shifted its focus to decreasing tensions with the Soviets, even at the expense of relations with its allies. The Soviet concern with the German problem meant American support for West Germany's long-held goal of reunification with East Germany would receive far less attention and explicit support. Tensions with the United States on a range of issues, from the balance of payments to the Nuclear Nonproliferation Treaty, were one factor that caused the Erhard government to fall, replaced by the so-called Grand Coalition led by Kurt Georg Kiesinger. In West Germany, some questioned the reliability or even the wisdom of the close partnership with the United States.

Leadership differences magnified the structural challenges the Johnson administration faced in Europe. There was an irony in this struggle: As tensions with the Soviets decreased on the continent after the earlier 1960s, there was bound to be more willingness on all sides to pursue their own interests at the expense of alliance solidarity. Europeans, for their part, understandably sought to increase their freedom of movement and shape policies outside of the shadow of the bipolar superpower contest. Any American effort to establish détente with the Soviet Union, however, could make America's European allies nervous that a superpower condominium would dictate their own political and security situation without their say. In other words, European states wanted the security of America's protection and support, while also preserving some measure of strategic autonomy.

The Johnson administration faced a domestic problem as well, as the developing great-power peace and easing of Cold War tensions would increase the pressure to bring American forces in Europe home. Either factor could upset the finely tuned approach to the potentially dangerous German question, which relied on a robust United States military commitment against a common foe.

The Johnson administration handled these tensions with its European allies with impressive tact. It avoided major confrontations and did not allow disputes like those with France to escalate to full rupture. It supported the continued development of the European Economic Community (EEC) to promote further economic integration (which it hoped would lead to further political integration), despite the fact it discriminated against US trade. Most importantly, it supported a major effort to reassess and reform the mission of NATO, the core transatlantic security institution. NATO had been buffeted by internal crises almost from its origins, with the departure of France and the questions over West Germany's status leading some to question its future. Initiated by Pierre

Harmel, a former Belgian minister of foreign affairs, the "Report of the Council on the Future Tasks of the Alliance," or the Harmel Report, sought to reinvigorate and refocus NATO at a time of drift and crisis. The report, issued in 1967, was a success. It accepted and encouraged the Western alliance to seek détente with the Soviet Union and Warsaw Pact even as it adapted its military strategies to maintain deterrence. The Harmel Report also called for increased consultations within the alliance to allow for greater coordination between the United States and its European allies. While the Johnson administration did not lead this effort, its support was crucial, guaranteeing NATO's survival and even increased relevance in the face of important international changes. Transatlantic relations were stabilized and reset to fit new circumstances, providing the solid foundation for them to remain constant to this day.

If the Johnson administration can be criticized for anything in its European relations, it might be that it did not better manage the opportunities created by waning Cold War tensions with the East. LBJ began a wise policy termed "bridge-building," which aimed through small measures to build independent ties with communist countries in Eastern Europe. Announced in a speech in October 1966, President Johnson called for Western policy to shift away from a "narrow concept of coexistence to the broader vision of peaceful engagement."[10] A variety of small initiatives were undertaken with the goal of improving relations with countries like Poland, Hungary, and Romania, and perhaps loosening their ties to the Soviet Union. Few substantial results emerged from this policy, however.

Nor did President Johnson bring about a fundamental reorientation of relations with the Soviet Union. There were important efforts to reduce nuclear dangers, and the Nuclear Nonproliferation Treaty was a signal success. But regional rivalries remained and, in some areas, such as the Middle East, they intensified. The 1967 mini-summit in Glassboro produced good press but few lasting results. The worsening American military situation in Vietnam prevented either superpower from taking too big a risk.

President Johnson and his foreign policy team navigated the structural changes in the Cold War in Europe with skill if not imagination. The Western alliance stayed together, despite fraying relations between the

United States and the key European states, Great Britain, France, and West Germany. The United States continued to support European integration and allowed the key security institution, NATO, to creatively adapt to a changing environment. These outcomes were not inevitable: it is not hard to imagine circumstances where structural forces and personality clashes might have deeply poisoned transatlantic relations and led to a rupture, even an end to NATO. Today, the European Union (EU) has expanded and deepened without sacrificing relations with the United States, while a reformed and expanded NATO remains the bedrock of European security. President Johnson deserves more credit than he is given for stabilizing the relationship during a difficult period.

LBJ's characteristic boldness, however, disappeared when it came to the Cold War writ large. The major changes in the ideological competition between the Soviet Union and the United States would not appear until LBJ's successor, Richard Nixon, took office. It is interesting to ask whether the bold moves taken by Nixon and his national security adviser, Henry Kissinger – détente, the quadripartite agreement over Berlin, the opening to China, summitry, and the Antiballistic Missile and Strategic Arms Limitation Treaties, the winding down and eventual end of America's military engagement in Southeast Asia – might have been available to President Johnson with more foresight and vision.

NEW GLOBAL CHALLENGES: MONEY AND BOMBS

The changing geopolitical landscape faced by the Johnson administration would have been challenging under normal circumstances. Ironically, relaxing Cold War tensions between the superpowers generated pressures within the Western alliance that demanded skilled diplomacy by President Johnson and his team. Powerful tectonic forces, driven by intensifying globalization, made the international system and in particular managing America's European partners even more complex.

Globalization is an awkward and blunt word to describe a complex historical process that was by no means new in the 1960s. Increasing ties between societies and political entities, advanced through the movement of peoples, ideas, and goods, is as old as history itself. What changed during the Johnson period, however, was the emergence of global challenges that were not only above the ability of singular states to solve but also had impacts that transcended borders. Issues like environmental degradation, global telecommunications, migration and demographic change, and resource scarcity were beginning to catch the consciousness of policymakers and the larger public.

Two global concerns presented especially sharp challenges: the nuclear question and the functioning of the international monetary system. In some ways, these appeared to be conventional policy challenges. Nuclear weapons and their role in the international system were matters of national security. The role of the dollar and gold were functions of the international economy, and foreign economic policy was a central concern of American foreign policy since the nation's founding. Under the surface, however, both of these challenges reflected the powerful new role global forces would play moving forward. More importantly, the issues of nuclear weapons and international monetary relations became intertwined and inseparable, both with each other and with more traditional geopolitical concerns, in ways few could have anticipated.

Two cataclysmic events hung over the decision-making of all American policymakers in the 1960s: the memory of the intertwined disasters of the Great Depression and World War II. Policymakers had a shared view of what caused each, and why the first catastrophe – a financial and monetary collapse – led to the second, a global conflagration. These historical memories often guided how American policymakers thought about the US balance of payments deficit and its impact on both economic and national security issues.

The shared consensus about the Great Depression held that untrammeled and "speculative" monetary flows, unregulated banking and markets, and price instability generated the crisis that led first to the collapse of the New York Stock Exchange and the banking crisis in the United States.[11] The response the United States and other countries offered to this initial crisis – trade protectionism and tariffs, deflationary monetary policies, and a failure to cooperate – generated what came to be known as "beggar thy neighbor" policies, wherein each state sought to protect its own economic interests at the expense of the world economy. The United States turned inward,

Great Britain closed its gold window, and nascent democracies that depended upon trade like Germany and Japan turned to autarky and authoritarianism. Autarky bred geopolitical competition, hyper-nationalism, and ideological extremes, leading in time to war. While the true story of the origins of the Great Depression and World War II are, in retrospect, more complex, this causal narrative shaped the plans for postwar economic order developed in the United States, Great Britain, and elsewhere. The result was the Bretton Woods monetary system, established in the summer of 1944.

The standard accounts describe Bretton Woods as both the birthplace of two pillars of the postwar economic order – the International Bank for Reconstruction and Development, or the World Bank, and the International Monetary Fund (IMF) – and the blueprint for stable inter-national monetary rules, practices, and relations. In truth, the system that emerged after World War II was a hodgepodge. Contrary to standard accounts, its goal was not to revitalize globalization; rather, the focus was on national reconstruction, regional economic integration, and stability. Global exchange rates were fixed, based on the convertibility of the US dollar into gold at $35 an ounce. But unlike the international gold standard of the late nineteenth and early twentieth centuries, national governments did not rush to deflate their economies if they lost gold or their own currency. The IMF helped bridge balance of payments gaps, as did large-scale American aid. Most countries, however, managed their currencies, and the major Western European currencies did not become convertible into dollars until 1958.

Around the same time West European currencies become convertible (and not unrelatedly), the United States began recording larger balance of payments deficits, with an outflow of its dollars and gold. There were a variety of reasons for these balance of payments deficits, but both the Eisenhower and Kennedy administrations focused on the foreign exchange costs of American troops and their families headquartered abroad. It was galling to both presidents that the states that were accumu-lating the most dollars and gold – France, Japan, and especially West Germany – were the main beneficiaries of American security guarantees and protection. Furthermore, both presidents were greatly worried that, if not tended to, the balance of payments deficit and the outflow of dollars and gold could affect both the US and global economies. Memories of the 1930s – when policymakers pursued deflationary monetary policies and protectionist trade policies to tamp down balance of payments deficits – haunted both presidents.

President Johnson inherited the balance of payments deficit, dollar and gold outflows, and a perceived threat to global monetary stability. As the president told Senate Minority Leader Everett Dirksen, "the biggest problem I have outside of Vietnam is balance of payments."[12] He also faced the same choices as Eisenhower and Kennedy – redeployments, restrictions, or reform. LBJ – unlike Eisenhower and Kennedy – revealed little enthusiasm, at least initially, to remove troops from abroad for balance of payments purposes. The administration believed this move would send the wrong message to both European allies and the Soviet Union. Nor was the president interested in restrictions. The Kennedy administration had explored a variety of implicit and explicit capital account and trade controls to limit the dollar and gold outflow. Johnson, however, sought to expand global trade and, with it, the American economy. As Daniel Sargent has argued, LBJ would not "put the cause of monetary equilibrium ahead of his political goals."[13] This left reform as the only option. As he did in other areas of policy, Johnson abandoned his predecessor's more cautious approach for bolder proposals, for both good and ill.

Hints of American reform could be found in various interagency and international reports: the G-10 had produced a study on ways to increase global liquidity, while the United States created both a Long-Range International Payments Committee and a Report on Foreign Economic Policy chaired by former National Security Council staffer Carl Kaysen. The American reports understandably focused on the need for currency surplus countries, especially the Europeans, to manage their reserve dollars, perhaps with bonds, and not turn them into gold. This position, unpopular with the allies, took a hit when French President Charles de Gaulle decided to declare war on the American dollar in February 1965. The French charged that the dollar possessed "exorbitant privilege" in a system that "has enabled the United States to be indebted to foreign countries free of charge." De Gaulle played into European fears that America's deficit dollars were being used to purchase continental companies on the cheap and avoid disciplining their own economy. De Gaulle's call to rely on gold alone – and completely exclude the dollar as a reserve currency – was seen as a great threat to both America's position and the Bretton Woods system.

Johnson's secretary of treasury, Henry Fowler, responded with a bold plan for reform in a speech in Hot Springs, Virginia, the following summer. The most innovative recommendation was the creation of a new kind of international reserve, Special Drawing Rights (SDRs), that could supplement and, in some ways, replace gold. This would help achieve LBJ's goal of increasing, not decreasing, global liquidity, while avoiding measures that would restrict the American economy, limit overseas investment, or force a reduction in forces stationed abroad. The announcement, while derided in France and viewed with curiosity, if not skepticism, elsewhere in Europe, was widely hailed in the United States.

The Johnson administration's bold plan for reform and its effort to fight off de Gaulle's scheme might have worked if not for a few factors. When Fowler announced his plan in 1965, America's balance of payments deficit had markedly improved since the Kennedy and Eisenhower years. The situation, however, was soon to get worse: The costs of Vietnam, the Great Society, and ensuing inflationary pressures led, over the next three years, to ballooning dollar and gold outflows and an increased sense of crisis. Most alarming, however, was the deteriorating status of Great Britain's currency, sterling, mentioned earlier.

Why was sterling's weakness a danger to the dollar, and ultimately to the international monetary system? Sterling had been, throughout much of the nineteenth and early twentieth centuries, the primary global reserve currency and the foundation for global monetary relations. Two costly world wars, depression, a messy process of decolonization, and declining economic productivity weakened the currency. Yet many states that had once been part of Great Britain's former empire held the currency, whether willingly, though persuasion, or under pressure, and its convertibility was seen as a backstop to gold and the dollar as a source of international liquidity. But if its weakness was exposed, government and private actors would turn in their pounds for dollars or even gold, leaving the dollar open to attack.

The Johnson administration worked hard to get the British to improve their economic performance and rein in their own balance of payments deficit, while also reluctantly offering aid packages in 1964, 1965, and 1966 to stave off a devaluation of the pound. The Wilson government failed to correct the underlying weaknesses that created the British deficit, and when the 1967 war in the Middle East challenged access to the Suez Canal and the security of global oil supplies, the pressure on sterling became unrelenting. In November 1967, the British devalued the pound sterling from $2.80 to $2.40. With sterling weakened, capital markets turned next against the dollar.

The Johnson administration worked vigorously to protect the dollar, strong-arming European central banks into cooperation while announcing a strong balance of payments program on January 1, 1968, that included capital controls. At first the markets rallied, until images of the Tet Offensive, launched at the end of January, revealed how poorly the war in Vietnam was going. American gold drained from the treasury at an alarming pace, until Great Britain, at the request of the United States, closed the gold market. The administration called for an emergency conference for the middle of March 1968. A two-tiered market for gold was created, separating the private and the central bank market for gold, with the latter agreeing to stabilize the system. It was a temporary reprieve – a little more than four years later, President Nixon formally ended dollar–gold convertibility and allowed currency rates to be set by the open market. By 1969, however, this outcome, while in the future, was nearly a foregone conclusion, and the Johnson administration had neither achieved reform nor avoided restrictions to save the Bretton Woods system.

The administration did, however, avoid major redeployments. On one level, this is surprising – the balance of payments costs of American troops stationed abroad had long been identified as an ideal target to solve the monetary problems, especially as those forces were protecting countries that ran the largest deficits. In the end, however, international monetary issues were intertwined with the defense of Europe, the stability of West Germany, and nuclear nonproliferation. In a newly globalized era, LBJ appreciated that these issues could not be disconnected from each other. The Johnson administration ultimately stabilized and balanced all three concerns – the defense of Europe, limiting the spread of nuclear weapons, and improving America's foreign economic policies. Furthermore, and unlike his hero FDR, LBJ resisted the powerful temptation to turn away from the world to satisfy domestic concerns. The president kept a strong troop presence in Europe while working to maintain stable international monetary relations, precedents that served the United States well in future decades.

THE NUCLEAR QUESTION

To understand LBJ's reluctance to withdraw troops from NATO, one must understand the role nuclear weapons played in US grand strategy. Nuclear weapons presented both challenges and opportunities for American policymakers.[14] America's early monopoly and lead in nuclear weapons allowed it to defend far-flung allies and secure its strategic position in both Europe and East Asia without bankrupting the treasury with expensive and domestically unsustainable troop deployments abroad. American presidents, starting with Truman, put nuclear weapons at the center of their grand strategies. Doing this, however, generated difficulties. First, after the Truman administration used nuclear weapons against two Japanese cities in August 1945, their future was hard to fathom. The murderous destruction against civilians seemed unthinkable, a concern that only increased with the development of thermonuclear weapons in 1952, weapons whose destructive power was orders of magnitude larger than the bombs dropped on Hiroshima and Nagasaki. Second, once the Soviets developed their own atomic and thermonuclear weapons, along with an ability to use them in response to an attack by the United States, it was hard to imagine scenarios where the United States would be willing to employ them.

Despite being a core part of American grand strategy, nuclear weapons presented unique global challenges. The four-year impasse over Berlin's status (1958–62) and the October 1962 standoff over Soviet missiles in Cuba highlighted the increasing danger that a crisis could escalate into a nuclear war. Even absent a war, the Johnson administration inherited expensive and destabilizing nuclear arms races, both between the superpowers and through the proliferation of nuclear weapons to new states. To President Johnson's credit, he put questions surrounding nuclear weapons at the top of his agenda. As Thomas Schwartz has argued, historians "have not fully recognized the degree to which the Johnson administration was determined to reduce the threat of war with the Soviet Union from the very beginning and how this overriding objective influenced his foreign policy decisions."[15]

This desire to ease nuclear dangers took several forms. First, the Johnson administration explored a number of arms control arrangements. Both the United States and the Soviet Union agreed to freeze and reduce the production of fissionable materials. In early 1966, the superpowers concluded an agreement, the "Treaty on Principles Governing the Activities of States in the Exploration and Use of Outer Space, Including the Moon and Other Celestial Bodies," also known as the Outer Space Treaty, limiting the militarization of space. Led by the United States, NATO adjusted its strategy to rely less on the early and massive use of nuclear weapons in its defense of Western Europe to produce a more flexible, less immediately escalatory response. Secretary of Defense Robert McNamara resisted intense pressure from both the Joint Chiefs of Staff and Congress to deploy several expensive new nuclear weapons systems while slowing the increases in the size of America's strategic nuclear forces. Resources were put into fortifying US command-and-control capabilities, as well as improving nuclear safety measures. President Johnson 's boldest and most consequential efforts ran along two lines: limitations on strategic nuclear arms and missile defenses, and nuclear nonproliferation.

The administration had tried to negotiate strategic arms limitations throughout its tenure. In 1966 and 1967, these efforts intensified with exchanges of letters. The key issue was missile defense; pressure from the US Congress and public opinion was forcing the administration to consider the Nike-X antiballistic missile system. Led by McNamara, the administration doubted its effectiveness and cost, while worrying it could intensify the arms race. Ultimately, McNamara announced in a September 1967 speech that the United States would deploy a limited force, an awkward compromise that satisfied few. Discussions on limiting offensive strategic forces made greater progress, and in the summer of 1968, LBJ was set to hold a summit with the Soviet leadership with the goal of a major arms control treaty. The Soviet suppression of the protests in Czechoslovakia, however, forced him to forgo that effort. While President Johnson did not, in the end, succeed in achieving a strategic arms control treaty, the work of his administration laid the groundwork for the successful negotiations that would lead, eventually, to the foundational Antiballistic Missile and Strategic Arms Limitation (SALT) treaties in 1972.

The Johnson administration's greatest success in the nuclear realm – and arguably its greatest and longest-lasting foreign policy success – was in nuclear nonproliferation. In many ways, the global nuclear nonproliferation regime constructed by LBJ is both taken for granted and underappreciated. If you had told any smart observer in late 1963, when President Johnson took over the presidency, that sixty years later the number of nuclear weapons states remained in the single digits (and that nuclear weapons had not been used in battle), they would have been deeply skeptical but thrilled. That good outcome, however, was not inevitable; it involved difficult and bold choices by the president.

The turning-point in the debate came after the People's Republic of China detonated an atomic device in October 1964. Mao's China was seen as the ultimate rogue state, far more dangerous and potentially irrational than the Soviet Union. A select committee, chaired by former Undersecretary of Defense Roswell Gilpatric, issued a controversial report to the president in January 1965 that recommended a bold shift in policy to make nuclear nonproliferation a grand strategic priority. Many foreign policy officials inside and outside the government – including Secretary of State Dean Rusk and "wise man" John McCloy – were adamantly against the report's recommendations, which suggested cooperating with the Soviet Union, even at the expense of close allies who were interested in the bomb, to limit the spread of nuclear arms. Their more conventional position was understandable. At what point in modern history had any state or organization been able to stop independent states from acquiring a military technology that aided their security? Such a strategy risked not only failure, but as Americans had learned when trying to limit France's earlier nuclear ambitions, risked unnecessarily alienating foreign governments.

The United States and the Soviet Union began to explore a nonproliferation treaty with message exchanges. There were high obstacles, however. First, the United States had to convince its allies to accept its negotiating position; the French were opposed, the West Germans deeply concerned, and many others, ranging from Italy to Australia, were unconvinced. What would be the status of the Multilateral Force – a multinational, shared nuclear weapons capability – that would include West Germany and allow it to feel as if it was a fuller participant in NATO's nuclear decision-making? Would any effort to craft a Nuclear Nonproliferation Treaty (NPT) forever forestall any effort at a collective European nuclear force? What entity would be responsible for nuclear safeguards and inspections?

In the summer of 1965, the United States introduced a draft treaty to the Eighteen Nation Committee on Disarmament (ENCD), the United Nations entity created to deal with arms control. US diplomats spent much of the next two years navigating the complexities of nonproliferation amongst American allies, especially West Germany. By 1966, the Soviet Union had reluctantly agreed that NATO's Nuclear Planning Group – an entity created to allow the alliance's non-nuclear states to be briefed and consulted on nuclear matters – would not violate a future treaty. A joint superpower treaty was presented to the ENCD on August 24, 1966. A variety of difficult issues remained, and the Johnson administration continued to aggressively pursue negotiations with its allies and the Soviets to resolve the remaining issues. Ultimately, the United States, the Soviet Union, and Great Britain signed the treaty on July 1, 1968, opening the way for nations around the world to accede to it. Though rarely making headlines, the NPT is the most important nuclear arms control agreement ever crafted, with enormous consequences for global peace. It was neither easy nor inevitable, and President Johnson deserves far more credit than he typically receives for his controversial commitment to its negotiation and completion.

MANAGING ISSUES TRADITIONAL AND NEW

When the Johnson administration took the dramatic decision to make inhibiting the spread of nuclear weapons a top grand strategy priority, his choice generated sharp tensions, both inside his own government and with some allies. The Federal Republic of Germany was a primary focus of this nonproliferation effort, which irritated the West German government. West Germany had expressed interest in, if not their own independent nuclear weapon, then at least access to the bomb. Various efforts to facilitate this access – namely, the Multilateral Force – had foundered. An American–Soviet deal, made over their heads, to prevent them from acquiring the bomb, while doing nothing to facilitate German reunification, was a bitter pill to swallow.

To make matters worse, the West Germans had accumulated the largest surplus of US dollars. During the Kennedy administration, West Germany had agreed to fully offset its deficit by purchasing American military equipment, but Chancellor Erhard saw this arrangement as too onerous and tried to leave the deal. President Johnson, adhering to the advice of his secretary of treasury and secretary of defense, took a hardline position, which created a crisis that helped lead to Erhard's demise. The new government, the so-called Grand Coalition, made clear it would not continue the full offset deal. Would the United States withdraw its military forces in response? Making matters worse, the British government, facing its own balance of payments crisis, threated to pull out any of its military forces whose costs were not fully offset. In the context of de Gaulle's attacks on NATO and the United States, and the increasing isolationism of the American public driven by the worsening situation in Vietnam, the nexus between the balance of payments, conventional troop commitments, and the nuclear question created a crisis that threatened to unravel the postwar alliance.

Johnson responded by tapping distinguished "wise man" John McCloy to lead talks between the United States, Great Britain, and West Germany. Choosing McCloy demonstrated Johnson's willingness to consult with prestigious statesmen when navigating foreign policy. The negotiations were difficult: the United States wanted to protect its own monetary position, but not at the expense of unravelling the alliance. While removing American troops would be the easiest solution to the balance of payments situation, it would undermine West Germany's faith in the US commitment to defend it at the same time that it was asking the divided nation to swallow the bitter pill of non-nuclear status. Furthermore, the British, facing their own monetary difficulties, could not be allowed to abandon Western Europe.

In the end, a deal was cut. The West Germans agreed to formally commit to holding dollars and not to turn them in for gold, making explicit their practice of the past few years. The United States joined with

West Germany to alleviate British balance of payments deficits. Both the United States and Great Britain removed some forces, but this move was justified not as an economic necessity but as a redeployment based on a dramatically reduced threat of a Soviet invasion. Most importantly, while the United States continued to work with the Soviet Union on nuclear nonproliferation, West Germany and the United States reaffirmed their commitment to the NATO alliance and each other.

The Trilateral Negotiations of 1966–67 are rarely mentioned in histories of the period and are barely remembered. Yet they revealed the Johnson administration's deft handling of a series of problems that came together to generate a crisis. Two traditional challenges, a splintering alliance and the rise of Gaullist attacks on the United States, combined with increased isolationism and calls for the return of American troops by Congress, joined with two novel, transnational challenges, international monetary instability and nuclear proliferation, to shake the very foundation of the Cold War Western alliance. It requires little imagination to see that one, a combination, or all of these challenges could have led to an American retreat from the continent, a collapse of NATO, or a resurgent and unhealthy German nationalism. The Johnson administration avoided these calamities, while revealing how new, global issues could combine with traditional power-political competition to generate unsettling challenges. As Thomas Schwartz has argued, "Lyndon Johnson guided the United States with a policy that balanced the solidarity of the Western alliance with the need to stabilize the Cold War and reduce the nuclear danger."[16] Given the prominence of the Vietnam War, this deft diplomacy by the Johnson administration, which helped stabilize transatlantic relations through the end of the Cold War and beyond, has often been underappreciated.

CONCLUSION

President Lyndon Johnson and his administration are rarely lauded for their foreign policy accomplishments. The legacy of the disastrous war in Vietnam correctly overshadows all other successes and failures.

This judgment, however, should be tempered by several considerations. First, LBJ inherited a transatlantic alliance that was teetering. The leading countries of Europe, in particular France, Great Britain, and West Germany, presented personal leadership challenges and moved to pursue their own narrow interests, often at the expense of the alliance and the United States. These problems arose at a time when, ironically, the decreased threat from the Soviet Union weakened the bonds that kept these disparate countries together. Johnson demonstrated foresight and balanced restraint to maintain a teetering alliance, creating a firmer foundation for NATO that allows it to remain the key instrument of European security half a century later. Second, new global issues emerged, challenges that were not easy to understand or ameliorate through traditional paradigms, politics, or institutions. The 1960s saw many such challenges, but two stood out – nuclear weapons and globalized money. Sometimes, as with the question of nuclear proliferation, LBJ successfully crafted bold, innovative solutions. The Nuclear Nonproliferation Treaty remains the most important and lasting arms control treaty of any type ever negotiated. We live in a world with far fewer nuclear weapons states and less likelihood of nuclear war because of President Johnson's difficult but bold policy choices. On other issues, such as the strategic arms limitation treaty or the reform of the international monetary system, the administration did not, in its own time, solve the underlying problems. In both cases, however, the Johnson administration set the stage for many of the policy responses that were to be embraced, first by Nixon, and then future presidential administrations. Johnson laid the foundations for the Nixon administration to implement both the SALT Treaty and the August 15, 1971 decision to end the link between the US dollar and gold.

LBJ deftly navigated between the traditional Cold War issues and these new challenges surrounding international monetary relations and nuclear weapons. He maintained the Western alliance despite great pressure; by the end of his term, NATO not only was still together but was re-animated by a new strategic concept that was to guide it through the end of the Cold War and beyond. Relations with the Soviets stabilized and even improved. None of these accomplishments makes up for disastrous decision-making in Southeast Asia. It is important to remember, however, how hard it is to make successful grand strategy, and in the complex and dangerous world LBJ faced, that things easily could have turned out much worse.

CHAPTER 11

"Through a Narrow Glass": Compassion, Power, and Lyndon Johnson's Struggle to Make Sense of the Third World

Sheyda Jahanbani

Nations sink when they see [their] interest only through a narrow glass.

Lyndon B. Johnson, Annual Message to the Congress
on the State of the Union, January 12, 1966

To understand the legacies of LBJ's presidency for how we think about the so-called "Third World," let us travel back to a bitterly cold day in central Texas in 1973. Just ten days before his weary heart gave its last, a visibly ailing Lyndon Baines Johnson found himself sitting across from Walter Cronkite for the last time. The conversation centered on the evolution of LBJ's attitudes and policies on civil rights. Contrary to his previous appearances, in which he had predictably oscillated between blandishment, defensiveness, and outright intimidation, this LBJ was thoughtful and open. Between coughing fits, a surprisingly honest Johnson shared regrets about his timidity on the issue of Black civil rights in his years in the Senate. "I took my own rights for granted and I did not see and feel and was not as concerned with my fellow man as I later became," he readily admitted. He expressed his deep appreciation for the efforts of Black leaders to teach him and, eventually, to trust him. Perhaps most surprisingly, he sympathized with Black Americans' impatience with the pace of change, even the far-reaching laws he had enacted as president. In this conversation, in short, we witness something rather unusual in political history: an opportunity to see a man of power express genuine compassion for people on the margins of political power and reflect upon his own limitations in feeling and acting upon it.[1]

The humble tone of LBJ's words – the last he would utter to the nation he had once led – hardly seems fitting for a man well known for his domineering style. But half a century later, in an era in which compassion seems to be dangerously undervalued in American political life, LBJ's capacity for humility seems worthy of thoughtful consideration. Indeed, compassion was a central part of his political identity, driving at least in part many of the hundreds of pieces of legislation he initiated to aid poor and marginalized Americans. Evidenced by those policy achievements, we see the wisdom in the observation of LBJ's foremost biographer, Robert Caro, who writes that Johnson possessed "a rare capacity to make compassion meaningful."[2]

And yet what is most striking about his last exchange with Cronkite to a scholar of US foreign relations is that there is no analog on the subject of Johnson's policies toward the poor and marginalized abroad. Of course, he had done an obligatory hour with the veteran newsman on the war in Vietnam, but the LBJ who showed up for that conversation had been combative, defensive, and frustrated. Why? Where was the disconnect for Johnson between the struggles of the marginalized at home and those of the peasants of Southeast Asia?

Lyndon Johnson, perhaps more than any other president before or since, was confronted with the enormous challenge of representing liberal democracy at a moment in which billions of people were sorting through the wreckage left behind by four centuries of domination and exploitation. Yet he seemed to have little capacity to empathize with the struggles of relatively powerless people beyond his own shores. Would the tragedy of his war in Vietnam – and, by extension, his domestic policies – have turned out differently had he been able to do so? Could the death and destruction caused by Richard Nixon's continuation of the war in Southeast Asia have been avoided? Would the United States have been able to use its global leadership to ensure a more genuinely democratic world? We are left to wonder.

That Johnson could not marry his capacity for compassion with his global ambitions more successfully was not for want of trying. He proposed a global analog to his Great Society, promising that the United

States would lead a worldwide war on hunger, disease, and ignorance for the benefit of all. But he often chose to deploy the power of the United States to pursue immediate national security objectives no matter the cost to the long-term cause of promoting democracy, putting the need for stability before the principle of self-determination. Why did LBJ hold these priorities?

In this essay, I seek to answer that question by exploring the impact that Johnson's personality and worldview had on his approach to the Third World. Elevating the significance of any one individual's temperament and perspective as causal factors in history can lead to simplistic conclusions, but deploying this method here may offer insight precisely because little else explains the rather wild fluctuations of Johnson's approach. His predecessor's policies had been no more coherent. Over his 1,000 days in office, John F. Kennedy and his aides experimented with a mixed bag of policies toward the various countries of the decolonizing world. What was consistent, however, was Kennedy's process: he welcomed debate among his advisers and relied on his own pragmatism when the time came to make decisions.[3] Moreover, as historians Robert Rakove and Fredrik Logevall have demonstrated, Kennedy possessed a defter understanding of decolonization as a world historical process owing to both his Irish heritage and his wide-ranging travels in the 1950s.[4]

LBJ inherited Kennedy's assortment of policies and programs but neither the process by which Kennedy determined them nor the historical consciousness that framed his thinking. In the Oval Office, Johnson had no appetite for hosting debate sessions. He rarely questioned the advice of trusted experts. He took criticism personally and often cast even mild dissenters out from his inner circle – and his political instincts made him chronically impatient. These factors mattered when it came to his policies toward the Third World. Yet Johnson's capacity for compassion meant that, despite his insensitivity to the historical significance of decolonization or the ideological complexities of revolutionary nationalism, he did feel deeply for the poor and marginalized in the Third World and wanted to find ways to improve their lives.

With the exception of Caro and authors of a few sentimental accounts, scholars of LBJ's presidency have not attended overly much to how his sensitivity to the needs and desires of common people shaped the foreign policy he worked to build; nor have they scrutinized his failures of compassion.[5] Yet Johnson *himself* wanted us to judge him by this standard. "This administration is going to be a compassionate administration," he declared in January of 1964.[6] So, as we consider the characteristics of "LBJ's America" in this volume, we should not overlook this important part of the story of Lyndon Johnson and the legacy he left behind. In his 1966 State of the Union address, in which he sought to parry criticism of his plans to spend more money on both his global Great Society and the war in Vietnam, LBJ asserted that *both* were in the national interest because doing good and doing well should not be mutually exclusive. "Nations sink," he warned, "when they see that interest only through a narrow glass."[7] No president can lead entirely based on sentiment, of course, but great leaders can expand the way citizens understand their own national interests. Johnson earnestly endeavored to do just that. At home, these efforts resulted in a human rights revolution. In the Third World, however, he never found a way to see through anything but that narrow glass for very long. To be fair, few leaders have. Where we need their vision the most, even our most compassionate leaders seem unwilling to help us see our national interests more expansively. That the American people allowed George W. Bush, the self-styled "compassionate conservative," and Barack Obama, whose own father came from one of those postcolonial societies, to replicate LBJ's disastrous war in Vietnam in Iraq and Afghanistan two decades later should, I think, tell us something about how, in this respect at least, LBJ's America remains the only America we have.

A GREAT SOCIETY FOR THE WORLD?

While Lyndon Johnson may not have been as adept at presidential speechmaking as John F. Kennedy, he articulated a soaring vision of what a compassionate global foreign policy might look like, and he worked to fulfill the promise of American largesse. As LBJ declared to India's ambassador to the US in the autumn of 1965, "what I am doing in this country this year, I would like to do worldwide. My foreign policy is the Great Society."[8] Later, he made the point publicly. "We mean to show that our dream of a great society does not stop at the water's edge, that it is not just an American dream. All are welcome to share in it and all are invited to contribute to it. The most urgent work of our times – the most urgent work of all time – is to give that dream reality."[9] These were not empty words. Throughout his presidency, even as the war in Vietnam began to consume more and more of his attention, Johnson pledged himself to building a global Great Society. His administration pioneered innovative efforts to promote economic development, better health, more accessible education, and an end to hunger throughout the Third World. From his earliest days in politics, Johnson hewed to the principle that government could and should serve human interests, especially in a country as wealthy as the United States. As such, he adopted Franklin Delano Roosevelt's more expansive conception of national security, one that promoted an activist role for the state in advancing the general welfare of all.[10] This objective became the consensus view among liberal internationalists after 1945, inspiring the Marshall Plan, as well as Harry Truman's promise to provide technical assistance to the postcolonial countries and a host of other foreign aid endeavors. In 1960, John F. Kennedy placed special emphasis on the imperative to alleviate poverty in the decolonizing world, making it a central objective of his foreign policy. Johnson dreamt of outshining both his mentor and his predecessor.

The first pillar of LBJ's global Great Society was economic development. As Kennedy's vice president, Johnson had provided some of the most persuasive arguments both to and on behalf of the world's poor. In goodwill tours to Asia, Africa, and the Middle East, Johnson made a point of talking to everyday people about their struggles (see Figure 11.1). Whether it was stopping by a fruit stand in Beirut to talk to a teenage boy selling watermelons or telling a fisherman in a Senegalese village about how he understood their plight because of his experiences with rural poverty in Texas – he often quoted statistics about rural poverty in his home state – LBJ promoted the kind of development that he believed in, a commonsensical approach rooted in satisfying the bread-and-butter needs of struggling people.

Although some in the Kennedy administration thought Johnson's style artless, no less than Walt W. Rostow, JFK's deputy national security adviser

11.1. During a May 1961 trip to India, Vice President Lyndon Johnson showed his usual enthusiasm for mingling with poor people in Third World nations. He gives away a ballpoint pen during a stop at a village near Agra.
Credit: US Embassy New Delhi

and perhaps the foremost expert on economic development in the government, identified Johnson as the man who made "the best single speech on foreign aid I've ever heard by anyone."[11] In that speech, given to a group of American advertising executives, LBJ shared his insight into the needs of the world's poor. "About all the average fellow wants," he told the assembled men:

> is a chance to work from daylight to dark, to provide some food for the stomachs of his children, some clothes for their backs, and a roof over their heads and a place for them to worship in, maybe a little recreation, and to maintain the freedom and dignity of the individual. . .. I believe all those people that I saw in Africa and Asia want the same thing.[12]

As Rostow saw it, Johnson's message was effective precisely because it was rooted in personal experience. "He made the link between what he had seen in our own country and seen as a young man in Texas with these poor people out in Asia. And he spoke of how much could be done in the span of one man's lifetime."

While he never seems to have explored the complexities of development theory or practice with the eggheads he inherited from Kennedy, Johnson, as president, possessed some confidence that he knew what they were talking about; he had, after all, spent three decades "developing" a backward part of the United States. From his experience in the South, he believed that the greatest obstacle to economic growth was the problem of untapped resources. He had witnessed the transformative power of the New Deal state's development programs like the Tennessee Valley Authority and wanted to build similar programs abroad.[13]

Johnson also believed that, deep down, poor people everywhere were guided by the same motives and wanted the same things from politicians. "To Johnson," Doris Kearns Goodwin wrote, "there were foreign customs, foreign religions, foreign governments, but there were no foreign cultures, only different ways of pursuing universal desires – in this case, the transition from rags to riches."[14] Government could provide the capital and the technology to unleash the power of human and natural resources for the betterment of the Third World, just as it had done in the South. He believed in this mission deeply. Historian Nick Cullather tells us that "as much as Johnson disdained the intellectual theorizing that surrounded development policy, he was powerfully drawn to its visionary ambition."[15]

For LBJ, these principles manifested most fully in the Peace Corps. Although John F. Kennedy's profile graces Norman Rockwell's Peace Corps painting, Lyndon Johnson considered the Corps one of the crowning jewels of his global Great Society. Perhaps because the Peace Corps bore such a strong resemblance to FDR's National Youth Administration (NYA) and reminded LBJ of the transformative year he spent as the NYA's Texas director, he supported it with a kind of enthusiasm and commitment that he mustered only rarely during his tenure as vice president.[16] One of JFK's signal promises to young voters on the campaign trail in 1960, the idea had originally been Senator Hubert Humphrey's (D-Minnesota). Kennedy had adopted it in his stump speeches to energize college students. Even in brief sketch, the Peace

Corps became so popular that Kennedy had no choice but to follow through on establishing it as a program, which he did by Executive Order in March 1961.[17] What form the Peace Corps would take after that was not JFK's concern. Surprisingly, it was Johnson's. When the Peace Corps' first director, Sargent Shriver, faced pressure from Kennedy and his cabinet to place the Peace Corps under the aegis of the State Department, it was Lyndon Johnson who steeled his spine in defending the program's independence. When Shriver's entreaties to Kennedy faltered, it was Johnson who personally lobbied the president – something he almost never did – to maintain the Peace Corps' autonomy. And when Shriver, preparing to navigate the legislation establishing the Corps as an independent agency through Congress, found himself abandoned by an irritated JFK, LBJ helped him find a safe route through the Capitol's perilous waters.[18] In doing so, he became, in Shriver's words, a "founding father" of the program.[19]

From his first days as vice president to his last as president, LBJ kept his eye on the Peace Corps, offering his support when it was needed and boasting its achievements when he felt all else might be lost.[20] Johnson's war in Vietnam diminished the popularity of the Peace Corps and shrank the size of its volunteer army.[21] Yet its example still inspired *him*. In his last months as president, he was still willing to talk to advisers about ways to build on the Corps' success. Even in March of 1968, surrounded by the ruins of his global Great Society and a growing sense that his presidency would fail, Johnson pointed to the Peace Corps as an enduring symbol of the future in which he still believed. "If you would confirm your faith in the American future," he told Congress, "take a look at the Peace Corps."[22]

Beyond development, Johnson showed real perspicacity about the emergence of social problems that explicitly transcended national boundaries.[23] In January 1966, he stood before both houses of Congress at the rostrum of the House chamber and promised to "conduct a worldwide attack on the problems of hunger and disease and ignorance."[24] Although his level of interest in addressing these problems waxed and waned depending upon what other preoccupations demanded his attention, Johnson consistently articulated them as explicitly global and directed his administration to explore solutions that could benefit the Third World, as well as align with long-term US national security objectives. Johnson proposed three pieces of legislation to address the problems he enumerated in that speech: the International Health Act, the International Education Act, and the Food for Freedom Act. All these proposals created new administrative capacities within the US state to fight global social problems, and all were built, at least to some extent, on the Peace Corps model that Johnson so admired.

The second pillar of his global Great Society was his campaign to improve public health worldwide. In the words of historian Erez Manela, LBJ's decision to eradicate smallpox "may well have been one of the administration's most significant decisions in terms of its global human impact."[25] It was also one of his most personal. On one of his goodwill tours as vice president, Johnson observed the ravages of disease on poor communities in the Global South firsthand. Having invited his longtime physician and friend, James Cain, to join the trip, Johnson requested that Cain produce a memorandum outlining the most pressing health challenges in the underdeveloped countries.[26] That report left a lasting impression. International organizations had been building an administrative and technical infrastructure to identify and treat infectious diseases such as measles, smallpox, and polio since the 1920s without much support from the US government. In 1964, Johnson declared his intention to join a United Nations initiative – the International Year of Cooperation – and devote the resources of the US government to eradicating smallpox around the world.[27] "Smallpox," historian Scott Reinhardt explains, "presented itself as the perfect target for the ambitions of Johnson's Global Great Society: a universal disease subject to the powers of universal liberalism."[28]

A year later, Johnson proposed an International Health Act (IHA) to formally globalize the Great Society's health and nutrition programs. Congress balked at this ambitious proposal and killed the IHA before it got to the floor. Johnson grew less patient with international partners whose support for American foreign policy might not be total. Yet the foundation that international health advocates had built, coupled with the wheels Johnson had put into motion, enabled the smallpox campaign to carry on apace. By 1979, the World Health Assembly declared smallpox to be eradicated. Johnson's decisive support played an enormous role in that species-wide achievement.

Befitting Johnson's formative experience as a schoolteacher in Cotulla, Texas, education became the third pillar of his Global Great Society. Starting in 1964, he pursued legislation that pumped vast new investments into early childhood, elementary, secondary, and higher education at home.[29] But his ambitions went beyond those reforms. In January 1966, he proposed the International Education Act (IEA). Developed by education leaders in the US from both the public and private sectors, the IEA promised more robust programs to enhance knowledge of foreign languages and cultures in US schools, enable greater cooperation and exchange between American universities and institutions of higher education abroad, and offer technical expertise to educators in the Third World. The IEA also established an "Exchange Peace Corps," in which teachers from developing countries would be given an opportunity to teach American schoolchildren their languages.[30] The IEA passed both houses of Congress without fanfare – the *New York Times* called it the "least discussed piece of legislation passed by Congress this year" – and was signed into law by LBJ in October 1966, but bizarrely funds were never appropriated to enable the policies.[31] As one of the education experts working on the bill explained, Johnson made a few high-profile speeches but was otherwise too "distracted and tired by reason of the war" to expend much energy seeing the proposal through.[32] Despite its fate, the IEA represented one of the boldest of Johnson's global welfare proposals. That it languished in the no-man's land between the executive and legislative branches, signed into law but unfunded, and that Johnson made no meaningful effort to bridge that gap, reveals much about the fate of his overarching vision for the world's poor.[33]

The final pillar of Johnson's global Great Society was an attack on hunger. "Food for Freedom" had its origins in the Food for Peace program that Johnson's vice president, Hubert Humphrey, had championed in the Senate in the 1950s. For farm state internationalists like Humphrey, the American tradition of offering food aid to hungry nations took care of two problems at once: surplus crops that reduced the price of food US farmers could earn at home, and humanitarian crises abroad that threatened to cause political instability. Public Law 480, as the law became known, proved, in historian Kristin Ahlberg's words, that "self-interest and altruism were not mutually exclusive."[34] As one of the most ardent liberals in the Senate, Humphrey spent the Eisenhower years working to improve the program's capacity to serve US foreign policy toward the decolonizing world. When JFK was elected, Humphrey found a benefactor for the program. Kennedy expanded Food for Peace and appointed George McGovern, one of Humphrey's fellow prairie liberals, to run it.

The program earned enthusiastic support from Lyndon Johnson, for whom the simplicity of feeding hungry people held great appeal. Indeed, Johnson embraced the program so warmly that, when it came up for reauthorization during his presidency, he sought to further expand it as an explicitly humanitarian undertaking rather than a way to manage domestic surpluses. Johnson took a personal role in developing the legislation. He saw the initiative as a way to enact more effective development programs. Offering food aid to developing countries could serve as a carrot to encourage foreign governments to implement sometimes politically painful agricultural reforms. In the war on hunger, "the key to victory," Johnson explained, "is self-help."[35] This was not a new concept in foreign aid, but Johnson's insistence on using food aid to achieve commitments from foreign countries to enact Western-style agricultural reforms was somewhat novel, even if it demonstrates the way that his preference for exerting power over Third World countries shaped even his global Great Society.

On the day that President Johnson delivered his International Health Act, International Education Act, and Food for Freedom programs to Congress, the *New York Times'* Felix Belair Jr. opened his piece on this "world aid drive" with a rather damning observation. "President Johnson told Congress today that the appalling conditions of the underdeveloped half of the world 'challenge our own security and threaten the future of the world,'" Belair wrote. "He then requested the smallest appropriation for improving them in the 18-year history of the foreign aid program."[36] This owed, in no small part, to the skyrocketing costs of his war in Vietnam and his War on Poverty at home. Indeed, as LBJ's promises to the world's poor grew more grandiose, his ability to fulfill them seemed to falter ever more. As much as he dreamed of – and promised – a global Great Society, Johnson's sense of his own limits militated against success. His efforts to see beyond the narrow glass of national interest failed, and his capacity for compassion was overwhelmed by the fear of losing power.

A WORLD OF ROCKS AND HARD PLACES

For as much dreaming as Johnson did, he was consistently dogged by his sense of reality – especially the political realities that he was so accustomed to anticipating. But Johnson was not always accurate in these judgments, and, as president, his faith in his own ability to help the country see reality differently faltered. This was especially true in the case of the US relationship with the countries of the Third World.

Perhaps the problem was that Johnson himself could not imagine seeing differently. He was certainly impatient with those who wanted him to try. In the spring of 1965, shaken by Johnson's decision to order air strikes in North Vietnam, then-Senator George McGovern (D-South Dakota) called the White House and asked for a meeting with the president. McGovern was regarded by many as an expert on the decolonizing world. A decorated World War II combat veteran, he had earned a PhD in History from Northwestern and had been a professor before pursuing a life in politics. He wanted to offer the president some historical perspective as Johnson deepened US involvement in Southeast Asia. As McGovern later recalled, LBJ was ready to parry any criticisms from the senator, who had been the first member of Congress to question US military involvement in Vietnam back in September 1963. When McGovern persisted, Johnson began cursing at him. "Goddamn it, George, you and Fulbright and all you history teachers down there. I haven't got the time to fuck around with history."[37]

Alas, while LBJ may not have had time to "fuck around with history," history, it would seem, had time to fuck around with him. More than any president, he was confronted with a world that had been transformed by nearly three decades of ferocious historical change, a world remade by decolonization. In 1955, while Johnson was preoccupied with a major political crisis early in his career as Senate Majority Leader, the United Nations counted some sixty member states. In 1960, when he left the

Senate to become vice president, that number had swelled to ninety-nine. By 1968, as his presidency neared its end, UN membership had grown to 126 independent countries. In place of a world with Western Europe reliably located at its center was this new and dizzying map of "Third World" countries, each embarked on a struggle, in the words of the French demographer who coined the term, to "become something."[38] As we have seen, these circumstances provoked some of Johnson's more imaginative policy thinking, but, ultimately, he seemed unable to grasp their full import and appreciate their significance.

To be fair to LBJ, few midcentury Americans possessed the ability to see revolutionary nationalism as a political and social phenomenon in its own right rather than as a troublesome sideshow to the ongoing Cold War struggle. For much of his career, the entire encounter between the United States and the decolonizing world had been framed as part of the Cold War. As such, it was subject to the logic of that conflict, a logic that, to Johnson, seemed very clear. "Whether Communist or Fascist, or simply a pistol-packing racketeer, the one thing a bully understands is force and the one thing he fears is courage," Johnson contended in a speech in support of the Truman Doctrine in 1947.[39] The "painful lesson" that LBJ had learned from World War II was that appeasement was the deadly offspring of an isolationism that almost cost democracy its life.[40] As World War II transitioned into the Cold War in the late 1940s, Johnson absorbed the doctrine of containment as a way to ensure that the United States did not slide back into isolationism. He saw this position as both pragmatic from an electoral perspective and correct in terms of foreign policy. His foreign policy positions emphasized maintaining strategic superiority over the Soviet Union and reassuring allies in Western Europe of America's resolve, both of which often mitigated against a deft approach to the decolonizing world.[41] The Cold War was, in his view, a zero-sum game in which overwhelming strategic advantage was the only winning hand. Ironically, as president, he successfully initiated a de-escalation of tensions with the Soviet Union, but he transferred the containment framework to the Third World and never really questioned that decision.[42]

In addition to his insensitivity to history, understanding Third World nationalism demanded that LBJ take a global perspective especially difficult to gain in the daunting context of domestic Cold War politics, the context in which he slept, ate, and breathed. Above and beyond any geopolitical insights he gained by observing how Washington fought the Soviets abroad, what LBJ learned about the Cold War during the 1950s was how it poisoned politics at home. In his first term in the Senate, Johnson had a front-row seat for the circus that ensued in Washington after the Chinese communists triumphed in their civil war against the US-backed Nationalist government.[43] As a devoted New Deal Democrat, LBJ watched as President Truman's ambitious domestic reform agenda fell victim to Cold War politics. The extent to which these experiences seared his consciousness can be discerned by his habit of bringing up Truman's "loss" of China as a reason to stay the course in Vietnam.[44] These fears did not just fixate on the extent to which perceived foreign policy blunders might alienate congressional allies from supporting his domestic reform program. Johnson's anxieties about the political impacts of foreign policy decisions went much farther than that; indeed, he expressed fears that he would be impeached if he withdrew from Vietnam or failed to stop Castroism in the Western Hemisphere.[45] For a consummate student of American political history, LBJ had to know that calls to impeach Truman, though they came, never gained any traction. No president had been impeached for any foreign policy decision ever before, yet the specter lingered over LBJ.

Finally, more than just the exigencies of the Cold War, there were older, deeper forces shaping Johnson's comprehension of decolonization. As historian Michael Hunt has persuasively argued, a central tenet of US foreign policy since the founding of the Republic has been an antipathy to social revolution. Tracing this core idea to the writings of Adams and Jefferson, Hunt shows us that no subsequent revolution ever seemed to rise to the standard set for US foreign policy thinkers by the American Revolution. This tendency proved especially portentous for Americans navigating post-1945 decolonization. By this time, "the causes of revolution – the problems of a peasantry, prolonged and exhausting wars, resentments engendered by foreign rule – were either largely alien or increasingly remote to Americans."[46] As such, and relying on the formula US foreign policymakers had developed starting just a few decades after the founding of the country, midcentury Americans perceived two choices when confronted with revolutions abroad: they sought either to guide them, or, failing that, to stop them.[47] Johnson did not deviate from this approach. He grew frustrated when nationalist leaders questioned his motives or resisted his influence, and he struggled to see why they continued to carp about history and spout ideological maxims when so many of their desperately poor peoples yearned for the basic comforts of food and shelter. This *insensitivity* to history often overshadowed his profound *sensitivity* for the poor. LBJ, and the country he led, never did resolve this tension.

These constraints on Johnson's thinking about the extraordinarily complex questions raised by decolonization were further tightened by his broader theory of politics. In the many accounts of LBJ, two tropes recur that help us understand how his extraordinarily adroit political mind worked. They reveal both why he accomplished so much, on the one hand, and why his presidency is forever equated with tragedy – especially in the Third World – on the other.

The first trope was that the world was full of impossible trade-offs, often articulated by Johnson in a construction that put him between the proverbial rock and a hard place. Despite his public bombast, Johnson was profoundly fatalistic about the inevitable costs of making any decision at all, no matter how seemingly insignificant. In an extended passage in Doris Kearns Goodwin's biography, LBJ utters many versions of this formulation, describing his sense that a different course in Vietnam would have meant the failure of his Great Society. "I was bound to be crucified either way I moved," he lamented.[48] This tension has become central to much recent scholarship on LBJ's fateful decision to commit US troops to South Vietnam, but the validity of his concerns remains controversial.[49] Either way, this was not a perspective restricted to the war in Vietnam – he saw rocks and hard places everywhere. "If I send in the Marines," LBJ told an aide in regard to a proposed intervention in the Dominican Republic in 1965, "I can't live in the hemisphere. If I don't, I can't live at home."[50] (See Figure 11.2.) It seems that Johnson, a politician so very good at winning, could speak only in the language of "lose-lose" propositions. This tendency caused him to exaggerate the risks at home of more nuanced foreign policy positions abroad. The zero-sum nature of the global Cold War, so important to his own political

11.2. US troops search a suspect in the Dominican Republic during the military intervention on the island in 1965. US forces helped end civil conflict and install a new conservative regime.
Credit: Getty Images

evolution in the 1940s and 1950s, was thus reinforced, in LBJ's view, by his deeply held conviction that he was damned no matter what he did.

The second recurring trope in LBJ's political worldview was his impression that taking the ideas and ideologies of his interlocutors seriously was a luxury he never had time to afford. It appears in stories like the one Senator McGovern told about that visit to the Oval Office in the spring of 1965. But it also appears in LBJ's political tactics; he believed that political leaders of all stripes were more interested in short-term results than in long-term ideological projects, and he struggled to shake himself free from that conviction even when the evidence proved otherwise. In a telling comment, Johnson once described his frustration with French President Charles de Gaulle and "people like him, who let high rhetoric and big issues take the place of accomplishments."[51] He sought to give Third World leaders "accomplishments" they could take home to their people. But, for LBJ, "accomplishments" were always tangible – bread for the proverbial butter – not arguments won or symbolic gestures made. The North Vietnamese rebuffed LBJ's offer of a "TVA on the Mekong" not because the North Vietnamese wanted to continue to live in poverty but because they were motivated by something beyond material interests.[52] He could not grasp such commitments. Johnson's deep faith in the efficacy of transactional politics served him well in the Senate and, as president, it emboldened him to fight for civil rights at home and for a host of new programs that he hoped would transform the lives of everyday people. But it also limited Johnson's capacity for compassion with people motivated by history and ideology, and reduced his ability to think beyond a reductive carrot-and-stick approach to diplomacy. As LBJ's national security adviser, McGeorge Bundy, memorably recalled, "Johnson treated Third World leaders like Senators. He presumed they were all reasonable men who could be persuaded to compromise on almost any issue if the right combination of threats and incentives was employed."[53] This tendency exacerbated his impatience when his desired results did not come to pass, another liability in trying to navigate the complexities of decolonization.

In another chapter in this volume, an eminent scholar of the US war in Vietnam explores LBJ's particular failures in that prolonged confrontation, but, for my purposes, Johnson's inability to find a way out of Vietnam reveals his own comfort with a certain kind of diplomacy vis-à-vis Third World countries, one based largely on exerting power. Johnson's political toolkit had always included this skill. Early on, he had developed a keen sense for how to identify friends and enemies, and how to use rewards and punishments to keep the former and scare the latter. The ease with which he slipped into this mode made it especially hard for him to see *through* it, to use his capacity for compassion to determine what his counterparts were really trying to communicate and to find imaginative solutions to diplomatic problems. Indeed, despite his sincere impulse to dream up a new world of peace and prosperity for all and his fealty to the notion that all common folk, whether they lived in Ghana or West Virginia, wanted the same things, Johnson believed deeply in power as the only *truly* universal language. While he may not have displayed self-awareness very often, Johnson did seem to recognize these skills in himself. "I do understand power, whatever else may be said of me," he told an aide. "I know where to look for it, and how to use it."[54]

Johnson's reliance on raw power in his interactions with the countries of the Third World shows us most convincingly how his capacity for compassion and understanding could sometimes so profoundly fail him. In contrast to his deft management of alliances in Europe, Johnson rarely seemed able to make sense of the motivations and interests of the nationalist leaders he worked with in the Third World. He was especially aggressive with nationalist leaders in the Western Hemisphere and believed that toughness should guide his interactions with Latin America at every turn lest he be taken advantage of by opportunists. From his efforts to exert pressure on Panama's President Robert Chiari during an outbreak of protests against the United States over its control of the Canal to his fateful decision to approve the first US military intervention in the Western Hemisphere in three decades in the Dominican Republic, Johnson often tried to bully his way through conflicts in the region.[55] Even when he resisted his worst instincts to intimidate and cajole, Johnson found himself resorting to pressure more than conciliation or understanding.

Far beyond the Western Hemisphere, Johnson turned to intimidation tactics with Third World leaders because he often found them to be unreadable and thus unpredictable. The leaders of the non-aligned countries – notably India, Egypt, and Indonesia – were especially infuriating to LBJ. Because he discounted ideology as a motivating factor for human behavior, he saw the unpredictability of leaders working to pursue non-alignment as a cover for old-fashioned shake-downs. Even when he made a personal connection with a nationalist leader, as he did with India's Indira Gandhi, Johnson found it almost impossible to take the perspectives and circumstances of his Third World counterparts seriously, to use his nearly unmatched political intelligence to consider the conundrums they faced at home, for instance. When he wanted India to undertake more aggressive agricultural reforms, Johnson used his Food for Peace aid to pressure Prime Minister Gandhi, with whom he had seemingly cultivated a warm friendship, to accede to US demands for agricultural reform in order to continue receiving food aid. Beyond using what leverage he had to achieve a long-term objective, Johnson demanded that Gandhi publicly proclaim her country in desperate need of food, going so far as to drum up the appearances of a famine, no matter the political consequences she might face. Using leverage is the work of statecraft, but this raw exertion of power was insensitive to the political context Indian leaders found themselves in and gave no consideration to the long-term consequences of promoting to the American people an image of a postcolonial democracy that could not feed its own people.[56]

Johnson was somehow capable of making sense of the whims, desires, beliefs, and values of 535 very different inhabitants of the US Capitol, but he struggled to grasp the interests and ideologies that shaped the politics of much of the postcolonial world. His habits as president exacerbated this shortcoming. After becoming president, LBJ cut himself off from the kinds of encounters with the masses abroad that he had enjoyed as vice president, limiting himself almost exclusively to working with elites.[57] Long gone were scenes like those of Johnson glad-handing fruit vendors on the streets of Beirut or camel-drivers in Karachi.[58] To some extent, Johnson simply stopped talking – and listening – to people from the Third World beyond very occasional diplomatic visits with policymakers. This allowed his resentments to fester, his misconceptions to go unchallenged, and his anxieties to multiply.

It would take many pages to document the multiple ways in which Johnson deployed power to control his interactions with the Third World – he did this from Indonesia to Iran to Panama to Brazil to Rhodesia to a hundred other places. But what these examples point to is a pattern of LBJ falling back into both fear and certainty, fear of being taken advantage of or otherwise weakened by his counterparts and certainty that he understood the context in which they were operating and the motivations that guided them. In this context, we should not be surprised that Johnson presided over a period of growing authoritarianism in the Third World; he felt like he was on safer ground with leaders whose motives made sense to him, and those were often the ones who were reliable in pursuit of their own power. From the Shah of Iran to military dictators in Brazil, Johnson showed a decided preference for leaders who could guarantee stability – even if they willfully undermined democracy.[59]

CONCLUSION

In one of his many interviews with Doris Kearns Goodwin, Johnson offered a telling reflection. "When I first became President," he told Kearns Goodwin, "I realized that if only I could take the next step and become dictator of the whole world, then I could really make things happen. Every hungry person would be fed, every ignorant child educated, every jobless man employed. And then I knew I could accomplish my greatest wish, the wish for eternal peace."[60] That Johnson dreamed of possessing unchecked authority to do what he thought was right not just for his own people but for the people of the world demonstrates his failure to understand the significance of sovereignty and self-determination to the peoples of the postcolonial world.

Of course, for many Third World leaders in the 1960s, it might have come as a surprise to discover that Johnson was *not* the "dictator of the whole world." After all, for Indira Gandhi of India and Suharto of Indonesia, among others, it was Lyndon Johnson who decided who they could talk to and who they could not; who got what kind of help meeting their own national needs and who did not; what rules they had to follow and what priorities they had to pursue. It was Lyndon Johnson who possessed not only the power to give and take resources away, but who also wielded the threat of force, a threat that was especially concrete for a generation of leaders who had watched the United States make "regime change" a policy of its own.[61] Unable to see this, Johnson often struggled to convince Third World leaders that what was good for the United States was also good for them, and he grew enormously frustrated when they dared to doubt it; American presidents still do.

And yet we have to countenance the undeniable fact that, despite his dreams of dictatorial power, Lyndon Baines Johnson, the "Big Daddy of the Pedernales," served not as patriarch but as midwife to an unprecedented efflorescence of participatory democracy – one limited to the borders of his own country.[62] Despite its many shortcomings, what Johnson offered with his domestic Great Society was a democratic vision of the United States that exceeded even the ambitions of his lodestar, Franklin D. Roosevelt. Beyond ambition, however, his efforts yielded transformative results. Between LBJ's embrace of the civil rights movement and support for legislation that movement leaders demanded, the Community Action Programs of his War on Poverty, volunteer programs like Foster Grandparents and Volunteers in Service to America (VISTA), and his aggressive investment in educating poor people and improving the health of the aged and disabled, he, as president, invited Americans to participate in the life of their country and to share the fruits of its wealth and power.[63] This was not the product of Johnson's beneficence; social movements, building pressure for decades under the mantle of mainstream indifference, finally broke through the surface to bring force to bear on politicians like LBJ. But he had a choice to open a door or add another bolt to it – and, by cracking it open just a little bit, he invited a few more guests to the table. Because of this choice, during LBJ's tenure in the White House, the United States came closer to *being* a participatory democracy than it had ever done before.

Yet LBJ did not choose to open that door when it came to the billions of people who sought their self-determination in the Third World. Why not? Here, we must return to that final conversation between Johnson and Walter Cronkite, a conversation that revealed so powerfully the connection between compassion and understanding in Johnson's leadership. With people of color in the United States, his early experiences in a Cotulla, Texas, schoolhouse provoked his compassion. That compassion fed a curiosity that turned into a willingness to listen. It was not a complete conversion, but the LBJ who sat across from Cronkite in 1973 was not the same man as the one who had been so evasive about civil rights in the 1950s.

This process had no equivalent when it came to the poor and oppressed of the Third World. Johnson didn't know them, didn't listen to them, and didn't learn from them. He certainly recognized the value of compassion as a tool of global leadership, as he explained in October 1966. "From the Marshall Plan to now," he wrote, "[our] policy has rested upon the claims of compassion and common sense – and on the certain knowledge that only people with rising faith in the future will build secure and peaceful lands." But he could not find a way to get there when it came to the really existing peoples of the vast Third World.[64]

Historians and biographers like to remind us that Johnson once remarked that "foreigners are not like the folks I am used to."[65] This quotation has been used to illustrate his lack of confidence in foreign affairs but also, more lazily, to suggest that Johnson was fundamentally uninterested in the world beyond his own country.[66] I contend that this isn't what that line tells us: It tells us instead that, as much as Johnson might have wanted to extend his dreams of a better future across the globe, he didn't know how. To be sure, he felt badly for the benighted masses he saw on those tours throughout Asia and Africa in his days as vice president; no doubt, he wanted to help them, he wanted America to "work" for them as it had worked for the poor in his own beloved Texas Hill Country. But he did not know how to make this manifest because he did not *know* them, and he did not know how to learn.

Lyndon Johnson, at a pivotal moment in the history of the world, did see through a narrow glass of indifference to lead his country toward a more compassionate tomorrow. But his ability to discern the wounds of discrimination and injustice at home sat alongside his willful blindness to the dreams of freedom and hopes for equality of the masses of people who had been similarly marginalized by colonialism and exploitation. He did not seem to comprehend that, sometimes – indeed, we might say often – what serves US interests simply does *not* serve the interests of countries in the Third World. Even on issues as seemingly universal as climate change and global health, we have seen in our own time how divergent the national interests – and national responsibilities – are between the United States and the countries of the Global South. To find global solutions to the challenges that face humanity requires an American leadership that listens more than it speaks and that understands before it acts. It requires an American leadership that knows other cultures, other languages, other histories, and other perspectives. And it requires an American leadership that recognizes the shape of its own power as others see it. Had LBJ been able to speak to Cronkite as frankly about his inabilities to fully comprehend the experiences of those poor peasants in India and Vietnam as he did of his experiences with Black Americans, his presidency might have left a very different legacy, one that showed his America that to truly see beyond the narrow glass of national interest means first perceiving one's own reflection more clearly.

Afterword: LBJ's America

Melody C. Barnes

"The stories we tell ourselves about ourselves" define and shape American culture.[1] The truth is noble and ignoble, and often there's friction between American history and American memory, particularly the characterization of events and decisions that are fundamentally antithetical to our democratic aspirations. That friction prompts us to create narratives to reconcile our aspirations with the reality of American life. Sometimes fiction is better than truth, particularly when history is painful, or would upend our conception of ourselves and our culture, or require us to change in ways inconvenient, uncomfortable, or unprofitable. We back away, avert our eyes, and create new stories until something or someone forces us to reckon with the past in ways that push America forward – at least until the reckoning becomes an existential threat and provokes a backlash, and the cycle begins again.

Harnessing the power of the presidency, Lyndon Baines Johnson required America to wrestle with its past. Together, the powerful social movements of the 1960s and his Great Society catalyzed a cycle of reckoning and discomfort that changed America until the war in Vietnam, along with anger and angst about government, identity, and power, brought it to an end. And as Great Society legislation ground to a halt and the war continued, America turned away from LBJ, too.

We've tried to forget him and, in some cases, what his presidency achieved and helped unearth. We've failed to come to terms with the America that was revealed. For some it's better to look at a shining city on a hill than confront a smoldering country. For others, Johnson is an inadequate and uncomfortable arbiter of robust American democracy.

But we ignore him – the successes, the mistakes, the pain, the contradictions, the turbulence, and the progress – at our peril. The Johnson years have much to teach us, as America in the 1960s and today's America have much in common. Those two consequential periods in American life are tightly bound together, proving that while history doesn't repeat itself, it often rhymes.

America marched out of the 1950s and into the 1960s content and confident – or so it would seem. A war had been won, incomes were rising, citizens were better educated, more families were buying homes and cars and taking vacations. But, on the international stage, America's global superpower status was being tested; on the heels of the Korean War, Vietnam was a growing and confounding challenge. And domestically, the calm above the surface belied what was bubbling beneath it and had been ignored. Things were better for more Americans than ever before but too many were on the outside of American political and economic life and had been there for too long. A period of reckoning was imminent, and Lyndon Baines Johnson would help catalyze and wrestle with all that followed.

Popular culture and political lore cast Johnson as a cunning, homespun, often crude, Texas bully, a masterful legislator who aided and abetted white supremacists early in his career. While all of those things are true, the facts are more complicated than the often-one-dimensional depiction of Johnson and his legacy. Johnson pursued his ambition to be president battling personal demons, self-inflicted wounds, and obstacles pushed in his path by others. Once the son of a pillar of the community in tiny Johnson City, Texas, Johnson would learn the feeling, taste, and smell of failure when his father literally "lost the ranch." Social ruin followed economic disaster, and the ripple effect shaped the currents of Johnson's life. He was a laughingstock and resented much of what followed. Lyndon Johnson knew what it meant to be an outsider and to fail. He was interested in neither and began climbing the ladder of power armed with the highs and lows of his life, including the experience he called formative – teaching poor, Mexican American children in Cotulla, Texas.

Feared and respected as Senate Majority Leader, Vice President Johnson was reduced to a joke and – if he was lucky – an afterthought.

According to Johnson biographer Robert Caro, "Say, whatever happened to Lyndon Johnson?" was a question asked over cocktails in the most powerful homes in Washington, DC, during the Kennedy administration. During the three years sandwiched between Johnson's domination of the United States Senate and his ascent to the Oval Office, he was so profoundly diminished that he seemed broken and almost forgotten.

But once the beloved, young, urbane Jack Kennedy was assassinated in Texas, Johnson assumed the presidency and used government, the Oval Office, and power amassed over twenty-five years to try to redress the economic hardship and outsider status that placed millions on America's periphery. Johnson wanted to expand upon Franklin Roosevelt's New Deal, which was robust but didn't do enough – not for women or people of color or the impoverished or immigrants. He reveled in and wielded his power even as he set out to change the power dynamic in American life.

An unmatched student of the legislative process, he drove the Great Society locomotive, urging Congress to pass one landmark bill after another touching every aspect of American life – the arts, childhood nutrition, civil rights, education, the environment, government transparency, health care, rural economic development, and the list goes on. Yet for many, Johnson's name is simply synonymous with one of America's darkest foreign policy hours: Vietnam. That failure is often articulated as his entire legacy and his accomplishments attributed to President Kennedy and others.

Yet the five years when Lyndon Johnson occupied the Oval Office turned American life upside down – our culture, our politics, and citizens' relationship to government. They changed the way Americans saw themselves and forced the country to wrestle with a new understanding of who is a citizen. Old political alliances were broken and new ones formed. Old ways were challenged, and norms began to fray. The America that appeared content and peaceful also proved to be angry, distrustful, nervous, and demanding as very different views of American identity, politics, and governing pushed to the surface. That period in history – the bold and simultaneously inadequate efforts to align the promises of democracy with the reality of American life – continues to affect and confound us decades later and has a direct bearing on the anger, angst, and deep polarization that have America teetering on the edge today.

For that, much of America hasn't forgiven and certainly remains uncomfortable with Lyndon Johnson. For many on the left, the stench of his early congressional voting record remains, and his good work didn't go far enough. Many on the right believe Johnson went too far ushering in the federal government where it didn't belong, supplanting individual liberty, and letting chaos overrun American cities. And for all, his presidency was overcome by the bad and the ugly of Vietnam. Martin Luther King Jr.'s searing commentary during his memorable speech at Riverside Church captured the anguish on the left, and blistering attacks from Barry Goldwater, Ronald Reagan, and others were a pointed blow to Johnson's efforts to prove that Democrats could be strong at home and abroad. America was left with a new, uncomfortable view of itself, given to us by the larger-than-life, sometimes coarse, politically deft, cowboy hat–wearing Texan who came to power after Camelot.

Today, we find ourselves in a period that rhymes with the Johnson era. It wasn't that long ago that America appeared prosperous and confident. Many things seemed to be working for many people – the technology sector was booming, the Dow was up, Americans were buying homes, we weren't at war. And then it all seemed to change. Our sense of economic security began unraveling. Yawning income inequality became painfully apparent and sparked resentment that won't be tamped down. Fewer Americans believe in the American Dream after watching the economic bubble burst and the financial sector and home ownership come crashing down in 2008. Economic fear met bitterness when only those on the lower rungs of the ladder appeared to pay the price. Deaths of despair continue to rise, layered on top of generations of despair in communities of color also plagued by mass incarceration and violence. The promise of the first African American president created a backlash, unleashing anger directed toward racial and ethnic minorities, as well as frustration in some quarters of the progressive community. Those who saw immigrants as a threat to jobs have been joined by those who perceive immigrants as a threat to America and "real" Americans. Those born after 2001 only know America at or precariously close to war. And like the 1950s and

1960s, much of what erupted in the 2000s was rooted in what had been there all along.

America today, as in the 1960s, is tumultuous. Armed with our memories and different conceptions of how we got here, we're struggling to define our problems, and the answers appear unknowable and out of reach. But instead of actively looking away from the past, we can choose to learn from it. Remembering Lyndon Johnson and his presidency – the good and the bad – offers us the opportunity to reposition government as an ally, not an enemy, and to acknowledge and confront the historically toxic relationship that binds power, politics, and American identity so we can move closer to our democratic aspirations.

GOVERNMENT AS AN ALLY

America was founded on contested ideas about government and its role in the lives of its citizens. Revolutionaries challenged a king. Those who penned the Articles of Confederation were so desperate to avoid anything that looked like a national government that they tried to govern based on a "firm league of friendship." The document wasn't worth the paper it was written on and was ultimately replaced by a constitution that tried to balance state and individual rights with the authority granted to a new central government. Our second attempt to constitute a new nation stuck, but Americans have never stopped debating the role of government in daily life. Twice those debates erupted into a violent attack on the United States government – a civil war that began in 1861 and an attempt to prevent the peaceful transfer of power at the US Capitol in 2021.

America's love–hate relationship with federal government endures, but citizens have held more charitable views about Washington, DC, than they do today. When Lyndon Johnson took the oath of office, government was held in high regard. According to the Pew Research Center, trust in the federal government reached its all-time high in 1964, with 77 percent of Americans saying they trusted those in Washington to do the right thing "nearly always or most of the time." Johnson shared the public's trust and believed government could – and should – be used as a tool to improve lives and empower people. A self-proclaimed Franklin

Roosevelt acolyte, he witnessed policies in the 1930s and 1940s that helped put Americans back to work, reduced poverty, created labor protections, and more. But Johnson also realized that Roosevelt's solutions failed to improve the lives of millions who remained on the margins of society.

Even as much of America grew more prosperous in the 1950s, Washington policymakers were coming face-to-face with the reality of "the other America" that author and political scientist Michael Harrington described in 1962 as a place impervious to hope and "populated by the failures ... by old people suddenly confronted with the torments of loneliness and poverty, and by minorities facing a wall of prejudice."[2] It was an America familiar to Lyndon Johnson, who sought to change it by building American cities as a source of vibrant community, protecting the environment for future generations, educating a growing population to counter poverty, and joining the battle for civil rights. He was clear that government didn't have all of the answers but that his government would assemble the best people to find them, launching a new federalism built on cooperation between local and federal government. For Johnson, the federal government wasn't evil; it tapped into the ingenuity of those willing to serve. Government didn't thwart progress; it used size and scale to take on challenges antithetical to the promise of America and too big for any one sector or state to solve. In his estimation, government was poised to help create a Great Society for all its citizens.

Since 1964, Americans' views have trended downward, with periods of highs and lows. Vietnam left its mark on everyone. On the left, it created a drumbeat that America was neither great nor good. Hundreds of thousands of protestors decried human rights violations during a war that made no sense and seemed to have no end. Not only were young men dying, but the brutal irony was apparent to many: at home, Black and brown soldiers were being denied many of the rights they were dying to secure for the citizens of Vietnam. In fact, the Great Society efforts that seemed promising were being suffocated because attention and resources were being devoted to the war. Fredrik Logevall's characterization of the Johnson presidency as Shakespearean probably would have resonated with movement leaders in the 1960s who believed America's deepening engagement in Vietnam was a disaster of our making, with

Lyndon Johnson in the driver's seat. As Martin Luther King Jr. queried before a national audience, why couldn't we say we'd made a mistake? Americans would ask similar questions about the Iraq War years later.

For others on the left, American government was meeting expectations – too little and far too late. From the Black Power movement to the Kerner Commission, the critique was sharp. The Commission's report, requested and later pushed aside by President Johnson, called for "a commitment to national action – compassionate, massive and sustained, backed by the resources of the most powerful and the richest nation on this earth. From every American it will require new attitudes, new understanding, and above all, new will."[3] Johnson, who was being consumed by the war, saw the report as a rebuke after championing the Civil Rights Act, the Voting Rights Act, and War on Poverty legislation, and he didn't – and probably couldn't, given the resources, national mood, and the loss of momentum in Congress – act on its recommendations. The Commission's prescient comments on American life went unheeded.

Vietnam, followed by Watergate, growing economic inequality, the Iraq War, and more setbacks leave many Americans distrustful and frustrated with government today. And while some, just to the left and the right of center, see America as durable and government as a force for good, many also believe democracy and democratic institutions are a sham. While there have been moments of progress, the journey is too long and the hurdles insurmountable. As Thad Williamson and I wrote in *Community Wealth Building and the Reconstruction of American Democracy*, from the left the critique is that "bolder aspirations for what America might become are largely pointless, because the powerful, rich, white elites who have held power from the beginning and hold most of the power now will never let such aspirations come to fruition."[4]

On the right, Johnson's solution to America's problems was a red cape dangled before a new conservative movement. Not your grandfather's conservatism – and not Ike Eisenhower's either – a sharpened worldview was being refined for public consumption. It rested on a few core ideas: economic activity unrestrained by government; the primacy of morality, including a traditional culture that supported institutions from the family to schools, churches, and businesses; and a more hawkish foreign policy. The new conservatism didn't immediately produce election-day victories, but it was bold, self-assured, and appealing to many. The difference between liberalism and conservatism became sharper, with each side claiming answers to the questions confounding America, and, soon, Republicans would reap the benefit at the polls.

What happened on the right from 1945 into the 1960s and beyond was the marriage of intellectual and organizational firepower and concerns about America's direction. At every turn, the role of the federal government was being questioned, and those philosophical debates shaped policy and political battles. Conservatives were full-throated in their belief that Johnson had gone too far, and as Nicole Hemmer points out, Johnson's work had become dangerous, "a new raft of programs that would lash Americans even more tightly to the federal government." Ultimately, they had to shift to "making liberalism less appealing and finding the right combination of policies, rhetoric, and ideas that would tempt more Americans into the conservative camp." As Marc Selverstone writes, Johnson became toxic for Democrats, but "Republicans on the other hand, sought to invoke LBJ as an object lesson during the country's rightward political shift." Ronald Reagan became one of their most powerful standard bearers, and in his 1981 inaugural address delivered the argument from which the notion of ambitious government has failed to recover in the minds of many: "In this present crisis, government is not the solution to our problem; government is the problem." Government – not the issues challenging the lives of citizens – became the target of our ire.

Years later, in her book *Strangers in Their Own Land*, Arlie Russell Hochschild tells us why antipathy toward government catalyzed the rise of the conservative Tea Party movement in the early 2000s. Americans who feel that they've done everything right patiently waited in line to achieve the American Dream only to find "line cutters" – African Americans, women, the LGBTQ community, and others – pushing them further behind. Adding insult to injury, the federal government is aiding and abetting the line cutting. According to those Russell Hochschild interviewed, "the right looks to the public sector as a service desk for a growing class of idle 'takers.'"[5] Values, rules, and culture are also being denigrated. Russell Hochschild writes:

> You are a stranger in your own land. You do not recognize yourself in how others see you. It is a struggle to feel seen and honored. And to feel honored you have to feel – and feel seen as – moving forward. But through no fault of your own, and in ways that are hidden, you are slipping backward.[6]

Men and women who believe the American Dream is slipping away align with those untouched by economic hardship but deeply concerned about the changes threatening the "American way of life." Government is out of step and hostile toward their nostalgia for an America they believe was more confident, economically secure, and rooted in traditional mores.

No matter the reason, government is a foe that should get out of the way. According to a May 2021 Pew Research Center report about the federal government's responsibility to provide social services in seven areas, a majority of Republicans support a government role in only two – ensuring clean air and water, and providing high-quality K-12 education. Over 75 percent of Republicans believe the government is doing too many things better left to business and individuals.

And yet the Affordable Care Act (ACA) tells an important story. The ACA – like health-care legislation since the Truman era – was labeled a threat to liberty. The "socialism" moniker resonated, while angst about "big government" led to the now infamous "Take your government hands off my Medicare" protest signs and helped fuel the Tea Party movement and populism on the right. But the unintended message embedded in that sign must not be ignored. Many Americans (unknowingly) embraced government's role in health care as they simultaneously rallied against the *idea* of the ACA. Over time, governors – including some conservatives – embraced Medicaid expansion, particularly after the COVID-19 pandemic began. The philosophical questions are real, but we also know that elected and appointed leaders and the public – left and right – embrace government when it responds to their needs.

Over time, Americans have sorted themselves across clear political lines and into more homogeneous groups with divided views about government. Never again has trust reached the level it did over fifty years ago. Since 2007, no more than 30 percent of Americans have expressed trust in government, and in 2022 trust hovers just above 20 percent.[7]

A growing number of Americans perceive government as an agent on behalf of some people "but not me," and when a significant number hold that belief, whether or not a majority, the consequences are dire for governing and democracy. In May 2021, most Americans – 52 percent – were "frustrated" with government, while 17 percent were angry and just 29 percent were content. And now, we have some sense of what that frustration and anger might mean, given the insurrection at the Capitol on January 6, 2021. That day is a chilling reminder that a number of Americans are willing to act violently based on their strongly held beliefs, even when many of those beliefs are rooted in myths.

In fact, there's a growing anger and justification of violence against the government. In the 1990s, 90 percent of Americans believed that violence was never justified against the government but, by 2010, 16 percent of Americans believed that it was. That number increased to 23 percent in 2015, and in 2022, according to a *Washington Post*–University of Maryland poll, about one in three Americans – 33 percent – believe violence against the government can sometimes be justified. That's not only an increase in number but also a new partisan divide, as 40 percent of Republicans and 41 percent of independents say violence is acceptable. A majority, 62 percent of Americans, believe violence is never justified, but that's also a new low.[8]

Our most significant challenges today include the narrative we've created about government and the political sorting we've done in response. Both prevent us from conducting an honest assessment of what government has and hasn't done for people and why; governance is calcified, devoid of robust debate and productive legislating. But our unvarnished history reveals that government isn't inherently good or bad. Government has created and diminished opportunity, supported and denied economic security and wealth building, and expanded and contracted freedom. The choice is ours. Government animated by the common good can be an ally, and treating it as the enemy harms the body politic.

The Great Society is an example. No one would argue that it was perfect. There were unintended consequences, mistakes, and sometimes bad choices. For different reasons, many on the right and many on the left were disappointed and angry. But progress was made. As Congresswoman Barbara Jordan said about Lyndon Johnson at the end of her life, "[h]e stripped the government of its neutrality and made it an agent on behalf of the people."[9]

The Great Society brought millions of Americans into mainstream civic and economic life even as it inflamed views about our government. Historian Josh Zeitz notes that the story doesn't end with passage of legislation, including the Civil Rights Act of 1964 and the Voting Rights Act of 1965, or the War on Poverty policies. Rather, the years *after* passage of those and other laws are the story of progress rarely told and almost lost in American memory: the integration of thousands of school districts and thousands and thousands of medical facilities. According to Zeitz, in 1965, 6.7 percent of African Americans in Mississippi and 19 percent in Alabama were registered to vote. In 1970, two-thirds of African Americans were registered, and most could cast their ballot unimpeded. And between 1960 and 2010, the poverty rate dropped 26 percent because of Great Society benefits like food stamps, Medicaid, and housing subsidies, as well as the Nixon-supported earned income tax credit. Two-thirds of the decline occurred before 1980.

Johnson's policies began to breathe life into America's founding promises as demonization of government began to permeate our culture. But in spite of the skepticism, and worse, the Great Society illustrated that government plays a necessary role in improving lives and that government can be a force for good. The mistakes and challenges aren't evidence that we should cast government as the enemy but rather that we must be vigilant about getting government right.

POWER, POLITICS, AND AMERICAN IDENTITY

America's founding argument – that it is self-evident that all men are created equal and endowed with certain unalienable rights – catalyzed a revolution and a battle for power between Britain and its thirteen colonies. Although democracy won, the contest for power in America endures. Where people with different beliefs and desires exist, there will be a struggle for control and – if history is our guide – for domination.

Checks and balances, the articulation of individual liberties, a belief in majority rule, and protection of minority rights are intended to mitigate the worst human instincts, including tyranny and the rise of authoritarian rule. But today, many Americans wonder whether our historical rules and norms are (or were ever) enough. Among our chief concerns: the realization that our inability to fully embrace our unique, multi-ethnic American identity plays a particularly destructive role in the struggle for power.

From the beginning, a cramped, anti-democratic definition of American citizenship was woven into the fabric of the body politic. Laws, policies, and practices followed suit, fueling conflict as America expanded to the west, confronted slavery and Reconstruction, gave women the right to vote, and, as Madeline Hsu argues, crafted immigration policy. The leitmotif runs through American history. Political scientist Rogers Smith asks us to consider the implications for daily life:

> And what contributed to the friction in American life? ... [t]hrough most of US history, lawmakers pervasively and unapologetically structured U.S. citizenship in terms of illiberal and undemocratic racial, ethnic, and gender hierarchies, for reasons rooted in basic, enduring imperatives of political life.[10]

Given this history, is it possible for us to fully embrace the diversity of our civic community? And at a minimum, can we de-weaponize race and ethnicity so they're not used to exclude people from the body politic?

Lyndon Johnson's example and legacy are deeply connected to those questions. Johnson understood power at least as well as anyone who has occupied the Oval Office. He actively sought, acquired, and used it to advance his career toward the prize he always craved: the presidency. As he told his teenage classmates during recess one day: "Someday, I'm going to be President of the United States." And when they laughed and said they wouldn't vote for him, he retorted, "I won't need your votes."[11]

Whether Johnson's classmates became his supporters, we'll never know, but we do know that he built a base of power in Texas and among his fellow Southerners, casting votes in Congress to cement that base. Until 1957, he had a "perfect" anti–civil rights voting record. He opposed legislation crafted to end the poll tax, segregation in the armed services, and even lynching because, in Johnson's words, "the federal government has no more business enacting a law against one form of murder than against another." The Southern Bloc relied on him. Powerful Senator Richard Russell and House Speaker Sam Rayburn were his mentors, the bankers, contractors, and oil men of Texas his backers. He cultivated those relationships and, over time, he managed them while supporting the more moderate positions he (and they) knew he had to adopt if he was going to run for president. It was a study in the fierce effort to amass and use power for a purpose. For Lyndon Johnson the purpose was the presidency of the United States, and once he secured that prize, it was to expand opportunity – civic and economic – to many who had been marginalized.

But LBJ's legacy as president is a parable for us today. His actions – as a central protagonist against the Mississippi Freedom Democratic Party (MFDP) in 1964 and for the passage of the Voting Rights Act of 1965 – illustrate that unless we embrace our multi-ethnic American identity, we will continue to act in ways counter to our stated democratic aspirations.

With the highly effective civil rights movement, Lyndon Johnson began to recast American life. In the podcast *LBJ and the Great Society* Vanderbilt historian Rhonda Williams describes what some movement leaders hoped for in LBJ: "Martin Luther King recognized the political skill of Lyndon Baines Johnson, approached him with the hope that he would see the moral conscience of the nation needed leadership, that someone had to be the statesman, and lead the nation on a new path." Johnson, who placed civil rights at the center of his agenda immediately after the assassination of President Kennedy, responded, and was essential to the Voting Rights Act of 1965 becoming law. He believed voting was central to African Americans moving into the mainstream of American life as citizens, taking control of their destiny and, yes, gaining power. Hubert Humphrey remembered a conversation with Johnson:

"Let me tell you something Hubert. All this civil rights talk," he [Johnson] said. "The thing that we've got to do is get those Blacks the vote." Johnson went on to say, "Now you fellows are trying to get them public accommodations. You want them to ride in a bus," and he'd go over all the little things, "but what they need is the vote." He said, "That's what I'm gonna get 'em. When they get the vote power, they got the power."[12]

315

Once in the White House, Johnson wasn't a reluctant warrior for the legislation, although he was always playing the political chessboard, calculating strategy and tactics. Even as Johnson encouraged Martin Luther King Jr. to ramp up the public campaign for voting rights, he tried to persuade him that other Great Society bills must take precedence in the queue. Like presidents before and after, Johnson's pragmatic efforts to juggle the legislative calendar failed to take into consideration the irresistible momentum for – and in this case, Alabama law enforcement's response to – the morality and urgency of the cause. But he wasn't lukewarm on voting rights, and even as he tried to slow the legislative process, he was also contemplating the exercise of executive authority.

For Lyndon Johnson, passage of the Voting Rights Act would be the crown jewel in his civil rights agenda. He called it the most important thing he would do even as he told his aide, Bill Moyers, that he knew the legislation would cost Democrats the South for a generation. He understood that citizenship had been narrowed to exclude millions of Americans by virtue of their race and ethnicity, leaving them without the tools necessary to help shape the nation and participate in democracy. However, the painful irony is that Johnson also worked to undermine the civil rights progress that he sought legislatively.

Politically, 1964 was a tumultuous year. Senator Barry Goldwater was rising to claim the Republican nomination with a full-throated articulation of a new conservatism. His philosophy and rhetoric sent the Republican Party reeling as moderates like New York Governor Nelson Rockefeller aggressively rejected the party's new direction and hoped to "push the GOP elephant forward" in response. Democrats, including President Johnson – particularly President Johnson – had their own problems. Who would be LBJ's running mate in 1964? Bobby Kennedy – attorney general; brother of the beloved, slain president; and Johnson's nemesis – wanted the job, but the antipathy between the two men was mutual. Johnson also believed Kennedy would cost him Southern votes that were already hanging by a thread. What would be the effect if Kennedy was on the ticket? What would be the consequences if he were not?

With those questions front and center, Johnson saw the MFDP as another threat among the constellation of issues that could derail his effort to win the White House and advance his Great Society agenda, including civil rights. The MFDP saw the world quite differently. Its effort to unseat the segregated, all-white Mississippi delegation at the Democratic National Convention was a fight for the most fundamental principles of personhood and citizenship. MFDP leader Fannie Lou Hamer told the Democratic National Committee's Credentials Committee:

> [I]f the Freedom Democratic Party is not seated now, I question America. Is this the America, the land of the free and the home of the brave where we have to sleep with our telephones off the hooks because our lives be threatened daily, because we want to live as decent human beings, in America?[13]

Johnson made a different calculation. It was his assessment that the MFDP's demands had to be set aside for another day. He believed his political life and the Democratic Party were on the line, and his reading of American culture and the political conundrum in which he found himself led him to undercut the very principles he was fighting for in Congress.

A few weeks after the convention, Johnson breathed a sigh of relief that the MFDP hadn't been successful. In a conversation with United Auto Workers president, March on Washington organizer, and civil rights organization funder Walter Reuther, Johnson said what had just transpired could have led to the "greatest debacle" in party history. Historian Kent Germany summarizes the exchange between LBJ and Reuther:

> Had the MFDP succeeded [LBJ said], it would have run "all those white folks out" and would have "put us back to the Emancipation Proclamation 100 years ago." Reuther agreed, explaining that the party would have "been ruined on both ends of the problem.... We'd have lost the South, and the North would have said, 'What the hell? The Freedom Riders have captured the Democratic Party."[14]

Were Johnson's actions and sentiments "just" politics, not conviction? Perhaps. But the moral of these events is that as long as politics turns on views of American identity that exclude citizens based on the race-based

American caste system, progress will be thwarted as our politics remain at odds with democratic principles. It's a battle we continue to fight in the twenty-first century. Sociologist and *Culture Wars* author James Davison Hunter argues that "[Race] has reemerged [today] in part because just as the earlier manifestations of the culture war were ultimately a struggle to define the meaning of America, this is also."[15] Race and ethnicity are central issues for America, prompting the questions: Who is an American? Who is considered a citizen, not only by birth or naturalization but based on American culture? And what is the relationship between the answers to those questions and the exercise of power in the United States?

Today, we wrestle with these questions in the America that LBJ helped create. Since the late 1960s, those historically marginalized – armed with new legislative and legal tools, organizing strategies, and allies – are better positioned to demand more from government and political life. However, the migration from the political margins to the mainstream, while further democratizing the country, has exacerbated polarization. Steven Levitsky and Daniel Ziblatt capture the historical arc in their 2018 book, *How Democracies Die*:

> [The] norms sustaining our political system rested, to a considerable degree, on racial exclusion. The stability of the period between the end of Reconstruction and the 1980s were rooted in an original sin: the Compromise of 1877 and its aftermath, which permitted the de-democratization of the South and the consolidation of Jim Crow. Racial exclusion contributed directly to the partisan civility and cooperation that came to characterize twentieth-century American politics. The "solid South" emerged as a powerful conservative force within the Democratic Party, simultaneously vetoing civil rights and serving as a bridge to Republicans. Southern Democrats' ideological proximity to conservative Republicans reduced polarization and facilitated bipartisanship. But it did so at the great cost of keeping civil rights – and America's full democratization – off the political agenda.
>
> America's democratic norms, then, were born in a context of exclusion. As long as the political community was restricted largely to whites, Democrats and Republicans had much in common. Neither party was likely

to view the other as an existential threat. The process of racial inclusion that began after World War II and culminated in the 1964 Civil Rights Act and 1965 Voting Rights Act would, at long last, fully democratize the United States. But it would also polarize it, posing the greatest challenge to established forms of mutual toleration and forbearance since Reconstruction.[16]

What's emerged is a cold civil war for power fueled by American identity, and the rights and the responsibilities of citizenship are at stake. The Voting Rights Act, necessary to the path to power for people of color, was partially dismantled by the Supreme Court, and with many of its protections gone, state-based retrenchment is on the rise. In 2021, at least 19 states passed 34 laws restricting access to voting, and over 440 bills with provisions restricting voting access have been introduced in 49 states.[17]

Similarly, even as we call ourselves a nation of immigrants, our two-decade-old effort to update and rationalize our immigration laws is in stalemate. Millions of lives and the American economy are at stake, but, for many, so are American identity and political power. Immigrants crossing our southern border aren't just seen as a threat to American workers; they're perceived as a threat to American culture and election outcomes. Immigrants – specifically immigrants coming across the United States' southern border – are welcomed through the back door as the front door remains double-locked. Madeline Hsu highlights the hypocrisy that remains in our immigration system even after the 1965 law addressed some – but not all – of its problems. Public policy is constrained by politics contorted by our views of American identity.

James Davison Hunter points to the Supreme Court's infamous *Dred Scott* decision, the Civil War, and the laws and policies that followed to illustrate the challenge:

> *Dred Scott* was an attempt to impose a consensus by law; it took the Civil War *and* the 13th and 14th and 15th Amendments to overturn *Dred Scott*. And yet that was also an imposition of solidarity by law and by force. The failures of Reconstruction and the emergence of Jim Crow and "Black Codes" and all of that was proof that politics couldn't solve culture; it couldn't solve the cultural tensions, and so what you end up with is a struggle for civil rights.
>
> My view is that the reason why we're continuing to see this press toward racial reckoning is because it's never been addressed culturally.[18]

Lyndon Johnson's legacy includes laws that are essential to the promise of democracy. But as an advocate for those policies while an opponent of the MFDP, he undermined the practice of the principles he sought to inscribe into law. Culture animated politics and undercut policy. Those impulses jeopardize LBJ's civil rights legacy over fifty-five years later. Then, as now, our narrow view of American identity remains a catalyst and a weapon in the inevitable struggle for political power in our democracy.

LBJ AND THE WAY FORWARD

Marc Selverstone urges us to consider that "[Johnson's] manifold flaws, inconsistencies, and paradoxes, and their impact on his policymaking, now sit on a broader canvas that incorporates the increasing complexity of the America he sought to govern and the world he tried to understand." After fifty-five years, what lessons does Lyndon Johnson have to teach us?

I believe he urges us to reconsider our war on government. We can point to government's failures, though our lists will differ. But government is not the enemy. Held to a high standard, it can be and has been an agent of change and a force for good when only the federal government, with its size and scale, could make the difference.

Johnson also tells us, as he did during his last public speech in December 1972, that while we've made progress, it's been too slow. Progress has been captured by a culture that resists a full embrace of our true American identity and relies on memory and narratives inconsistent with history. LBJ shows how even advocates for progress can be held hostage to those conceptions of American identity and illuminates the importance of confronting this essential and challenging issue if we're ever to become a true democracy.

Perhaps this is a new moment for Lyndon Baines Johnson, a chance to take a new look at those five years when he occupied the Oval Office, not to portray him through a gauzy, rose-colored light, but to take a good, honest look and absorb all that his legacy has to reveal to us.

Whatever became of Lyndon Johnson – complex, contradictory, aspirational, power-obsessed, empathetic, cunning Lyndon Johnson? The answer is that he is us.

Acknowledgments

Anthologies are inherently collaborative enterprises, and we naturally wish to thank the sensational group of historians who contributed to this project. We were humbled by the fact that every scholar whom we approached – a veritable dream team – agreed to write a chapter. We owe a debt of gratitude as well to three anonymous scholars who evaluated the proposal for this project. Their comments and suggestions shaped the finished product in innumerable ways.

We also wish to thank our colleagues at the LBJ Presidential Library and LBJ Foundation, institutions we are privileged to lead even as we moonlight as historians of American politics, foreign policy, and the presidency. We would be remiss if we did not single out Jay Godwin for his help in selecting photos and Hannah Green for doing so much to keep this project on track. Every contributor to this book owes thanks to the remarkable team of archivists who make the LBJ Presidential Library such a great place to conduct research: Claudia Anderson, Chris Banks, Jennifer Cuddeback, Sarah Cunningham, Jenna De Graffenried, Allen Fisher, Ian Frederick-Rothwell, Lara Hall, Brian McNerney, Alexis Percle, Scott Seely, Carrie Tallichet Smith, Liza Talbot, and John Wilson. We are also indebted to the trustees of the LBJ Foundation, who generously supported this project.

At Cambridge University Press, we wish to thank Cecelia Cancellaro for her unflagging encouragement at every step and her ambitious vision of what this book could be. We are grateful as well to Victoria Phillips for her expert guidance throughout the sometimes challenging process of meshing so many pieces into a finished product. In the closing stages, it was a pleasure to work with our stellar copy-editor, Christopher Jackson, and our endlessly helpful content manager, Laura Simmons.

Notes

INTRODUCTION

1. "Remarks to Key Officials of the Internal Revenue Service," February 11, 1964, *Public Papers of the President of the United States: Lyndon B. Johnson, 1963–1964*, vol. 1 (Washington, DC: US Government Printing Office, 1965), 286.

2. Reagan inaugural address, January 20, 1981, https://www.reaganlibrary.gov/archives/speech/inaugural-address-1981.

3. For a summary of these trends, see Robert D. Putnam with Shaylyn Romney Garrett, *The Upswing: How America Came Together a Century Ago and How We Can Do It Again* (New York: Simon and Schuster, 2020), 99–108.

4. Filmmakers Ken Burns and Lynn Novick made the point neatly in "How the Vietnam War Broke the American Presidency," *The Atlantic*, October 2017, https://www.theatlantic.com/magazine/archive/2017/10/how-americans-lost-faith-in-the-presidency/537897/.

5. On these themes, see Francis J. Gavin and Mark Atwood Lawrence, eds., *Beyond the Cold War: Lyndon Johnson and the New Global Challenges of the 1960s* (New York: Oxford University Press, 2014).

6. For an overview of scholarship on LBJ, see Kent B. Germany, "Historians and the Many Lyndon Johnsons: A Review Essay," *Journal of Southern History* 75, no.4 (November 2009): 1001–1028, and Mitchell B. Lerner, ed., *A Companion to Lyndon Johnson* (Malden, MA: Wiley-Blackwell, 2012). Among the most authoritative biographies cited repeatedly in this collection are Robert A. Caro, *The Years of Lyndon Johnson*, 4 vols. (1982–2014); Robert Dallek, *Flawed Giant: Lyndon Johnson and His Times, 1961–1973* (New York: Oxford University Press, 1998); Robert Dallek, *Lone Star Rising: Lyndon Johnson and His Times, 1908–1960* (New York: Oxford University Press, 1991); Doris Kearns Goodwin, *Lyndon Johnson and the American Dream* (New York: St. Martin's, 1976); and Randall B. Woods, *LBJ: Architect of American Ambition* (New York: Free Press, 2006).

7. Merle Miller, *Lyndon: An Oral Biography* (New York: G. P. Putnam's Sons, 1980), 8.

8. See especially Robert A. Caro, *The Years of Lyndon Johnson*, vol. 1: *The Path to Power* (New York: Vintage, 1982), chapters 29–32.

9. Germany, "Historians and the Many Lyndon Johnsons," 1005–1006.

10. Larry J. Sabato, *The Kennedy Half Century: The Presidency, Assassination, and Lasting Legacy of John F. Kennedy* (New York: Bloomsbury, 2013), 406–407.

11. On the release of the LBJ tapes, see Michael J. Beschloss, "Editor's Note," in Beschloss, ed., *Taking Charge: The Johnson White House Tapes, 1963–1964* (New York: Simon and Schuster, 1997), 547–553.

12. For example, David Kaiser, *American Tragedy: Kennedy, Johnson, and the Origins of the Vietnam War* (Cambridge, MA: Harvard University Press, 2000); Fredrik Logevall, *Choosing War: The Lost Chance for Peace and the Escalation of War in Vietnam* (Berkeley, CA: University of California Press, 1999); and H. R. McMaster, *Dereliction of Duty: Johnson, McNamara, the Joint Chiefs of Staff, and the Lies That Led to Vietnam* (New York: Harper, 1998).

13. "The Great Society at Fifty," *Washington Post*, May 17, 2014, https://www.washington post.com/sf/national/2014/05/17/the-great-society-at-50/.

14. Obama speech, LBJ Presidential Library, April 10, 2014, https://obamawhitehouse.ar chives.gov/the-press-office/2014/04/10/remarks-president-lbj-presidential-library-civ il-rights-summit.

15. Edward Rothstein, "Legacy Evolving at a Presidential Library," *New York Times*, April 9, 2014.

16. C-SPAN, "Presidential Historians Survey," https://www.c-span.org/presidentsur vey2021/?page=overall.

17. Robert Schenkkan, *All the Way: A Play* (New York: Grove, 2014), and *All the Way*, directed by Jay Roach (HBO Films, 2016).

18. *LBJ*, directed by Rob Reiner (Acacia Entertainment, 2016).

19. *Path to War*, directed by John Frankenheimer (HBO, 2002); *Selma*, directed by Ava DuVernay (Paramount, 2014); and *The Crown* (Netflix, 2016–2022).

20. For the link to Trump, see Josh Zeitz, "The Real Legacy in Jeopardy under the New Congress? LBJ's," *Politico*, November 23, 2016, https://www.politico.com/magazine/s tory/2016/11/new-congress-trump-lbj-214480/.

21. Ron Elving, "Can Biden Join FDR and LBJ in the Democratic Party's Pantheon?" National Public Radio, April 17, 2021, https://www.npr.org/2021/04/17/985980593 /can-biden-join-fdr-and-lbj-in-the-democratic-partys-pantheon?utm_source=dlvr.it&ut m_medium=twitter, and Susan B. Glasser, "Is Biden Really the Second Coming of FDR and LBJ?" *New Yorker*, April 1, 2021, https://www.newyorker.com/news/letter-from-bi dens-washington/is-biden-really-the-second-coming-of-fdr-and-lbj.

22. Adam Liptak, "Civil Rights Law Protects Gay and Transgender Workers, Supreme Court Rules," *New York Times*, June 15, 2020, https://www.nytimes.com/2020/06/15/ us/gay-transgender-workers-supreme-court.html.

23. Matt Lewis, "Joe Biden Wants to Be LBJ, But LBJ's Presidency Was a Disaster," *The Daily Beast*, August 17, 2021, https://www.thedailybeast.com/joe-biden-wants-to-be-lbj-but-l yndon-johnsons-presidency-was-a-disaster?ref=scroll.

24. For critical views of the War on Poverty, see Nicholas Eberstadt, "The Great Society at 50," *The Weekly Standard*, May 9, 2014, https://www.aei.org/articles/the-great-society-at- 50/, and Amity Shlaes, *Great Society: A New History* (New York: Harper, 2019).

25. LBJ Presidential Library, Oval Office museum exhibit, recorded message from President Johnson, October 1968.

CHAPTER 1   POWER AND PURPOSE: LBJ IN THE PRESIDENCY

1. Peter Dreier, "Bill Moyers," *The Progressive*, March 11, 2014.

2. This assessment draws on overviews of the literature from Mitchell B. Lerner, *Looking back at LBJ: White House Politics in a New Light* (Lawrence, KS: University Press of Kansas, 2005), 1–19; Kent B. Germany, "Historians and the Many Lyndon Johnsons: A Review Essay," *The Journal of Southern History* 75, no. 4 (November 2009): 1006; Andrew L. Johns, "The Legacy of Lyndon B. Johnson," in Mitchell B. Lerner, ed., *A Companion to Lyndon B. Johnson* (Malden, MA: Wiley-Blackwell, 2012), 506; and additional chapters in the Lerner *Companion*.

3. Robert Dallek, *Flawed Giant: Lyndon Johnson and His Times, 1961–1973* (New York: Oxford University Press, 1998); Robert A. Caro, *The Years of Lyndon Johnson*, vol. 3: *Master of the Senate* (New York: Knopf, 2002); Randall B. Woods, *LBJ: Architect of American Ambition* (New York: Free Press, 2006); Paul Keith Conkin, *Big Daddy from the Pedernales: Lyndon Baines Johnson* (New York: Twayne, 1986).

4. Dallek, *Flawed Giant*, 4; Woods, *LBJ*, 27.

5. Irwin Unger and Debi Unger, *LBJ: A Life* (New York: John Wiley & Sons, 1999), 244.

6. See Robert A. Caro, *The Years of Lyndon Johnson*, vol. 4: *The Passage of Power*, 176–190; Dallek, *Flawed Giant*, 8–12, 44–46.

7. Marc J. Selverstone, "The Vice Presidency," in Lerner, ed., *A Companion to Lyndon B. Johnson*, 38–56.

8. Horace Busby, "Reflections on a Leader," in Kenneth W. Thompson, ed., *The Johnson Presidency: Twenty Intimate Perspectives of Lyndon B. Johnson* (Lanham, MD: University Press of America, 1986), 25; see also Rowland Evans and Robert Novak, *Lyndon B. Johnson: The Exercise of Power* (London: George Allen and Unwin, 1967), 332, and Woods, *LBJ*, 414.

9. Johnson would not occupy the Oval Office until November 26, and his family would not move into the White House until December 7.

10. See Caro, *Passage of Power*, 409–414.

11. "Lyndon Johnson and Lady Bird Johnson (preceded by Office Conversation with Jack Valenti and Bill Moyers) on 7 March 1964," Tape WH6403.05, Citation #2395, *Presidential Recordings Digital Edition* (hereafter *PRDE*) [*Toward the Great Society*, vol. 4, ed. Robert David Johnson and Kent B. Germany]: https://prde.upress.virginia.edu/conversations/9040336/.

12. Julia Sweig, *Lady Bird Johnson: Hiding in Plain Sight* (New York: Random House, 2021), xv–xiii, 101–106.

13. This account of Johnson's day draws on Jack Valenti, *A Very Human President* (New York: W. W. Norton, 1975), 159–177; Joseph Califano Jr., *The Triumph & Tragedy of Lyndon Johnson: The White House Years* (New York: Simon and Schuster, 1991), 27–30; and W. Marvin Watson with Sherwin Markman, *Chief of Staff: Lyndon Johnson and His Presidency* (New York: St. Martin's Press, 2004), 89–93.

14. Califano, *Triumph & Tragedy*, 29.

15. Nancy Kegan Smith, "Presidential Task Force Operation during the Johnson Administration," *Presidential Studies Quarterly* 15, no. 2 (spring 1985): 320–329.

16. David C. Humphrey, "Tuesday Lunch at the Johnson White House: A Preliminary Assessment," *Diplomatic History* 8 no. 1 (January 1984): 81–101.

17. Smithsonian, "Lyndon Johnson and the 'Johnson Treatment,'" *Face to Face: National Portrait Gallery Blog*, https://npg.si.edu/blog/lyndon-johnson-and-johnson-treatment.

18. Merle Miller, *Lyndon: An Oral Biography* (New York: G. P. Putnam's Sons, 1980), 174.

19. "Lyndon Johnson and Richard Russell (President Johnson Joined by Albert Mousund) on 29 November 1963," Tape K6311.06, PNOs 14, 15, and 16, *PRDE* [*The Kennedy Assassination and the Transfer of Power*, vol. 1, ed. Max Holland]: http://prde.upress.virginia.edu/conversations/9010184; "Lyndon Johnson and Charles Halleck on 22 June 1964," Tape WH6406.12, Citation #3810, *PRDE* [*Mississippi Burning and the Passage of the Civil Rights Act*, vol. 7, ed. Guian A. McKee]: https://prde.upress.virginia.edu/conversations/9070157/; "Lyndon Johnson and Sargent Shriver on 1 February 1964," Tape WH6402.01, Citation #1804, *PRDE* [*Toward the Great Society*, vol. 4, ed. Robert David Johnson and Kent B. Germany]: http://prde.upress.virginia.edu/conversations/9040003.

20. Brian D. Sweany, "LBJ's Living Legacy," *Texas Monthly*, August 2000.

21. Woods, *LBJ*, 572–573.

22. "Lyndon Johnson and Walter Reuther on 9 August 1964," Conversation WH6408-15–4839–4840, *PRDE* [*Lyndon B. Johnson: Civil Rights, Vietnam, and the War on Poverty*, ed. David G. Coleman, et al.]. See also Woods, *LBJ*, 554; for Johnson's use of a similar metaphor to describe the Tonkin Gulf incident, see Gordon M. Goldstein, *Lessons in Disaster: McGeorge Bundy and the Path to War in Vietnam* (New York: Times Books, 2008), 123.

23. Kent Germany, "'I'm Not Lying about That One': Manhood, LBJ, and the Politics of Speaking Southern," *Miller Center Report* (summer 2002): 32–39.

24. Jack McNulty, "Words Mattered: Johnson the Communicator," in Thomas W. Cowger and Sherwin J. Markman, eds., *Lyndon Johnson Remembered: An Intimate Portrait of a Presidency* (New York: Rowman & Littlefield, 2003), 61.

25. Califano, *Triumph & Tragedy*, 11, 26.

26. "Lyndon Johnson and McGeorge Bundy on 20 October 1964," Conversation WH6410-13–5921, *PRDE* [*Lyndon B. Johnson: The Election of 1964*, ed. Kent B. Germany, et al.].

27. Watson, *Chief of Staff*, 77.

28. Larry Berman, "Johnson and the White House Staff," in Robert A. Divine, ed., *Exploring the Johnson Years* (Austin, TX: University of Texas Press, 1981), 191–194.

29. "Lyndon Johnson and John S. Knight on 20 October 1964," Conversation WH6410-13–5922–5923, *PRDE* [*Lyndon B. Johnson: The Election of 1964*, ed. Kent B. Germany, et al.].

30. "Remarks of President Johnson at the LBJ Presidential Library Dedication, May 22, 1971": www.lbjlibrary.net/collections/selected-speeches/post-presidential/05-22-1971.html.

31. Laura Kalman, *Abe Fortas: A Biography* (New Haven, CT: Yale University Press, 1990), 205.

32. David Culbert, "Johnson and the Media," in Divine, ed., *Exploring the Johnson Years*, 219.

33. Woods, *LBJ*, 459.

34. See Watson, *Chief of Staff*, 114.

35. See several conversations from October 14, 1964 through October 23, 1964 in *PRDE* [*The Election of 1964*, ed. Kent B. Germany, et al.].

36. Woods, *LBJ*, 744.

37. Berman, "Johnson and the White House Staff," 190–198.

38. Presidential Approval Ratings – Gallup Historical Statistics and Trends, https://news .gallup.com/poll/116677/presidential-approval-ratings-gallup-historical-statistics-tren ds.aspx.

39. Woods notes that the "credibility gap" may well have emerged earlier in his presidency in response to machinations concerning the 1965 federal budget. Woods, *LBJ*, 448.

40. Hal K. Rothman, *LBJ's Texas White House: "Our Heart's Home"* (College Station: Texas A&M University Press, 2001), 54–55.

41. Lyndon B. Johnson National Historic Park, Texas: https://www.nps.gov/nr/travel/ presidents/lyndon_b_johnson_nhp.html.

42. "Lyndon B. Johnson and Henry H. 'Joe' Fowler on 24 March 1968," Conversation WH6803-05–12844–12845–12846–12847, *PRDE* [*Johnson Telephone Tapes: 1968*, ed. Kent B. Germany, Nicole Hemmer, and Ken Hughes]: http://prde.upress.virginia.ed u/conversations/4011067.

43. For example, see "Lyndon Johnson, James Rowe, and Jack Valenti on 6 August 1964," Conversation WH5408-09–4777, 4778, *PRDE* [*Lyndon B. Johnson: Vietnam*, ed. David G. Coleman, Kent B. Germany, and Marc J. Selverstone]: http://prde.upress.virginia.ed u/conversations/4000589.

44. Califano, *Triumph & Tragedy*, 113–114; Woods, *LBJ*, 684.

45. For an example of Johnson coaching Nixon on how to respond to Humphrey's more dovish positioning on Vietnam, see "Lyndon B. Johnson, Richard M. Nixon, James R. 'Jim' Jones, and Walt W. Rostow on 30 September 1968," Conversation WH6809-04– 13432–13433, *PRDE* [*Johnson Telephone Tapes: 1968*, ed. Kent B. Germany, Nicole Hemmer, and Ken Hughes]: http://prde.upress.virginia.edu/conversations/4005497.

46. "Lyndon B. Johnson and Hubert H. Humphrey on 29 August 1968," Conversation WH6808-04–13330–13331, *PRDE* [*Johnson Telephone Tapes: 1968*, ed. Kent B. Germany, Nicole Hemmer, and Ken Hughes]: http://prde.upress.virginia.edu/conversations/ 4006019.

47. See John A. Farrell, *Richard Nixon: The Life* (New York: Doubleday, 2017), 342–345; Ken Hughes, ed., *Chasing Shadows: The Nixon Tapes, the Chennault Affair, and the Origins of Watergate* (Charlottesville, VA: University of Virginia Press, 2014); "Lyndon Johnson and Everett Dirksen on 2 November 1968," Conversation WH6811-01– 13706, *PRDE* [*Chasing Shadows*, ed. Ken Hughes]: http://prde.upress.virginia.edu/co nversations/4006123.

48. Rothman, *LBJ's Texas White House*, 235.

49. For a broader assessment of Johnson's health challenges, see Robert E. Gilbert, "The Political Effects of Presidential Illness: The Case of Lyndon B. Johnson," *Political Psychology* 16, no. 4 (December 1995): 761–776.

50. Bruce Shulman, "Lyndon Johnson Left Office as a Deeply Unpopular President. So Why Is He So Admired Today?" *Washington Post*, March 30, 2018.

51. "Address before a Joint Session of Congress on the State of the Union," *Public Papers of the Presidents of the United States: Ronald Reagan, 1988* (Washington, DC: 1990), vol. 1, 87.

52. "Address before a Joint Session of the Congress on the State of the Union," January 23, 1996, *Public Papers of the Presidents of the United States: William J. Clinton, 1996*, vol. 1 (Washington, DC: US Government Printing Office, 1997), 79.

53. Paul R. Henggeler, *In His Steps: Lyndon Johnson and the Kennedy Mystique* (Chicago, IL: Ivan R. Dee, 1991), and Jeff Shesol, *Mutual Contempt: Lyndon Johnson, Robert Kennedy, and the Feud That Defined a Decade* (New York: W. W. Norton, 1997).

54. *JFK*, directed by Oliver Stone (1991); John Newman, *JFK and Vietnam: Deception, Intrigue, and the Struggle for Power* (New York: Warner Books, 1992); Robert S. McNamara with Brian VanDeMark, *In Retrospect: The Tragedy and Lessons of Vietnam* (New York: Vintage Books, 1995).

55. *The LBJ Telephone Tapes: Inside the Presidency of Lyndon Baines Johnson*, http://lbjtapes .org; "The Presidential Recordings of Lyndon B. Johnson," *PRDE*: https://prde.upress .virginia.edu/content/johnson.

56. "LBJ's War," https://www.pri.org/programs/lbjs-war; "LBJ and the Great Society," https://lbjgreatsociety.org/. Full disclosure: I contributed to both productions.

57. Julian E. Zelizer, "What Hollywood Forgets about LBJ," *The Atlantic*, October 17, 2017.

58. Presidential Historians Survey 2021, https://www.c-span.org/presidentsurvey2021/; https://scri.siena.edu/us-presidents-study-historical-rankings/.

59. Allen J. Matusow, *The Unraveling of America: A History of Liberalism in the 1960s* (New York: Harper & Row, 1984).

60. Shulman, "Lyndon Johnson Left Office as a Deeply Unpopular President."

CHAPTER 2 LBJ AND THE CONTOURS OF AMERICAN LIBERALISM

1. For an interesting biographical essay that examines his evolution through liberal politics, see the introduction for Bruce J. Schulman, *Lyndon B. Johnson and American Liberalism: A Brief Biography with Documents* (Boston, MA: Bedford Books, 2007).

2. William Chafe, Raymond Gavins, and Robert Korstad, eds., *Remembering Jim Crow: African Americans Tell about Life in the Segregated South* (New York: New Press, 2001), 109, and American Presidency Project, www.presidency.ucsb.edu/documents/remarks-the-wel hausen-elementary-school-cotulla-texas.

3. Robert Dallek, *Lyndon B. Johnson: Portrait of a President* (New York: Oxford University Press, 2005), 26.

4. "A Roadside Shovel Salute That Caught F.D.R.'s Eye," *Life*, August 14, 1964.

5. Sidney Milkis and Jerome Mileur, "Lyndon Johnson, The Great Society, and the Twilight of the Modern Presidency," in Milkis and Mileur, eds., *The Great Society and the High Tide of Liberalism* (Amherst, MA: University of Massachusetts Press, 2005), 2.

6. Julian E. Zelizer, *On Capitol Hill: The Struggle to Reform Congress and Its Consequences, 1946–2000* (New York: Cambridge University Press, 2000), 27.

7. Ibid., 27–28.

8. William Leuchtenberg, *In the Shadow of FDR: From Harry Truman to Barack Obama*, 4th ed. (Ithaca: Cornell University Press, 2010), 130.

9. Randall B. Woods, *LBJ: Architect of American Ambition* (New York: Simon and Schuster, 2006), 145.

10. Michael Kazin, *What It Took to Win: A History of the Democratic Party* (New York:Farrar, Straus and Giroux, 2022), 188.

11. Ira Katznelson, *When Affirmative Action Was White: An Untold History of Racial Inequality* (New York: Norton, 2005).

12. Robert A. Caro, *The Years of Lyndon Johnson*, vol. 2: *Means of Ascent* (New York: Knopf, 1990).

13. Julian E. Zelizer, *Arsenal of Democracy: The Politics of National Security – From World War II to the War on Terrorism* (New York: Basic Books, 2010).

14. Robert A. Caro, *The Years of Lyndon Johnson*, vol. 3: *Master of the Senate* (New York: Knopf, 2002), 472.

15. Timothy Thurber, *The Politics of Equality: Hubert Humphrey and the African American Freedom Struggle* (New York: Columbia University Press, 1999), 62.

16. Schulman, *Lyndon B. Johnson and American Liberalism*, 52.

17. Caro, *Master of the Senate*.

18. Cited in Zelizer, *On Capitol Hill*.

19. Zelizer, *Arsenal of Democracy*, 127, 138.

20. Zelizer, *Arsenal of Democracy*, 139, and Caro, Master of the Senate, 1024.

21. Woods, *LBJ*, 561.

22. Telephone Conversation, Lyndon Johnson and Robert McNamara, August 3, 1964, White House Presidential Tapes, LBJ Presidential Library.

23. Charles Peters, *Lyndon B. Johnson* (New York: Times Books, 2010), 96.

24. John Lewis with Michael D'Orso, *Walking with the Wind: A Memoir of the Movement* (New York: Simon & Schuster, 2015), 291, and Stokely Carmichael and Charles V. Hamilton, *Black Power: The Politics of Liberation in America* (New York: Random House, 1971).

25. www.livingroomcandidate.org.

26. Charles Mohrs, "Johnson Sees U.S. Choice: Either 'Center' or 'Fringe,'" *New York Times*, September 24, 1964.

27. Julian E. Zelizer, *The Fierce Urgency of Now: Lyndon Johnson, Congress, and the Battle for the Great Society* (New York: Penguin Press, 2015), 163.

28. Ibid., 159–163.

29. Timothy J. Minchin and John A. Salmond, *After the Dream: Black and White Southerners since 1965* (Lexington: University of Kentucky Press, 2011), 28–29; Zelizer, *Fierce Urgency of Now*, 220; 321, and Zelizer, "So Far away from 1965," *Perspectives*, August 24, 2020, https://www.usccr.gov/files/pubs/msdelta ch3.htm#:~:text=Black%20voter%20registration%2C%20particularly%20in,some%20provisions%20addressing%20voting%20rights.

30. For a full discussion of these and other bills, see Zelizer, *Fierce Urgency of Now*, 163–223.

31. Fredrik Logevall, *Choosing War: The Lost Chance for Peace and the Escalation of War in Vietnam* (Berkeley, CA: University of California Press, 1999).

32. Zelizer, *Arsenal of Democracy.*, 185

33. Zelizer, *Fierce Urgency of Now*, 163–223.

34. Zelizer, *Fierce Urgency of Now*, 225–261.

35. Johnson speech, April 11, 1968, www.presidency.ucsb.edu/documents/remarks-upon-s igning-the-civil-rights-act.

36. Elizabeth Hinton, *From the War on Poverty to the War on Crime: The Making of Mass Incarceration in America* (Cambridge, MA: Harvard University Press, 2016), and Zelizer, "Introduction to the 2016 Edition," xii–xxxvi.

37. Zelizer, "Introduction to the 2016 Edition," *The Kerner Report: The National Advisory Commission on Civil Rights* (Princeton, NJ: Princeton University Press, 2016), xiii–xxxvi.

38. Michael Kazin, "Stop the Revisionism: LBJ Was No Liberal Hero," *New Republic*, April 11, 2014.

CHAPTER 3 LYNDON JOHNSON AND THE TRANSFORMATION OF COLD WAR CONSERVATISM

1. "The Week," *National Review*, December 17, 1963, 509.

2. John Chamberlain, "Which Way with LBJ?" *National Review*, December 17, 1963, 525–527.

3. Recent literature on the US right has worked to integrate the fringe and mainstream narratives more fully and show how blurred the lines were between the two. See, for instance, John S. Huntington, *Far-Right Vanguard: The Radical Roots of Modern Conservatism* (Philadelphia, PA: University of Pennsylvania Press, 2021) and Edward H. Miller, *A Conspiratorial Life: Robert Welch, the John Birch Society, and the Revolution of American Conservatism* (Chicago, IL: University of Chicago Press, 2022).

4. The "fusionism" approach, described in George Nash's intellectual history of the movement, has appeared as the basic ideological framework in most histories of US conservatism published since. George Nash, *The Conservative Intellectual Movement in America since 1945* (New York: Basic Books, 1976).

5. Lisa McGirr mapped the right's grassroots organizing in *Suburban Warriors: The Origins of the New American Right* (Princeton, NJ: Princeton University Press, 2001). On the Andrews campaign, see Nicole Hemmer, *Messengers of the Right: Conservative Media and the Transformation of American Politics* (Philadelphia, PA: University of Pennsylvania Press, 2016), 133–138.

6. William Buckley and Brent Bozell, *McCarthy and His Enemies: The Record and Its Meaning* (Chicago, IL: Regnery, 1954). On the right and unions, see Kim Phillips-Fein, *Invisible Hands: The Making of the Conservative Movement from the New Deal to Reagan* (New York: Norton, 2009) and Elizabeth Tandy Shermer, *Sunbelt Capitalism: Phoenix and the Transformation of American Politics* (Philadelphia, PA: University of Pennsylvania Press, 2013).

7. William Buckley, "Why the South Must Prevail," *National Review*, August 24, 1957, 148–149. On early Cold War conservatism and white supremacy, racism, and civil rights, see William P. Hustwit, *James J. Kilpatrick: Salesman for Segregation* (Chapel Hill, NC: University of North Carolina Press, 2011); Dan T. Carter, *The Politics of Rage: George Wallace, the Origins of the New Conservatism, and the Transformation of American Politics* (New York:

Simon and Schuster, 1995); and Emma J. Folwell, *The War on Poverty in Mississippi: From Massive Resistance to New Conservatism* (Jackson, MS: University of Mississippi Press, 2020).

8. Hemmer, *Messengers of the Right*, 137–139.

9. On Goldwater, see, for instance, McGirr, *Suburban Warriors*; Rick Perlstein, *Before the Storm: Barry Goldwater and the Unmaking of the American Consensus* (New York: Hill and Wang, 2001); Elizabeth Tandy Shermer, ed., *Barry Goldwater and the Remaking of the American Political Landscape* (Tuscon, AZ: University of Arizona Press, 2013).

10. Joshua Zeitz, *Building the Great Society: Inside Lyndon Johnson's White House* (New York: Viking, 2018).

11. Edward H. Miller, *Nut Country: Right-Wing Dallas and the Birth of the Southern Strategy* (Chicago, IL: University of Chicago Press, 2015).

12. Barry Goldwater, *The Forgotten American: A Statement of Proposed Republican Principles, Programs and Objectives* (Washington, DC: Human Events, Inc., 1961), 57–64.

13. Ibid.

14. "Transcript of Goldwater's Speech Accepting Republican Presidential Nomination," *New York Times*, July 17, 1964, 10.

15. Michael W. Flamm, *Law and Order: Street Crime, Civil Unrest, and the Crisis of Liberalism in the 1960s* (New York: Columbia University Press, 2005), 32.

16. J. Evetts Haley, *A Texan Looks at Lyndon: A Study in Illegitimate Power* (Canyon, TX: Palo Duro, 1964).

17. Rodney Crowther, "Two Health Plans Clash in Congress," *Baltimore Sun*, March 4, 1965, 6; Manion Forum Broadcast 540, "The 'Eldercare' Plan – Comprehensive, Efficient and Locally Administered," February 7, 1965; Manion Forum Broadcast 545, "Eldercare of Medicare? A Comparison of Costs, Controls and Benefits," March 14, 1965.

18. Manion to F. Leroy Hill, November 16, 1965, Box 21, Folder 1, Clarence E. Manion Papers, Chicago History Museum, Chicago, IL.

19. On the *National Review* editors' internal debates on the Birch Society editorial, see Hemmer, *Messengers of the Right*, 192–195.

20. Emil Herber to Manion, October 6, 1965, and Manion to Herber, October 8, 1965, Box 20, Folder 5, Clarence E. Manion Papers, Chicago History Museum, Chicago, IL.

21. On the uprisings, see Flamm, *Law and Order*, and Elizabeth Hinton, *America on Fire: The Untold History of Police Violence and Black Rebellion since the 1960s* (New York: Liveright, 2021).

22. Justin Vaïsse, *Neoconservatism: The Biography of a Movement* (Cambridge, MA: Belknap Press, 2010).

23. Thomas W. Evans, *The Education of Ronald Reagan: The General Electric Years and the Untold Story of His Conversion to Conservatism* (New York: Columbia University Press, 2006), 111–125.

24. Reagan gubernatorial campaign ad, "Ronald Reagan and a Need for Action!" January 4, 1966.

25. Ibid.

26. Donald T. Critchlow, *Phyllis Schlafly and Grassroots Conservatism* (Princeton, NJ: Princeton University Press, 2005).

27. On Wallace, see Carter, *The Politics of Rage.*

28. Frank S. Meyer, "The Populism of George Wallace," *National Review*, May 16, 1967, 527.

29. Barry Goldwater, "Don't Waste a Vote on Wallace, *National Review*, October 22, 1968, 1060–1061.

30. John Ashbrook, "And Anyway Is Wallace a Conservative?" *National Review*, October 22, 1968, 1048–1049.

31. Molly Michelmore, *Tax and Spend: The Welfare State, Tax Politics, and the Limits of American Liberalism* (Philadelphia, PA: University of Pennsylvania Press, 2012), 148; W. Elliott Brownlee and C. Eugene Steuerle, "Taxation," in W. Elliott Brownlee and Hugh Davis Graham, eds., *The Reagan Presidency: Pragmatic Conservatism and Its Legacies* (Lawrence, KS: University Press of Kansas, 2003), 161–168.

CHAPTER 4   THE GREAT SOCIETY AND THE BELOVED COMMUNITY: LYNDON JOHNSON, MARTIN LUTHER KING JR., AND THE PARTNERSHIP THAT TRANSFORMED ANATION

1. Nick Kotz, *Judgment Days: Lyndon Baines Johnson, Martin Luther King Jr., and the Laws That Changed America* (New York: Houghton Mifflin, 2005).

2. Peniel E. Joseph, *The Sword and the Shield: The Revolutionary Lives of Malcolm X and Martin Luther King Jr.* (New York: Basic Books, 2021), 206–207.

3. For example, ibid. 58, 62–64, 78–79, 174, 309.

4. See ibid.

5. Randall B. Woods, *LBJ: Architect of American Ambition* (New York: Free Press, 2006), 187–188.

6. Robert A. Caro, *The Years of Lyndon Johnson*, vol. 3: *Master of the Senate* (New York: Knopf, 2002), 711–715.

7. Johnson speech, May 30, 1963, https://www.lbjlibrary.org/object/text/remarks-vice-president-memorial-day-gettysburg-pennsylvania-05-30-1963.

8. For King's conception of radical Black citizenship, see Joseph, *Sword and the Shield*, 16, 266–306.

9. Ibid., 164–167.

10. Taylor Branch, *Parting the Waters: America in the King Years, 1954–1963* (New York: Simon and Schuster, 1988), 918.

11. Kotz, *Judgment Days*, 65–66.

12. Ibid., 66–67.

13. Keisha N. Blain, *Until I Am Free: Fannie Lou Hamer's Enduring Message to America* (Boston, MA: Beacon Press, 2021), 58.

14. Joshua Zeitz, *Building the Great Society: Inside Lyndon Johnson's White House* (New York: Viking Press, 2018), 189.

15. "Special Message to Congress: The American Promise," March 15, 1965, *Public Papers of the Presidents: Lyndon B. Johnson, 1965*, vol. 1 (Washington, DC: US Government Printing Office, 1966), 281–287.

16. James M. Washington, ed., *A Testament of Hope: The Essential Writings and Speeches of Martin Luther King, Jr.* (New York: HarperCollins, 1991), 295.

17. King–Johnson Conversation, August 20, 1965, Tape WH6508-07–8578, LBJ Presidential Library.

18. Joseph, *Sword and Shield*, 249–250.

19. Kotz, *Judgment Days*, 360.

20. Peniel E. Joseph, *Stokely: A Life* (New York: Basic Books, 2014), 105–123.

21. Taylor Branch, *At Canaan's Edge: America in the King Years, 1965–1968* (New York: Simon and Schuster, 2006), 595.

22. Jelani Cobb with Matthew Guariglia, eds., *The Essential Kerner Commission Report: The Landmark Study on Race, Inequality, and Police Violence* (New York: Liveright, 2021), xvii.

23. Steven M. Gillon, *Separate and Unequal: The Kerner Commission and the Unraveling of American Liberalism* (New York: Basic Books, 2018).

24. Cobb with Guariglia, eds., *Essential Kerner Commission Report*, 137, 140.

25. Ibid., 264–273.

26. "Statement by the President on the Assassination of Dr. Martin Luther King Jr.," April 4, 1968, *Public Papers of the Presidents: Lyndon B. Johnson, 1968–1969*, vol. 1 (Washington, DC: US Government Printing Office, 1970), 493.

27. Elizabeth Hinton, *From the War on Poverty to the War on Crime: The Making of Mass Incarceration in America* (Cambridge, MA: Harvard University Press, 2016), 118–119.

28. "Transcript of Johnson's Statement on Signing Crime and Safety Bill," *New York Times*, June 28, 1968, 23.

29. Hinton, *From the War on Poverty to the War on Crime*, 115–133.

30. For discussion of this period, see Peniel E. Joseph, *The Third Reconstruction: America's Struggle for Racial Justice in the Twenty-First Century* (New York: Basic Books, 2022).

31. Joseph, *Sword and the Shield*, 308.

32. See Michael Eric Dyson, *I May Not Get There with You: The True Martin Luther King Jr.* (New York: Free Press, 2000); Joseph, *Sword and the Shield*; Sylvie Laurent, *King and the Other America: The Poor People's Campaign and the Quest for Economic Equality* (Berkeley, CA: University of California Press, 2019); Brandon M. Terry and Tommie Shelby, eds., *To Shape a New World: Essays on the Political Philosophy of Martin Luther King Jr.* (Cambridge, MA: Harvard University Press, 2018); and Cornel West, ed., *The Radical King* (Boston, MA: Beacon Press, 2015).

CHAPTER 5 LYNDON JOHNSON, MEXICAN AMERICANS, AND THE BORDER

1. Lyndon B. Johnson, "Remarks at the Welhausen Elementary School, Cotulla, Texas," November 7, 1966. See https://www.presidency.ucsb.edu/documents/remarks-the-wel hausen-elementary-school-cotulla-texas.

2. Ibid.

3. Julie Leininger Pycior, *LBJ & Mexican Americans: The Paradox of Power* (Austin, TX: University of Texas Press, 1997), 7.

4. David Montejano, *Anglos and Mexicans in the Making of Texas, 1836–1986* (Austin, TX: University of Texas Press, 1987), 178.

5. Robert A. Caro, *The Years of Lyndon Johnson*, vol. 1: *The Path to Power* (New York: Vintage, 1990), 166–172.

6. Pycior, *LBJ & Mexican Americans*, xiii.

7. Henry A. Ramos, *The American GI Forum: In Pursuit of the Dream, 1948–1983* (Houston: Arte Público Press, 1998), 9–10.

8. Héctor P. García, in "Dr. Hector States His Beliefs and Talks about the Movement," at https://www.drhectorpgarciafoundation.org/dr_garcia_on_lyndon_johnson_the_felix_longoria_affair_and_his_purpose.

9. Montejano, *Anglos and Mexicans in the Making of Texas*, chapter 6.

10. Geraldo Cadava, *The Hispanic Republican: The Shaping of an American Political Identity, from Nixon to Trump* (New York: Ecco, 2020), chapter 1.

11. Ignacio M. García, *Viva Kennedy: Mexican Americans in Search of Camelot* (College Station, TX: Texas A&M University Press, 2000), chapters 2–4.

12. Mario T. García, *The Making of a Mexican American Mayor: Raymond L. Telles of El Paso and the Origins of Latino Political Power* (Tucson, AZ: University of Arizona Press, 2018).

13. Cynthia Orozco, "Viva Kennedy–Viva Johnson Clubs," *Handbook of Texas*, published by the Texas State Historical Association. See https://www.tshaonline.org/handbook/e ntries/viva-kennedy-viva-johnson-clubs.

14. Cadava, *The Hispanic Republican*, chapter 2.

15. Ibid.

16. "Title VII of the Civil Rights Act of 1964." See https://www.eeoc.gov/statutes/title-vii-civil-rights-act-1964#:~:text=Title%20VII%20prohibits%20employment%20discrimin ation,religion%2C%20sex%20and%20national%20origin.

17. Pycior, *LBJ & Mexican Americans*, 146.

18. Cadava, *The Hispanic Republican*, chapter 3.

19. Ibid., 147.

20. Greg Grandin, *Empire's Workshop: Latin America, the United States, and the Rise of the New Imperialism* (New York: Metropolitan Books, 2006).

21. Geraldo Cadava, *Standing on Common Ground: The Making of a Sunbelt Borderland* (Cambridge, MA: Harvard University Press, 2013), chapter 5.

22. Mae M. Ngai, *Impossible Subjects: Illegal Aliens and the Making of Modern America* (Princeton, NJ: Princeton University Press, 2004), chapter 1.

23. Leah Wright Rigueur, *The Loneliness of the Black Republican: Pragmatic Politics and the Pursuit of Power* (Princeton, NJ: Princeton University Press, 2015), chapter 2.

24. Ana Minian, *Undocumented Lives: The Untold Story of Mexican Migration* (Cambridge, MA: Harvard University Press, 2018), introduction.

25. "Good Neighbor Policy, 1933," https://history.state.gov/milestones/1921-1936/good-neighbor.

26. Paul Kramer, "A Border Crosses," *New Yorker*, September 20, 2014, https://www.new yorker.com/news/news-desk/moving-mexican-border.

27. Meeting between President Johnson and President López Mateos, "Memorandum of Conversation," February 21, 1964. See https://history.state.gov/historicaldocuments/frus1964-68v31/d346.

28. Kelly Lytle Hernández, "The Crimes and Consequences of Illegal Immigration: A Cross-Border Examination of Operation Wetback, 1943–1954," *Western Historical Quarterly*, 37, no. 4 (winter 2006): 421–444.

29. Ngai, *Impossible Subjects*, chapter 1.

30. Philip E. Wolgin, "Family Reunification Is the Bedrock of U.S. Immigration Policy," *Center for American Progress*, February 12, 2018. See https://www.americanprogress.org/article/family-reunification-bedrock-u-s-immigration-policy/.

31. Lyndon B. Johnson, "Remarks at the Signing of the Immigration Bill, Liberty Island, New York," October 3, 1965. See https://www.presidency.ucsb.edu/documents/remarks-the-signing-the-immigration-bill-liberty-island-new-york. Online by Gerhard Peters and John T. Woolley, The American Presidency Project.

32. Sean Parulian Harvey, "Assembly Lines: *Maquiladoras*, Poverty, and the Environment in the U.S.–Mexico Borderlands, 1966–1972," PhD Dissertation, Northwestern University, Department of History, 2020.

33. Jefferson Cowie, *Capital Moves: RCA's Seventy-Year Quest for Cheap Labor* (New York: New Press, 2001), chapters 4 and 6. For a later but related NAFTA-fueled story, see Chad Broughton, *Boom, Bust, Exodus: The Rust Belt, the Maquilas, and a Tale of Two Cities* (New York: Oxford University Press, 2015).

34. Harvey, "Assembly Lines," chapter 5.

35. Lyndon B. Johnson, quoted in Benjamin Francis-Fallon, *The Rise of the Latino Vote: A History* (Cambridge, MA: Harvard University Press, 2019), 121.

36. Lyndon B. Johnson, "Remarks at the Swearing in of Vicente T. Ximenes as a Member of the Equal Employment Opportunity Commission," June 9, 1967. See https://www.presidency.ucsb.edu/documents/remarks-the-swearing-vicente-t-ximenes-member-the-equal-employment-opportunity-commission. For more on the formation of the ICMAA, see G. Cristina Mora, *Making Hispanics: How Activists, Bureaucrats, and Media Constructed a New American* (Chicago: University of Chicago Press, 2014), chapter 1.

37. Rodolfo "Corky" Gonzáles, "Yo Soy Joaquín," 1967. See https://www.latinamericanstudies.org/latinos/joaquin.htm.

38. Mora, *Making Hispanics*, 28.

39. Ibid, 28.

40. Ibid, 24.

41. Lyndon B. Johnson, "Proclamation 3869 – National Hispanic Heritage Week, 1968," September 17, 1968. See https://www.presidency.ucsb.edu/documents/proclamation-3869-national-hispanic-heritage-week-1968. Online by Gerhard Peters and John T. Woolley, The American Presidency Project.

42. Leo Janos, "The Last Days of the President," *The Atlantic*, July 1973, https://www.theatlantic.com/magazine/archive/1973/07/the-last-days-of-the-president/376281/.

CHAPTER 6   THE WAR ON POVERTY: HOW QUALITATIVE

LIBERALISM PREVAILED

1. Walter Heller Oral History, February 20, 1970, 13–15, LBJ Presidential Library.
2. Nicholas Lemann, *The Promised Land: The Great Black Migration and How It Changed America* (New York: Vintage, 1999), 141.
3. Michael L. Gilette, *Launching the War on Poverty: An Oral History* (New York: Oxford University Press, 2010), 15.
4. Richard N. Goodwin, *Remembering America: A Voice from the Sixties* (New York: Little Brown Company, 1988), 270.
5. James T. Patterson, *Grand Expectations: The United States, 1945–1974* (New York: Oxford University Press, 1996), 312, 451. This growth was felt across the board, with the bottom two quintiles increasing its share of national income by 4 percent. See *Historical Statistics of the United States*, Table Be 39–46; Table Be 1–18, https://www.census.gov/library/p ublications/1975/compendia/hist_stats_colonial-1970.html.
6. Patterson, *Grand Expectations*, 312. Between 1936 and 1972 the proportion of families living in owner-occupied homes increased from 44 percent to 63 percent. See Kenneth Jackson, *Crabgrass Frontier: The Suburbanization of the United States* (New York: Oxford University Press, 1987), 205.
7. Between 1950 and 1970 the proportion of the workforce engaged in that qualified as white-collar increased from 30.5 percent to 41 percent. See Morris Janowitz, *The Last Half-Century: Societal Change and Politics in America* (Chicago, IL: University of Chicago Press, 1978), 127.
8. Joshua Zeitz, "Back to the Barricades," *American Heritage Magazine* (October 2001): 70–75.
9. Alvin Hansen, "Economic Progress and Declining Population Growth," *American Economic Review*, 29 (March 1939): 4.
10. "Reuther Challenges 'Our Fear of Abundance,'" *New York Times*, September 16, 1945.
11. Robert M. Collins, *More: The Politics of Economic Growth in Postwar America* (New York: Oxford University Press, 2000), 17–18.
12. Richard Hofstadter, *The Paranoid Style in American Politics:And Other Essays* (Cambridge, MA: Harvard University Press, 1996), 42.
13. Michael Harrington, *The Other America: Poverty in the United States* (New York: Macmillan, 1962), 10.
14. James T. Patterson, *America's Struggle against Poverty, 1900–1994* (Cambridge, MA: Harvard University Press, 1981), 129.
15. Gilette, *Launching the War on Poverty*, 3.
16. Ibid., 6.
17. Robert Dallek, *Flawed Giant: Lyndon Johnson and His Times, 1961–1973* (New York: Oxford University Press, 1998), 75.
18. Jule Sugarman Oral History, March 14, 1969, 12–16, LBJ Presidential Library.
19. Ibid., 14–15; John Andrew III, *Lyndon Johnson and the Great Society* (Chicago, IL: Ivan R. Dee, 1998), 76–77.

20. Jule Sugarman Oral History, March, 14, 1969, 14–15, LBJ Presidential Library; Andrew III, *Lyndon Johnson and the Great Society*, 76–77.

21. Edward D. Berkowitz, *Mr. Social Security: The Life of Wilbur J. Cohen* (Lawrence, KS: University Press of Kansas, 1995), 167.

22. James L. Sundquist, *Politics and Policy: The Eisenhower, Kennedy and Johnson Years* (Washington, DC: Brookings Institution, 1968), 290, 298.

23. Ibid., 288–289.

24. Randall B. Woods, *Prisoners of Hope: Lyndon Johnson, The Great Society, and the Limits of Liberalism* (New York Basic: Books, 2016), 146.

25. Ibid., 153–154.

26. Bridget Terry Long, "Supporting Higher Education," in Martha J. Bailey and Sheldon Danziger, eds., *Legacies of the War on Poverty* (New York: Russell Sage Foundation, 2013), 97.

27. Woods, *Prisoners of Hope*, 144.

28. Harry S. Truman, Annual Message to the Congress on the State of the Union, January 5, 1949; Alonzo Hamby, *Beyond the New Deal: Harry S. Truman and American Liberalism* (New York: Columbia University Press, 1976), 293.

29. Julian E. Zelizer, *The Fierce Urgency of Now: Lyndon Johnson, Congress, and the Battle for the Great Society* (New York: Penguin Press, 2015), 175; Sundquist, *Politics and Policy*, 159–160.

30. Elizabeth Cascio and Sarah Reber, "The K-12 Education Battle," in Bailey and Danziger, eds., *Legacies of the War on Poverty*, 68.

31. Sundquist, *Politics and Policy*, 155.

32. Ibid., 178, 187; Zelizer, *The Fierce Urgency of Now*, 181.

33. Joshua M. Zeitz, *White Ethnic New York: Jews, Catholics, and the Shaping of Post-War Politics* (Chapel Hill, NC: University of North Carolina Press, 2007), 11–38; Woods, *Prisoners of Hope*, 137.

34. Sundquist, *Politics and Policy*, 189.

35. Woods, *Prisoners of Hope*, 138.

36. Allen J. Matusow, *The Unraveling of America: A History of Liberalism in the 1960s* (New York: Harper & Row, 1984), 221.

37. Andrew III, *Lyndon Johnson and the Great Society*, 119–120.

38. Patrick McGuinn and Frederick Hess, "Freedom from Ignorance? The Great Society and the Evolution of the Elementary and Secondary Education Act of 1965," in Sidney M. Milkis and Jerome M. Mileur, eds., *The Great Society and the High Tide of American Liberalism* (Amherst, MA: University of Massachusetts Press, 2005), 302–303.

39. Scott Stossel, *The Life and Times of Sargent Shriver* (Washington, DC: Smithsonian Books, 2004), 411; Andrew III, *Lyndon Johnson and the Great Society*, 73.

40. Scott Stossel, *Life and Times*, 408.

41. Lemann, *The Promised Land*, 165–167; Andrew III, *Lyndon Johnson and the Great Society*, 73.

42. Gilette, *Launching the War on Poverty*, 247.

43. Lemann, *The Promised Land*, 167.

44. Ibid., 165.

45. "The Office of Economic Opportunity during the Administration of Lyndon Johnson: Administrative History," 22–24, LBJ Presidential Library; Andrew III, *Lyndon Johnson and the Great Society*, 61–62.

46. Rick Perlstein, *Before the Storm: Barry Goldwater and the Unmaking of the American Consensus* (New York: Hill and Wang, 2001), 317–321; Dan T. Carter, *The Politics of Rage: George Wallace, the Origins of the New Conservatism, and the Transformation of American Politics* (New York: Simon and Schuster, 1995), 202–203.

47. Perlstein, *Before the Storm*, 321, 342–344; Theodore H. White, *The Making of the President, 1964* (New York: Atheneum, 1973), 245.

48. On housing discrimination, see Jackson, *Crabgrass Frontier*, chapter 11; Harold X. Connolly, *A Ghetto Grows in Brooklyn* (New York, 1977); Craig Steven Wilder, *A Covenant with Color: Race and Social Power in Brooklyn* (New York, 2000), chapter 9.

49. Memorandum, Richard Scammon to Bill Moyers, July 21, 1964, Box 3, Office Files of Bill Moyers, LBJ Presidential Library.

50. Andrew III, *Lyndon Johnson and the Great Society*, 109–111.

51. Rick Perlstein, *Nixonland: The Rise of a President and the Fracturing of America* (New York: Scribner, 2008), 197–198.

52. George Reedy, *The Twilight of the Presidency: From Johnson to Reagan*, rev. ed. (New York: New American Library, 1987), 167.

53. Brian VanDeMark, *Into the Quagmire: Lyndon Johnson and the Escalation of the Vietnam War* (New York: Oxford University Press, 1995), 155.

54. "Consumer Price Index, 1913–," Federal Reserve Bank of Minneapolis (https://www .minneapolisfed.org/about-us/monetary-policy/inflation-calculator/consumer-price-index-1913-), and "Labor Force Statistics from the Current Population Survey," Bureau of Labor Statistics, Department of Labor (https://www.bls.gov/cps/).

55. Joseph Califano Jr., *The Triumph & Tragedy of Lyndon Johnson: The White House Years* (New York: Simon and Schuster, 1991), 61–148.

56. "Reagan Blames 'Great Society' for Economic Woes," *New York Times*, May 10, 1983.

57. Bailey and Danziger, eds., *Legacies of the War on Poverty*, 12–14.

58. Matusow, *The Unraveling of America*, 239; Patterson, *America's Struggle against Poverty*, 192–194; Joan Hoff, *Nixon Reconsidered* (New York: Basic Books, 1994), 115–119.

59. Irwin Unger, *The Best of Intentions: The Triumphs and Failures of the Great Society under Kennedy, Johnson, and Nixon* (New York: Doubleday, 1996), 195; Gareth Davies, *From Opportunity to Entitlement: The Transformation and Decline of Great Society Liberalism* (Lawrence, KS: University Press of Kansas, 1996), 97–102.

60. US Bureau of Labor Statistics, "Union Membership in the United States" (September 2016), 2, 4, https://www.bls.gov/spotlight/2016/union-membership-in-the-united-sta tes/home.htm; Jacob Hacker, "Failing the Middle Class: The Real Dangers to the American Middle Class," *Challenge* 50, no. 3 (May–June 2007): 26–42.

61. US Department of Agriculture, SNAP Data Tables, www.fns.usda.gov/pd/supplemental-nutrition-assistance-program-snap; Centers for Medicare & Medicaid Services (CMS), Latest Enrollment Figures, December 21, 2021, https://www.cms.gov/newsroom/news-alert/cms-releases-latest-enrollment-figures-medicare-medicaid-and-childrens-health-ins

urance-program-chip; "National School Lunch Program," USDA Economic Research Service, www.ers.usda.gov/topics/food-nutrition-assistance/child-nutrition-programs/national-school-lunch-program; "CMS Fast Facts," US Department of Health and Human Services, www.cms.gov/Research-Statistics-Data-and-Systems/Statistics-Trends-and-Reports/CMS-Fast-Facts.

62. Bridget Terry Long, "Supporting Higher Education," 95.
63. Ibid., 101.
64. Ibid., 95, 103–104.

CHAPTER 7 LBJ'S SUPREME COURT

1. Ethan Bronner, *Battle for Justice: How the Bork Nomination Shook America* (New York: W. W. Norton, 1989).
2. See, for instance, call to Walter Reuther, August 5, 1964, 2:54 P.M., WH6408.07, PNO 6, #4727.
3. See Gerald Rosenberg, *The Hollow Hope: Can Courts Bring about Social Change?* (Chicago, IL: University of Chicago Press, 1991), 4; Stephen Reinhardt, "Guess Who's Not Coming to Dinner!!," *Michigan Law Review* 91 (1993): 1175–1182, 1181; *Brown v. Board of Education*, 347 U.S. 483 (1954); 349 U.S. 294 (1955).
4. Laura Kalman, *The Strange Career of Legal Liberalism* (New Haven, CT: Yale University Press, 1996), 13–22; Morton Horwitz, "The Warren Court and the Pursuit of Justice," *Washington & Lee Law Review* 50 (1993): 5–13, 11; Bernard Schwartz, *Super Chief: Earl Warren and His Supreme Court – A Judicial Biography* (New York: New York University Press, 1983), 326.
5. Garrison Nelson with Maggie Steakley and James Montague, *Pathways to the Supreme Court: From the Arena to the Monastery* (New York: Palgrave Macmillan, 2013), 71.
6. Nomination of Arthur Goldberg, Hearings before the Committee on the Judiciary, US Senate, Eighty-Seventh Congress, Second Session on Nomination of Arthur J. Goldberg, of Illinois, to Be Associate Justice of the Supreme Court of the United States, September 11 and 13, 1962 (Washington, DC: US Government Printing Office, 1962), 22, 24; Barry Goldwater to the President, August 30, 1962, WHCF, Box 194 Ex FG 535/A, Kennedy Library.
7. *Abington School District v. Schempp*, 374 U.S. 203 (1963); *NAACP v. Button*, 371 U.S. 415 (1963); *Gideon v. Wainwright*, 372 U.S. 335 (1963); *Wong Sun v. United States*, 371 U.S. 471 (1963); *Ker v. California*, 374 U.S. 23 (1963); *Fay v. Noia*, 372 U.S. 391 (1963); *Gray v. Sanders*, 372 U.S. 368, 381 (1963); *Griffin v. County School Board of Prince Edward County*, 377 U.S. 218 (1964); *Edwards v. South Carolina*, 372 U.S. 229 (1963); *Griffin v. Maryland*, 378 U.S. 130 (1964); *Robinson v. Florida*, 378 U.S. 153 (1964); *Barr v. City of Columbia*, 378 U.S. 146 (1964); *Bell v. Maryland*, 378 U.S. 226 (1964); *Bouie v. City of Columbia*, 378 U.S. 347 (1964); *Hamm v. City of Rock Hill*, 379 U.S. 306 (1964); *McLaughlin v. Florida*, 379 U.S. 184 (1964); *Heart of Atlanta Motel v. U.S.*, 379 U.S. 241 (1964); *Katzenbach v. McClung*, 379 U.S. 294 (1964); *New York Times v. Sullivan*, 376 U.S. 254 (1964); *Jacobellis v. Ohio*, 378 U.S. 184 (1964); *Quantity of Books v. Kansas*, 378 U.S. 205 (1964); *Aptheker v. Secretary of State*, 378 U.S. 500 (1964); *Malloy v. Hogan*, 378 U.S. 1 (1964); *Massiah v. U.S.*, 377 U.S. 201 (1964); Fred Rodell, "The 'Warren Court' Stands Its Ground," *New York Times Magazine*, September 27, 1964.

8. Charles Mohr, "Goldwater Sees Presidency Peril," *New York Times*, September 12, 1964; Robert Thompson, "School Prayers Given Support by Goldwater," *Los Angeles Times*, October 11, 1964; Charles Mohr, "Goldwater Says He'd Curb Court," *New York Times*, September 16, 1964.

9. See, for instance, Frank Porter, "Prominent Lawyers Rebuke Goldwater: Many Bar Leaders," *Washington Post*, October 12, 1964; "Goldwater Scored for Court Attack," *New York Times*, September 3, 1964; Drew Pearson, "Goldwater Court Plan Claimed," *Los Angeles Times*, August 4, 1964; Brad Snyder, "How the Conservatives Canonized *Brown v. Board of Education*," *Rutgers Law Review* 52 (2000): 383–494.

10. Jim Cannon to Messrs. Elliott, Lansner, Bernstein, Bradlee, Iselin, Roberts, Miss Sain, "Talk with President Johnson on July 14, 1965," Box 32, Theodore White Papers, Kennedy Library; Alexander Wohl, *Father, Son, and the Constitution: How Justice Tom Clark and Attorney General Ramsey Clark Shaped American Democracy* (Lawrence, KS: University Press of Kansas, 2013), 288.

11. Robert Dallek, *Flawed Giant: Lyndon Johnson and His Times, 1961–1973* (New York: Oxford University Press, 1998), 233; Lady Bird Johnson, Tape-Recorded Diary, January 13, 1965, https://www.discoverlbj.org/item/ctjd-19650113.

12. *Dred Scott v. Sandford*, 60 U.S. 393 (1857); Merlo Pusey, "Dred Scott Was Court's Worst Blunder," *Washington Post*, March 3, 1957.

13. To Richard Russell, January 22, 1965, 11:15 A.M., WH6501.04, PNO 6–7, #6741–42; Max Frankel, *The Times of My Life and My Life with The Times* (New York: Random House, 1999), 291 ("pecker").

14. Barbara Perry, *A "Representative" Supreme Court? The Impact of Race, Religion, and Gender on Appointments* (Westport, CT: Greenwood, 1991).

15. John Kenneth Galbraith, *A Life in Our Times* (Boston, MA: Houghton Mifflin, 1981), 456–457; call to Richard Russell, July 19, 1965, 6:09 P.M., WH6507.04, PNO 13, #8352; Arthur Goldberg Oral History, 1, LBJ Presidential Library.

16. Lady Bird Johnson, Tape-Recorded Diary, July 21, 1965, https://discoverlbj.org/item/ctjd-19650721; Joseph Califano Jr., *The Triumph & Tragedy of Lyndon Johnson: The White House Years* (New York: Simon and Schuster, 1991), 48.

17. Laura Kalman, *Abe Fortas: A Biography* (New Haven, CT: Yale University Press, 1990), 245; "Nomination of Abe Fortas, of Tennessee, to Be an Associate Justice of the Supreme Court of the United States," *US Senate Judiciary Committee, August 5, 1965* (Washington, DC: US Government Printing Office, 1965).

18. *Brown v. Louisiana*, 383 U.S. 131, 142 (1966); *Miranda v. Arizona*, 384 U.S. 436, 501 (1966).

19. Kalman, *Abe Fortas*, 312 ("uncomfortable"); Califano, *Triumph & Tragedy*, 315.

20. Laura Kalman, *The Long Reach of the Sixties: LBJ, Nixon, and the Making of the Contemporary Supreme Court* (New York: Oxford University Press, 2019), 74–82; call to Abe Fortas, October 3, 1966, 8:16 A.M., WH6610.02, PNO 1, #10912.

21. Juan Williams, *Thurgood Marshall: American Revolutionary* (New York: Times Books, 1998), xiv; Carl Rowan, *Dream Makers, Dream Breakers: The World of Justice Thurgood Marshall* (Boston, MA: Little, Brown 1993), 218; call to Thurgood Marshall, July 7,

1965, 1:30 P.M., WH6507.01, PNO 7, #8307; call to John Galbraith, July 20, 1965, 12:06 P.M., WH6507.05, PNO 10, #8362.

22. Nicholas Katzenbach, *Some of It Was Fun: Working with RFK and LBJ* (New York: W. W. Norton, 2008), 211–213; call from Abe Fortas, September 22, 1966, 8:30 A.M., WH6609.11, PNO 3–4, #10821–22; call to Everett Dirksen, September 21, 1966, 11:41 A.M., WH6609.10 PNO 10, #10817; call to Everett Dirksen, September 22, 1966, 5:00 P. M., WH6609.11, PNO 7, #10825.

23. Call from Abe Fortas, September 22, 1966, 8:30 A.M., WH6609.11, PNO 3–4, #10821– 22; call from Ramsey Clark, January 25, 1967, 8:22 P.M., WH6701.09, PNO 2, #11408; Seth Stern and Stephen Wermiel, *Justice Brennan: Liberal Champion* (Boston, MA: Houghton Mifflin, 2010), 287–289; Roger Newman, *Hugo Black: A Biography* (New York: Pantheon, 1994), 570.

24. Linda Greene, "The Confirmation of Thurgood Marshall to the United States Supreme Court," *Harvard Blackletter Journal* 6 (1989): 27–50; Roy Reed, "Marshall Named for High Court, Its First Negro," *New York Times,* June 14, 1967; Herman Talmadge to Jesse Kite Sr., April 23, 1968, Series VII.A., Box 341, Riots, Talmadge Papers, University of Georgia, and L. M. Todd, August 3, 1967, ibid.

25. Nomination of Thurgood Marshall, Hearings before the Committee on the Judiciary, US Senate, 90th Congress, First Session, on the Nomination of Thurgood Marshall, of New York, to be an Associate Justice of the Supreme Court of the United States, July 13, 14, 18, 19, and 24, 1967, 3–14, 55, 158, 161–76; Kenneth Kmiec, "The Origin and Current Meanings of Judicial Activism," *California Law Review* 92 (2004): 1441–1478, 1445–1449.

26. Greene, "The Confirmation of Thurgood Marshall," 48–49.

27. Fred Graham, "The Law: Marshall and the Activists," *New York Times,* September 3, 1967; John MacKenzie, "Supreme Court Was Main Target in Marshall Quiz," *Washington Post,* September 4, 1967; Ronald Ostrow, "Marshall Target of South's Frustration," *Los Angeles Times,* July 18, 1967.

28. Jim Jones, Memorandum for the Record, June 13, 1968, EX FG535, Box 360, LBJ Presidential Library; "Nixon Links Court to Rise in Crime," *New York Times,* May 31, 1968; "Nixon, in Texas, Sharpens His Attack," *New York Times,* November 3, 1968; Califano, *Triumph & Tragedy,* 307.

29. Kalman, *Abe Fortas,* 327; Clark Clifford, *Counsel to the President: A Memoir* (New York: Random House, 1991), 555–556.

30. Lyndon Johnson, *The Vantage Point: Perspectives on the Presidency* (New York: Holt, Rinehart, and Winston, 1971), 545; call to Everett Dirksen, June 27, 1968, 3:57 P.M. WH6806.04, PNO 6, #13147; call to Mike Mansfield, June 26, 1968, 9:44 A.M., WH6806.04, PNO 5, #13145.

31. *Terry v. Ohio,* 392 U.S. 1 (1968); Abe Fortas, *Concerning Dissent and Civil Disobedience* (New York: A Signet Special Broadside published by the New American Library, 1968), 52–55.

32. Kalman, *Abe Fortas,* 329–330; Bruce Murphy, *Fortas: The Rise and Ruin of a Supreme Court Justice* (New York: Morrow, 1988), 292–299; Drew Pearson and Jack Anderson, "Fortas Support Is Keyed to SACB," *Washington Post,* July 11, 1968; call to Everett Dirksen, July 11, 1968, 8:26 A. M. WH6807.01, PNO 5, #13205.

33. Warren Christopher, Memorandum for Larry Temple, The Fortas and Thornberry Nominations, December 20, 1968, Box 3, Fortas–Thornberry MSS, LBJ Presidential Library (hereafter Fortas–Thornberry MSS); Mike Manatos, Memoranda for the President, June 25–26, 1968, Box 1, Fortas–Thornberry MSS; Robert Griffin, "The Senate Stands Taller: The Fortas Case" (Griffin's unpublished memoir of the Fortas fight; hereafter "The Fortas Case"), Box 284, Griffin MSS, Michigan State University; "Approval of High Court Nominees May Rest on Southern Fears of Warren's Staying On," *Wall Street Journal*, June 28, 1968.

34. "The Political Court," *Wall Street Journal*, June 27, 1968; Bob Fleming, Memorandum for the President, June 26, 1968, 7:15 P.M., Box 1, Fortas–Thornberry MSS; Don Irwin, "Fortas Naming Timed Wrong, Nixon Asserts," *Los Angeles Times*, June 27, 1968; "Subsiding Tempest," *Washington Post*, July 4, 1968; Griffin, "The Fortas Case."

35. Nominations of Abe Fortas and Homer Thornberry, Part I, Hearings before the Committee on the Judiciary, US Senate, 90th Congress, Second Session, on Nomination of Abe Fortas, of Tennessee, to be Chief Justice of the United States and Nomination of Homer Thornberry, of Texas, to be Associate Justice of the Supreme Court of the United States, July 11, 12, 16, 17, 18, 19, 20, 22, and 23, 1968, Part 1, 58, 54, 103.

36. Ibid., 103–106; Califano, *Triumph & Tragedy*, 313, 315; Murphy, *Fortas*, 378–406; Kalman, *Abe Fortas*, 337–339.

37. Nominations of Abe Fortas and Homer Thornberry, Part 1, 166.

38. Corrina Lain, "Countermajoritarian Hero or Zero? Rethinking the Warren Court's Role in the Criminal Procedure Revolution," *University of Pennsylvania Law Review* 152 (2004): 1361–1452.

39. Griffin, "The Fortas Case"; Nominations of Abe Fortas and Homer Thornberry, Part 1, 126–162.

40. Nominations of Abe Fortas and Homer Thornberry, Part 1, 191–192; Meg Greenfield, "In 1968, Read 'Crime' for 'Communism': Law and Order Issue Stirs Memories of Fifties," *Los Angeles Times*, August 25, 1968; Griffin, "The Fortas Case"; *Mallory v. US*, 354 U.S. 449 (1957); James Clayton, "The Mallory Story: From Death Cell to Freedom," *Washington Post*, June 30, 1957; John McKenzie, "Fortas Berated for Two Hours," *Washington Post*, July 19, 1968.

41. John MacKenzie, "4 Noted Attorneys Endorse Fortas," *Washington Post*, August 3, 1968; Fred Graham, "Law Dean Assails Critics of Fortas," *New York Times*, August 7, 1968; "Head of Bar Assails Griffin for Battle against Fortas," *New York Times*, August 13, 1968; Louis Harris, "Fortas Backed in Poll but Court in Disfavor," *Atlanta Constitution*, August 12, 1968; Murphy, *Fortas*, 447.

42. Mark Silverstein, *Judicious Choices: The Politics of Supreme Court Confirmations*, 2nd ed. (New York: W. W. Norton, 2007), 26–27; John James Lucier to Strom Thurmond, July 19, 1968, Box 45, Fortas Speech/Statement Drafts/Folder 1, Legislative Assistant Series, Thurmond MSS, Clemson University.

43. Nominations of Abe Fortas and Homer Thornberry, Part 1, 277, 2511; Fred Graham, "Thornberry Bars Senate Questions on Past Decisions," *New York Times*, 1968; Griffin, "The Fortas Case."

44. Hugh Jones, "The Defeat of the Nomination of Abe Fortas as Chief Justice of the United States: A Case Study in Judicial Politics," PhD Dissertation, Johns Hopkins University, 1979, 201, 274, n. 148, 256–258, 281–282.

45. Brian Frye, "The Dialectic of Obscenity," *Hamline Law Review* 35 (2012): 229–278; James Kilpatrick, "Fortas: His Confirmation Could Turn on Film Decision Alone," *Los Angeles Times*, August 13, 1968; "Strom Thurmond Reports to the People: Fortas on Filth," August 5, 1968, vol. XIV, No. 28, Box 508, Folder 60, McClellan MSS, Oachita Baptist University (hereafter McClellan MSS); Marjorie Hunter, "Returning Democrats Are in for Trouble," *New York Times*, September 1, 1968.

46. Ronald Ostrow and Robert Jackson, "Even Supporters Question Fortas' Accepting Fee," *Los Angeles Times*, September 21, 1968; Philip Dodd, "Fortas Dealt New Blow," *Chicago Tribune*, September 28, 1968; Richard Russell to Lyndon B. Johnson, September 26, 1968, Box 3, Fortas–Thornberry MSS; Mike Manatos, Memorandum for the President, September 16, 1968, Fortas–Thornberry MSS; Griffin, "The Fortas Case."

47. Califano, *Triumph & Tragedy*, 316–317; Fred Graham, "The Votes Are Not There for Fortas," *New York Times*, September 29, 1968.

48. Johnson, *The Vantage Point*, 546.

49. "Sen. Griffin Wins Once Lonely Battle to Block Court Change," *Chicago Tribune*, October 3, 1968; Phyllis Schlafly, "What the Vote on Abe Fortas Means," December 1, 1968, Box 528, McClellan MSS; Patrick Buchanan, *The Greatest Comeback: How Richard Nixon Rose from Defeat to Create the New Majority* (New York: Crown, 2014), 278; Whitney Strub, *Perversion for Profit: The Politics of Pornography and the Rise of the New Right* (New York: Columbia University Press, 2010), 7, 20; Kalman, *Abe Fortas*, 356, 357 (Fortas, Johnson).

50. Ronald Ostrow, "Scholars See Trouble Ahead for High Court: Battle over Fortas Nomination Could Be Signal That Greater Difficulties Are Due," *Los Angeles Times*, October 3, 1968.

51. Thomas Keck, "Party Politics or Judicial Independence? The Regime Politics Literature Hits the Law Schools," *Law and Social Inquiry* 511 (2007): 32.

52. Jeffrey Rosen, "Even Stephen," *New Republic*, June 5, 1994, https://newrepublic.com/article/73758/even-stephen; Silverstein, *Judicious Choices*, 80; John Rollett, "Forum: Reversed on Appeal: The Uncertain Future of President Obama's 'Empathy Standard'," https://www.yalelawjournal.org/forum/reversed-on-appeal-the-uncertain-future-of-president-obamas-qempathy-standardq; "Presidential Candidates on Judicial Selection," American Bar Association, August 8, 2008, https://www.c-span.org/video/?280373-2/presidential-candidates-judicial-selection; "Remarks to the White House Press Pool and an Exchange with Reporters," April 28, 2010, https://www.presidency.ucsb.edu/documents/remarks-the-white-house-press-pool-and-exchange-with-reporters; Charlie Savage and Sheryl Stolberg, "Obama Says Liberal Courts May Have Overreached," *New York Times*, April 30, 2010.

53. Lee Epstein, Jack Knight, and Andrew Martin, "The Norm of Prior Judicial Experiences and Its Consequences for Career Diversity on the U.S. Supreme Court," *California Law Review* 91 (2003): 903–966; Emily Bazelon and John Witt, "Notebook: Senate Republicans and the Supreme Court: Where Is This Headed Exactly?" *New York Times Magazine*,

February 24, 2016, https://www.nytimes.com/2016/02/24/magazine/senate-repub
licans-and-the-supreme-court-where-is-this-headed-exactly.html; A. E. Dick Howard, "The
Changing Face of the Supreme Court," *Virginia Law Review* 101 (2015): 231–316, 256.

54. Amber Phillips, "Obama Just Chose Merrick Garland for the Supreme Court.
Republicans Still Won't Confirm Him," *Washington Post*, March 16, 2016, https://www
.washingtonpost.com/news/the-fix/wp/2016/02/13/can-republicans-really-block-oba
mas-supreme-court-nomination-for-a-year-probably/; Robert Kagan, "What If Abe Fortas
Had Been More Discreet?" in Nelson Polsby, ed., *What If? Explorations in Social-Science
Fiction* (Lexington, MA: Lewis, 1982), 153–180, 179–180; Frank Michelman, "The
Supreme Court, 1968 Term: Foreword: On Protecting the Poor through the
Fourteenth Amendment," *Harvard Law Review* 83 (1969): 7–282.

55. Kalman, *The Long Reach of the Sixties*, 188–198.

56. "Conversation with Newsmen on the Nomination of the Chief Justice," May 22, 1969,
https://www.presidency.ucsb.edu/documents/conversation-with-newsmen-the-nom
ination-the-chief-justice-the-united-states.

57. Vincent Blasi, ed., *The Burger Court: The Counter-Revolution That Wasn't* (New Haven, CT:
Yale University Press, 1983); Linda Greenhouse and Michael Graetz, *The Burger Court
and the Rise of the Judicial Right* (New York: Simon and Schuster, 2016).

58. Patrick Buchanan, Memorandum for the Chief of Staff, July 10, 1985, 2 FG051, 275543,
Reagan Library; David Greenberg, "Supreme Court Cronyism: Bush Restarts a Long
and Troubled Tradition," *Slate* (October 5, 2005), https://slate.com/news-and-polit
ics/2005/10/supreme-court-cronyism.html; "Remarks by the President and Solicitor
General Elena Kagan at the Nomination of Solicitor General Elena Kagan to the
Supreme Court," May 10, 2010, https://obamawhitehouse.archives.gov/the-press-offic
e/remarks-president-and-solicitor-general-elena-kagan-nomination-solicitor-general-el.

59. Mark Walsh, "Supreme Court Nominations: 'You'll Get Justice Kagan, You Won't Get
Justice Marshall,'" June 29, 2010, www.abajournal.com/news/article/sessions_to_kaga
n_i_would_have_to_classify_you_as_a_legal_progressive/; Dana Milbank, "Kagan May
Get Confirmed, But Thurgood Marshall Can Forget It," *Washington Post*, June 29, 2010,
https://www.washingtonpost.com/wp-dyn/content/article/2010/06/28/A
R2010062805129.html.

CHAPTER 8 "IF I CANNOT GET A WHOLE LOAF, I WILL GET WHAT BREAD I CAN":

LBJ AND THE HART–CELLER IMMIGRATION ACT OF 1965

The quotation in the chapter title is from Meg Greenfield, "The Melting Pot of Francis E.
Walter," *The Reporter*, October 26, 1961, 24. My thanks to Mae Ngai for providing a copy of
this article. Dirksen referred to his reluctant vote for yet another token reform gesture that
authorized US participation in the 1960 World Refugee Year.

1. As summed up by David Reimers, *Still the Golden Door: The Third World Comes to America*
(New York: Columbia University Press, 1985), 67, Johnson "had evidenced no great
interest in immigration reform as a senator. However, as in other areas of political life,
Johnson became more liberal as President than he had been as a senator from the state

of Texas." See Daniel Tichenor, *Dividing Lines: The Politics of Immigration Control in America* (Princeton, NJ: Princeton University Press, 2009), 212–213.

2. Irving Bernstein, *Guns or Butter: The Presidency of Lyndon Johnson* (Oxford: Oxford University Press, 1996), 252, quotes Kennedy's aide, Myers Feldman: "When he became President, Johnson was uninformed about immigration reform" and "I had to educate both President Johnson and [his assistant] Jack Valenti."

3. See Hiroshi Motomura, *Immigration outside the Law* (New York: Oxford University Press, 2014).

4. Maddalena Marinari, "'Americans Must Show Justice in Immigration Policies Too': The Passage of the 1965 Immigration Act," *The Journal of Policy History* 26, no. 2 (April 2014): 219–221; James G. Gimpel and James R. Edwards, *The Congressional Politics of Immigration Reform* (Boston, MA: Allyn and Bacon, 1998); Aristide R. Zolberg, *A Nation by Design: Immigration Policy in the Fashioning of America* (Cambridge, MA: Harvard University Press, 2006), 324.

5. Johnson also used the "half a loaf" metaphor to express his disappointment with the limited reforms enacted by the 1957 Civil Rights Act, signaling his commitment to continue to fight for stronger measures. In *The Vantage Point: Perspectives of the Presidency, 1963–1969* (New York: Holt, Rinehart, and Winston, 1971), 156, Johnson wrote: "I felt the need for change as Majority Leader when I led the Senate fight for the Civil Rights Act of 1957. We obtained only half a loaf in that fight, but it was an essential half-loaf, the first civil rights legislation in eighty-two years." My thanks to archivist Allen Fisher for tracking down this reference and to editor Mark Lawrence for directing my attention to it.

6. David FitzGerald and David Cook-Martín, *Culling the Masses: The Democratic Origins of Racist Immigration Policy in the Americas* (Cambridge, MA: Harvard University Press, 2014), 40.

7. See Hidetaka Hirota, *Expelling the Poor: Atlantic Seaboard States and the Nineteenth-Century Origins of American Immigration Policy* (New York: Oxford University Press, 2017).

8. The 1790 Nationality Act barred Asian immigrants from gaining citizenship by naturalization, a right confined only to "free white persons." Anti-Asian laws targeted them as "aliens ineligible for citizenship."

9. Beth Lew-Williams, "Before Restriction Became Exclusion: America's Experiment in Diplomatic Immigration Control," *Pacific Historical Review* 83, no.1 (February 2014): 24–56, and Gordon Chang, "China and the Pursuit of America's Destiny: Nineteenth-Century Imagining and Why Immigration Restriction Took So Long," *Journal of Asian American Studies* 15, no. 2 (June 2012): 145–169.

10. Veto Message, March 2, 1897, Messages and Papers of the Presidents, Grover Cleveland, April 28, 2017. See https://www.presidency.ucsb.edu/documents/veto-message-31. Online by Gerhard Peters and John T. Woolley, The American Presidency Project.

11. Katherine Benton-Cohen, *Inventing the Immigration Problem: The Dillingham Commission and Its Legacy* (Cambridge, MA: Harvard University Press, 2018).

12. Mae M. Ngai, *Impossible Subjects: Illegal Aliens and the Making of Modern America* (Princeton, NJ: Princeton University Press, 2005), 245; Zolberg, *A Nation by Design*, 334.

13. Tichenor, *Dividing Lines*, 177–178.

14. Maddalena Marinari, "Divided and Conquered: Immigration Reform Advocates and the Passage of the 1952 Immigration and Nationality Act," *Journal of American Ethnic History* 35, no. 3 (spring 2016): 9.

15. Jethro Lieberman, *Are Americans Extinct?* (New York: Walker, 1968), 106.

16. Ibid.

17. Ibid., 109; for the Humphrey–Lehman draft bill, see https://www.trumanlibrary.gov/library/research-files/summary-humphrey-lehman-draft-bill.

18. "President Truman's Veto of the McCarran–Walter Act, June 25, 1952," https://www.ruhr-uni-bochum.de/gna/Quellensammlung/10/10_presidenttrumansveto_1952.htm.

19. *Whom We Shall Welcome: Report of the President's Commission on Immigration and Naturalization* (n.p., 1953), xii, 263–264.

20. Senator Pat McCarran, *Congressional Record*, March 2, 1953, 1518.

21. Greenfield, "The Melting Pot," 25.

22. Lieberman, *Are Americans Extinct?*, 115.

23. Robert A. Caro, *The Years of Lyndon Johnson*, vol. 3: *Master of the Senate* (Vintage Books, 2002), 757–760.

24. Letter from JFK to LBJ, June 29, 1955, Senate Files, Legislation Files '53–'60: '53–'55, Immigration 6/3/55–8/2/55, JFK Pre P Box 647.

25. Robert Dallek, *Lone Star Rising: Lyndon Johnson and His Times 1908–1960* (New York: Oxford University Press, 1991), 485.

26. Dwight D. Eisenhower, "Annual Message to the Congress on the State of the Union," January 5, 1956, https://www.presidency.ucsb.edu/documents/annual-message-the-congress-the-state-the-union-11.

27. Murrey Marder, "New Alien Law Lost in Rush to Adjourn," *Washington Post and Times Herald*, August 1, 1956, 20. Immigration-studies accounts do not mention the 1956 Johnson–Dirksen amendment, except for Donna Gabaccia and Maddalena Marinari, "American Immigration Policy," in Mitchell B. Lerner, ed., *A Companion to Lyndon B. Johnson* (Oxford: Blackwell Publishing, 2012), 215, which cites Lieberman, *Are Americans Extinct?*, 116–117. The fullest secondary account appears in Ruth Wasem, "The Struggle for Fairness: National Origins Quotas and the Immigration Act of 1965" (forthcoming), which the author generously shared with me.

28. Also see "Compromise Offered on Immigration Law," *Washington Post and Times Herald*, July 27, 1956, 16.

29. Allen Drury, "Immigration Bill Passed by Senate," *New York Times*, July 27, 1956.

30. Marder, "New Alien Law," 20. See *Congressional Quarterly, Congress and the Nation, 1945–1964: A Review of Government and Politics in the Postwar Years* (Washington, DC: US Government Publishing Office, 1965), 229. My thanks to archivist Brian McNerney for this reference.

31. Statement of Senator John F. Kennedy (Dem.-Massachusetts) upon Introducing S2410 on the floor of the Senate, Thursday, June 27, 1957, Senate Files, Legislation Files '53–'60, 56–57, Immigration Legislation 6/19/57-7/8/57, JFK Pre P Box 610.

32. Lieberman, *Are Americans Extinct?*, 118–119.

33. Greenfield, "The Melting Pot," 24.

34. Myer Feldman Memorandum to Frederick G. Dutton, February 2, 1961, "LE/IM" JFK White House Subject Files Box 482, Enclosure.

35. Greenfield, "The Melting Pot," 24.

36. Zolberg, *A Nation by Design*, 317.

37. Lieberman, *Are Americans Extinct?*, 120.

38. Lieberman, *Are Americans Extinct?*, 130.

39. Tichenor, *Dividing Lines*, 212–213. Also see Lieberman, *Are Americans Extinct?*, 132. Johnson's archive contains very little about his personal views of the immigration reform effort.

40. Lyndon B. Johnson, "Remarks to Representatives of Organizations Interested in Immigration and the Problems of Refugees," January 13, 1964. See https://www.presidency.ucsb.edu/node/242246. Online by Gerhard Peters and John T. Woolley, The American Presidency Project.

41. Karen Tumulty, "LBJ's Presidency Gets Another Look as Civil Rights Law Marks Its 50th Anniversary," *Washington Post*, April 8, 2014 .

42. Lyndon B. Johnson, "Annual Message to the Congress on the State of the Union," January 4, 1965. See https://www.presidency.ucsb.edu/documents/annual-message-the-congress-the-state-the-union-26.

43. Lyndon B. Johnson, "Special Message to the Congress on Immigration," January 13, 1965, https://www.presidency.ucsb.edu/documents/special-message-the-congress-immigration-0; Lieberman, *Are Americans Extinct?*, 130, 133; Marinari, "Americans Must Show Justice," 233–236.

44. Although the law is named for Hart and Celler, Feighan's *New York Times* obituary identifies him as the real author of the law. Wolfgang Saxon, "Ex-Rep. Michael A. Feighan, 87; Architect of '65 Immigration Law," *New York Times*, March 20, 1992, https://www.nytimes.com/1992/03/20/us/ex-rep-michael-a-feighan-87-architect-of-65-immigration-law.html?searchResultPosition=1. Lieberman, *Are Americans Extinct?*, 160; Marinari, "Americans Must Show Justice," 229.

45. Julia Sweig, *Lady Bird Johnson: Hiding in Plain Sight* (New York: Random House, 2021), chapters 9 and 10.

46. Reimers, *Still the Golden Door*, 75–77.

47. The President's News Conference, August 25, 1965, https://www.presidency.ucsb.edu/documents/letter-the-president-the-senate-and-the-speaker-the-house-proposing-bill-simplify-the.

48. Cited in Reimers, *Still the Golden Door*, 81.

49. Abba P. Schwartz, Letter to Robert F. Kennedy, September 20, 1965, RFK Senate Papers Subject File, 1965 Box 27, JFK Presidential Library; Reimers, *Still the Golden Door*, 65.

50. Lieberman, *Are Americans Extinct?*, 163–164; Reimers, *Still the Golden Door*, 71.

51. Stephen D. Lerner, "Johnson to Sign Immigration Bill; National Origins Quota System Ends: First Quotas for Hemisphere," *Harvard Crimson*, October 1, 1965; Reimers, *Still the Golden Door*, 79–80; Kevin R. Johnson, "The Beginning of the End: The Immigration Act

of 1965 and the Emergence of the Modern U.S.–Mexico Border State," in Gabriel Chin and Rose Cuison Villazor, eds., *The Immigration and Nationality Act of 1965: Legislating a New America* (Cambridge: Cambridge University Press, 2015), 116–170.

52. Lyndon B. Johnson, "Remarks at the Signing of the Immigration Bill, Liberty Island, New York," October 3, 1965. See https://www.presidency.ucsb.edu/documents/rem arks-the-signing-the-immigration-bill-liberty-island-new-york.

53. Pew Research Center: Hispanic Trends, "Modern Immigration Wave Brings 59 Million to U.S., Driving Population Growth and Change through 2065: Views of Immigration's Impact on U.S. Society Mixed," September 28, 2015, https://www.pewresearch.org/h ispanic/2015/09/28/modern-immigration-wave-brings-59-million-to-u-s-driving-popu lation-growth-and-change-through-2065/.

54. Andrew Kohut, Pew Research Center, "From the Archives: In '60s, Americans Gave Thumbs-Up to Immigration Law That Changed the Nation," September 20, 2019. Originally released February 14, 2015, https://www.pewresearch .org/fact-tank/2019/09/20/in-1965-majority-of-americans-favored-immigration-and-nationality-act-2/ Accessed on November 24, 2020.

55. Pew Research Center, "Modern Immigration Wave."

56. Gabriel Chin, "Were the Immigration and Nationality Act Amendments of 1965 Antiracist?" in Chin and Villazor, eds., *Immigration and Nationality Act*, 16, 26; James G. Gimple and James R. Edwards, *The Congressional Politics of Immigration Reform* (Boston, MA: Allyn and Bacon, 1998), 105–106.

57. Brinley Thomas, "'Modern' Migration," in Walter Adams ed., *The Brain Drain* (New York: Macmillan, 1968), 38.

58. Pew Research Center, "Modern Immigration Wave."

59. Zolberg, *A Nation by Design*, 317.

60. Ngai, *Impossible Subjects*, 245.

61. Chin and Villazor, "Introduction," in Chin and Villazor, eds., *Immigration and Nationality Act*, 4.

62. Johnson, "The Beginning of the End," 124–125; Zolberg, *A Nation by Design*, 245.

63. Zolberg, *A Nation by Design*, 245.

64. Johnson, "The Beginning of the End," 129.

65. Zolberg, *A Nation by Design*, 321, 327.

66. Reimers, *Still the Golden Door*, 74; Leticia M. Saucedo, "The Impact of 1965 Immigration and Nationality Act on the Evolution of Temporary Guest Worker Programs, or How the 1965 Act Punted on Creating a Rightful Place for Mexican Worker Migration," in Chin and Villazor, eds., *Immigration and Nationality Act*, 304–305.

67. Johnson, "The Beginning of the End," 136, 139, 147.

68. Douglas S. Massey and Karen A. Pren, "Unintended Consequences of US Immigration Policy: Explaining the Post-1965 Surge from Latin America," *Population and Development Review* 38, no. 1 (2012): 3–5.

69. Bernstein, *Guns or Butter*, 258.

70. See Ana Minian, *Undocumented Lives: The Untold Story of Mexican Migration* (Cambridge, MA: Harvard University Press, 2018), 52–56.

71. Johnson, "The Beginning of the End," 141.

72. Reimers, *Still the Golden Door*, 74, 81.

73. Bill Ong Hing, "African Migration to the United States: Assigned to the Back of the Bus," in Chin and Villazor, eds., *Immigration and Nationality Act*, 61.

74. US Department of State, Bureau of Consular Affairs, *Visa Bulletin* 10, no. 49, January 2021 (Washington, DC: US Government Printing Office), 2, https://travel.state.gov/content/travel/en/legal/visa-law0/visa-bulletin/2021/visa-bulletin-for-january-2021.html.

75. Saucedo, "Impact," 293; Massey and Pren, "Unintended Consequences," 3–5.

76. US Undocumented Immigrant Population Estimates, June 22, 2022, https://immigration.procon.org/us-undocumented-immigrant-population-estimates/.

CHAPTER 9 "IT'S ALWAYS HARD TO CUT LOSSES": THE POLITICS OF ESCALATION IN VIETNAM

1. LBJ–Bundy telcon, September 8, 1964, in Michael J. Beschloss, ed., *Taking Charge: The Johnson White House Tapes, 1963–1964* (New York: Simon and Schuster, 1997), 364–365; LBJ–McNamara telcon, February 26, 1965, in Michael J. Beschloss, *Reaching for Glory: Lyndon Johnson's Secret White House Tapes, 1964–1965* (New York: Simon and Schuster, 2001), 194; LBJ–Russell telcon, March 6, 1965, in ibid., 210–213.

2. See Fredrik Logevall, *Choosing War: The Lost Chance for Peace and the Escalation of War in Vietnam* (Berkeley, CA: University of California Press, 1999).

3. William H. Chafe, *The Unfinished Journey: America since World War II*, 3rd ed. (New York: Oxford University Press, 1991), 271; Ronnie Dugger, *The Politician: The Life and Times of Lyndon Johnson* (New York: Norton, 1992).

4. John Prados, *Vietnam: The History of an Unwinnable War* (Lawrence: University Press of Kansas, 2009), 32–33.

5. Logevall, *Choosing War*, 76; Doris Kearns, *Lyndon Johnson and the American Dream* (New York: Harper & Row, 1976), 252–253.

6. Memo for the Record, November 24, 1963, *FRUS, 1961–1963*, IV, 635–637; Lyndon B. Johnson, *The Vantage Point: Perspectives of the Presidency* (New York: Holt, Rinehart, and Winston, 1971), 43–44.

7. Robert McNamara, *In Retrospect: The Tragedy and Lessons of Vietnam* (New York: Times Books, 1995), 102; David Nes telephone interview with the author, February 20, 1994; Anne E. Blair, *Lodge in Vietnam: A Patriot Abroad* (New Haven, CT: Yale University Press, 1995), 119. LBJ's determination is also evident in LBJ–Donald Cook telcon, November 20, 1963, Beschloss, ed., *Taking Charge*, 73–74. See also the president's comments at the State Department on December 5, as recorded in the *New York Times*, December 6, 1963.

8. George E. Reedy, *Lyndon B. Johnson: A Memoir* (New York: Andrews and McMeel, 1982), 25.

9. See Logevall, *Choosing War*, chapter 5.

10. Beschloss, *Taking Charge*, 362–373.

11. McNamara, *In Retrospect*.

12. George C. Herring, *LBJ and Vietnam: A Different Kind of War* (Austin, TX: University of Texas Press, 1994), 131.

13. On this debate, see Francis M. Bator, "No Good Choices: LBJ and the Vietnam/Great Society Connection," *Diplomatic History* 32 (June 2008): 309–340; and Fredrik Logevall, "Comment on Francis M. Bator, 'No Good Choices: LBJ and the Vietnam/Great Society Connection,'" *Diplomatic History* 32, no. 3 (June 2008): 355–359.

14. Charles E. Neu, *America's Lost War: Vietnam: 1945–1975* (Wheeling, IL: Harlan Davidson, 2005), 86.

15. The memorandum is reprinted in full in Hubert H. Humphrey, *The Education of a Public Man: My Life and Politics* (Garden City, NJ: Doubleday, 1976), 320–324. For Johnson's response, see Carl Solberg, *Hubert Humphrey: A Biography* (New York: Norton, 1984), 287–288; and Humphrey, *Education of a Public Man*, 327.

16. Fredrik Logevall, "Presidential Address: Structure, Contingency, and the War in Vietnam," *Diplomatic History* 39 (January 2015): 14.

17. H. W. Brands, *The Wages of Globalism: Lyndon Johnson and the Limits of American Power* (New York: Oxford University Press, 1995), 245.

18. Quoted in Fredrik Logevall, "Rethinking 'McNamara's War,'" *New York Times*, November 28, 2017.

19. Mark Atwood Lawrence, *The Vietnam War: A Concise International History* (New York: Oxford University Press, 2010), 117.

20. McNamara, *In Retrospect*, 261.

21. Leslie H. Gelb, "Robert McNamara," *Time*, July 20, 2009.

22. McNamara, *In Retrospect*.

23. George C. Herring, ed., *The Secret Diplomacy of the Vietnam War: The Negotiating Volumes of the Pentagon Papers* (Austin, TX: University of Texas Press, 1983), 536–544, 717–771; Lloyd C. Gardner, *Pay Any Price: Lyndon Johnson and the Vietnam Wars* (Chicago, IL: Ivan R. Dee, 1995), 385–394.

24. Warsaw to Utrikesdepartementet, September 8, 1967, HP1, #XV, Utrikesdepartementets Arkiv, Stockholm. See also Robert McNamara, James G. Blight, and Robert K. Brigham, *Argument without End: In Search of Answers to the Vietnam Tragedy* (New York: Public Affairs, 1999), 296.

25. Walter Cronkite, *A Reporter's Life* (New York: Ballantine, 1996), 256.

26. Campbell Craig and Fredrik Logevall, *America's Cold War: The Politics of Insecurity* (Cambridge, MA: Belknap/Harvard University Press, 2009), 249.

27. Walter Isaacson and Evan Thomas, *Wise Men: Six Friends and the World They Made* (New York: Simon and Schuster, 1986), 689.

28. Ibid., 684; George Herring, *America's Longest War: The United States and Vietnam, 1950–1975*, 6th ed. (New York: McGraw-Hill, 2019), 249–250.

29. Mark Perry, *Four Stars: The Inside Story of the Forty-Year Battle between the Joint Chiefs of Staff and America's Civilian Leaders* (Boston, MA: Houghton Mifflin, 1989), 196.

30. Robert Dallek, *Flawed Giant: Lyndon Johnson and His Times, 1961–1973* (New York: Oxford University Press, 1998), 536–537.

31. Daniel Ellsberg, *Secrets: A Memoir of Vietnam and the Pentagon Papers* (New York: Viking, 2002), 216.

32. Allan E. Goodman, *The Lost Peace: America's Search for a Negotiated Settlement of the Vietnam War* (Palo Alto, CA: Hoover Institution Press, 1978), 69.

33. Herring, *America's Longest War*, 258; Clark Clifford, "A Viet Nam Reappraisal: The Personal History of One Man's View and How It Evolved," *Foreign Affairs* 47 (July 1969): 614–615; Clark Clifford, *Counsel to the President: A Memoir* (New York: Random House, 1991), 551.

34. Clifford, *Counsel to the President*, 571.

35. Walter LaFeber, *The Deadly Bet: LBJ, Vietnam, and the 1968 Election* (Lanham, MD: Rowman & Littlefield, 2005), 158.

36. Ellsberg, *Secrets*, 224.

CHAPTER 10   LYNDON JOHNSON AND THE SHIFTING GLOBAL ORDER

1. Robert Dallek, *Franklin D. Roosevelt and American Foreign Policy, 1932–1945* (New York: Oxford University Press 1979).

2. FDR's foreign policy legacy would have appeared quite mixed if he had served only two terms, and even less impressive if he had served in the White House only as long as LBJ did.

3. Randall B. Woods, *LBJ: Architect of American Ambition* (New York: Free Press, 2006), 483.

4. Fredrik Logevall, *Choosing War: The Lost Chance for Peace and the Escalation of War in Vietnam* (Berkeley, CA: University of California Press, 1999).

5. A concept I explore in Francis J. Gavin, "History and Policy," *International Journal* 63, no. 1 (winter, 2007/2008): 162–177.

6. Frank Costigliola, "US Foreign Policy from Kennedy to Johnson," in Melvyn P. Leffler and Odd Arne Westad, eds., *The Cambridge History of the Cold War: Volume II, Crises and Détente* (Cambridge: Cambridge University Press, 2011), 112–133.

7. Woods, *LBJ*, 483.

8. This discussion builds upon the excellent analysis of a large literature. See especially Melvyn P. Leffler, *A Preponderance of Power: National Security, the Truman Administration and the Cold War* (Stanford, CA: Stanford University Press, 2000); Melvyn P. Leffler and Odd Arne Westad, eds., *The Cambridge History of the Cold War* (Cambridge: Cambridge University Press, 2010); Marc Trachtenberg, *A Constructed Peace: The Making of the European Settlement, 1945–1963* (Princeton, NJ: Princeton University Press, 1999).

9. For an outstanding analysis of how LBJ navigated transatlantic challenges and tensions, see Thomas Alan Schwartz, *Lyndon Johnson and Europe: In the Shadow of Vietnam* (Cambridge, MA: Harvard University Press, 2003).

10. Lyndon B. Johnson, "Remarks in New York City before the National Conference of Editorial Writers," October 7, 1966, https://www.presidency.ucsb.edu/documents/remar

ks-new-york-city-before-the-national-conference-editorial-writers. Online by Gerhard Peters and John T. Woolley, The American Presidency Project.

11. This discussion of the background for the balance of payments deficit and dollar and gold outflow, and the Johnson administration's response, is based on Francis J. Gavin, *Gold, Dollars, and Power: The Politics of International Monetary Relations, 1958–1971* (Chapel Hill, NC: University of North Carolina Press, 2004).

12. Ibid., 117.

13. Daniel Sargent, "Lyndon Johnson and the Challenges of Economic Globalization," in Francis J. Gavin and Mark Atwood Lawrence, eds., *Beyond the Cold War: Lyndon Johnson and the New Global Challenges of the 1960s* (New York: Oxford University Press, 2014), 21.

14. The ensuing discussion draws on Francis J. Gavin, *Nuclear Statecraft: History and Strategy in America's Atomic Age* (Ithaca, NY: Cornell University Press, 2012); Francis J. Gavin, *Nuclear Weapons and American Grand Strategy* (Washington, DC: Brookings Institution Press, 2020).

15. Thomas Alan Schwartz, "Moving beyond the Cold War: The Johnson Administration, Bridge-Building, and Détente," in Gavin and Lawrence, eds., *Beyond the Cold War*, 79.

16. Schwartz, *Lyndon Johnson and Europe*, 236–237.

CHAPTER 11 "THROUGH A NARROW GLASS": COMPASSION, POWER, AND LYNDON JOHNSON'S STRUGGLE TO MAKE SENSE OF THE THIRD WORLD

1. *LBJ, The Last Interview*, Lyndon B. Johnson and Walter Cronkite (Carousel Films, Inc., 1973), https://www.youtube.com/watch?v=YrtWwBreRwg.

2. Robert A. Caro, *The Years of Lyndon Johnson*, vol. 3: *Master of the Senate* (New York: Vintage Books, 2003), xxi.

3. See Mark Atwood Lawrence, "Chapter 1: The Liberal Inheritance," in Lawrence, *The End of Ambition: The United States and the Third World in the Vietnam Era* (Princeton, NJ: Princeton University Press, 2021), 1–15.

4. For an exploration of Kennedy's evolving perspective on decolonization, see Robert B. Rakove, *Kennedy, Johnson, and the Nonaligned World*, repr. ed. (Cambridge and New York: Cambridge University Press, 2014). In his biography of Kennedy, Fredrik Logevall also explores Kennedy's interactions with the countries of the Third World in the decade before he became president and their significance for his worldview. See Fredrik Logevall, *JFK: Coming of Age in the American Century, 1917–1956* (New York: Random House, 2020), chapter 17.

5. Caro devotes an entire chapter of *Master of the Senate* to "The Compassion of Lyndon Johnson." See Caro, *Master of the Senate,* chapter 31, 711–740. For one such sentimental biography, see Philip Reed Rulon, *The Compassionate Samaritan: The Life of Lyndon Baines Johnson* (Chicago, IL: Nelson-Hall, 1981).

6. Lyndon B. Johnson, "Remarks to the National Planning Committee of the Machinists Non-Partisan Political League," January 28, 1964. See https://www.presidency.ucsb.ed u/node/240094. Befitting her lifelong insistence that the morality of historical actors should be among our central considerations as scholars, historian Marilyn Young

reminds us that Johnson's defenders also pointed to his compassion as a source of his decision-making. See Marilyn B Young, "Comment on Francis M. Bator's 'No Good Choices': LBJ and the Vietnam/Great Society Connection," *Diplomatic History* 32, no. 3 (June 2008): 347–350.

7. Lyndon B. Johnson, "Annual Message to the Congress on the State of the Union," January 12, 1966. See https://www.presidency.ucsb.edu/node/238437.

8. Memorandum for the Record, "The President's Meeting with Indian Ambassador B. K. Nehru, 6pm, 9 September 1965 (off the record)," in Gabrielle S. Mallon and Louis J. Smith, eds., *Foreign Relations of the United States, 1964–1968*, vol. 25: *South Asia* (Washington, DC: US Government Printing Office, 2000), Document 195.

9. Lyndon B. Johnson, "The President's Prologue and Epilogue to 'This America,'" October 3, 1966. See https://www.presidency.ucsb.edu/node/238391.

10. See Andrew Preston, "Monsters Everywhere: A Genealogy of National Security," *Diplomatic History* 38, no. 3 (June 2014): 477–500, https://doi-org.www2.lib.ku.edu/1 0.1093/dh/dhu018.

11. Oral history transcript, Walt W. Rostow, interview 1 (I), 3/21/1969, by Paige E. Mulhollan, LBJ Presidential Library Oral Histories, 4–5, LBJ Presidential Library, htt ps://www.discoverlbj.org/item/oh-rostoww-19690321-1-74-242.

12. "Remarks by Lyndon B. Johnson at the Annual Washington Conference of the Advertising Council," June 6, 1961, VP Aides Files of George Reedy, "Memos – 1961 [2 of 4]," Box 6, Lyndon Baines Johnson Library, Austin, Texas.

13. For more on LBJ's belief in the universal applicability of the TVA, see David Ekbladh, "A TVA on the Mekong," in Ekbladh, *The Great American Mission: Modernization and the Construction of an American World Order*, chapter 6 (Princeton, NJ: Princeton University Press, 2009), 190–226.

14. Doris Kearns Goodwin, *Lyndon Johnson and the American Dream*, 3rd repr. (New York: Thomas Dunne Books, 2019), 194; for more on LBJ's vice-presidential diplomacy, see Mitchell Lerner, "'A Big Tree of Peace and Justice': The Vice Presidential Travels of Lyndon Johnson," *Diplomatic History* 34, no. 2 (April 2010): 357–393, and "The Vice Presidency: All the Way with LBJ," *Time*, April 14, 1961, http://content.time.com/tim e/subscriber/article/0,33009,872238-1,00.html.

15. Nick Cullather, "LBJ's Third War: The War on Hunger," in Francis J. Gavin and Mark Atwood Lawrence, eds., *Beyond the Cold War: Lyndon Johnson and the New Global Challenges of the 1960s* (New York: Oxford University Press, 2014), 120.

16. LBJ's tenure as director of the National Youth Administration (NYA) in Texas was central to his rise to national visibility in the Democratic Party. See Robert Dallek, "The Making of a Congressman," in Dallek, *Lone Star Rising: Lyndon Johnson and His Times, 1908–1960* (New York: Oxford University Press, 1991), 125–159, and Doris Kearns Goodwin, "The Making of a Politician," in Kearns Goodwin, *Lyndon Johnson and the American Dream*, 72–101. For a more detailed treatment of LBJ's administrative work as Texas NYA director – especially his efforts to serve Black constituents through the program – see Christie L. Bourgeois, "Stepping over Lines: Lyndon Johnson, Black

Texans, and the National Youth Administration, 1935–1937," *The Southwestern Historical Quarterly* 91, no. 2 (October 1987): 149–172.

17. See Gerald Rice, *The Bold Experiment: JFK's Peace Corps* (Notre Dame, IN: University of Notre Dame Press, 1985).

18. For a history of the Peace Corps that documents Johnson's role in the organization's founding and survival, see Elizabeth Cobbs Hoffman, *All You Need Is Love: The Peace Corps and the Spirit of the 1960s* (Cambridge, MA: Harvard University Press, 1998).

19. See Harris Wofford, *Of Kennedys and Kings: Making Sense of the Sixties* (Pittsburgh, PA: University of Pittsburgh Press, 1992), 266.

20. On LBJ's enduring support for the Peace Corps, see Elizabeth Cobbs Hoffman, "Slippery Slopes," in Cobbs Hoffman, *All You Need Is Love*, chapter 7, 183–217.

21. See Cobbs Hoffman, *All You Need Is Love*, 200–202.

22. Lyndon B. Johnson, "Message to the Congress Transmitting the Sixth Annual Report of the Peace Corps," March 1, 1968. See https://www.presidency.ucsb.edu/node/237551.

23. Francis J. Gavin and Mark Atwood Lawrence, "Introduction," in Gavin and Lawrence, eds., *Beyond the Cold War*, 1–17.

24. Lyndon B. Johnson, "Annual Message to the Congress on the State of the Union," January 12, 1966. See https://www.presidency.ucsb.edu/node/238437.

25. Erez Manela, "Globalizing the Great Society: Lyndon Johnson and the Pursuit of Smallpox Eradication," in Gavin and Lawrence, eds., *Beyond the Cold War*, 166.

26. Oral history transcript, James Cain, interview 1 (I), 2/22/1970, by David G. McComb, LBJ Presidential Library Oral Histories, LBJ Presidential Library, https://www.disco verlbj.org/item/oh-cainj-19700222-1-73-34.

27. The authoritative treatment of Johnson's global smallpox eradication campaign is Bob H. Reinhardt, *The End of a Global Pox: America and the Eradication of Smallpox in the Cold War Era* (Chapel Hill, NC: University of North Carolina Press, 2015). See also Bob H. Reinhardt, "The Global Great Society and the US Commitment to Smallpox Eradication," *Endeavour* 34, no. 4 (December 2010): 164–172.

28. Reinhardt, "The Global Great Society," 168.

29. For a helpful summary of Johnson's education policy in the United States, see Lawrence McAndrews, "Education Reform," in Mitchell B. Lerner, ed., *A Companion to Lyndon Johnson* (Hoboken, NJ: John Wiley & Sons, 2011). McAndrews offers a more thorough treatment in *The Era of Education: The Presidents and the Schools, 1965–2001* (Champagne-Urbana, IL: University of Illinois Press, 2008).

30. See David Busch, "The Politics of International Volunteerism: The Peace Corps and Volunteers to America in the 1960s," *Diplomatic History* 42, no. 4 (September 2018): 669–693, and Sheyda F. A. Jahanbani, "One Global War on Poverty: The Johnson Administration Fights Poverty and Home and Abroad, 1964–1968," in Gavin and Lawrence, eds., *Beyond the Cold War*, 97–118.

31. Fred Hechinger, "Education: Pro and Con on International Exchange," *New York Times*, December 18, 1966, E11.

32. Paul A. Miller, quoted in Theodore Vestal, *International Education: Its History and Promise for the Future* (Westport, CT: Praeger, 1994), 107.

33. Very little has been written about the International Education Act. For a brief account of its origins and fate, see Liping Bu, *Making the World like Us: Education, Cultural Expansion, and the American Century* (Westport, CT: Praeger, 2003), 221–247.

34. Kristin L. Ahlberg, *Transplanting the Great Society: Lyndon Johnson and Food for Peace* (Columbia, MO: University of Missouri Press, 2008), 17.

35. Lyndon B. Johnson, "Special Message to the Congress: Food for Freedom," February 10, 1966. See https://www.presidency.ucsb.edu/node/238330.

36. Felix Belair Jr., "President Urges World Aid Drive, but Trims Funds," *New York Times*, February 2, 1966, 1.

37. McGovern quoted Johnson in a private interview with historian Randall Woods. See Randall Woods, *Fulbright: A Biography* (New York: Cambridge University Press, 1995), 364–365.

38. Alfred Sauvy, "Trois Mondes, Une Planète," *L'Observateur* 118, August 14, 1952, 14.

39. Representative Lyndon B. Johnson, speaking on H.R. 2616, 80th Congress, 1st Session, *Congressional Record*, May 7, 1947, 4696 (Washington, DC: US Government Printing Office, 1947).

40. Lyndon Baines Johnson, *The Vantage Point* (New York: Holt, Rinehart, and Winton, 1971), 47.

41. On the centrality of Western Europe to postwar US foreign policy, see Charles Maier, "The Politics of Productivity: Foundations of American International Economic Policy after World War II," *International Organization* 31 (August 1977): 607–633. For LBJ's policies toward Western Europe, see Thomas Alan Schwartz, *Lyndon Johnson and Europe: In the Shadow of Vietnam* (Cambridge, MA: Harvard University Press, 2003).

42. For an especially useful exploration of this theme, see Peter Felten, "Yankee, Go Home and Take Me with You: Lyndon Johnson and the Dominican Republic," in H. W. Brands, ed., *The Foreign Policies of Lyndon Johnson: Beyond Vietnam* (College Station, TX: Texas A&M University Press, 1999).

43. For the impact of "failed US policy" in China on US relations with the Third World more broadly, see Odd Arne Westad, *The Global Cold War: Third World Interventions and the Making of Our Times* (New York: Cambridge University Press, 2011), 117–118.

44. Robert Dallek, *Flawed Giant: Lyndon Johnson and His Times, 1961–1973* (New York: Oxford University Press, 1998), 99.

45. Michael J. Beschloss, ed., *Taking Charge: The Johnson White House Tapes, 1963–1964* (New York: Simon and Schuster, 1997), 369.

46. Michael H. Hunt, *Ideology and US Foreign Policy* (New Haven, CT: Yale University Press, 2009), 116.

47. Ibid., 123.

48. Kearns Goodwin, *Lyndon Johnson and the American Dream*, 251.

49. See Fredrik Logevall, *Choosing War: The Lost Chance for Peace and the Escalation of War in Vietnam* (Berkeley, CA: University of California Press, 1999). See also Fredrik Logevall, "Fredrik Logevall Comment on Francis M. Bator's 'No Good Choices: LBJ and the Vietnam/Great Society Connection,'" *Diplomatic History* 32, no. 3 (June 2008): 355–359, https://www.jstor.org/stable/24915876.

50. Quoted in Brands, *Wages of Globalism*, 58.

51. Kearns Goodwin, *Lyndon Johnson and the American Dream*, 195.

52. See Ekbladh, *The Great American Mission*, for more on this project. For Johnson's attitudes toward it, see Lloyd Gardner, *Pay Any Price: Lyndon Johnson and the Wars for Vietnam* (Chicago, IL: Ivan R. Dee, 1995).

53. William J. Burns, *Economic Aid and American Policy toward Egypt, 1955–1981* (Albany, NY: SUNY Press, 1985), 152.

54. Caro, *Master of the Senate*, xx.

55. Michael E. Latham, "Imperial Legacy and Cold War Credibility: Lyndon Johnson and the Panama Crisis," *Peace & Change* 27, no. 4 (October 2002): 499–527.

56. On this episode, see Cullather, "LBJ's Third War," 118–141; Kristin L. Ahlberg, "Machiavelli with a Heart: The Johnson Administration's Food for Peace Program in India, 1965–1966," *Diplomatic History* 31, no. 4 (September 2007): 665–700; H. W. Brands, "When the Twain Met – Head-on," in Brands, *The Wages of Globalism* (New York: Oxford University Press, 1995).

57. Lawrence, *The End of Ambition*, 82.

58. Robert J. McMahon, "Towards Disillusionment and Disengagement in South Asia," in Warren I. Cohen and Nancy Bernkopf Tucker, eds., *Lyndon Johnson Confronts the World: American Foreign Policy 1963–1968* (New York: Cambridge University press, 2012), 137; see also Lerner, "'A Big Tree of Peace and Justice,'" 363.

59. See Lawrence, *The End of Ambition*.

60. Kearns Goodwin, *Lyndon Johnson and the American Dream*, 194.

61. For an overview of US international interventions, see Stephen Kinzer, *Overthrow: America's Century of Regime Change from Hawaii to Iraq* (New York: Henry Holt & Company, 2007).

62. Paul Keith Conkin, *Big Daddy from the Pedernales: Lyndon Baines Johnson* (New York: Twayne, 1986).

63. On the relationship between Johnson's domestic reforms and participatory democracy, see Sidney Milkis and Jerome M. Mileur, eds., *The Great Society and the High Tide of Liberalism* (Amherst, MA: University of Massachusetts Press, 2005).

64. Lyndon B. Johnson, "The President's Prologue and Epilogue to 'This America,'" October 3, 1966. See https://www.presidency.ucsb.edu/node/238330.

65. Johnson quoted in Eric F. Goldman, *The Tragedy of Lyndon Johnson* (New York: Dell, 1969), 447.

66. See Dallek, *Flawed Giant*, 86–87.

AFTERWORD: LBJ'S AMERICA

1. Clifford Geertz, *The Interpretation of Culture* (London: Hutchinson, 1975).

2. Michael Harrington, *The Other America: Poverty in the United States* (New York: Macmillan, 1962).

3. Kerner Commission, *Report of the National Advisory Commission on Civil Disorders* (Washington, DC: US Government Printing Office, 1968).

4. Melody C. Barnes, Corey D. B. Walker, and Thad M. Williamson, eds., *Community Wealth Building and the Reconstruction of American Democracy* (Cheltenham: Edward Elgar Publishing, 2020), 16.

5. Arlie Russell Hochschild, *Strangers in Their Own Land* (New York: The New Press, 2016).

6. Ibid., 144.

7. Pew Research Center, *Public Trust in Government: 1958–2022* (Washington, DC: Pew Research Center, 2022).

8. M. Kornfield and M. Alfaro, "1 in 3 Americans Say Violence against Government Can Be Justified, Citing Fears of Political Schism, Pandemic," *Washington Post*, January 1, 2022, https://www.washingtonpost.com/politics/2022/01/01/1-3-americans-say-violence-against-government-can-be-justified-citing-fears-political-schism-pandemic/.

9. Harry Middleton, "LBJ: Still Casting a Long Shadow," *Prologue Magazine* 40, no. 2 (summer 2008).

10. Rogers M. Smith, *Civic Ideals* (New Haven, CT: Yale University Press, 1997).

11. Robert A. Caro, *The Years of Lyndon Johnson*, vol. 4: *The Passage of Power* (New York: Vintage Books, 2014).

12. M. Barnes (host), "Give Us the Ballot," audio podcast episode, S2 Ep. 5 of *LBJ and the Great Society*, PRX, March 3, 2020, https://lbjsgreatsociety.org/episodes/s2-ep-5-give-us-the-ballot-s1!4983d.

13. Fannie Lou Hamer (1917–77), "Testimony before the Credentials Committee, Democratic National Convention," August 22, 1964, American Public Media, https://americanradioworks.publicradio.org/features/sayitplain/flhamer.html.

14. Presidential Recordings Digital Edition, https://prde.upress.virginia.edu/content/CivilRights.

15. Z. Stanton, "How the 'Culture War' Could Break Democracy," Politico.com, May 20, 2021, https://www.politico.com/news/magazine/2021/05/20/culture-war-politics-2021-democracy-analysis-489900.

16. Steven Levitsky and Daniel Ziblatt, *How Democracies Die* (New York: Crown, 2018), 144.

17. Brennan Center for Justice, *Voting Laws Roundup: December 2021* (New York: Brennan Center for Justice, 2022), https://www.brennancenter.org/our-work/research-reports/voting-laws-roundup-december-2021.

18. Stanton, "How the 'Culture War' Could Break Democracy."

Index